Policy-Making in a Transf[

M. Evren Tok • Lolwah R.M. Alkhater • Leslie A. Pal

# Policy-Making in a Transformative State

The Case of Qatar

palgrave
macmillan

*Editors*
M. Evren Tok
Hamad Bin Khalifa University,
Doha, Qatar

Leslie A. Pal
Carleton University
Ottawa, Ontario, Canada

Lolwah R.M. Alkhater
Qatar Foundation for Education,
Science, and Community Development

ISBN 978-1-137-46638-9   ISBN 978-1-137-46639-6  (eBook)
DOI 10.1057/978-1-137-46639-6

Library of Congress Control Number: 2016945721

© The Editor(s) (if applicable) and The Author(s) 2016
The author(s) has/have asserted their right(s) to be identified as the author(s) of this work in accordance with the Copyright, Designs and Patents Act 1988.
This work is subject to copyright. All rights are solely and exclusively licensed by the Publisher, whether the whole or part of the material is concerned, specifically the rights of translation, reprinting, reuse of illustrations, recitation, broadcasting, reproduction on microfilms or in any other physical way, and transmission or information storage and retrieval, electronic adaptation, computer software, or by similar or dissimilar methodology now known or hereafter developed.
The use of general descriptive names, registered names, trademarks, service marks, etc. in this publication does not imply, even in the absence of a specific statement, that such names are exempt from the relevant protective laws and regulations and therefore free for general use.
The publisher, the authors and the editors are safe to assume that the advice and information in this book are believed to be true and accurate at the date of publication. Neither the publisher nor the authors or the editors give a warranty, express or implied, with respect to the material contained herein or for any errors or omissions that may have been made.

Cover image © Art of Travel / Alamy Stock Photo

Printed on acid-free paper

This Palgrave Macmillan imprint is published by Springer Nature
The registered company is Macmillan Publishers Ltd. London

# Acknowledgements

The journey for this book began many years ago in seminars, lectures, and discussions organized through the Public Policy in Islam Program of Qatar Faculty Islamic Studies, Hamad Bin Khalifa University. A key, recurring issue was the application of current models of policy analysis to the uniqueness of Qatar's policy-making processes and its grand passions formalized in the Qatar National Vision, "transforming Qatar into an advanced country by 2030." The country is grappling with standard policy challenges (e.g., health, education, and economic development) but in very special circumstances. And yet there is almost no sustained scholarly attention or analysis of these challenges. To date, the work on Qatar has been preoccupied with its foreign policies and its oil and gas economy. We decided to remedy that by focusing on the policy process in Qatar, its internal dynamics and tensions, and its results and prospects. We decided on a theme of Qatar as a *transformative state*, a policy-making system that combines the features of a Gulf monarchy: a modern governance machinery, unrivalled resources, and remarkable ambition.

From the very beginning of the project, we decided that we would do our best to enlist Qatari as well as non-Qatari contributions. For a variety of reasons, much of the scholarship on the Gulf region has been written by outsiders, and we wanted to balance that with an "internal perspective" from analysts who have been, in some cases, directly engaged in policy development or who work and live in Qatar. Additionally, we held two authors workshops in Qatar to encourage cross-fertilization and strengthen the book's thematic focus.

Apart from chapter authors, we have significantly benefited from the work of graduate students of Qatar Faculty of Islamic Studies, Public Policy in Islam Program. We are grateful to Sara Al Mohannadi, Sultan Al Kuwari, Abdulla Al Shaiba, and Haya Burshaid, who acted as theme leaders and helped develop the initial thematic scaffolding for the book. Jennifer Spence at Carleton University also aided invaluably in organizing and editing the bibliography.

We are grateful to the Qatar Faculty of Islamic Studies and two consecutive Deans, Dr. Hatem Al Karanshawy and Dr. Aisha Yusuf Al Mannai, for their unwavering support throughout the project. We extend our special gratitude to Her Highness, Shaikha Moza bint Nasser for providing her valuable feedback on the initial stages of the book.

We commenced this book with the intention of showcasing the "uniqueness" of Qatar, but readers will acknowledge that Qatar as a transformative state is not only about the special nature of the Qatari experience. We believe that there is a lot to learn from the Qatari experience about transformational policy-making, and this experience brings valuable lessons for the region and other developing countries.

M. Evren Tok
Lolwah R.M. Alkhater
Leslie A. Pal

# Contents

1 Policy-Making in a Transformative State: The
   Case of Qatar  1
   M. Evren Tok, Lolwah R.M. Alkhater, and Leslie A. Pal

2 Qatar's Constitutional and Legal System  37
   Hassan Al-Sayed

3 Policy-Making in Qatar: The Macro-Policy Framework  65
   Jocelyn Sage Mitchell and Leslie A. Pal

4 Qatar's Borrowed K-12 Education Reform in Context  97
   Lolwah R.M. Alkhater

5 Transforming Qatar's PSE: Achievements and
   Concessions  131
   Ahmed Baghdady

6 Fragmentation and Continuity in Qatar's Urbanism:
   Towards a Hub Vision  155
   Ashraf M. Salama and Florian Wiedmann

| | | |
|---|---|---|
| 7 | **Health Policy-Making in a Transformative State**<br>Faleh Mohamed Hussain Ali, Orsida Gjebrea, Chloe Sifton,<br>Abdulrahman Alkuwari, and Rifat Atun | 179 |
| 8 | **The Qatari Family at the Intersection of Policies**<br>Lina M. Kassem and Esraa Al-Muftah | 213 |
| 9 | **Public Policy and Identity**<br>Amal Mohammed Al-Malki | 241 |
| 10 | **Demographic Policies and Human Capital Challenges**<br>Hend Al Muftah | 271 |
| 11 | **Integrated Water, Energy, and Food Governance:<br>A Qatari Perspective**<br>Rabi H. Mohtar | 295 |
| 12 | **Macroeconomic Stabilization Policies and<br>Sustainable Growth in Qatar**<br>Khalid Rashid Alkhater | 309 |
| 13 | **Qatar's Global-Local Nexus: From Soft to<br>Nested Power?**<br>Abdulaziz Al Horr, Ghalia Al Thani, M. Evren Tok,<br>Hany Besada, Ben O'Bright, and Jason McSparren | 347 |
| 14 | **Conclusions**<br>Lolwah R.M. Alkhater, M. Evren Tok, and Leslie A. Pal | 367 |
| **Index** | | 395 |

# List of Contributors

*Abdulaziz Al Horr*  Qatar Finance and Business Academy (QFBA), Doha, Qatar

*Hend Al Muftah*  Doha Institute for Graduate Studies, Doha, Qatar

*Ghalia Al Thani*  International Cooperation Department, National Human Rights Committee of Qatar, Doha, Qatar

*Faleh Mohamed Hussain Ali*  Policy Affairs of the Supreme Council of Health (SCH) Qatar, Doha, Qatar

*Lolwah R.M. Alkhater*  Qatar Foundation and RAND-Qatar Policy Institute, Doha, Qatar

*Khalid Rashid Alkhater*  Department of Research and Monetary Policy, Qatar Central Bank (QCB), Doha, Qatar

*Abdulrahman Alkuwari*  Former Minister of Public Health, Qatar, Doha, Qatar

*Amal Mohammed Al-Malki*  College of Humanities and Social Sciences, Hamad bin Khalifa University-Qatar Foundation, Doha, Qatar

*Esraa Al-Muftah*  University of British Columbia, Vancouver, BC, Canada
Qatar University, Doha, Qatar

*Hassan Al-Sayed*  Qatar University, Doha, Qatar
College of Law, Doha, Qatar

*Rifat Atun*  Harvard University, Cambridge, MA, USA
Harvard School of Public Health, Boston, MA, USA

*Ahmed Baghdady*  Qatar National Research Fund, Doha, Qatar
RAND-Qatar Policy Institute, Doha, Qatar

*Hany Besada* African Mineral Development Centre (AMDC), United Nations University Institute for Natural Resources in Africa, Ottawa, ON, Canada
Economic Commission for Africa (UNECA) United Nations University Institute for Natural Resources in Africa, Ottawa, ON, Canada
Institute of African Studies Carleton University, Ottawa, ON, Canada
Centre on Governance University of Ottawa, Ottawa, ON, Canada

*Orsida Gjebrea* Office of the Assistant Secretary, Supreme Council of Health (SCH) Qatar, Doha, Qatar

*Lina Kassem* Department of International Affairs, Qatar University, Doha, Qatar

*Jocelyn Sage Mitchell* Northwestern University in Qatar, Doha, Qatar

*Jason McSparren*, Global Governance & Human Security McCormack Graduate School of Policy and Governance University of Massachusetts, Boston

*Rabi H. Mohtar* Texas AM University, College Station, TX, USA
Qatar Environment and Energy Research Institute (QEERI), Qatar Foundation, Ar-Rayyan, Qatar

*Ben O'Bright* Centre on Governance, University of Ottawa, Ottawa, ON, Canada

*Leslie A. Pal* School of Public Policy and Administration, Carleton University, Ottawa, ON, Canada

*Ashraf M. Salama* Department of Architecture, University of Strathclyde, Glasgow, UK

*Chloe Sifton* Supreme Council of Health (SCH) Qatar, Doha, Qatar

*M. Evren Tok* Public Policy in Islam Program, Qatar Faculty of Islamic Studies, Hamad bin Khalifa University, Doha, Qatar

*Florian Wiedmann* Department of Architecture, University of Strathclyde, Glasgow, UK

# List of Abbreviations

| | |
|---|---|
| ABET | Accreditation Board for Engineering and Technology |
| AHDR | Arab Human Development Report |
| ALESCO | Arab League Educational, Cultural and Scientific Organization |
| AR-DRGs | Australian Refined Diagnosis Related Groups |
| CCQ | Community College of Qatar |
| CEDAW | The Convention on the Elimination of all Forms of Discrimination Against Women |
| CNOOC | China National Offshore Oil Company |
| CPO | Central Planning Organization |
| DIAC | Dubai International Academic City |
| DNV | Dubai Knowledge Village |
| EIU | Economist Intelligence Unit |
| EU | European Union |
| FIFA | Federation of International Football Association |
| GCC | Gulf Cooperation Council |
| GDP | Gross Domestic Product |
| GSDP | General Secretariat for Development Planning |
| HBKU | Hamad Bin Khalifa University |
| HEI | Higher Education Institute |
| HMC | Hamad Medical Complex |
| ILO | International Labour Organization |
| IMF | International Monetary Fund |
| isQua | International Society for Quality in Healthcare |
| LNG | Liquefied Natural Gas |
| MENA | Middle East and North Africa |
| MMUP | Ministry of Municipalities and Urban Planning |
| MOE | Ministry of Education |

| | |
|---|---|
| MPH | Ministry of Public Health |
| NGO | Non-Governmental Organization |
| NHA | National Health Authority |
| NHIC | National Health Insurance Company |
| OECD | Organization of Economic Cooperation and Development |
| PBM | Pharmaceutical Benefit Management |
| PDP | Physical Development Plan |
| PDQL | Petroleum Development Qatar Limited |
| PSE | Post-Secondary Education |
| QCB | Qatar Central Bank |
| QCBDR | Qatar Central Bank Deposit Rate |
| QCHP | Qatar Council for Healthcare Practitioners |
| QF | Qatar Foundation for Education, Science and Community |
| QHFMP | Qatar Healthcare Facilities Master Plan |
| QIA | Qatar Investment Authority |
| QIF | Qatar Investment Fund |
| QMA | Qatar Monetary Agency |
| QNDS | Qatar National Development Strategy |
| QNFSP | Qatar National Food Security Program |
| QNMHS | Qatar National Mental Health Strategy |
| QNV 2030 | Qatar National Vision 2030 |
| QP | Qatar Petroleum |
| QR | Qatari Riyal |
| QU | Qatar University |
| SCH | Supreme Council of Health |
| SEC | Supreme Council on Education |
| SWF | Sovereign Wealth Fund |
| THE | Total Healthcare Expenditure |
| UAE | United Arab Emirates |
| WECG | World's Economic Center of Gravity |
| WEF | Water Energy Food |
| WGI | World Governance Indicators |
| WHO | World Health Organization |
| ZLB | Zero Lower Bound |

# List of Figures

| | | |
|---|---|---|
| Fig. 1.1 | Qatar Time Line | 10 |
| Fig. 1.2 | WGI Qatar 2003, 2008, 2013 | 15 |
| Fig. 1.3 | WGI Qatar and MENA, 2013 | 15 |
| Fig. 3.1 | Qatar's 20 Key Challenges (GSDP 2011a: 266) | 77 |
| Fig. 3.2 | Drivers and Levers of Public Management (GSDP 2011a: 244) | 85 |
| Fig. 4.1 | Ministry of Education Organization Chart | 107 |
| Fig. 4.2 | Organizational Structure of the Reform in 2002 | 107 |
| Fig. 4.3 | Student Performance: 2008 and 2011 | 120 |
| Fig. 6.1 | Interview questions | 159 |
| Fig. 6.2 | Five main categories of investment | 160 |
| Fig. 6.3 | Questionnaire results | 164 |
| Fig. 6.4 | Questionnaire Results | 168 |
| Fig. 6.5 | Map of Current Megaprojects | 169 |
| Fig. 6.6 | Waterfront High-Rises in West Bay | 171 |
| Fig. 6.7 | Impact of investment strategies on urbanism | 173 |
| Fig. 6.8 | The New Form of Urban Governance in Qatar | 175 |
| Fig. 7.1 | WHO Health Systems Framework | 180 |
| Fig. 7.2 | Patient Satisfaction, by Nationality, 2012–2014 | 186 |
| Fig. 7.3 | Total Health Expenditure (in thousands, current Qatari riyals, 2005–2013 | 188 |
| Fig. 7.4 | THE per Capita (current US dollars at average exchange rate), 2013 | 189 |
| Fig. 7.5 | Out-of-Pocket Health Spending as a Share of THE (%), 2009–2013 | 190 |
| Fig. 7.6 | Burden of Health Spending (% household spending), by Nationality and Occupation, 2012–2014 | 190 |
| Fig. 7.7 | Healthcare Coverage (%), by Nationality, 2012–2014 | 191 |

| | | |
|---|---|---|
| Fig. 10.1 | Distribution of Employment by Nationality in the GCC | 280 |
| Fig. 11.1 | Example environmental governance | 305 |
| Fig. 12.1 | Real Sector (GDP and Trade) | 312 |
| Fig. 12.2 | Financial Sector | 312 |
| Fig. 12.3 | Government Revenue and Expenditure | 313 |
| Fig. 12.4 | Annual inflation in Qatar | 314 |
| Fig. 12.5 | Oil-GDP Nexus: Qatar versus USA | 323 |
| Fig. 12.6 | Share of Country Groups in Qatar's Exports | 324 |
| Fig. 12.7 | Inflation Rate Divergence: 2001–2011 | 325 |
| Fig. 12.8 | Policy Divergence | 329 |
| Fig. 12.9 | Inflation Rates in GCC Countries | 330 |
| Fig. 12.10 | Qatar's Policy and Money Market Rates | 331 |
| Fig. 12.11 | Current versus Long-Run Macro-policy Frameworks | 338 |
| Fig. 13.1 | Qatar's nested power | 356 |
| Fig. 14.1 | Qatar Policy-Making System | 373 |

# List of Tables

| | | |
|---|---|---|
| Table 4.1 | Educational statistics 2004/2005–2007/2008 | 109 |
| Table 8.1 | List of Institutions and Legislation Related to Family and Women | 221 |
| Table 8.2 | Qatari Women in the Labor Force. Increasing proportion of Qatari women in the labor force working outside government sector | 223 |
| Table 8.3 | Institutional Changes in Family Policy | 230 |
| Table 10.1 | Population growth in Qatar, 1908–2014 | 274 |

# List of Boxes

Box 12.1  GCC Economic Model  319
Box 12.2  Growth and Policy Model, and Inflationary Channels
          in Qatar  326

CHAPTER 1

# Policy-Making in a Transformative State: The Case of Qatar

*M. Evren Tok, Lolwah R.M. Alkhater, and Leslie A. Pal*

Qatar, a tiny sheikhdom on the Gulf, has drawn—often deliberately—international interest far out of proportion to its size, in part because of its intriguing contradictions. With a national citizenry of only around 300,000 out of a total population of 2.3 million (most of whom are foreign workers), it has the world's highest per capita GDP, the third largest reserves of natural gas, and is the largest exporter of liquefied natural gas (LNG). Despite its hydrocarbon wealth, it has a national vision to transform the country into a knowledge economy by 2030, and it has engaged in projects, partnerships, and events that reach far beyond natural gas exports. Qatar bid (unsuccessfully) for both the 2016 and the 2020 Summer Olympics, and it bid for and won the FIFA World Cup for 2022. FIFA and economic diversification are behind an estimated $220 billion infrastructure investment program that has made Doha, the capital city, a giant construction zone. Under its brand as a Western ally, Qatar has become

M.E. Tok (✉)
Public Policy in Islam Program, Qatar Faculty of Islamic Studies,
Hamad bin Khalifa University, Doha, Qatar

L.R.M. Alkhater
Qatar Foundation and RAND-Qatar Policy Institute, Doha, Qatar

L.A. Pal
School of Public Policy and Administration,
Carleton University, Ottawa, ON, Canada

© The Author(s) 2016
M.E. Tok et al. (eds.), *Policy-Making in a Transformative State*,
DOI 10.1057/978-1-137-46639-6_1

home to the forward headquarters of the U.S. Central Command, as well as several American military bases, including the largest prepositioning base outside the continental United States (Blanchard 2014). And yet, with approximately 12,000 personnel, Qatar's armed forces are the second smallest in the Middle East, just slightly ahead of Bahrain. At the same time, it has been a significant supporter of the Muslim Brotherhood in the region after the Arab Spring.

Qatar's first modern boys school was opened in 1948 (Al-Kobaisi 1979), but it now has an "Education City" that hosts branches of Texas A&M University, Weill Cornell Medical College, Carnegie Mellon University, Northwestern University, and HEC (Hautes Études Commerciale) Paris, among other institutions. Like its neighbor, Saudi Arabia, it practices the more conservative Wahhabist version of Sunni Islam, but women have greater freedoms, occupying some leadership positions in various government and non-governmental organizations. Doha is an unremitting construction zone, with sparkling office towers, modern hospitals, and sports arenas rising from the sand. In formal terms it is a constitutional monarchy, but in reality all key decisions are made by the ruling Al-Thani family. Parliamentary elections have been promised but repeatedly postponed, and political freedoms are carefully constrained. Nonetheless, Qatar evinces none of the instability that afflicts nearby Yemen or Bahrain. Despite being a hereditary sheikhdom, it ranks quite high on the standard governance indicators (e.g., the World Bank's Worldwide Governance Indicators) and funds the largely independent news organization, Al Jazeera.

Qatar has been the object of analysis as part of studies of the Middle East and the Gulf (Davidson 2012, 2011; Kadhim 2013; Kamrava 2011; Nugée and Subacchi 2008; Peterson 1988; Potter 2009), and as a focus of study in itself (Crystal 1995; Fromherz 2012; Gray 2013; Kamrava 2013c; Mitchell 2013). This prevailing work on Qatar has relied on two broad lenses. We discuss them in more detail below, but for the moment, they can be summarized simply as the political economy of oil (including its economic and political effects) and international relations/regional studies. The two overlap of course, but the first focuses on the "resource curse" and "rentier state" effects of reliance on vast amounts of oil and gas, while the second is about the external push for power and security by an otherwise small state.

This book draws on these approaches, but its focus and contribution are different. We explore in detail how public policy is made in Qatar, within the context of what we will call a *transformative* state. If we simply assume that Qatar is an autocracy, ruled completely by the Al-Thani family, the answer to the policy-making question is also quite simple: policy is what the Emir Sheikh Tamim bin Hamad Al-Thani says it is. As the chapters in this book will show, the real answer is more complicated, and indeed other analysts have tried to come to grips with the nuances of the Qatari reality by using qualified descriptions of the system such as "late rentier," "pluralized autocracy," "tribal democracy," or "soft authoritarian." Most importantly, for our analysis, Qatar is deliberately engaged in a rapid process of societal transformation. That process has its contradictions and tensions, particularly with regards to achieving a balance between Islam, social traditions, and modernity. But it also has a specific policy dynamic of generating ideas and institutions, developing policy and program designs, and implementation and coordination.

In grappling with this, it is important to understand the starting point. Qatar became independent in 1971, after being a British protectorate since 1916. On the economic side, its key reservoir of natural gas, the North Field, was only discovered in 1971 and then took 20 years to develop, with the first export of LNG to Japan in 1997. As an oil producer, Qatar had been a minor player. Its unprecedented gas revenues began to build only in the mid-2000s, and even then Qatar had to make strategic decisions on other gas liquids development, creation of production facilities, and shipping capacity and markets. On the governmental side, its first ministry—the Ministry of Education—was founded in 1957, and a recognizable ministerial structure of government only emerged in the 1960s. Its current constitution came into force in 2005. In short—and we could multiply the examples—the economic, social, and political development of Qatar has been extraordinarily rapid, gathering intensity since the 2000s, once significant LNG revenues began to roll in. Managing that development is a major challenge.

The Qatar National Vision 2030, published in 2008, has the goal of "transforming Qatar into an advanced country by 2030." Fostering achievements in health, education, transportation, and other services, as well as expanding and transforming the economy, requires drawing on the most advanced ideas and human resources and transferring and adapting those ideas (and sometimes the people who have them). It requires designing policies and programs and then developing the institutional mechanisms and processes of implementation. And when that transformation is occurring in all sectors simultaneously, it also requires macro-policy and program oversight and strategic direction. Getting these governance institutions right is no easy task, even with almost limitless financial resources: "The reality was that it was taking much longer to develop the institutions and administrative capacities of a modern state than it had taken to build an internationally competitive hydrocarbon industry" (Ibrahim & Harrigan 2012: 3).

In other words, this book is less about "tiny state vs. big ambitions" or "autocracy vs. democracy" than it is about the state's capacity to design and implement a comprehensive, rapid transformation and transition to an advanced state and society. As such, each chapter of this book breaks new ground in exploring a key policy area, the specific policy institutions and processes that drive it, as well as preliminary results. Together, they provide a unique portrait of Qatar, with pointillist detail on issues and mechanisms of transformation, as well as the conflicts and tensions that accompany them.

A summary of the chapters follows below, but we first provide some background on Qatar for readers unfamiliar with it, as well as the key lenses that have been used to date to come to grips with this unusual country. In the book's conclusion, we will return to these themes and, in particular, to the "uniqueness" of Qatar. Is there anything that we can generally learn from Qatar about transformational policy-making ? Is it a pure case, a unique outlier, or does its experience have lessons for the region and other developing transforming states? With the plunge in 2015 of oil and gas prices, and a possible plateauing of those prices at around $50/barrel, how will Qatar handle the current and future costs of its transformation?

## Historical Background

The modern history[1] of Qatar begins in 1868 with the resolution of hostilities between the tribes in Qatar and Bahrain. That resolution was in the form of a peace treaty brokered by the British, which recognized the Al-Thani family as the ruler of the Qatar peninsula. Ottoman interest in the region led to an agreement in 1876, giving the Qataris the protection of a small Ottoman garrison. The Ottomans, fearing British attack during World War I, withdrew the garrison in 1915, and in 1916 Sheikh Abdullah bin Jassim Al-Thani signed a protectorate agreement with the British that lasted until Qatar's independence in 1971 (for the text of the 1868 and 1916 treaties, see Zahlan 1979). The immediate effect of the agreement was to affirm Al-Thani as the ruler of Qatar (Kéchichian 2008: 186), but it also gave the country an extended period of peace and stability, most importantly, as oil and gas began to be developed in the 1950s.

Up to the 1930s, the economy had revolved almost completely around pearls and some fishing. The Depression and the Japanese development of cultured pearls devastated the Qatari economy, leading to almost two decades of destitution. Oil exploration in the immediate region started in the 1920s, and the first Qatari production concession was signed in 1935 with the Anglo-Persian Oil Company (which had had an exploration concession since 1926), which then formed the Petroleum Development Qatar Limited (PDQL) (Crystal 1995: 145–47). Oil was discovered in 1939, but large-scale production and export did not begin until 1949 (Kéchichian 2008: 189). It "came as a godsend and marked the beginning of the transformation from a tribal society to a recognizable political entity that would become increasingly modern" (Bahry 2013: 252).

The influx of foreign workers and the overnight creation of an oil extraction industry in what had been a sleepy, impoverished tribal society led to predictable turbulence. Frequent strikes led PDQL in 1955 to give preferential hiring to Qatari nationals, which was followed in 1956 by the proclamation by the Sheikh to regulate non-Qatari owned businesses, and ultimately, by a series of labor laws starting in the 1960s, the establishment of preferential hiring for Qataris (Crystal 1995: 145). Unrest was evident in the ruling family as well. Ruling families in the region are more like clans or tribes, with loose hierarchy and often unclear rules of succession. The Al-Thanis began to compete internally over economic resources generated by the boom in the 1950s, leading eventually to what Herb calls a "dynastic monarchy" in which most of the key positions of state are held by family members (Herb 1999: 109–26).

Even though, under the 1916 treaty, Qatar was a protectorate of Britain (along with the other "trucial states," the sheikhdoms that became the UAE along with Oman and Bahrain), the British had little political impact and even less interest in Qatar, believing that its oil reserves were insignificant. A succession crisis in 1948, coupled with dissension in the extended Al-Thani family over claims to oil revenues and allowances, was resolved when Ali bin Abdallah became Sheikh in 1949 and agreed to the appointment of a British Political Officer and Advisor to Qatar. The crisis gave the British the leverage to "impose advisors and set in place an administrative structure" on what was virtually a bureaucratic "blank slate" (Crystal 1995: 121). A police force, infrastructure, and social services were gradually built during the 1950s.

Another succession crisis occurred in 1960, again largely because of internecine family struggles over revenue distribution, and Ali abdicated in favor of his son, Ahmad. This violated the 1949 succession agreement that had stated that Khalifa bin Hamad, Ali's nephew, would be Heir Apparent. Ahmad faced the regime's most severe test to date in 1963, with an uprising by a "National Unity Front" consisting of oil workers (who called a strike), disgruntled family members, and Arab nationalists. The uprising was put down, but Ahmad was himself overthrown by Khalifa in a peaceful coup in 1972, shortly after the country became independent in 1971. Khalifa launched a series of major budgetary and social policy reforms that "poured large amounts of money into education, health care, and other programs that would benefit the less wealthy Qatari" (Crystal 1995: 157). He also launched economic diversification initiatives (e.g., fertilizers and steel production) that largely failed (Nafi 1983), though the development of gas reserves and LNG export was later to become the backbone of Qatar's immense wealth. The state government structure was streamlined with independence, going from thirty-three departments to ten ministries, and Khalifa put members of his side of the family in charge. Writing in 1995, Crystal's judgment was that the result was state expansion (with government employment being essentially a form of welfare) and a "nearly uncontrolled bureaucracy."

In 1995, Khalifa was in turn deposed by his son, now The Father Emir His Highness Sheikh Hamad bin Khalifa Al-Thani and at the time the Heir Apparent. The chapters in this book explore different aspects of policy development under Hamad, but his signature contributions to Qatar's policy landscape have been limited liberalization and democratization, constitutional reform, and the Qatar National Vision to transform Qatar into a knowledge economy by 2030. Hamad has been called "perhaps the country's most energetic and transformative leader" (Kamrava 2013c: 105) and the most astute in managing the intra-familial disputes that have afflicted all of the Gulf monarchies (Herb 1999: 109–26). In 2013, Hamad abdicated in favor of his son Tamim, the Heir Apparent. This was surprising not only because it was the first normalized succession after two coups, but because Hamad was relatively young at 61, and Tamim was only 33. The Gulf monarchial pattern is closer to the octogenarian model of Saudi Arabia, which underwent its own succession in 2015 from King Abdullah to his "younger" half-brother, King Salman, who was 79 at time. It is also known for more turbulent and unpredictable successions, to which Qatar itself had been prey.

## Contemporary Context and Constitution

This section provides some basic facts and figures about Qatar that will set the context for more detailed treatments in subsequent chapters. A key point for readers unfamiliar with the Gulf is that the states in the region vary significantly, and sometimes dramatically. The six Gulf monarchies have distinct historical trajectories, institutions, and demographic and resource mixes, and to treat them simply as monochromatic monarchies is misleading. One key distinction, for example, is in the distribution and extent of oil and gas reserves (Krane 2013). Qatar is not even an oil state in the strict sense any longer, since it has carved out its niche in LNG. Though all the states are Islamic, the mix of Sunni and Shi'a varies, with Qatar and Saudi Arabia being largely Sunni (the more conservative, Wahhabist version). Yemen has a significant Shi'a minority, while Bahrain has a majority Shi'a population with a Sunni monarchy. At the same time, many countries in the region do share similar challenges—food and water security, sizeable expatriate workforces, rapidly growing populations, geopolitical tensions, and conflicts in the region. Qatar therefore has both unique characteristics as well as ones that it shares with other Gulf states.

The population in early 2016 was 2.3 million, with a severe imbalance of 75 % male, though that is completely an artifact of the largely male expatriate labor force. As a measure of the rocketing growth of the population, in 2010 the census counted only 1,670,389, with a 33 % increase in only four years. If we go back further in time, the pace of population change is even more striking. In 1940, after the Depression and the collapse of the pearl fishery, the entire population of Qatar was estimated at 16,000. In the 1930s, there might have been only one South Asian expat living in Doha, a barber from Balushistan (Fromherz 2012: 11).

Qatar's constitution, which became law in 2004, was ratified in a referendum in 2003; however, there were only 150,000 "nationals" (citizens), and of those only 71,400 were eligible to vote (Kamrava 2013c: 124). It has also had five elections (1999, 2003, 2007, 2011, and 2015) to the Central Municipal Council (29 members). The 2011 elections had 35,000 eligible voters. Uniquely for the Gulf, women were permitted to vote as well (Lambert 2011). The most recent election was held on May 13, 2015. Of the 29 seats, three were filled by acclamation, and so 26 were contested. Five women ran, and two were elected for the Council's fifth term, 2015–2019. This time, however, there were only 21,014 registered voters, of which only 14,509 voted.

The Constitution declares that Qatar's "religion is Islam and Shari'a law shall be a main source of its legislations (sic). Its political system is democratic" (Art. 1). It is notable that the document refers to Shari'a as "a" source, and not "the" source—a change that was made from the provisional draft to the one voted in the referendum. Another key feature is a clause on succession, given the trouble that it had caused in Qatari history and that of other Gulf monarchies (Kéchichian 2008). Article 8 states: "The rule of the State is hereditary in the family of Al-Thani and in the line of the male descendants of Hamad Bin Khalifa Bin Hamad Bin Abdullah Bin Jassim. The rule shall be inherited by the son named as Heir Apparent by the Emir. In the case that there is no such son, the prerogatives of rule shall pass to the member of the family named by the Emir as Heir Apparent." Supporting this article is one that establishes a "Council of the Ruling Family" (Art. 14), which, upon the demise or incapacity of the Emir, meets to declare the vacancy and the Heir Apparent as Emir. This concentration of the "rule of the State" in the Al-Thani family has its ambiguous complements in article 59, which states that the "people are the source of power," and in article 60, which states that the system of government is "based on the separation of powers."

Executive authority is vested in the Emir (Art. 62), and he is the head of state (Art. 64), the Commander in Chief (Art. 65), and the representative of the state in international affairs (Art. 66). His list of powers (Art. 67) includes setting the policy agenda for the Council of Ministers, ratifying legislation, presiding over the Council of Ministers, appointing and terminating the service of civil servants and military personnel, and establishing the organization of government (ministries and other bodies). He can declare martial law (Art. 69), and in exceptional cases issue decrees that have the force of law (Art. 70). The Prime Minister is appointed by and serves at the pleasure of the Emir (Art. 72). Ministers in the Council of Ministers are nominated by the Prime Minister but appointed by the Emir (Art. 73). They do not necessarily have to sit in the legislature, but they are accountable to it (Art. 111). The list of powers of the Council of Ministers (Art. 121) includes the usual cabinet functions: proposal of draft laws and decrees to the legislature, proposals on the organization of government and the financial and administrative system in the government, budgets, and oversight of international relations. However, members of the Council are collectively and individually "responsible before the Emir" (Art. 123).[2] When the new Emir announced his cabinet on June 26, 2013, it consisted of 20 ministers. One was a woman (the third in Qatari history). The Prime Minister and Interior Minister was, and remains, Sheikh Abdullah bin Nasser bin Khalifa Al-Thani.

The legislative authority in Qatar is the Shura Council Council (Art. 76). It is to consist of 45 members, 30 of whom are to be elected and 15 to be appointed by the Emir. Elections to the legislature are to be established in law, but they have been postponed repeatedly. The Council is to be elected for four-year terms, though the Emir has the power to dissolve it and call new elections (Art. 104). Article 106 has a double veto provision: the Emir may veto draft legislation and return it, but if passed by two-thirds of the Council, he must ratify and promulgate it. However, he may nonetheless, even with a two-thirds vote, indefinitely suspend the legislation for the "higher interests of the country."

The amending procedure may be launched by the Emir or one-third of the Shura Council, and if accepted by a majority of the Council, it can be passed after debate by a two-thirds vote. The Emir, however, must approve of the amendment for it to go into force, and moreover, amendments cannot be made to the constitutional provisions on the rule of state, inheritance, or the functions of the Emir. It is not clear whether this is pertinent to the amendment procedure, but the Emir also has the right (Art. 75) to "seek public opinion" through referenda.

Western constitutions and constitutional law are today overwhelmingly viewed through the prism of human or individual rights. The Qatar Constitution refers (in its English translation) to "rights" twenty times, but the substantive list of rights (or protections, even if the term "rights" is not used) are found in Part 3: Public Rights and Duties. The key provisions that would be expected in a modern constitution are all there: equality of citizens in rights and duties (Art. 34); equality of "all persons" before the law and without discrimination "whatsoever" on "grounds of sex, race, language or religion" (Art. 35); protection against unlawful arrest or detention (Art. 36); protection of privacy (Art. 37); the right to elect and be elected (Art. 42); the right of assembly (Art. 44) and of association (Art. 45); freedom of expression (Art. 48); freedom of religion (Art. 50).

However, in all important cases, these rights are constitutionally qualified by the phrase "in accordance with the conditions and circumstances set forth in law." To take freedom of the press as an example, the 1979 law on Publications and Publishing requires all press publications to have a license, makes it a criminal offense to criticize the personality of the Emir,[3] or any material that could "endanger the internal and external

| Date | Event |
| --- | --- |
| 1868 | The British broker a peace treaty between Qatari and Bahrain rulers that recognizes Sheikh Muhammed bin Al-Thani as the legitimate ruler of Qatar. |
| 1871 | Sheikh Jassim bin Muhammed Al-Thani signs an agreement with the Ottomans, who place a small garrison in Doha. |
| 1915 | Ottomans leave Qatar, fearing attack by the British during World War I. |
| 1916 | Sheikh Abdullah bin Jassim Al-Thani signs protectorate agreement with the British. This lasted until independence in 1971. |
| 1928 | First official court (as opposed to simply the Sheikh holding hearings) established – Islamic Law Court. |
| 1935 | First concession signed with Anglo-Persian Oil Company, which then formed the Petroleum Qatar Development Limited |
| 1946 | First hospital established – Rumailah – headed by British doctor |
| 1949 | Arrival of a British officer who was to organize security and police. Followed by the arrival of a British "advisor" to the Sheikh, who helped establish departments (police, customs, land registry, water, electricity, postal service. |
| 1949 | First boy's (1949) school established. Led to creation in 1957 of a |

**Fig. 1.1** Qatar Time Line

| 1955 | Ministry of Education. This was the first ministry in the history of Qatar. |
| 1957 | This was followed in the 1960s by the development of other ministries. |
| 1963 | Uprising and demonstration by "United National Front" – Qatari nationalists and Baathists. |
| 1964 | Sheikh Ahmad Al-Thani establishes an unelected Advisory Council (*Majlis al-Shura*), representing different branches of the ruling family. |
| 1970 | First constitution introduced – the "Basic Law." It established a cabinet, with the Crown Prince as Prime Minister. |
| 3 September 1971 | The British protectorate ends, and Qatar becomes independent country. |
| 22 February 1972 | Sheikh Khalifa Al-Thani stages bloodless coup over his uncle, Sheikh Ahmad, who had ruled since the abdication of his father Ali in 1960. |
| 1976 | Oil industry nationalized and brought under the Qatar National Petroleum Company. |
| 27 June 1995 | Sheikh Hamad Al-Thani stages bloodless coup over his father, Sheikh Khalifa. Launches a major series of reforms. |
| 1995 | Establishing Qatar Foundation for Education, Science and Community Development followed by opening the Education City branch campuses of world-class universities like Weil Cornell, Carnegie Mellon and many others mainly between 2001 and 2005, although VCU Qatar was established much earlier in 1998, while both HEC-Paris and UCL |

(*continued*)

|  | branch campuses were founded later in 2011. Qatar Foundation also hosts many other research- and education-related institutions such as Qatar National Library and Qatar National Research Fund, the main research catalyst in the country, and community development initiatives such as Awsaj Academy for kids with learning challenges, and cultural initiatives such as Qatar Philharmonic Orchestra. |
| --- | --- |
| February 1996 | Sheikh Khalifa (the father of Sheikh Hamad) fails in a counter-coup to take back the government. Turned back. |
| 16 November 1998 | Sheikh Hamad bin Khalifa Al-Thani announces that he would like a new constitution to replace the "temporary" one, with an elected Parliament of men and women. Appoints a 32-member committee to draft new constitution. Presented in 2002, voted on in referendum in 2003, signed by Emir in 2004 and proclaimed in 2005. |
| 1998 | Establishing the Supreme Council for Family Affairs as the first Supreme Council in Qatar. This institution is unique in two ways; it is the first specialized institution with a mandate to design family policies, and it is the first entity outside the traditional bureaucratic setting (i.e. not a member of the Council of Ministers, yet reports directly to the Emir) to have policy-making authority. This authority was reinforced by the fact that it was headed by the current Emir Shaikh Tamim (then the Heir Apparent) with the Father Emir's (then the Emir) wife Shaikha Moza bint Nasser as his deputy. This arrangement aimed to get around |

*(continued)*

| | |
|---|---|
| | the old bureaucracy with a more effective organization. The idea was replicated later on in many other sectors like Education, Health, ICT, Economy and the Judiciary system, but each of these Supreme Councils went through a different trajectory. |
| 8 March 1999 | First elections held for municipal government council where both men and women could vote and run. First time in GCC. No women elected. Council elections were held again in 2003 and 2007 |
| 2003 | Referendum on new constitution |
| 2003 | RAND establishes an office in Qatar in partnership with Qatar Foundation to play a significant role in advising on many policies. RAND-Qatar Policy Institute was closed down in 2013 |
| 2004 | Introduction of new "independent schools" based on RAND advice ("Education for a New Era") |
| June 2005 | New constitution takes effect, though with the important absence of the elected Shura Council |
| 2008 | Supreme Constitutional Court appointed. |
| 1 November 2011 | Sheikh Hamad announces first general election to be held in 2013. Postponed. |
| 25 June 2013 | Sheikh Tamim becomes Emir after the abdication of his father, Sheikh Hamad. |

security of the State," be "prejudicial to the heads of states or disruptive to the bilateral relationships with Sister Arab and friendly countries," contain any "ridicule of or contempt toward any of the religions or their doctrines" or materials "prejudicial to ethics," and finally, and most comprehensively, any "material which the Minister of Information requests the editor-in-chief or proprietor of the press publication not be published." Another example is freedom of association. The 2004 Law on Private Associations and Foundations requires all such organizations to be registered by the Ministry of Social Affairs, in itself not unusual since even the most democratic countries require some regulation of charities, foundations, and professional associations, but the law also bans political parties and trade unions (Law No. 12, 2004, on Organizing Associations, and Private Organizations). It is also important to recognize that laws and rights apply differently to nationals (citizens) and foreigners. According to the Nationality Law (Law No. 38, 2005, On the Acquisition of Qatari Nationality), a Qatari national is someone who was a resident in the country as of 1930 or has descendants traced through the father that were residents. Qatari citizenship is defined restrictively and narrowly, due to the huge proportion of expats in the population and to the extraordinary benefits that come with Qatari citizenship (Babar 2014).

Legislation routinely distinguishes between nationals and foreigners, most notoriously in the *kafala* or sponsorship system, used throughout the Gulf states, whereby employers are responsible for the visa and legal status of their workers, including the granting of exit visas should they wish to leave the country (for a particularly personalized portrait of the system, see Beydoun and Baum 2012).

Unsurprisingly, in light of these constitutional provisions, assessments of governance in Qatar have been critical, though somewhat mixed (Rosman-Stollman 2009; also see Chapter 2 for more detail). Freedom House rates Qatar as "unfree." The World Bank, on the other hand, in its Worldwide Governance Indicators (WGI), measures governance on six dimensions (voice and accountability, political stability and absence of violence, government effectiveness, regulatory quality, rule of law, and control of corruption). Figure 1.2 shows that Qatar ranks, as we would expect, low on the first, but well above the sixtieth percentile on the others. In comparison with the MENA region, Fig. 1.3 shows a dramatic superiority on all dimensions except voice and accountability. But even here, by the standards of the region, there have been limited elections, a relatively benign and light-handed security apparatus, relatively free access to international

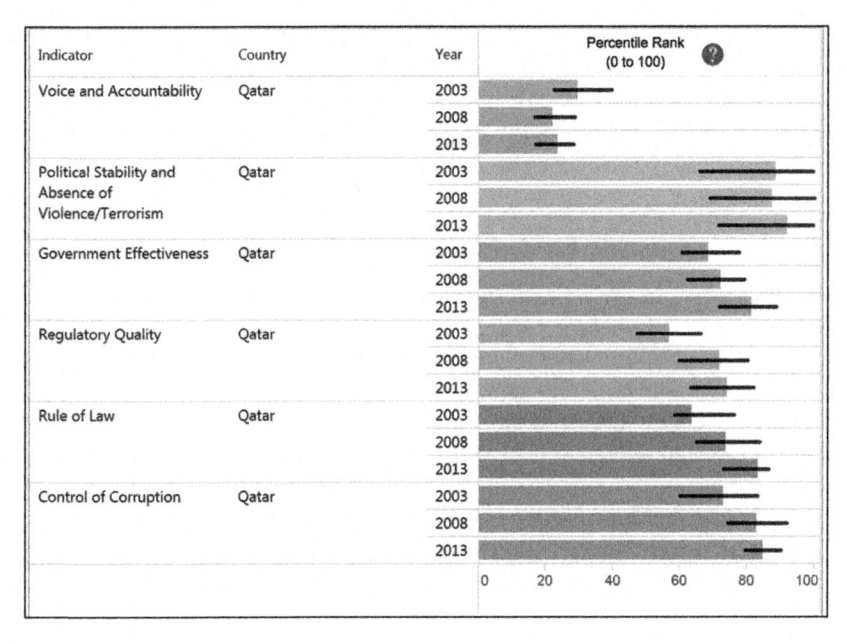

POLICY-MAKING IN A TRANSFORMATIVE STATE: THE CASE OF QATAR 15

| Indicator | Country | Year | Percentile Rank (0 to 100) |
|---|---|---|---|
| Voice and Accountability | Qatar | 2003 | |
| | | 2008 | |
| | | 2013 | |
| Political Stability and Absence of Violence/Terrorism | Qatar | 2003 | |
| | | 2008 | |
| | | 2013 | |
| Government Effectiveness | Qatar | 2003 | |
| | | 2008 | |
| | | 2013 | |
| Regulatory Quality | Qatar | 2003 | |
| | | 2008 | |
| | | 2013 | |
| Rule of Law | Qatar | 2003 | |
| | | 2008 | |
| | | 2013 | |
| Control of Corruption | Qatar | 2003 | |
| | | 2008 | |
| | | 2013 | |

**Fig. 1.2** WGI Qatar 2003, 2008, 2013

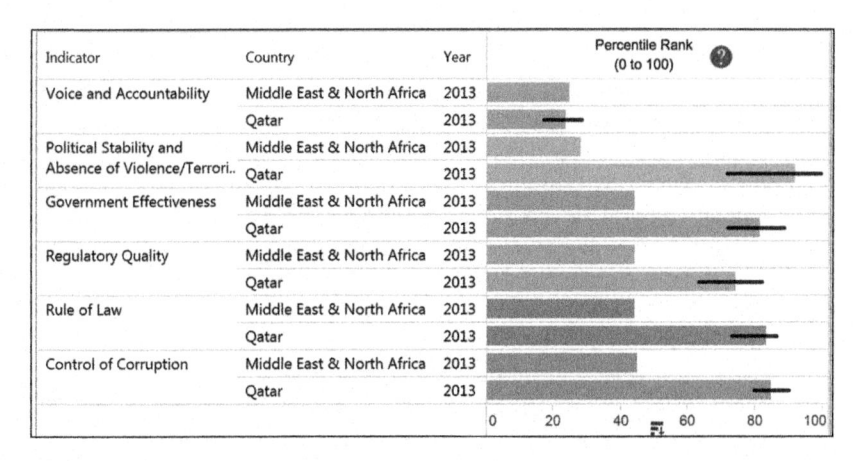

| Indicator | Country | Year | Percentile Rank (0 to 100) |
|---|---|---|---|
| Voice and Accountability | Middle East & North Africa | 2013 | |
| | Qatar | 2013 | |
| Political Stability and Absence of Violence/Terrori.. | Middle East & North Africa | 2013 | |
| | Qatar | 2013 | |
| Government Effectiveness | Middle East & North Africa | 2013 | |
| | Qatar | 2013 | |
| Regulatory Quality | Middle East & North Africa | 2013 | |
| | Qatar | 2013 | |
| Rule of Law | Middle East & North Africa | 2013 | |
| | Qatar | 2013 | |
| Control of Corruption | Middle East & North Africa | 2013 | |
| | Qatar | 2013 | |

**Fig. 1.3** WGI Qatar and MENA, 2013

media and internet, and a largely independent if government-funded Al Jazeera. Other assessments of the quality of governance in Qatar and the region come to the same conclusions, again highlighting the Father Emir Sheikh Hamad's role in nudging toward what is, by regional standards, a "liberal" regime (Hudson 1977; Najem & Hertherington 2003).

## Understanding Qatar: A Transformational State

Qatar was almost invisible on the scholarly and political radar before 2000. While Qatar had become wealthy through oil, the unprecedented revenue flows from LNG only began in the mid-2000s. Emir Sheikh Khalifa had started his reign in 1972 with reformist impulses, but kept a low international profile, showed little ambition to have Qatar punch above its weight, and embarked on relatively modest domestic economic development projects. As Emir, Sheikh Hamad changed all that dramatically and helped create the multiple, apparent contradictions that have attracted fresh analytical attention in the last decade. The attraction for analysts, of course, is based on how these contradictions seem to confound the usual background expectations:

1. Small state, big money: There are about 300,000 Qatari nationals. Resource wealth has made them, virtually overnight, the richest people on the planet. Small states do not usually get that rich, that quickly.
2. Small state, big international ambitions: Qatar has built an international profile and brand out of all proportion to its diminutive size: engaged actively (and some would argue, sometimes unhelpfully) in regional conflicts like Sudan, Lebanon, Palestine, Syria, Iraq and Egypt, hosting international sporting events and conferences, and using its sovereign wealth funds to purchase flagship assets such as Harrods of London.
3. Small national population, sea of expats: How does a country manage the influx of a wave of (mostly South Asian, blue collar, male) workers at least six times the size of the native population?
4. Democratic governance, monarchy: While Qatar technically is a constitutional monarchy where the Emir is subject to the rule of law and a legislature, in practice the monarchy is close to absolute. And yet the constitution, political discourse, and some of the relaxed

political realities of the country all point to quasi-democratic aspirations. The background expectation is that modern regimes will collapse unless they grant some form of popular participation, either purely as a mechanism for feedback and adjustment, or as a popular demand for political rights. Qatar seems untroubled by significant opposition.
5. Arab Islamic state, modern (Western-like) lifestyle: The Muslim world has several examples, such as Indonesia and Malaysia, of flexible, if not always easy, accommodations between Islamic tradition and aspects of Western lifestyles that seem to accompany modernity (e.g., equality between men and women; permissive sexual attitudes and behavior; gay and lesbian rights). Most of the Gulf states have various traditions, and Qatar shares with Saudi Arabia the more conservative Wahhabist version of Sunnism. And yet Qatar seems to be navigating these tensions relatively smoothly.

Other puzzles might be cited, but these are the most pressing and entangled of the prevailing observations of Qatar. Therefore, the following questions arise: How can these contradictions be understood? How can their dynamics and pressures be assessed? As we mentioned, Qatar has only pulsed on the analytical radar in the last decade, but generally, it has been assessed through one of two lenses: (1) the political economy of oil and (2) the dynamics of international relations and geo-politics. The lens of international relations theory has focused on the Middle East and its obvious internal conflicts and how those project onto global geopolitics (the literature is huge, but an introduction is provided in Kamrava 2013a). A subset of that work, specific to Qatar, has explored the mechanisms of Qatar's international "branding" or its "soft" or "subtle power" (Cooper and Momani 2011). Both these lenses focus on the two first contradictions or puzzles listed above. This lens is less an explanation of Qatar than an observation about its unusually active and visible diplomacy. For international relations scholars, this is part of an interesting question about the diplomatic capacity of small states (Cooper & Shaw 2009). Qatar not only has the financial capacity, but apparently the will and the strategy to play an out-sized role both globally and regionally. Its diplomacy has also been seen as a tool to manage political loyalties and diversify its economy. The focus of this book is on domestic policy, but Chapter 13 does address Qatar's global role and will engage directly with the international relations/geo-political lens on the country.

From the point of view of explaining Qatar, and understanding its policy dynamics, the political economy of oil has been the most important lens. This optic actually embraces two related but distinct approaches, each with a slightly different emphasis, and we will take some time here to outline them because of their importance in the field. The first is a literature and debate over the resource curse that can afflict countries with a large proportion of their revenues derived from natural resource extraction, primarily oil and gas (Auty 1990; Chaudhry 1997; Crystal 1995; Davidson 2009; Foley 2010; Herb 2014; Hertog 2010; Humphreys et al. 2007; Legrenzi and Momani 2011; Ross 2001, 2012; Sachs and Warner 2001). On the economic level, the challenge is how to absorb vast resource wealth in an appropriate development that actually supports and sustains the national economy. There is a host of economic pathologies that flow with high resource revenues, from high inflation to suppression of other domestic production sectors. The political effects can be just as damaging, from corruption to civil wars. A species of this approach, "rentier state theory," focuses the analysis of the resource curse on the Arab oil states, particularly the Gulf monarchies. The background expectation, as we noted above, is that populations eventually rebel against concentrations of unaccountable political power, and the Gulf monarchies and the Chinese Communist Party are the two most vivid examples, though the monarchies are more perplexing because they make not even a pretense of popular legitimacy (China, is after all, the "People's Republic").

The answer has been that the Gulf monarchies are a peculiar form of economic and state system, a rentier state where the flows of revenues from oil and gas resources are so huge that they can be used to buy acquiescence (Beblawi 1987; Beblawi & Luciani 1987; Luciani 1987, 1990; Mahdavy 1970). The meaning of "rent" in economics is somewhat ambiguous, being in one sense a return to a factor of production above production costs, and in another, a return due to a privilege (e.g., a patent) or ownership (hence the common sense notion of rent as something paid to an owner of land or property). In some cases, the amount of rent is a function of the value placed on some thing, which itself may be a function of scarcity, fashion, or any other number of factors not related to actual production costs and profits. In reality, "rents" are always mixed in with the price and profits of normal goods and services, for example if they are scarce (gems or land or housing) or first-to-market through innovation. In the case of natural resources, these may simply be considered "gifts of nature" and if demand is high (for whatever reason), the revenues or "rents" are commensurably high as well, and, most importantly, they are well above the cost of production. A rentier economy is one that relies heavily on rentier income, which is typically produced through exports to international markets and with relatively low production costs or processes. In such an economy, wealth is "accrued" rather than "earned"—the production costs and infrastructure around oil export in the Gulf are minimal, for example, in comparison to the extraction of shale oil.

A rentier state, given that most natural resources are owned by the state—and in the case of the Gulf monarchies, by the ruling families—is a peculiar beast. Beblawi (1987) argued that the Arab oil states represented the rentier state *par excellence:* rent captured by the state is distributed among the population, with cascading layers of beneficiaries creating a hierarchy of rentiers; tribal traditions of buying loyalty are reinforced; public goods are disbursed as the "ruler's benevolence"; citizens do not demand political participation because they receive (often lavish) benefits without taxation; the state becomes the major employer in the economy; there is an uneasy coexistence of nationals and expatriates because the expats are needed both in the extraction of the resource, but increasingly in the management of the booming economy and its ancillary expansion and development. Beblawi had no illusions about the internal complexity, stresses, and contradictions of a rentier economy, but the classic version of the thesis tended to connect resources with authoritarian rule: "The availability of resource rents accruing from abroad strengthens the incumbent's chances to retain power, through either coercion, use of government expenditure to buy off opposition, or simply better opportunities to deliver services and engage in populist policies" (Luciani 2012: 4). This authoritarian rule is presumed to suffocate all opposition, either through formal mechanisms like restrictive laws and an invasive security apparatus, or simple acquiescence to personal wealth and abundant public services, received without much effort and virtually no taxation.

The reality is more complex, and so recent versions of the rentier state have become more nuanced. The Arab Spring reverberated enough even in the Gulf states that the notion of a completely quiescent population was clearly inaccurate (Al-Kuwari 2012; Althani 2012). Empirical evidence, specifically policy case studies, began to show that there was a variety of ways in which local populations could push back, register dissent, and effect policy change by the authorities (Foley 2010; Okruhlik 1999). The Qatar case in particular has forced reconsideration of the paradigm. Empirical evidence shows several notable instances of political dissatisfaction, and a more complicated relationship between elites, state authorities, and citizens (Mitchell 2013). Davidson (2012) argued that the "ruling bargain" in the six Gulf monarchies each differed, depending on circumstances and particularly the quantity of rents, and that Qatar was in fact an outlier and its future was "rosier" than that of the other monarchies. Kamrava (2013c) in particular has tried to draw a more nuanced, and cautiously positive, portrait of Qatar. He notes that Qatar is certainly a rentier state in the conventional sense in that it distributes rents through a patronage system of benefits, but he argues that it is unusual to the degree that it distributes that rent in multiple forms (e.g., land, interest free loans, guaranteed state employment and salaries, and high quality social services for nominal fees). Among its other "pillars of power" are an astute Emir (Hamad) and a relatively light-handed security apparatus: "The state may be autocratic ... but it is also responsive to popular sensibilities." In terms of theories about why and how autocracies remain in power, Qatar seems to have combined a workable mix of legitimacy, "low intensity repression," and co-optation of other possible competing elites (Gerschewski 2013).

The focus of this book is different. While we acknowledge that the state's control of a vast amount of hydrocarbon wealth affects the policy-making dynamic of the polity in crucial ways, we are interested in the *dynamics of policy-making* in a rentier state context, with Qatar as our case study. This springs from the simple but unexamined fact that rentier states have to *do things* with their money. The "high quality services" that supposedly buy off the citizenry, like health and education, are extremely complicated to design and implement. The same is true of housing, transportation, and communications infrastructure, especially since these are being built rapidly and simultaneously. Cities, roads, schools, hospitals, arenas—and the complex society that accompanies them—rise overnight from the sand and sea. Policy choices have to be made, and programs have to be designed and then implemented. This requires substantial and sophisticated state capacities if it is to be done well.

We suggest that Qatar is not merely developing services to placate and pacify its citizens. The scale of its ambitions is what we call here *transformative*. The Qatar National Vision 2030, for example, has the goal of "transforming Qatar into an advanced country by 2030, capable of sustaining its own development and providing for a high standard of living for all of its people for generations to come." Kamrava (2013c: 10) notes how Qatar is engaged in "a frantic effort to construct an entirely new society." He calls

Emir Sheihk Hamad's accomplishments "transformative," and the resulting state agenda "catalytic" (following Weiss 1998) and reflecting an ideology of "high modernism" identified through 20th century authoritarian planning and development disasters by Scott (1998). The Qatari version has been more tempered in that it is less authoritarian and has shown more respect for local tradition, as opposed to a blind faith in rationalistic science. Because the Qatar experiment lacks some of this modernist tinge *à la Scott* (though not all), we prefer the term "transformative."

The Qatar National Development Strategy (2011–2016), discussed in various chapters, is breathtaking in its scope and ambition. It wants indeed to transform Qatar into an "advanced country," but by that it means "one of the best" advanced countries—not an Italy or an Iceland, but a Denmark, or perhaps "Denmark plus." This is reinforced daily in Doha—the road barriers that hive off construction projects all have "Qatar Deserves the Best" emblazoned on them. The "best" means the best and most advanced health care, the best and most advanced educational system, the best and most advanced environmental standards (paradoxically, a country with the world's third largest gas reserves wants to go green), and so on. Scott's "high modernist" projects come rightly to mind, since Qatar has goals, and hubris, on the same scale as the transformation of the Soviet Union to an industrial economy, or the building of the modern Le Corbusier city. This ambition is even inscribed in the Constitution. The Council of Ministers is to prepare an annual report, accompanied by "a plan drawing up the most adequate ways for achieving comprehensive development of the State, providing the necessary conditions for its development and prosperity" (Art. 121, sec. 11).

The notion of a transformative state—perhaps because of its association with the overweening disasters of "high modernism," or because it assumes a dominant "comprehensive political authority" (Migdal 2001: 113) absent from most Western states—has not been explored in the literature. Where comprehensive authority has been exercised in the development context, it is usually described as disastrous in much the same terms as Scott's analysis (Easterly 2006, 2013; Moyo 2009). On the other hand, there are examples of successful economic and governance transformations in Singapore (Yew 2000) and China (Coase and Wang 2012), and at least reviving pockets of academic interest in entrepreneurial states (Mazzucato 2013). In the policy literature, there has also been some focus on the challenges of "wicked problems" (Levin, et al. 2012; Rittel and Webber 1973)—another way of posing the issue of transformation. In one area in particular—climate change—some analysts have argued that "this changes everything" and that major social and economic transformations are needed to save the planet (Klein 2014).

In this book, we will focus on Qatar as a transformative state. We define a transformative state as *one that seeks to introduce and implement, over a comparatively short time, a radical reconfiguration of social, economic, and political institutions in a country*. We cannot assess the ultimate success of this agenda—it is too soon—but we are interested in the policy dynamics of its development and implementation. By this we mean the choices made in specific policy fields; the processes and personnel engaged in developing solutions and strategies; the implementation resources, mechanisms, and tools; and the reception and engagement of stakeholders and societal actors. In this we are probing the *capacity* of the Qatari state to undertake its agenda. Capacity as a key dimension in governance has attracted more attention recently (Fukuyama 2013; Holt and Manning 2014), and it draws us away from, and we hope beyond, the rentier state *problématique* of governance as authority relations and institutions to check or control that authority. From that perspective, of course, Qatar is simply an authoritarian state and consequently ranks low on governance measures that emphasize voice and accountability. Our interest is in government effectiveness or capacity, its ability to carry out its ambitious and transformative agenda. A full understanding of governance in Qatar requires an understanding of these policy dynamics, ones that have only been explored on the surface. Whether these dynamics are entirely unique to Qatar, or whether they cast some light on transformative projects in other states or policy fields, is something that we take up in the conclusion.

## Overview

In Chapter 2, Hassan Al-Sayed provides a detailed examination of Qatar's constitutional and legislative system. Of course, the starting point in understanding that system is that Qatar is a monarchy, ruled by the Al-Thani family and tribe. The central question, from both a constitutional and a policy-making perspective, is how absolute that monarchy is, how constrained it is in law and in practice. As with the ancient monarchies of Europe, historically Qatar's monarchy (as with the other Gulf sheikdoms) has been absolute (though constrained by specific Arabic principles and conventions on consultations and councils). Since statehood in 1971,

Qatar has had two constitutions. The first was the Provisional Basic Law of 1970, drafted entirely by the Emir and his advisors, and without public input. It was amended several times, so its successive versions came to be known as the Amended Provisional Basic Law. It remained in place until the current Constitution was adopted by popular referendum in 2003 and ratified on June 8, 2004. The chapter examines the various provisions of the current Constitution, particularly the balance of power between the Shura Council (the legislature) and the Emir and his Council of Ministers. It is clear that the balance is strongly tipped in favor of the Emir. He appoints the Prime Minister and Council of Ministers, and he can dismiss them. All legislation must be ratified by the Emir. The Shura Council is only partly elected—of its 45 members, 15 are to be appointed by the Emir. Even at that, the provisions for the election of the Council have been repeatedly delayed, so all the members are currently appointed by the Emir. The chapter details the ways in which even the formal powers of the Shura Council can be easily neutralized by the Emir. He also controls appointments to all the courts, including the Supreme Constitutional Court (which, while appointed in 2008, has never sat). Finally, the chapter points out that certain key legislative areas are exempt from administrative law review, including matters of Qatari nationality, Emiri decrees, "protection of society" legislation, and press and association. There is no doubt, therefore, that while Qatar is a constitutional monarchy in name, it remains a highly centralized political system in practice. The issue is how this maps against the policy-making system, a system that requires the careful and detailed design of programs and their implementation to fulfill national agendas and deliver complicated modern public services. This is a related, but different story that is the focus of this book.

In Chapter 3, Jocelyn Sage Mitchell and Leslie A. Pal explore the design and implementation of the Qatar National Vision 2030 (QNV) and Qatar National Development Strategy, 2011–2016 (QNDS)—the foundations of the state's modern transformative agenda. Of course, oil revenues had been flowing into the country since the first exports in 1949, and though they were modest in comparison with some of the richer Gulf monarchies, they did provide a basis for development, especially under Emir Khalifa. The development of the North Field gas reserves, however, brought a different phase, and waves of revenues began to build in the 2000s. What to do with them? The chapter shows that there was clearly a key moment at which the ruling family, the Emir in particular, decided that a national development strategy had to be developed, in conjunction with new policy-making institutions for both the design and implementation of that strategy. The General Secretariat for Development Planning was established, international experts were recruited not simply as consultants but as government staff, and entirely new forms of policy development and coordination were established. The QNDS was a state-of-the-art document, notable for its ambition and scope, but it had the extraordinary foundation of almost limitless financial resources. The chapter shows the difficult tensions that existed in trying to design coordinative central government machinery (e.g., a functioning cabinet and ministries) in a system still dominated by the Emir and the ruling family. A key question is whether the QNDS was the product of a moment—the personality of the Emir, the riches that came with high oil prices and engagement across key actors—or whether it is sustainable in the form of the next development phase to 2030.

Two chapters address education. In Chapter 4, Lolwah R.M. Alkhater explores the reforms to the K-12 educational system in Qatar. Modern schools developed in the 1950s as Qatar itself developed through the economic stimulus of oil. The Ministry of Education was established in 1957 and started standardizing and systematizing pre-university education, including the development of its own curriculum and textbooks in 1965, and the establishment of the first institute to prepare local teachers in 1966. Within twenty years, public education covered the entire population, accommodating males and females (though in gender-segregated schools) and citizens and non-citizens in primary, preparatory, and secondary levels. In the 1990s several incomplete and partial reforms took place including the establishment of the Scientific Schools in 1999. In 2004 a major transformational agenda—"Education for a New Era"—was launched by the newly established Supreme Education Council during the tenure of Sheikha Al-Mohmoud, the first female Minister in the history of Qatar. The RAND Corporation had been contracted in 2001 to advise on the reform, and the authorities decided on the charter school model (termed Independent Schools). This required the creation of a Supreme Council on Education (SEC) in 2002 to oversee the conversion of all public schools under the authority of the Ministry of Education into independent schools. It took until 2011 to achieve that conversion, and one year later an additional reform was introduced to provide school vouchers. As the chapter points out, this was in effect a major decentralization, since each independent school had a separate contract with the SEC and was responsible for its own finances, curriculum, and teaching resources, while remaining compliant with overall SEC educational standards. The model was heavily market-oriented and had all the familiar aspirations of autonomy, parental choice, and competitive pressures for specialization as well as excellence. But it was disruptive and generated an unprecedented (from a rentier state theory perspective) public criticism. The rapid pace of the reform, the duality of decision-making (Ministry of Education and Supreme Education Council), and the complexity of the transformation from the traditional deep-rooted centralization into the visionary (though blurry) decentralization, besides many other factors discussed in the chapter, created a unstable policy scene. This instability and rivalry between the old system and new have negatively affected students' performance, learning quality, and the overall organization of the K-12 education. Although all schools became independent schools in 2011, marking the end of the Ministry of Education and turning the SEC into a solo decision-maker, technically Education for a New Era is no longer in effect. Starting from 2012 the SEC launched a series of reversal decisions that effectively abandoned the charter reform model. (In January 2016 the SEC was disbanded by Emir decree, in favour of a single Ministry model.)

In Chapter 5, Ahmed Baghdady analyzes the massive attempts that have been made to develop a domestic post-secondary educational sector from scratch and virtually overnight. It focuses on three related initiatives: (1) establishing university branch campuses and the creation of the Education City, (2) reforming Qatar University, and (3) reforming the government higher education scholarship system. The de facto and early post-secondary policy choice for most of the GCC states was simply to send qualified students abroad, but demand rapidly increased and was coupled with a growing sense that there needed to be domestic universities, for both nationalistic as well as pedagogical reasons. Qatar University was established in 1977, and like its counterparts in the GCC adopted and followed models from other well-established post-secondary institutions in the Middle East. The next phase was to attract world-class universities to establish branch campuses, with the UAE and Qatar as outstanding examples of this strategy. The Qatar Foundation was established in 1995, headed by Sheikha Moza Bint Nasser, and it invited six universities to be the core of its Education City, paying for all their start-up costs and infrastructure. This initiative was not simply about post-secondary education, but ultimately about economic diversification toward a knowledge-based economy, as outlined in the QNV and QNDS. In 2011, these branch campuses and programs were brought under the umbrella of Hamad bin Khalifa University (HBKU), an arrangement that is still evolving but is intended to consolidate the different programs in a "multi-varsity" model. Reforms to Qatar University and to the scholarship program were undertaken at almost the same time as the development of the Education City, and the chapter outlines the implementation challenges and the mounting societal resistance to such rapid transformation, particularly in the initial drive to quality that actually restricted some university spaces. This has led to some reforms to Qatar University (e.g., reintroducing Arabic instruction) and the creation of a community college option.

We then move to urban development and health care. In Chapter 6, Ashraf Salama and Florian Wiedmann show the strains of accommodating such rapid population growth, with its unique demographics, in a small urban space like Doha, while at the same time trying to transform that space into a modern, regional hub. The chapter argues that the new urban development era in Qatar and the Gulf region is a major shift from oil-driven development toward the creation of "dynamic service hubs" for a post-hydrocarbon future. In the Doha case, massive development projects had to be coupled with new administrative vehicles both to implement the developments themselves and to manage the new "built environment" that has sprung from the desert. As we see with education, this involved—again, counter-intuitively from the understanding of Qatar as a centralized monarchy—a substantial degree of decentralization. In urban policy, this has led to "city-within-a-city" projects managed by private sector consortia and linked through public sector infrastructure such as the new rail line and road systems. This has been accompanied by a deregulation of the real estate market and a shift from centralized urban governance to "multi-layered cooperation among various stakeholders." The list of simultaneous development projects has turned Doha into a massive construction site: Lusail City, West Bay, Education City, the rail line, stadiums for the FIFA World Cup in 2022, Hamad International Airport, Souq Waqif (now almost complete), Katara Cultural Village, and three new museums (the National Museum, the Orientalist Museum, and the Olympic and Sports Museum). Salama and Wiedmann point out that these investment decisions, often driven by members of the ruling family with real estate interests of their own, overwhelmed the planning capacity of the Ministry of Municipal Affairs and Agriculture. Planning regulations were regularly interpreted as guidelines and constantly revised, and master developers were given extensive rights to implement their own projects without requiring government planning approvals. This rapid and uncoordinated growth has led to some stunning if somewhat isolated successes—the Corniche, the Souq Waqif, Education City, and the Pearl. But these successes reside within an urban landscape characterized by a low density center surrounded by urban peripheries, gated developments such as the Pearl, an inconsistent urban morphology of high- and low-rise buildings, and often low-quality construction. Efforts are being made, however, to develop a more coordinated master plan in line with the QNV and to harness these transformational energies.

Health care is addressed in Chapter 7. Demographic pressures have been the key driver in this field, both for the provision of the full range of modern medical services, as well as the facilities to deliver those services. As an indicator of the challenge, the population grew by 81 % between 2005 and 2009, while the number of health facilities and hospital beds increased only slightly. Intense efforts to address this gap began in the late 2000s, marked by the creation of the Supreme Council of Health in 2009. Between 2009 and 2012, however, three new public hospitals were opened, bringing the national total to 13: eight public hospitals, one semipublic hospital, and four private hospitals. The chapter provides detailed evidence on the marked success of these efforts across the range of usual indicators of the population health status. The number of health personnel per 100,000 population increased as well and by 2012 had exceeded OECD averages. All of this was, of course, based on ballooning expenditures in the sector, but this was a deliberate, transformative strategy of creating (as the QNV stated) "a comprehensive, world-class healthcare system whose services are accessible to the whole population." It has to be remembered that the intricate healthcare systems that are taken for granted in developed countries—primary care facilities, hospitals, diversified and extensive healthcare professionals, clinics, private providers of key medical services—all had to be created, quickly, from scratch. Also, a national insurance scheme with coverage for both Qataris and non-Qataris had to be designed and implemented. Not surprisingly, and similar to other key policy initiatives that have the highest national priority, decision-making powers for the sector were lodged with the Supreme Council of Health and its Board of Directors, chaired by the then Heir Apparent. The chapter judges these efforts to be, on the whole, a success, in part because of the concentration of authority in the Supreme Council. Challenges remain, principally with ensuring the application of standards, health care promotion, the development of primary care, and extending the national insurance scheme, Seha, to include the entire population (covering both nationals and non-nationals will be a GCC first).

Next, we examine the transformation in the social sphere in two related dimensions: the Qatari family and the role of women, as well as the issue of Qatari social identity. Some of this transformation is a deliberate strategy—for example, forging a healthy and educated population as measured by modern, international standards. Some of it is a reaction to and effect of transformations in other spheres, such as the economy, immigration, and factors such as information technology. Chapter 8, by Lina Kassem and Esraa Al-Muftah, examines Qatar's reshaping and buttressing of the family. The QNV itself highlighted the challenge of balancing modernization around local culture and traditions, but the chapter argues that the traditional extended, tribal family has been undermined by the transformative agenda. As other chapters have noted, tribal allegiances continue to play an important role in Qatar and in the GCC states, but land distribution and tenure has broken down the contiguity of family members and increasingly shifted most of the key social protective functions of the family to the state. Kassem and Al-Muftah argue that the family remains a key value for Qataris, and it is highlighted in the QNV and QNDS, even as the expectation is that it will "modernize," in part through the enhanced role (within traditional boundaries) of women. However, the Qatari family is threatened by declining birthrates, lower marriage and higher divorce rates, reliance on domestic servants for child-rearing, a high migrant population, and contradictory pressures on women to have more children and participate in the labor force. State policy seems to be torn between full-bore modernization in the economy and education, and a muddle of efforts to encourage strong families (and hence, key traditional roles for women), for example, through the Permanent Population Committee.

In Chapter 9, Amal Al-Malki explores the process of forging a new Qatari national identity to align with a transformed society and culture. Al-Malki is careful to emphasize that national identities are "constructs," not some preordained and static quality given by history. After the discovery of oil, the national identity in Qatar has been framed successively against the backdrop of larger collectivities such as the "Arab identity" and then the "Gulf identity." In the last twenty years, the complicated international and regional context has led to an emphasis on local and national identities and the distinctiveness of each of the Gulf states. National projects have been launched to reimagine communities, history, and identity, often creating a tension between outward projections and local authenticities. One of those tensions is in citizenship: it is deliberately restrictive in order to protect a small and culturally vulnerable native population, but it affects long-time residents (many of them Arab) who see Qatar as their home but can never be full citizens. Another tension is the second-class citizenship of women, particularly women who marry non-Qataris and cannot pass their citizenship on to their children. The Qatari national project has developed a discourse of balancing "tradition with modernity," a discourse that Al-Malki argues is being molded to equate identity with state (and hence, royal family) development, as well as a narrative of "tribalism" connected to sand and sea. But this discourse and narrative is not uncontested or even uniquely dominant. The chapter outlines responses that articulate identity in a different key: either in traditional terms or in emerging and more mixed identities as articulated by Qatari youth in traditional and new social media, such as blogs (particularly ones by women). Al-Malki contrasts this with state efforts in heritage projects such as museums and the Katara Village, which project a single history of a single people—all in the face of a real society that is in fact multi-ethnic and multicultural, with, as she puts it "colour patches that don't necessarily complement each other." She concludes that the current national project needs to develop a richer and more inclusive model of citizenship if it is to be sustainable.

Three chapters address different aspects of development and economic policies and sustainability. In Chapter 10, Hend Al Muftah examines demographic policies and human capital challenges. In Chapter 11, Rabi Mohtar analyzes the water-food-energy security nexus. Chapter 12, by Khalid Alkhater, rounds out the discussion with a view of macroeconomic policy development, especially monetary and exchange rate policy, in the face of declining oil and gas revenues.

In brief, this trio of chapters probes Qatar's people, resources, and broad economic policies. Demographic issues are touched on in various chapters, but Al-Muftah outlines them in detail. It is more than a matter of going from small to large; it is the disproportionate size of the expat population, at about 90 % of the total population, and the gender imbalance. The labor force reliance on expats has led to the Qatarization policy, first introduced in the 1970s in the oil and gas sector, and then built momentum with different quotas for the private and public sectors. This has been supplemented by a series of measures to restrict and control the reliance on foreign workers. The chapter argues that these might be successful, but only if Qatarization moves from a numerical, quota-based framework to one that focuses on the quality of human resources. This has implications for a range of labor market related policies, including education. Chapter 11 on the water-food-energy nexus complements Chapter 10 in surveying the strain that population growth has put on these key resources. Qatar is drawing down its already limited natural water supplies, imports almost all of its food, and is one of the world's most intensive per capita energy users, with massive growth in annual consumption rates. The chapter argues that the three resources are interconnected and have to be addressed through a nexus of integrated policies. The chapter has a case study on Qatar's Food Security Plan, which is a step in the nexus direction but has implementation gaps. Finally, Chapter 12 shifts to a macroeconomic perspective in examining the fiscal and monetary policy tools at Qatar's disposal for its transformational project. Alkhater points out that since 1973, shortly after independence, Qatar established the Qatar Monetary Authority and its own currency, the riyal. The riyal was de facto pegged to the US dollar, in part to project monetary credibility and in part of stabilize government revenues (generated through oil and gas exports, which are denominated in dollars). Though these were clearly advantages at the time, they did strip the government of two important economic policy instruments: monetary policy (interest rates) and exchange rate policy. In terms of macroeconomic policy, that left the government with only one instrument to deal with booms and busts, fiscal policy. Even so, since Qatar has essentially no income tax, it only had the spending side of this instrument. Nonetheless, this instrument worked quite well during the period when the USA dominated the global economy, especially oil and gas consumption. If the US economy declined, so did the demand and hence the price for oil. As a result, the GCC economies declined as well; they were essentially synchronized. Whatever the US government did to stimulate or cool its economy fed through to the GCC with an equivalent effect. This has changed in the last twenty years as global demand for oil has been gradually driven more and more by Asian (particularly China) and emerging economies. The global financial crisis in 2008 further exacerbated the "de-synchronization" of the US and GCC economies—what was good in terms of monetary and exchange rate policy for the USA was no longer necessarily good for the GCC. This has been clear since 2008, when the US Federal Reserve has been trying to revive the moribund American economy, even while Qatar has been booming and trying to deal with an overheated economy. Alkhater urges a more independent monetary policy, one that equips the government to manage a more sustainable and stable growth path.

Chapter 13 shift to Qatar's regional and global role, by Abdulaziz Al-Horr, Ghalia Al-Thani, M. Evren Tok, and Hany Besada. It argues that Qatar has deliberately used an approach of "nested power" to pursue and achieve its foreign and domestic policy goals. While "soft power" is a concept developed by international relations specialists, it tends to see non-military instruments as relatively anemic and disaggregated. This chapter shows how the Qatari government has used a variety of tools and resources in a coordinated and multi-dimensional way that go well beyond military capacity and even economic clout through hydrocarbon exports. Qatar, as other chapters have shown, has invested heavily in education and in state-owned enterprises in the oil and gas sector. In addition, it backed and has continued to support the Al Jazeera news network, a sovereign fund investment portfolio in prestigious properties, a national airline, and even investments and aid in developing countries. The FIFA World Cup, despite the various controversies that surround it, was the clearest stab at international branding of Qatar as a sports hub and a regional leader yet somehow "Western friendly." As with all its transformative endeavors, the key question is whether this is sustainable, given the shifts in strategic leadership and the inherent challenge of both "punching above its weight" and punching in all directions simultaneously.

We take up the issue of policy sustainability in our concluding chapter.

## Notes

1. For a pre-1868 history, see Rahman (2006).
2. Though not mentioned in the Constitution, the executive structure also makes use of Supreme Councils (SC). In January 2015, there were two: SC for Health and SC of Education. Both Councils were disbanded in early 2016 by Emir decree.
3. This clause was used in 2012 to sentence a poet, Mohammed Rashid Hassan Nasser al-Ajami, to life imprisonment. The sentence was later commuted to 15 years.

## Bibliography. Qatar: Policy Making in a Transformative State

Al-Kobaisi, Abdulla Juma. 1979. *The Development of Education in Qatar, 1950–1977, with an Analysis of Some Educational Problems*. Durham, UK: University of Durham, School of Education.
Al-Kuwari, Rabia bin Sabah. 2012. The open meeting with HH Sheikha Moza at QU for developing the national university [in Arabic]. *Al Sharq Newspaper*, May 13.
Althani, M.A.J. 2012. *The Arab Spring and the Gulf States: Time to Embrace Change*. London: Profile Books.
Auty, R.M. 1990. *Resource-Based Industrialization: Sowing the Oil in Eight Developing Countries*. Oxford: Oxford University Press.
Babar, Zahra. 2014. The cost of belonging: Citizenship construction in the State of Qatar. *Middle East Journal* 68(3): 403–420.
Bahry, L. 2013. Qatar: Democratic reforms and global status. In *Governance in the Middle East and North Africa: A Handbook*, ed. A. Kadhim, 250–274. London: Routledge.
Beblawi, H. 1987. The rentier state in the Arab world. In *The Rentier State*, eds. H. Beblawi and G. Luciani, 49–62. London: Croom Helm.
Beydoun, N. M., & Baum, J. (2012). *The Glass Palace: Illusions of Freedom and Democracy in Qatar*. New York: Algora Publishing.
Blanchard, C. M. (2014). Qatar: Background and U.S. relations. *Congressional Research Service Report*, 5.
Chaudhry, Kiren Aziz. 1997. *The Price of Wealth: Economics and Institutions in the Middle East*. Ithaca: Cornell University Press.
Coase, R., and N. Wang. 2012. *How China Became Capitalist*. Houndmills, Basingstoke: Palgrave Macmillan.
Cooper, Andrew F., and Bessma Momani. 2011. Qatar and the expanded contours of small state diplomacy. *International Spectator* 46(2): 127–142.
Cooper, Andrew F., and Timothy M. Shaw. 2009. Diplomacy of small states at the start of the twenty-first century: How vulnerable? How resilient? In *The Diplomacies of Small States: Between Vulnerability and Resilience*, eds. Andrew F. Cooper, and Timothy M. Shaw, 1–18. Houndmills, Basingstoke: Palgrave Macmillan.
Crystal, Jill. 1995. *Oil and Politics in the Gulf: Rulers and Merchants in Kuwait and Qatar*, Rev. edn. Cambridge: Cambridge University Press.
Davidson, C.M. 2009. *Abu Dhabi: Oil and Beyond*. London: Hurst and Company.
Davidson, C. M. Ed. 2011. *Power and Politics in the Persian Gulf States*. London: Hurst and Company.
Davidson, Christopher M. 2012. *After the Sheikhs: The Coming Collapse of the Gulf Monarchies*. London: Hurst and Company.

Easterly, W. 2006. *The White Man's Burden: Why the West's Efforts to Aid the Rest have Done so Much Ill and So Little Good*. New York: Penguin.
Foley, S. 2010. *The Arab Gulf States: Beyond Oil and Islam*. Boulder, CO: Lynne Rienner Publishers.
Fromherz, Allen J. 2012. *Qatar: A Modern History*. London: I.B. Tauris.
Fukuyama, F. 2013. Commentary: What is governance? *Governance* 26(3): 347–368.
Gerschewski, J. 2013. The three pillars of stability: Legitimation, repression, and co-optation in autocratic regimes. *Democratization* 20(1): 13–38.
Gray, Matthew. 2013. *Qatar: Politics and the Challenges of Development*. Boulder, CO: Lynne Rienner Publishers.
Herb, Michael. 1999. *All in the Family: Absolutism, Revolution, and Democracy in the Middle East Monarchies*. Albany, NY: State University of New York.
———. 2013. *The Tyranny of Experts: Economists, Dictators, and the Forgotten Rights of the Poor*. New York: Basic Books.
———. 2014. *The Wages of Oil: Parliaments and Economic Development in Kuwait and the UAE*. Ithaca, NY: Cornell University Press.
Hertog, Steffen. 2010. *Princes, Brokers, and Bureaucrats: Oil and the State in Saudi Arabia*. New York: Cornell University Press.
Holt, J., and N. Manning. 2014. Fukuyama is right about measuring state quality: Now what? *Governance* 27(4): 717–728.
Hudson, M.C. 1977. *Arab Politics: The Search for Legitimacy*. New Haven: Yale University Press.
Humphreys, M., J. Sachs, and J.E. Stiglitz. 2007. *Escaping the Resource Curse*. New York: Columbia University Press.
Kadhim, A., ed. 2013. *Governance in the Middle East and North Africa: A Handbook*. London: Routledge.
Ibrahim, Ibrahim, and Frank Harrigan. 2012. Qatar's economy: Past, present and future. *QScience Connect* 9: 1–24.
Kamrava, Mehran. 2011. Mediation and Qatari foreign policy. *Middle East Journal* 65(4): 539–556.
Kamrava, M. 2013a. *The Modern Middle East: A Political History since the First World War*, 3 edn. Berkeley, CA: University of California Press.
———. 2013b. *Qatar: Small State, Big Politics*. Ithaca, NY: Cornell University Press.
Kéchichian, J.A. 2008. *Power and Succession in Arab Monarchies: A Reference Guide*. London: Lynne Rienner Publishers.
Klein, N. 2014. *This Changes Everything: Capitalism vs. The Climate*. New York: Simon and Schuster.
Krane, Jim. 2013. *Stability versus Sustainability: Energy Policy in the Gulf Monarchies*. EPRG Working Paper 1302. Cambridge Cambridge Working Paper in Economics. Retrieved from http://www.eprg.group.cam.ac.uk

Lambert, J. 2011. Political reform in Qatar: Participation, legitimacy and security. *Middle East Policy* 18(1): 89–101.
Legrenzi, M., and B. Momani, eds. 2011. *Shifting Geo-Economic Power of the Gulf: Oil, Finance, and Institutions.* Farnham: Ashgate.
Levin, K., B. Cashore, S. Bernstein, and G. Auld. 2012. Overcoming the tragedy of super wicked problems: Constraining our future selves to ameliorate global climate change. *Policy Sciences* 45(2): 123–152.
Luciani, Giacomo. 1987. Allocation vs. production states: A theoretical framework. In *The Rentier State*, eds. Hazem Beblawi, and Giacomo Luciani, 63–82. London: Croom Helm.
———. 2012. Introduction: The resource curse and the Gulf development challenges. In *Resources Blessed: Diversification and the Gulf Development Model*, ed. Giacomo Luciani, 1–28. Berlin: Gerlach Press.
Mahdavy, Hussein. 1970. The patterns and problems of economic development in rentier states: The case of Iran. In *Studies of Economic History of the Middle East*, ed. M.A. Cook, 428–467. London: Oxford University Press.
Moyo, D. 2009. *Dead Aid: Why Aid is not Working and How There is a Better Way for Africa.* New York: Farrar, Straus and Giroux.
Migdal, Joel S 2001. *State in Society: Studying How States and Societies Transform and Constitute Each Other.* Cambridge: Cambridge University Press.
Mitchell, Jocelyn Sage. 2013. *Beyond Allocation: The Politics of Legitimacy in Qatar.* Ph.D., Graduate School of Arts and Science, Georgetown University.
Nafi, Z.A. 1983. *Economic and Social Development in Qatar.* London: Francis Pinter.
Najem, T.P., and M. Hertherington, eds. 2003. *Good Governance in the Middle East Oil Monarchies.* London: RoutledgeCurzon.
Nugée, J., and P. Subacchi, eds. 2008. *The Gulf Region: The New Hub of Global Financial Power.* London: Royal Institute of International Affairs.
Peterson, J.E. 1988. *The Arab Gulf States: Steps Toward Political Participation.* New York: Praeger and Center for Strategic and International Studies.
Potter, L.G., ed. 2009. *The Persian Gulf in History.* Basingstoke: Palgrave Macmillan.
Rahman, H. 2006. *The Emergence of Qatar: The Turbulent Years, 1627–1916.* London: Routledge.
Rittel, H.W.J., and M.M. Webber. 1973. Dilemmas in a general theory of planning. *Policy Sciences* 4(2): 155–169.
Rosman-Stollman, E. 2009. Qatar: Liberalization as foreign policy. In *Political Liberalization in the Persian Gulf*, ed. J. Teitelbaum, 187–209. New York: Columbia University Press.
Ross, Michael L. 2001. Does oil hinder democracy? *World Politics* 53(3): 325–361.

Ross, Michael L 2012. *The Oil Curse: How Petroleum Wealth Shapes the Development of Nations*. Princeton, NJ: Princeton University Press.
Sachs, J.D., and A.M. Warner. 2001. The curse of natural resources. *European Economic Review* 45(4–6): 827–838.
Scott, James C 1998. *Seeing Like a State: How Certain Schemes to Improve the Human Condition Have Failed*. New Haven: Yale University Press.
Yew, L.K. 2000. *From Third World to First: The Singapore Story: 1965–2000*. Singapore: Marshall Cavendish Editions.
Zahlan, R. 1979. *The Creation of Qatar*. London: Barnes and Noble.

CHAPTER 2

# Qatar's Constitutional and Legal System

## Hassan Al-Sayed

This chapter addresses the constitutional and legislative system in the State of Qatar. This system is the institutional foundation of the policy-making process in the country, and while there are a host of informal features and dynamics in that process (discussed in following chapters), they are all anchored in the country's basic legal architecture. The chapter outlines the key provisions of the Qatar Constitution, how legislation is proposed, debated and promulgated, who the competent political authorities are in the legislative process, and how effective the system is in constraining state authority. However, before delving into the details, it is essential first to understand the nature of Qatar's monarchical system and its influence on the legislative system.

### QATAR'S MONARCHICAL SYSTEM

The State of Qatar is a hereditary Emirate similar to the other GCC states. This means that the country is ruled by the Al-Thani family, specifically the descendants of HH the Emir, Sheikh Hamad Bin Khalifa Bin Hamad Bin Abdullah Bin Jassim Bin Mohamed Bin Thani. Such hereditary succession is what distinguishes a monarchy from a republic. Monarchies

H. Al-Sayed (✉)
Qatar University, Doha, Qatar
College of Law, Doha, Qatar

© The Author(s) 2016
M.E. Tok et al. (eds.), *Policy-Making in a Transformative State*,
DOI 10.1057/978-1-137-46639-6_2

around the world vary among absolute monarchy, limited monarchy, and constitutional monarchy, depending on the scope of substantial authority vested in the monarch.

In an absolute monarchy, the monarch has supreme power, despite the multiplicity of agencies and authorities in the country, which only serve as pro-forma political bodies appointed by the monarch. Consequently, these bodies are accountable to the monarch alone. Their role is administrative and regulatory, to enforce legislation either issued by the monarch or receiving his assent. In the case of absolute monarchy, there is no elected parliament; alternatively, there is an appointed council that can make non-binding recommendations. A limited monarchy, on the other hand, is one that may historically succeed the absolute monarchy (as with the Glorious Revolution of 1688 in the United Kingdom), whereby the ruler's powers are relatively reduced, thus restricting his functions in favor of a council. In a limited monarchy, the ruler still retains many powers, such as enacting legislation, appointing ministers, and defining their responsibility and accountability, as well as the right to dissolve the parliament. In parallel with such powers, a parliament is elected by the people to participate alongside the ruler in the legislative process and to perform a political role, that is, monitoring and holding the government accountable. As for the constitutional monarchy, the monarch's authority is further constrained to the benefit of the people, who are viewed as the ultimate source of such authority, and the monarch is left with ceremonial functions only. It is worth noting that having a constitution in a monarchy does not necessarily mean that it is a constitutional monarchy in the strict sense of the term; in fact, the constitution could be used to vest in the monarch the actual power and main governance functions. As a matter of fact, each monarchy could have a constitution; however, in a true constitutional monarchy, the people are sovereign and the ruler's powers are governed and restricted by the constitution, which guarantees freedoms (Fahmy 2006: 135).

To explore the influence of the monarchy underpinned by the Qatari Constitution on the legislative system, it is imperative to investigate the functions vested in HH the Emir by virtue of the Constitution, to see whether these functions are substantial or honorary. On the other hand, it is also necessary to explore the scope of the people's participation in legislation, knowing that the Constitution mandates that legislation be enacted by the Shura Council alone.

## The Emir and State Public Authorities

To clarify the relationship between the Emir and the State Public Authorities, it is essential to investigate the relationship between the Executive, the Legislature, and the Judiciary.

*The Executive* According to Art. 62 of the Constitution, "The Executive Authority shall be vested in the Emir and he shall be assisted by the Council of Ministers."[1] The Emir is the one who appoints the prime minister, usually from the Royal Family, and forms the government by virtue of an Emiri decree and as proposed by the prime minister (Art. 118). Furthermore, he devises the state public policy with the assistance of the Council of Ministers. The prime minister and the ministers will then be collectively and individually accountable to the Emir for executing the government's policy and performing their duties and authorities respectively (Art. 123). The Emir, for his part, may dismiss the prime minister and the ministers. Also, many of the Council resolutions must be submitted to him for ratification and publication, such as ratifying the regulations and resolutions which are issued or adopted by the Council to execute the law, establishing and governing government agencies and public entities, ensuring internal security, maintaining public order, approving of economic projects and means of execution, protecting national interests abroad, and governing foreign affairs.[2]

*The Legislature* The Emir's powers go beyond the Council and the Executive to reach the Legislature, that is, the Shura Council. In fact, the Constitution stipulates to the Emir substantial functions which undermine the effectiveness of the Shura Council. Such functions include appointing 15 of the Shura Council members, dismissing or accepting members' resignations, convening the Council through a decree (which is a substantial power as it prevents the Council from convening unless called to order by the Emir), closing the session, extending the legislature's term for another four years, adjourning the session, and dissolving the Shura Council.[3]

*The Judiciary* The Emir appoints the president of the Supreme Judiciary Council. According to the Judiciary Law, this Council provides its opinion regarding the appointment, promotion, transfer, secondment, and retirement of judges. Such key decisions will be influenced by the president appointed by the Emir. In addition to this, the Emir has the power to appoint the president and members of the Supreme Constitutional Court and may issue an Emiri decree to suspend any judge from service as per the Judiciary Law, for reasons pertaining to the "public interest," which is a vague expression that cannot be invalidated by any authority.[4]

In outlining the functions of the Emir, it becomes clear that his role in ruling and running the country's affairs is not ceremonial as in a true constitutional monarchy. On the contrary, he enjoys powers of utmost importance and has the final say as to making, approving, or ratifying legislation. It is worth noting as well that the Constitution, despite explicitly stating all such functions, leaves the door open for any additional functions, since Art. 67/10 of the Constitution stipulates that the Emir shall discharge "any other functions vested upon him by this Constitution or the law."

### Emir's Prerogatives in Legislation

The Emir's functions in term of legislation encompass the Constitution, the laws, and the regulations.

*Constitution* According to Art. 144 of the Constitution, The Emir "shall have the prerogative to apply for the amendment of one or more of the articles of this Constitution." Any amendment proposed by the Shura Council shall not enter into force before the approval of the Emir, who has the right to reject the same. If the proposal for amendment is rejected, the rejection shall be considered final and may not be overruled by the Shura Council.

*Laws* The Emir shall have the prerogative to ratify and promulgate a law. He may also reject and refer back a draft law to the Shura Council. The Emir may also suspend the enforcement of a law for the duration he views appropriate to serve the country's highest interests (Art. 106). In case the Shura Council is dissolved, the Emir assumes the functions of the Legislature entirely, assisted by the Council of Ministers (Art. 104).

*Regulations* The Emir may endorse the executive regulations and regulations specific to establishing and governing the work of government agencies and public entities. These regulations are known as the governing regulations.[5] The Emir may also issue emergency regulations (legal decrees), which are laws issued by him when the Shura Council is not convened and in exceptional circumstances that cannot afford any delay. Such emergency regulations are as legally valid as normal legislation (Art. 70).

## Shura Council's Prerogatives in Legislation

The Council's prerogatives in legislation may be divided into four main components:

1. The Council's role in the amendment of certain s of the **Constitution**. According to Art. 144 of the Constitution, the Shura Council may begin the amendment procedures by proposing and discussing amendments; however, "the said amendment shall not be into force before the approval of the Emir," which means that no article of the Constitution may be amended without the Emir's approval.
2. The Council's role in promulgating **ordinary laws**. According to the Constitution, each member of the Shura Council has the right to propose a law and the Council may discuss and endorse draft laws. Furthermore, in case the draft law is not ratified by the Emir, the latter will have to ratify the same in case the Shura Council succeeds in endorsing this draft law again. However, the Constitution renders such prerogatives challenging, as it prescribes a practically impossible majority of two-thirds (Arts. 105, 106) within the Shura Council to overrule the Emir's rejection of the draft law. For additional measure, the Constitution grants the Emir, in case such majority is achieved, the authority to suspend the enforcement of the ratified law for the duration he sees fit. As such, virtually no law may be promulgated against the Emir's will.
3. The Council's role in **legal decrees**: According to the Constitution, legal decrees issued by the monarch while the Shura Council is not in session must be "submitted to the Shura Council at the first meeting" to reach a decision about them. However, the Constitution restricts the authorities of the Council so as to keep such legal decrees in force, by facilitating their approval and complicating their rejection or amendment. Article 70 of the Constitution stipulates that "the Council may within a maximum period of forty days from the date of submission and with a two-thirds majority of its Members reject any of these decree-laws or request amendment thereof." Thus, exceeding such period will be considered as an approval of the legal decree by the Council.
4. According to the Constitution, the Emir and the Council of Ministers assume the functions of the legislature entirely while the Shura Council is dissolved, which may be a relatively a long period possibly reaching six months (Art. 104).

Based on the above, we conclude that the authorities of the Qatari Shura Council regarding legislation are extremely limited. When comparing the prerogatives of the Emir and the Shura Council, it becomes clear that the monarchy adopted by the Qatari Constitution is technically a constitutional one in the sense that its powers are limited by and balanced against the legislative and judicial branches, but in practice it is virtually absolute. The Constitution does include specific elements of a limited monarchy, but these are in fact ineffective in limiting the Emir's powers, particularly in terms of legislation.

### *Participation of the Qatari People in Drafting the Constitution*

Comparative analysis suggests four basic methods of drafting constitutions: (1) drafting by the ruler alone, (2) a participatory method that involves both the people and the ruler, (3) a democratic method whereby the constitution is derived from a constituent assembly, and (4) the constitutional referendum method. In the first, the ruler (monarch) will of course have advisors, but of his choosing. As for the participatory method, it generally consists of electing a council that drafts the constitution and then seeks the ruler's approval. The Constitution only enters into effect when the ruler and the elected council mutually approve it. With a constituent assembly, on the other hand, the constitution enters into effect once formulated and endorsed by the elected council, without having to seek the ruler's approval. Finally, the constitutional referendum method requires the approval of the entire citizenry through public referendum.

In the State of Qatar, the first constitution—the Provisional Basic Law of 1970—was drafted by the Emir and his advisors without public involvement. At the time, the political developments in the region and the UK's announcement that it would grant the Gulf sheikhdoms independence, led the Emir of Qatar to promulgate the Provisional Basic Law. This law was amended after Qatar's independence and its refusal to join the Arab Emirates Federation. The substantial amendments to the Provisional Basic Law were such that the law was more of a new Constitution, and it was called the Amended Provisional Basic Law. The amendment was effected by the Emir, again without public participation.

The Amended Provisional Basic Law remained in effect until the Permanent Constitution of the State of Qatar was adopted by public referendum in 2003. The idea of a new constitution was proposed in 1998 by HH Sheikh Hamad Bin Khalifah, the then Emir of Qatar, at the opening of the twenty-seventh ordinary session of the Shura Council.[6] In 1999, Emiri Decree No. 11 was issued to form and assign the functions of the Permanent Constitution Drafting Committee. The committee included 32 members appointed by the Emir. Article 3 of the Decree indicated that the draft Constitution be written within three years. The decree also allowed the committee to seek the assistance of experts by inviting them to attend its meetings, and to form sub-committees to assist the committee in performing its duties. The committee delivered the draft constitution within three years as prescribed in the decree. The draft Permanent Constitution and explanatory notes were submitted to Sheikh Hamad Bin Khalifa on July 2, 2002.

On April 15, 2003, the Emir issued Decree No. 38 calling for a citizens' referendum on the draft constitution. The referendum took place on April 29, 2003, with the agreement of the vast majority of those eligible to vote. The Permanent Constitution was ratified on June 8, 2004, though it is worth noting that the articles pertaining to the Shura Council have not to date been implemented.

Despite the fact that the Qatari Constitution was approved through public referendum, its popular endorsement was flawed due to several factors:

1. The committee entrusted with the development of the constitution was entirely appointed by the Emir, rather than being elected by the people.
2. The vast majority of those appointed members were ministers and figures of the Executive.[7] For example, the Committee did not include independent or unbiased members, which tips the Constitution balance in favor of the Executive rather than achieving balance among the three branches of the state.
3. Prior to the referendum on the draft Constitution, a promotional campaign was organized including seminars, programs, articles, TV reports, and interviews, all in encouraging a "yes" vote. The state media also played a role in this.
4. The committee supervising the referendum was not independent from the Executive; in fact, the referendum was managed and supervised by the Qatari Ministry of Interior.

The following sections will discuss the legislative process or cycle from "proposal" to "promulgation." As in any legislative system, laws first have to be proposed by the competent executive authority, discussed and debated in a legislature, and endorsed or passed by it, ratified in some fashion, and then promulgated and implemented.

## THE LEGISLATIVE PROCESS

### Who Has the Right to Propose Laws?

The proposal is the engine that drives the legislation process; without a proposal, no law can see the light (Al Saleh 2003: 466–68). Constitutions around the world have different approaches in deciding on the entities entitled to propose laws. Some constitutions, such as that of the Unites States, grant such right to the legislature exclusively. Other constitutions, on the other hand, grant such right to the executive branch solely, such being the case in non-parliamentary systems where Shura or State Councils are the only alternative to the Parliament despite lacking any parliamentary function.

Some constitutions grant the right of proposing laws to the legislature and the executive branch equally, so as to create a certain sort of balance, such as the Tunisian Constitution. Finally, there are constitutions that grant such right to numerous entities, such as the Brazilian Constitution, which authorizes the Parliament, the president, the Head of the Supreme Court, the State Attorney and the citizens to propose laws (Art. 61 of the Constitution of Brazil). In the State of Qatar, there were no legislative rules before 1962 to govern the legislative process including who had the right to propose laws. The few laws[8] issued prior to this date were derived from propositions made by the Emir himself, his son, Sheikh Ahmed, or his nephew, Sheikh Khalifa Bin Hamad ,who both played a significant role in assisting the Emir in administering the state affairs, particularly in the second half of the 1950s. The British Advisor may have had a role in proposing some laws as well.

When the law governing the Government Higher Administration was promulgated in 1962, some aspects of the legislative process became clearer. The Deputy Ruler was granted the function of proposing laws and decrees[9], being the one in charge of devising the state public policy which maximizes economic, social, cultural, and administrative development.[10]

The Deputy Ruler carried out his function of proposing laws independently, until the situation changed with the issuance of the Provisional Basic Law in 1970, which transferred the right of proposing laws to the

Council of Ministers alone. Article 37 of the Provisional Basic Law outlines the functions of the Council of Ministers including the following: "Proposing draft laws and decrees to be submitted to the Ruler for ratification and publication according to the provisions of this Law. Draft laws shall be submitted to the Shura Council for review and discussion before submitting the same to the Ruler." In 1972, the amendment of the Provisional Basic Law came to further confirm the exclusive right of the Council of Ministers to propose laws.[11]

On the other hand, the Legislature did not grant the members of the Shura Council the right to propose laws except after the Permanent Constitution of the State of Qatar was issued in 2004,[12] granting both the Legislature and the Executive the authority to propose laws. According to Art. 121 of the Constitution, the "proposal of draft laws and decrees" was among the Council of Ministers' functions, and according to Art. 105, the Shura Council shall also be authorized to propose laws, as it states: "Every Member of the Council shall have the right to propose bills..."

However, it should be noted that the procedure of proposing laws by the Shura Council may take much longer than the procedure of proposing laws by the Council of Ministers. In fact, the Constitution stipulates that the proposals made by the Shura Council members are to be submitted to the Cabinet to give its opinion on the matter during the same session or the next one.[13] The session is the period during which the Shura Council conducts its work, usually lasting eight months or so. Another difference between the Shura Council and the Cabinet proposals is that the latter has more leverage. In case the Shura Council rejects a proposal made by any of its members, the same proposal may not be re-submitted until the next annual term. Additionally, the Cabinet is free to re-submit a rejected proposal during the same session.[14]

### *Debate and Discussion of Draft Laws*

Discussion is a process that allows members of the Shura Council to review a draft law and identify any shortcomings, gaps, or contradictions in it, in order to address them before its endorsement, by making the necessary amendments (Art. 105). Discussions take place through general and public deliberations involving all the Council members. The general discussion is preceded by a thorough examination of the draft law by a specialized committee made up of several members of the Shura Council. The committee shall submit its findings to the Council, which shall go through the draft law and the committee's report to express its opinion regarding the relevance/irrelevance or consistency/contradiction of its provisions. By doing so, the voting and endorsement of the draft law are made easier.

In Qatar, the first Shura Council was established in 1964. Therefore, the discussion of drafts laws, as one phase of the legislative process, was never regarded as a possibility prior to this date. Discussions would rather take the form of a bilateral dialog between the Deputy Ruler and the Legal Advisor to the Cabinet,[15] in his capacity as President of the Legal Affairs Department, according to the Government Higher Administration Law.[16] The main function of this department was the "formulation of draft laws, decrees, regulations and executive regulations."[17] This [legal affairs] department submitted its reports and findings to the Deputy Ruler.[18]

After the establishment of the first Shura Council in Qatar, presided by the Emir and having among its members the Deputy Ruler and fifteen members of the Royal Family,[19] the Council was bestowed with the authority of "submitting recommendations regarding the issuance of laws."[20] Art. 10 of the Shura Council Incorporation Law stipulates that the government shall submit draft laws to the Council and seek its advice prior to issuing laws. The Emir would preside over the Shura Council sessions he attends and would chair the deliberations without taking part in the vote.[21] This Shura Council did not last long. The 1970 Constitution of the State of Qatar explicitly outlined the function of the Shura Council in discussing draft laws proposed by the Council of Ministers prior to their submission to the Ruler for ratification and publication.[22] The Amended Provisional Basic Law of 1972 further confirmed this function.[23]

When the Permanent Constitution of the State of Qatar was issued, it provided in its Art. 121/1 that draft laws should be submitted to the Shura Council for debates. Art. 97 of the Constitution stipulates that "the Shura Council shall make its internal regulations comprising its internal order and the conduct of its business, the work of committees, organization of sessions, rules of proceedings, voting and all functions stipulated in this Constitution." However, given that these regulations were not drafted as prescribed in the present Constitution, due to the suspension of the Constitutional provisions related to Shura Council, we will be analyzing the process of discussing draft laws according to the internal regulations issued by virtue of Art. 64 of the Amended Provisional Basic Law.

Draft laws are currently discussed through the Shura Council sessions which are, as a general rule (Art. 98), public sessions held weekly on Monday, for the Council to discuss the items listed on the agenda.[24]

Before discussing any draft law, the Shura Council President communicates the draft law to the Council members in preparation for its referral to the specialized committee for examination and advice.[25] The specialized committee entrusted with the examination of draft laws is one of the various Shura Council committees which are formed among its members during the first week of its annual term session, to assist the Council in performing its functions.[26] These committees are the Committee of Legal and Legislative Affairs, the Committee of Financial and Economic Affairs, the Committee of Services and Public Utilities, the Committee of Internal and External Affairs, and the Committee of Cultural and Media Affairs.[27]

In case the specialized committee in charge of studying and advising on the draft law considers that amendments should be recommended, it may request the assistance of the Committee of Legal and Legislative Affairs to advise on the amendment and convenient formulation. Then, the specialized committee refers the draft law and the corresponding recommendations to the Shura Council, which launches the discussions.[28]

According to the regulations, the draft law is discussed over two deliberation cycles; the first cycle of the deliberation sessions is usually lengthier and requires more effort than the second cycle of the deliberation sessions. The first deliberation cycle is also divided into two phases. The first phase consists of discussing the general provisions of the draft law without entering into the details of each clause, in order to secure for the Council initial approval of the draft law. This phase starts with reading the original draft law with the corresponding explanatory notes, if available, and the committee's report inclusive of relevant recommendations and amendments. The right to speak is first given to the rapporteur of the specialized committee, then to the Minister or his representative, then to the members.[29]

If the Council grants its initial approval of the draft law, it moves to the second phase of the first deliberation cycle, which consists of discussing the subject of the draft law by looking into the details of its clauses, one by one, by reading each article and considering suggestions and recommendations on the same.[30]

The regulations give each Council member the right to present suggestions regarding the provisions of the draft law, whether for adding, removing or replacing articles. Such suggestions are to be submitted in writing at least twenty-four hours prior to the discussion session, in order to allow sufficient time for the Committee of Legal and Legislative Affairs to review and advise on the submitted suggestions. However, with the

Council's consent, members may submit their suggestions right before or during the discussion session.[31]

If the proposed amendments are likely to affect the remainder of the draft law provisions, the president shall adjourn the discussions until the specialized committee completes its review and advises on the same.[32] After discussing each article and the proposed amendments, an opinion is given first on the amendments and then on the entire draft law. At this point, the first cycle of deliberations ends.[33]

The president of the Shura Council shall chair the sessions and discussions, grant the right to speak, close the session, propose items for vote, and announce the vote results. No member may speak unless he has sought and received permission to do so. The president will grant the permission to speak in the order in which the requests to speak were made. A member who has not yet expressed his opinion on the subject will be favored over a member who has. Any member who requests to speak may relinquish his turn in favor of another.[34]

The second deliberation cycle shall be limited to discussing amendments proposed by members to the draft law already voted for and endorsed by the Council during the first deliberation cycle. Procedures of discussing amendments in the second deliberation cycle are similar to those of the previous cycle.[35] Then, a final vote is sought on the draft law. If the Council approves the draft law, the discussion and voting phase ends and a new phase of the legislative process is launched, which is the ratification phase.[36]

Although the Shura Council is supposed to follow the foregoing procedures in discussing draft laws according to the regulations, the case is different in practice, as the Council only holds one session for deliberations, lasting for 30 minutes at most, after which the specialized committee's report about the draft law is opened for vote. This shortcut is most probably due to the members' ineffectiveness. Most of the Shura Council members have been Council members for more than fifteen years. Many members appear not to have read the session documents or the specialized committee's report, which would negatively affect the discussions, despite being an essential phase of the legislative process.

### *Emir's Powers of Ratification and Refusal*

Ratification is an essential part of the legislative process. It gives the competent authority the right to approve a draft law in order to promulgate the law. In Qatar, Art. 51 of the Amended Provisional Basic Law stipulated that the functions of the Shura Council shall include the discussion of draft laws proposed by the Council of Ministers and referred to the Shura Council, prior to submitting the same to the Emir for ratification and publication. Article 40 of the Amended Provisional Basic Law indicated that the Shura Council advises on how recommendations are formulated. From these two articles, the Emir's ratification is not a mere formality according to the Amended Provisional Basic Law, whose provisions regarding the Shura Council are still in force. Therefore, the Shura Council cannot overrule the Emir's decision in case he refuses to ratify the draft law.

However, will the situation change if the provisions of the Permanent Constitution related to the Shura Council are enforced? Article 106/1 of the Permanent Constitution stipulates that "any draft law passed by the Council shall be referred to the Emir for ratification," and Art. 67 outlines the functions discharged by the Emir, confirming that such functions include the "ratification and promulgation of laws, and no such law may be issued unless ratified by the Emir" But the question raised is the following: Is the Emir ratification of draft laws as per the Permanent Constitution as effective as in the Amended Provisional Basic Law? To answer this question, the two abovementioned articles of the Constitution should be construed in light of the other constitutional provisions.

Two paragraphs of Art. 106 of the Constitution stipulate that "If the Emir, declines to approve the draft law, he shall return it along with the reasons for such declination to the Council within a period of three months from the date of referral. In the event that a draft law is returned to the Council within the period specified and the Council passes the same once more with a two-thirds majority of all its Members, the Emir shall ratify and promulgate it." As a first impression, we notice from the previous text that the Permanent Constitution adopted a different approach than that the Amended Provisional Basic Law as it granted the Emir the right to reject a draft law and not to effectively ratify it. Thus, the Shura Council would be able to overrule this rejection if it succeeds in re-endorsing the draft law.

However, the Constitution requires the approval of two-thirds of the Council members in order to overrule the Emir's ejection of the draft law, and because many of the members are appointed and not elected, it makes it very hard, if not impossible, to secure this threshold. Article 77 of the Permanent Constitution stipulates that "the Shura Council shall consist of forty-five Members thirty of whom shall be elected by direct, general secret ballot; and the Emir shall appoint the remaining fifteen Members from amongst the Ministers or any other persons. The term of service of the appointed Members shall expire when these Members resign their seats or are relieved from their posts." According to the foregoing provision, the appointed members account for one-third of the total Council members. These members are ethically bound to the Emir as being the person who appointed them. Therefore, it is unlikely that they will vote against any matter that he had rejected.

It should be noted that the Constitution, in Art. 106, grants the Emir three months to return the declined draft law to the Shura Council. However, the Constitution does not address the possibility of the period expiring without the ratification or return of the draft law by the Emir. In other words, what if the period of three months expires while the Emir had neither returned the draft law to the Shura Council not ratified it? Will the draft law be considered ratified by law, as it is the case in other constitutions? For example, Egypt's Constitution of 2012, as amended in 2014, addressed this possibility in Art. 123, which states that "if the draft law is not returned to the Assembly within 30 days, it shall be considered as a valid law and subsequently published." The same period is prescribed in the Kuwait Constitution, which states that "the law shall be promulgated within 30 days of submitting the draft law to the Emir without receiving a request for reconsideration."[37]

In the Qatari Constitution there is no explicit provision stating that the law should be ratified and promulgated in case no action is taken by the Emir. The absence of such provision reduces the pertinence of Art. 106 and is regarded as a gap to suspend the promulgation of laws or indefinitely disregard the draft laws submitted to the Emir.

### *The Official Gazette*

The law enters into force following the draft law endorsement by the Shura Council and its ratification and promulgation by the Emir. For the law to be fairly executed and to govern relationships and disputes, it should be communicated to all individuals and entities in the Official Gazette. In Qatar, the Official Gazette was established by virtue of Law No. 1 of 1961, and it was especially intended for the publication of any newly issued legislation. The publication in this gazette cannot be replaced by the publication of the law through any other media such as the radio, television, or daily newspapers.

For the publication of the law in the Official Gazette, the Qatar Constitution sets out a deadline of two weeks at most from its promulgation date. Article 142 of the Qatar Permanent Constitution stipulates that "laws shall be published in the official Gazette after ratification and promulgation within two weeks of their issue." However, many laws are not usually published within the constitutional period for their publication (that is, two weeks of their issuance date). For example, the Law on Public Finance System, issued by virtue of Law No. 2 of 2015, was promulgated on March 10, 2015 but was not published until June 14, 2015 in issue No. 12 of the Gazette, that is, three months after its promulgation date. Likewise, the Code of Law Practice was published two months after its promulgation date. The same holds true for the Family Law, the Law on the Rule of Law and Inheritance Governance, the Law on Public Benefit Private Institutions, etc. Such examples show that any law is rarely published in the Gazette within two weeks of its promulgation as stipulated in the Constitution.

This contravention is probably due to two main reasons. The first is the time required to gather and classify laws and prepare and send copies thereof for printing. These steps contribute to delaying the publication in one way or another. The second reason is that often only a small number of laws are issued during a period of several weeks, making them hardly worth publishing in an entire issue of the newspaper. In these cases, the Gazette Division at the Ministry of Justice prefers to wait until more laws are promulgated to publish them at once in one issue.

Upon the actual publication of a law, it usually enters into force after a certain period of time of its publication date. In Qatar, the Permanent Constitution sets out a period of one month, as a general rule, from the date of publication. "As a general rule" means that this period may be either shorter or longer, particularly in cases where the law indicates the date of its entry into force. However, if the law itself does not indicate such period, the "general rule" date shall apply, that is, one month starting the publication date.[38]

Upon examining a number of Qatari laws, we find that these laws have different enforcement dates: some enter into force on the promulgation date, that is, before publication, while others enter into force on the publication date or within two to six months of promulgation. The date of entry into force is decided in a way to serve the public interest. If the public interest requires that the law is applied with no delay upon its promulgation, it enters into force on its promulgation date, for example, the decree issuing Law No. 9 of 2001 on the Exemption of Private Health Facilities from Customs Duties.[39] However, if the public interest requires giving people time to sort out and adjust their situation, the law enters into effect within a certain period of its publication to best serve the public interest. Such is the case of the Labor Law, which was set to enter into force within six months of its publication.[40]

The publication of the law is the final step of the legislative process, which started with the proposal, then the discussion, then the endorsement, then the ratification and promulgation. Afterwards, the law enters into practical execution and becomes part of individuals' and communities' lives, until amended or annulled.

## *Time Required to Promulgate a Law*

What is the average time needed to promulgate a law in Qatar? In order to answer this question, and in the absence of official statistics, we examined the phases of promulgating laws in the State of Qatar for the last ten years. However, given how hard it was to collect relevant information, the research was limited to studying the progress of draft laws after being announced in the media. Therefore, the answer does not cover the first steps of the law promulgation cycle, that is, the proposal and first formulation of the draft law. It rather starts at the date of announcing the law in the media, which includes the steps outlined above.

The research concluded that the average time needed to promulgate ordinary laws is one year and a half, noting that this period may be longer or shorter depending on whether the law is a mere amendment of the provisions of an existing law, or an entirely new law, or a new law to replace a previous law, or a law intended to govern economic or commercial affairs. For example, if we study the announced phases leading up to the promulgation of the Law on Electing the Shura Council members, we notice that the process was very slow. During its weekly meeting held on Wednesday, June 6, 2007, the Council of Ministers approved referring the draft law to the Shura Council. However, the Shura Council only studied the draft law and referred it to the competent committee after nine months of receiving it, namely on Monday, March 10, 2008. For its part, the competent committee at the Shura Council (which is the Committee of Legal and Legislative Affairs) held many meetings to discuss the draft law from

March 12, 2008, to May 6, 2008. This means that the Committee took almost two months to study the draft law, which exceeds the "general rule" period of one month, stipulated in Art. 30 of the Shura Council Internal Regulations. Then, on Monday, May 19, 2008, the Shura Council endorsed the Draft Law on Electing the Shura Council Members and submitted the same again to the Council of Ministers, which slept on it for four years until it was finally listed on its agenda on June 6, 2012, when the Council of Ministers agreed in its weekly meeting to start the necessary procedures for promulgating the law. The draft law is still on the shelf until today. Thus, it has been almost eight years since the Council of Ministers agreed to refer the draft law to the Shura Council; yet, the law has still not been promulgated at the time of writing.

By contrast, if we trace the announced phases of promulgating the Law on Establishing the Supreme Constitutional Court, we notice that the process was fast. The Council of Ministers approved of the draft law on Establishing the Supreme Constitutional Court during its weekly meeting held on Wednesday, May 14, 2008 and referred it to the Shura Council, which reviewed and approved its referral to the competent committee on May 26. The competent committee at the Shura Council (which is the Committee of Legal and Legislative Affairs) studied the draft law in one session held on Wednesday, May 28, and returned it to the Shura Council on June 2 to be approved on that same day and submitted to the Council of Ministers. The latter approved the promulgation of the law in its weekly meeting held on June 11, 2008. The law was subsequently promulgated after one week of its approval by the Council of Ministers on June 18, 2008. Thus, the time required to promulgate the said law did not exceed one month and a few days (from May 14 to June 18 2008). Once the law was promulgated, an Emiri order was issued to nominate a new president for the Cassation Court, and a second Emiri order was issued to nominate the former president of the Cassation Court as president of the Supreme Constitutional Court. However, once this change in posts was effected, the Constitutional Court Law was suspended. So despite promulgating the law at this high speed, the law has not yet taken effect and the Court has never convened.

### *The Constitutional Court*

In Qatar, the question of controlling the constitutionality of laws and regulations was never raised before the 1970s as there was no written

Constitution. On April 2, 1970, Qatar issued its short-lived Provisional Basic Law which was amended after the independence and after Sheikh Khalifa bin Hamad Al Thani acceded to power. The control over the constitutionality of laws and regulations was not raised under the Amended Provisional Basic Law, which did not include any provision stipulating for this kind of control, and no legislation was issued to assign any judicial or political body to carry out such role. On the other hand, courts never applied the abstention doctrine whereby a judge abstains from relying on a certain provision of a law or regulation in his judgment, due to its unconstitutionality.

There are two reasons why the control over constitutionality of laws and regulations was never raised under the Amended Provisional Basic Law. First, this law represented a rather flexible constitution. Article 67 stipulated that "the Emir may revise this Basic Law by amending, omitting or adding provisions as he may deem necessary for the higher interests of the State." The amendment to this law depended on the Emir's unilateral will of what he deemed appropriate for the higher interests of the state. Contrary to rigid constitutions, flexible constitutions do not enjoy procedural prevalence, and therefore, any contradiction between a provision in a law and the constitution shall not constitute an issue of essential importance (El-Gamal 1992). Second, under this law, there was no separation of powers, particularly the Legislature and the Executive. As a result, the Executive had control over the three legislative tools, namely the Constitution, the Law and the Regulations. The constituent authority was represented in the Emir who was the head of the Executive, having drafted the Amended Provisional Basic Law and had the exclusive and unilateral authority of revising or amending it. Accordingly, the question of controlling the constitutionality of laws and regulations could not be raised under the Amended Provisional Basic Law. But has the situation actually changed under the Permanent Constitution?

Unlike the Amended Provisional Basic Law, the Qatar Permanent Constitution is considered "rigid." Article 144 provides for strict and more complicated procedures to amend the Constitution compared to amending an ordinary law. Moreover, the Permanent Constitution grants the Shura Council a larger role in lawmaking, compared to its role under the Amended Provisional Basic Law. Therefore, this Council may stand to some extent as an autonomous body, as compared to its role under the Amended Provisional Basic Law, where it served as a secondary body subordinate to the Executive, whose role was to assist the Emir and the

Cabinet in making decisions.[41] Therefore, the question of controlling the constitutionality of laws and regulations is raised under the Permanent Constitution. In fact, Art. 140 goes as far as to state that "the law shall specify the judicial body for settling of disputes pertaining to the constitutionality of laws and regulations, define its powers and method of challenging and procedures to be followed before the said body. It shall also specify the consequences of judgment regarding unconstitutionality."

Based on the above provision, the Qatari Legislature initially issued Law No. 6 of 2007 on the Adjudication of Constitutional Disputes,[42] which entrusted the control over constitutionality of laws and regulations with a special division of the Cassation Court division. The last provision in this law stipulates that it shall be effective as of January 1, 2008; however, it has not entered into force, and the said division has not assumed its role as prescribed by the Legislature.[43] Six months later, new legislation was issued, namely Law No. 12 of 2008, whereby a Supreme Constitutional Court[44] was established, thus annulling the previous law. The reasons why the Legislature renounced the establishment of such division or why the law was repealed before its enforcement were never clarified. However, one can question whether the cancelation of the Law and the establishment of the Court in replacement of the division came as a result of some political circumstances at that time or as a desire to strengthen the principle of control over constitutionality of laws as some observers claim.[45] For example, the law establishing the Supreme Constitutional Court was drafted with remarkable speed (six weeks), after which, by Emiri order the former president of the Cassation Court was appointed the president of the new Constitutional Court. At that point the law on the Constitutional Court was suspended, and the Court has not convened since 2008. As a result, the role of the Cassation Court president was marginalized by appointing him president of a court destined to be ineffective from the very beginning.

Regarding the formation of the judicial body, the repealed Law on the Adjudication of Constitutional Disputes stipulated that the president of the Cassation Court is *ex-officio* president of the Constitutional Division. The remaining members of the Constitutional Division, whether original or alternate members, were appointed by virtue of an Emiri decree based on nominations made by the Supreme Judiciary Council.[46]

In contrast, the current law did not allocate to the Supreme Judiciary Council any role in selecting the members of the Constitutional Court. Article 2 of the Supreme Constitutional Court Law stipulates that the president and the six members of the court shall all be appointed by virtue of an Emiri order, which is in fact an instrument for the Emir to take unilateral decisions. This provision grants the Emir a substantial role in selecting the president and six members of the Supreme Constitutional Court, which could undermine the autonomy of the Constitutional Judiciary in Qatar, especially in that the new law authorizes a wider scope for the selection of members, without limiting it to judges alone, or even to Qataris alone. The 2015 report prepared by the UN Special Rapporteur on the Independence of Judges and Lawyers, Gabriela Knaul, notes that the Emir appoints all judges in courts, which creates "concerns as to the soundness of the current process of appointing judges," arguing that "such unilateralism may expose them to undue political pressure, given that appointments and nominations by the Emir himself greatly influence the judge stands and conduct, particularly when it comes to the representatives of the Executive" (Knaul 2015). If the Special Rapporteur expresses concerns over the appointment of judges in ordinary courts by virtue of an Emiri order based on the Supreme Judiciary Council nominations, her concerns will be multiplied over the unilateral appointment by the Emir of the Supreme Constitutional Court judges, even with no recommendations by the Supreme Judicial Council.

To strengthen the autonomy of the Constitutional Judiciary and to put Art. 140 of the Constitution into effect—emphasizing that the competent body for settling disputes is a judicial body—the majority of the Constitutional Court members should be selected by the Supreme Judiciary Council through secret ballot and according to a process that authorizes candidacy by cassation and appeal judges wishing to join the membership of the Constitutional Court. The Constitutional Court could also include among its members other jurists such as academic professors-in-law, an attorney at the Cassation Court, and a legal adviser to the Ministry of Justice in state affairs administration, to be appointed by an Emiri decree.

Finally, it is worth mentioning—with respect to filing constitutional suits by individuals—that both the previous and current laws stipulate that the court adjudicates on disputes related to the constitutionality of laws and regulations, stating that "during legal suit before a court or a judicial body, if the plaintiff petitions for legal proceedings to judge on the constitutionality of a provision of a certain law or regulation, and the respective court or body deems the petition substantive, the court shall hold off the legal suit and set a date not exceeding 60 days for the plaintiff to file constitutional action. If the action is not filed within this period, the petition will be nullified."

This provision clearly shows that, for individuals, the Qatari Legislature only requires a petition to challenge the constitutionality of a provision of a law or regulation. In other words, when an action is filed before a court or a body to adjudicate on a certain dispute, the plaintiff may petition for legal proceedings regarding the unconstitutionality of the law. As such, individuals may not file any such constitutional action directly before the Constitutional Court; they first have to file an action before an ordinary court then petition for constitutional action.

### *The Administrative Justice System*

Challenging administrative judgments has been separated from the jurisdiction of Qatari judiciary bodies for a long time. Although the civil court, called "Court of Justice," was created in the early 1970s and was preceded by other competent courts, it was not until 2007 that the Legislature explicitly stated that the Qatari Judiciary has jurisdiction to rule on petitions related to revoking final administrative judgments (Mansour 2011).

The Amended Provisional Basic Law (the previous constitution) did not include any provision specifying the competent judicial body to adjudicate on administrative disputes. However, Art. 138 of the Permanent Constitution states that "the law specifies the judicial body competent to adjudicate on administrative disputes, and outlines its regulations and the way it shall conduct its work."

In 2007, Law No. 7 of 2007 on Administrative Dispute Adjudication[47] was issued to establish administrative divisions in the Court of First Instance and the Court of Appeal, to be affiliated to the Supreme Judiciary Council. However, this long overdue law excluded many administrative disputes and decisions from its scope of competence,[48] including the following disputes:

1. Matters related to the Qatari Nationality: The Judiciary does not look into any decision related to the Qatari nationality, whether the cause of the dispute is challenging a judgment that unlawfully deprives a citizen of his or her nationality, or whether it is one that deprives them of their political rights for reasons related to nationality or from benefits accorded to them by law, such as land grants or housing loans.

2. Emiri orders, decisions, and decrees: The danger of excluding such decisions from judiciary control lies, as aforesaid, in the fact that the Emir's authorities in administrating the state affairs are substantial and that many decisions are taken unilaterally by him.
3. Decisions made under the Protection of Society Law: The Protection of Society Law is legislation issued as an exception from the Criminal Procedure Law and allows, if there is strong evidence, detaining a suspect without bringing him to public prosecution for two weeks, extendible to a similar term for a maximum of six months. This law, therefore, violates the constitutional principle that guarantees personal freedom and prohibits the apprehension, search, or detention of persons, or placing them under house arrest or placing restrictions on their freedom of residence or movement, except in accordance with the law.
4. Decisions made under the Law on Associations and Private Foundations: In other words, any decision that rejects the establishment of an association is immune against judiciary control. That is, undoubtedly, contrary to what has been established by the Qatari constitution regarding the establishment of associations.
5. Decisions made under the Print, Publication, and Newspaper and Magazine License Law: This prevents the Judiciary from hearing any appeal against a decision that undermines freedom of opinion, expression, press, and publication.

In addition, the law provides for immunity against judiciary examination for decisions regarding the entry, stay, and exclusion of foreigners or regarding the expropriation of property for public benefit, or the determination of the electoral region of electorates.

The immunity of decisions from judiciary control is a clear violation of the rule of law principle on the one hand, and curtails the right of prosecution on the other (Tolba 1986), which are two pillars for a state governed by the rule of law. Anchoring such immunity in the law and narrowing the Judiciary's scope of functions not only causes the public to lose confidence in the judiciary, it also violates Qatar's constitution, whose Art. 129 states that "the rule of law is the basis of ruling in the State..." Article 57 affirms that "abiding by the constitution and the laws issued by the governmental authorities are mandatory to the residents of Qatar or whosoever enters its territory," and Art. 135 provides for and ensures the right of prosecution to all.

## Conclusions

This chapter has presented an overview of the constitutional and legislative system in the State of Qatar, both its principles and its practice. We have demonstrated that no law can be issued without the Emir's consent, and we suggested that although the Qatari constitution was approved through popular referendum, it was a process directed from above, as has been its implementation. The chapter has also pointed out that the right to propose draft laws is currently confined to the Council of Ministers. However, in the event of enforcement of the Qatari constitution's suspended articles on the elected Shura Council, the member of the Shura Council will be entitled to propose draft laws as well.

The chapter has also shown some of the limitations of the actual legislative process. The discussion, debate, and drafting of laws by the Shura Council are not performed effectively in practice. Additionally, laws are not published in the Official Gazette within two weeks as stipulated in the Constitution. Studying the stages of law enactment, we found that the average period for promulgating a law is about one and a half years, which might be shortened or lengthened according to the Emir's will. Finally, the chapter shows that although the Qatari Legislature has issued the Supreme Constitutional Court Law, the Court itself has been suspended since 2008. Moreover, a large set of decisions have been excluded from the jurisdiction of the Administrative Division at the First Instance Court, as per the Law on Administrative Disputes Adjudication, which constitutes a violation of the rule of law and the right of prosecution.

As we noted at the beginning of this chapter, Qatar's policy-making system is anchored in its constitutional and legal architecture, but it cannot be reduced to it. The Emir, the ruling family, and key ministers clearly drive the policy process—and this chapter shows the legal underpinnings of those powers—but in doing so they rely on a wide array of advisory and implementing agencies which in turn face their own challenges in implementing a transformative policy agenda.

## Notes

1. To avoid confusion, the Council of Ministers will sometimes be referred to as the "Cabinet" when comparing it to the Shura Council.
2. See Emiri Decree No. (29) of 1996 regarding the Cabinet resolutions submitted to the Emir for ratification and publication. Published in the Official Gazette, Issue 12, of 1996.

3. All these functions are stipulated by the Permanent Constitution of the State of Qatar, whose provisions regarding the elected Shura Council are not yet enforced. Currently, this council is fully appointed by the Emir and performs an advisory role only.
4. Law 10 of 2003—Par. 5 of Art.63 on issuing the Judiciary Law.
5. Regarding the ratification by the Emir on the executive regulations, Par. 2 of Art. 121 of the Constitution stipulates the Cabinet functions of approving regulations and resolutions prepared by ministries and other government agencies, each according to their competency, to execute the laws according to their provisions. However, according to Par. 1 of Art. 1 of the Emiri Decree No. 29 of 1996 regarding the Cabinet resolutions that are submitted to the Emir for ratification and publication, "the regulations and the decrees issued or adopted by the Cabinet in implementation of the laws must be submitted to the Emir for ratification and publication." Regarding the regulations, Article 67 of the Constitution stipulates the functions of the Emir regarding the establishment and regulation of ministries and other government agencies, and the assignment of their functions. Par. 4 of Art. 121 of the Constitution stipulates that the Cabinet functions to propose the establishment and regulation of government agencies, authorities, and public institutions. However, according to Par. 2 of Art. One of the Emiri Decree No. 29 of 1996 regarding the Cabinet resolutions that are submitted to the Emir for ratification and publication, the regulations and resolutions issued or approved by the Cabinet regarding the establishment of agencies and public entities must be submitted to the Emir for ratification. Finally, regarding emergency regulations, Art. 70 of the Constitution authorizes the Emir, in exceptional circumstances that require urgent and expedient measures while the Shura Council is not in session, to issue decrees that are as powerful as a law.
6. That was on November 16, 1998. It was part of the Emir's speech: "In order to achieve this, we have decreed, with God's help to form a committee of qualified and competent individuals to develop a Permanent Constitution for the state where the basic items would be the formation of an elected parliament through direct public election in order to complete our endeavor to establish public participation as a foundation for the rule of law and to achieve the ultimate objective that guides our hopes and ambitions for the future."
7. The Drafting Committee of the Permanent Constitution included six members of the Royal Family, including HH Emir and former Minister, Hamad Bin Jassim Bin Jabr, and other members of the Executive such as the following: Abdullah Bin Hamad Al-Atiah, Deputy Prime Minister at the time, Ahmad Bin Abdullah Al Mahmoud, Minister of Energy, Hassan Bin Abdullah AlGhanem, Ali Bin Saeed AlKhayareen, Ahmed Bu Sherbak Al Mansouri, Mohamed Bin Saleh Al Sadah, Sultan Bin Hassan Al Dosari, and Ali Bin Fetais Al Marri.

8. For example, the Qatar Income Tax Decree (1954), Qatar Customs Laws (1955), Qatar Traffic Decree (1954), and the Constitution of Doha Municipal Council (1955).
9. Clauses 2 and 3 of Art. 1 of Law No. 1 of 1962 governing the Higher Administration of the Government.
10. Clause 1 of Art. 1 of the Law Governing the Higher Administration of the Government, ibid.
11. Article 34 of the Amended Provisional Basic Law, published in the Official Gazette, Issue: 5 of 1972.
12. The Constitution was ratified on June 8, 2004, but it was published in the Official Gazette after one year, Issue6 of 2005.
13. Art. 105 of Qatar Constitution.
14. Ibid.
15. Established by virtue of Law No. 1 of 1962 governed by the Higher Administration of Government.
16. The Department of Legal Affairs was presided by the government legal consultant Dr. Hasan Kamle, by virtue of Decree No. 1 of 1962, related to the appointment of the government legal consultant, published in the official gazette No. 1 of 1962. Mr. Hasan Kamel was also appointed as General Director of the Government at the same time, in addition to his initial position as Legal Advisor to the Government. See Resolution No. 1 of 1962, published in the Official Gazette, Issue: 1 of 1962. In 1967, the position of Legal Advisor to the Government was canceled and the position of Legal Affairs Director was created by virtue of Resolution No. (18) of 1967 related to the creation of the Legal Affairs Director position. Published in the Official Gazette, Issue7 of 1967.
17. Clause 6 of Art. 1 of the Resolution No. 4 of 1962 governing the functions of the Legal Affairs Department in the Government of Qatar, published in the Official Gazette, Issue1 of 1962.
18. Article 2 of the Resolution No. 4 of 1962 governing the functions of the Legal Affairs Department in the Government of Qatar.
19. See Law No. 6 of 1964 on the Establishment of the Shura Council, Arts. 2 and 3, published in the Official Gazette, Issue3 of 1964.
20. Article 9 of the Law on the Establishment of the Shura Council.
21. Article 16 of the Law on the Establishment of the Shura Council.
22. Article 55 of the Amended Basic Law (1970).
23. See clause (1) of Art. 33 and clause 3 of Art. 51 of the Amended Provisional Basic Law of 1972.
24. Article 36 of Law No. 6 of 1979 related to the Internal Regulations of the Shura Council. This law was issued on September 29, 1979, and published in the Official Gazette, Issue 5 of the same year. It was later called "the Shura Council Internal Regulations."

25. Article 105 of the Qatar Permanent Constitution and Art. 64 of the Shura Council Internal Regulations.
26. Article 15 of the Shura Council Internal Regulations; however, Art. 94 of Qatar Permanent Constitution stipulates that these committees shall be formed within two weeks, starting the annual session term of the Council, and not within one week, as the current practice of the present appointed Council.
27. Article 15 of the Shura Council Internal Regulations specifies these committees and outlines at least five members for each committee, provided that each member of the Council participates in one committee at least and two committees at most. Articles 19 to 23 specify the functions of these committees.
28. Article 65 of the Shura Council Internal Regulations.
29. Article 66 of the Shura Council Internal Regulations.
30. Article (66) of the Shura Council Internal Regulations; moreover, Arts. 67 to 72 govern the deliberation process in the second phase of the first deliberations cycle.
31. Article 67 of the Shura Council Internal Regulations.
32. Article 71 of the Shura Council Internal Regulations.
33. Article 69 of the Shura Council Internal Regulations.
34. Article 96 of Qatar Permanent Constitution stipulates that the order maintenance in the Council falls within the president's functions; Articles 47 to 50 of the Council's Internal Regulations provide for the president's power of managing sessions.
35. Article 73 of the Council's Internal Regulations.
36. Article 105 of the Council's Internal Regulations describes the mode of voting and confirms the public nature of the vote while authorizing the secret ballot as an exception to the general rule if requested by the government or the competent minister or the president or five members of the Shura Council.
37. See Art. 65 of Kuwait Constitution.
38. Some constitutions define, as a general rule, the date of publishing the law as the date of its entry into force. For example, the Basic Law of the Sultanate of Oman, issued in 1996, stipulates in Art. 74 that "the law enters into force on the date of its publications unless otherwise stipulated."
39. The decree issued on July 2, 2007, to promulgate Law No. 9 of 2001, published in Issue9 of the year 2001.
40. See Art. 4 of Law No. 4 of 2004, relevant to the promulgation of the Labor Law.
41. The Amended Provisional Basic Law of the State of Qatar, Art. 40 states that "the Advisory Council may give its opinion to the Emir and cabinet in performing their functions. This Council is called 'Advisory Council,' and expresses its opinion in the form of recommendations."

42. Issued on 3/26/2007 and published in the Official Gazette, Issue4 of the year 2007.
43. See Article 13 of the Law.
44. Law No. (12) /2008 on the establishment of the Supreme Constitutional Court, issued on 18/6/2008, and published in the Official Gazette, Issue: (8) of the year 2008.
45. Jadda (2013) considers that the establishment of a Constitutional Court "highlights the leaders' keenness on ensuring control over the constitutionality of laws thus preserving rights and freedoms within the society. By doing so, Qatar has entrusted the control duty with an independent constitutional court, rather than with the ordinary judiciary institutions. This action, by itself, strengthens the principle of control over the constitutionality of laws."
46. The Supreme Judiciary Council is composed of the president of the Court of Cassation, the president, and the senior vice presidents in the Court of Cassation, vice presidents, and the membership of the senior judges in the Court of Cassation, the president of the Court of Appeal, the oldest vice presidents in the Court of Appeal, and the president of the Court of the First Instance. The Council has many functions as stipulated in Article (23) of the Judiciary Law, the most important of which is ensuring the independence of the Judiciary, advising on the appointment, promotion, delegation, transfer, secondment and retirement of judges thereunder. The Council holds an ordinary meeting at least once a month.
47. Published in the Official Gazette, Issue4, May 13, 2007.
48. See Art. 3 of Administrative Dispute Adjudication Law.

## Bibliography. Qatar: Policy Making in a Transformative State

Al Saleh, Othman Abdulmalek. 2003. *Constitutional System and Political Institutions in Kuwait [in Arabic]*. Kuwait: Dar AlKutub.

El-Gamal, Yehia. 1992. *Al-Qada' Al-Dustoori fi Masr [The Constitutional Judiciary in Egypt]*. Cairo.

Fahmy, Mostafa Abu Zaid. 2006. *Political Regimes and Constitutional Law*. Alexandria: University Press House.

Knaul, Gabriella. 2015. *Report of the Special Rapporteur on the Independence of Judges and Lawyers*. New York: Office of High Commissioner for Human Rights, General Assembly, United Nations.

Mansour, Ahmed. 2011. *Authenticating Study on Historical Development of Qatari Court Jurisdiction in Administrative Disputes [in Arabic]*. Doha: Special issue attached to the Legal and Judiciary Journal, Center of Legal and Judiciary Studies, Qatar Ministry of Justice.

Tolba, Abdullah. 1986. *Administrative Law: Judiciary Control over the Administrative Work*. Damascus: Damascus University.

CHAPTER 3

# Policy-Making in Qatar: The Macro-Policy Framework

*Jocelyn Sage Mitchell and Leslie A. Pal*

This chapter discusses what many may consider an oxymoron: policy-making in a monarchy. To an outsider, policy in Qatar must simply be what the Emir says it is. Chapter 2 has outlined some of the institutional features of the Qatari political system, and while it is indeed led by the Al-Thani tribe and it is dominated by the emir, that is not the full story. Every political system, no matter how apparently centralized and controlled, has its factions, interests, power differentials, and internal dynamics. Overlaying this universal reality are several other specific factors: (1) the formal commitments that the Qatari state has made to democratization, albeit limited and delayed; (2) the evident examples of unrest in other countries in the region, starting with the Arab Spring, that have destabilized regimes or at least threatened them; and (3) the imperatives of managing rapid and massive social and economic development. These factors pose challenges even to a Gulf monarchy—essentially the same challenges that most governments face in developing, designing, and implementing public policies that will both satisfy their populations and generate enough wealth to sustain the polity.

---

J.S. Mitchell (✉)
Northwestern University in Qatar, Doha, Qatar

L.A. Pal
School of Public Policy and Administration, Carleton University, Ottawa, ON, Canada

© The Author(s) 2016
M.E. Tok et al. (eds.), *Policy-Making in a Transformative State*,
DOI 10.1057/978-1-137-46639-6_3

65

Other chapters in the book examine specific policy fields and their content and trajectories. This chapter assesses the policy-making system in Qatar from 40,000 meters up—what does the *macro-policy system* look like, and how does it work? The backdrop for our analysis is a body of theoretical work about how states like Qatar are supposed to function (rentier state theory) and scattered analyses of Qatar itself. Neither, in our view, is satisfactory, so this chapter breaks new empirical ground in providing both a detailed analysis of the strategic policy framework for Qatar and the policy machinery that gave birth to it. But it also nuances the theoretical discussion of rentier states and their transformational capacities. The first section of the chapter critically reviews this body of theoretical work. The second discusses two key documents that are designed to guide Qatar's economic and social development to 2030: the *Qatar National Vision 2030* (QNV) (General Secretariat for Development Planning (GSDP) 2008) and the *Qatar National Development Strategy, 2011–2016* (QNDS) (GSDP 2011a). The third section, based primarily on confidential interviews, explores the policy institutions and processes behind the national development strategy. Together, the revised theoretical framework and original fieldwork provide the basis for conclusions on the nature of the policy-making system in Qatar, its deficits and liabilities, and future directions for reform.

## POLICY-MAKING IN THE STATE OF QATAR: THEORIES AND PUZZLES

At an April 2011 fundraising event, US President Barack Obama spoke off the record—but on tape—on the per capita income of Qatar and its relation to authoritarianism: "There is no big move towards democracy in Qatar. You know part of the reason is that the per capita income of Qatar is $145,000 a year. That will dampen a lot of conflict—$145,000 a year!" (Khatri 2011). Obama's words reflect a common assumption about the political system in Qatar: that the state's control of hydrocarbon wealth (and lavish distribution to citizens) suppresses dissent in exchange for economic largesse.

How does the link between natural resource wealth and political acquiescence work? Rentier states like Qatar—states that derive more than 40 % of their budgets from certain types of exports, such as oil and gas—do not have to tax their citizens to produce revenue (Gause 1994: 42–44; Luciani 1987: 69–72; Mahdavy 1970). This financial autonomy, in theory, leads to political autonomy by severing the connection between taxation and representation; turning the American Revolution maxim around, rentier states offer no taxation and, hence, no representation. The only policy that matters for political stability is the allocation of the state's vast reserves of wealth among its receptive, but passive, citizens in the form of various social and economic benefits (Crystal 1995; Luciani 1987: 74; Ross 2001, 2012). With this framework in place, all other policy preferences—no matter how sweeping—can be determined by the state and shielded from citizen input or pressure.[1]

Rentier states, then, are seen as a special class of (neo-Weberian) polities: strong, autocratic states that use their financial autonomy from society to pursue their desired policies effectively and efficiently, particularly to keep the elites (in the GCC case, the monarchies) in power (Skocpol 1979: 32; Weber 1958: 83) and to transform their societies (Kamrava 2013). Rentier state theory, however, tends to make blanket statements about the power of these states to simultaneously stabilize and radically re-mold their societies. It needs to be emphasized that the "ruling bargain" between the elites and citizens is not only about sending checks or distributing cash. The "benefits" come in the form of programs—health services and hospitals, education and schools and universities, transportation, all manner of subsidies, and, above all, jobs. In the context of countries enjoying relatively recent resource rents, these programs involve major investments and sweeping socioeconomic development. Rentier state theory is largely silent on the policy processes that accompany these large-scale transformations, and it fails to explain the specific policy and programmatic mechanisms these states use to accomplish these goals.

Rentier state theory "rests on the mistaken assumption that the state apparatus is entirely self-contained, and can be immunised from the attitudes and actions of the surrounding population" (Beetham 2013: 118). We suggest here that rentier states not only "power" their ways through the policy-making arena—they must also "puzzle." In other words, even with vast financial independence from their domestic economy and society, rentier states still need to craft and implement their policies and programs. Despite the wide array of wealth and coercive power available to rentier states, the evidence nevertheless demonstrates that they often fail to fully implement their transformative and developmental agendas.

The example of oil-rich Saudi Arabia highlights the disconnect between rentier state theory and empirical reality. Hertog's (2010) in-depth analysis of policy-making in Saudi Arabia rejects the portrayal of the Kingdom as a static example of financial autonomy begetting political autonomy. Rather, Hertog demonstrates that autonomous state decisions made at the beginning of the oil wealth years resulted in unanticipated restrictions on the state's political autonomy in later years. Although he argues that, ultimately, the top levels of the Saudi state remain autonomous from society regarding their decision-making capabilities, he adds nuance to the literature by portraying the micro-level pushback that these decisions may receive. By focusing on the street-level state bureaucrats, who are directly responsible for implementation of the top-down decisions, policies, and reforms, Hertog provides a fuller picture of the policy-making environment in a rentier state, in which top-down preferences are modified, delayed, or even completely obstructed by various forms of resistance, reminiscent of Scott's (1985) "weapons of the weak."[2] Hertog's in-depth discussion of the policy distortions in a powerful rentier state illustrates the difficulty that rentier states may still face in implementing their sweeping visions.

It is at this intersection between theorized capacity and empirical limitations that we come to our case study of Qatar, one of the richest, smallest, most peaceful, and most stable rentier states in the world. Qatar has maintained its place atop the International Monetary Fund's (IMF) GDP per capita list since 2010 due to its substantial oil and gas resources; its exports of liquefied natural gas (LNG) in particular have allowed the state to continue allocating billions to welfare and economic benefits for its citizens (Mitchell 2013: 82–167), even as other Gulf states wrestle with budget cuts and energy shortfalls (Krane 2013). Further, the combination of a small and relatively homogeneous citizen population of predominantly Sunni Muslims and a unified ruling family (Davidson 2012; Herb 1999) without a rival source of political power, such as an entrenched indigenous religious elite (Başkan and Wright 2011; Seznec 2004), or an independent business class (Crystal 1995; Luciani 2007) has made Qatar the only state in the Middle East and North Africa region to avoid the large-scale political unrest of the Arab Spring (Farha 2015; Lucas 2014). If any rentier state could have transformative capacity in its policy-making, it should be Qatar. Indeed, the most recent literature has started to use the concept of "late rentier" states—ones with greater capacity and developmental or transformative agendas—and Qatar is one of the prime examples (Gray 2011).

Yet a brief example of the incomplete implementation and reversal of an important top-down initiative suggests some limits to this transformative capacity. Along with health, reform of the national education system tops the policy priority list, comprising the foundation for the human development goals outlined in the QNV and the QNDS. Education-related spending accounts for about 13 % of total government expenditure (GDSP 2012: 31). A large part of these expenditures were invested in sweeping national education reforms that began in the early 2000s, with the aim of indigenizing Qatar's private sector workforce and increasing local proficiency in English ("Qatari job seekers view manual labour as 'socially unacceptable'" 2012), among other goals. Spanning both the K–12 system as well as Qatar University, these reforms were initiated by the state in a top-down and unilateral manner quite in line with theoretical conceptions of a transformational rentier state. In fact, the reform proposed in the commissioned 2007 RAND–Qatar Policy Institute (an offshoot of RAND Corporation) study, *Education for a New Era* (Brewer et al. 2007) was so far-reaching and began so quickly that one Qatari official was quoted as calling it (favorably) "a total earthquake" (Glasser 2003).

Yet the story does not end here (see Chapter 4 for more details). Despite the "power" brought to the national education reforms by the state, Qatar was not able to "puzzle" toward successful implementation and consolidation of these policies. Concerns over cultural and linguistic preservation, academic standards, professionalization of teachers, student behavior, and the right of citizens to a college education were voiced in local Arabic newspapers ("91.8 percent of Qatari teachers find 'HEI's List' allowed students to disrespect their teachers" 2012; Al Sulaiti 2012; Al-Khater 2012; Al-Kuwari 2012), petitions ("Demands for administrative reform in QU" 2012), academic publications (Al-Kobaisi 2012), and even an award-winning short documentary (Al-Saadi et al. 2012). These anecdotal concerns should not be seen as an elite and unrepresentative sample of the Qatari population. Data from nationally representative mass attitude surveys of Qatari citizens, conducted in 2013 and 2014, highlight widespread concerns with the implementation of the national education reforms (Mitchell et al. 2013, 2014).[3] Specifically, the 2013 survey reported 29 % dissatisfaction with the current K–12 system and 18 % dissatisfaction with the current college education system. In both surveys, the majority of respondents desired more say in the reform process of both systems—between 54 and 58 % in 2013 and 64 % in 2014.[4] Showing that the state shared these concerns, the Qatari government backtracked on several key aspects of its reforms—most prominently switching back to Arabic language instruction for both K–12 and Qatar University for the start of the 2012–2013 academic year.

These unexpected reversals of Qatar's preferred education policies suggest that the theoretical conception of a transformative rentier state with unlimited capacity may not hold up under empirical scrutiny. Despite all of Qatar's resources, its financial autonomy from society, and the strength of its leadership, it remains an open question of whether Qatar currently has the institutional and human capacity to implement and consolidate its transformational goals.

In this chapter, we explore this puzzle further through an in-depth look at the process of creating and implementing the QNV and the QNDS. These policy frameworks are the government's vision of a radical socioeconomic transformation. As we will discuss, the state of Qatar highlighted the importance of societal consultation with regards to producing these policy plans, demonstrating that the state itself feels that society must be included—at least superficially—in the policy process to ensure "ownership" and adequate support for implementation. Yet questions remain: To what extent did societal consultation influence the creation of the national policy documents? How did societal actors and new bureaucratic institutions and processes help or hinder Qatar's policy-making capacity? Given that the rentier state may not be as autonomous and transformative as previously theorized, what do our findings mean for the successful implementation of the state's top policies?

## Strategic Policy Frameworks: QNV and QNDS

The idea of strategic policy frameworks or "national planning" to guide an entire country's development went largely out of fashion in the developed economies shortly after World War II (Shonfield 1965), although it lingered in the Soviet Bloc until 1991. Until recently, the closest most developed countries ever got to a "national plan" was through their budget, which typically both sets a government's fiscal framework and outlines priorities and sectoral strategies. In most of these countries, there certainly was an emphasis on policy oversight and coordination, but it was rarely framed as national planning (Ben-Gera 2004; Dahlström et al. 2011: 106–107; Peters et al. 1999). The 2008 financial crisis changed the policy terrain significantly, as governments embarked on unprecedented efforts of national economic rescue and stimulus. The EU, always a ready source of continent-wide plans and frameworks, has found itself essentially enforcing national economic adjustment strategies among its southern members, notably Greece. Additionally, the OECD has launched a program investigating "New Approaches to Economic Challenges," one of which is a "strategic state" that has the capacity to implement coordinated, long-term visions (OECD 2012).

The story in developing countries has been different, simply because "development" is, by definition, a national effort. Indeed, even as the collapse of communism was heralded as a neoliberal triumph and hence a repudiation of planning, others were noting that the East Asian successes seemed to be due to a muscular "developmental state" model (Öniş 1991). In the development field, national visions and national development strategies continue to enjoy support, and they indeed have been recommended by international agencies such as the UNDP (Center for Economic Research (Uzbekistan) 2014) and the World Bank, through its poverty reduction strategies and comprehensive development frameworks. Although South Korea, China, and Malaysia are prominent examples, countries as diverse as Kazakhstan, Kenya, Ireland, Latvia, Russia, and Brazil have all embarked on national strategic planning exercises. Accordingly, Qatar's QNV and the QNDS reflect international best practices in the field. In fact, Qatar's strategy was not merely economic development, but comprehensive social development as well.

The fact that Qatar has a coherent and comprehensive national development strategy suggests something about both the policy-making system and the challenges the country faces (discussed in the introduction to this book). Interestingly, several other Gulf states have similar and sometimes equally ambitious plans. As Ulrichsen (2011) points out, national visions and strategies began in the GCC in the mid-1990s, first with Bahrain and Oman (the two countries with the lowest oil reserves), followed by Qatar, Kuwait, Saudi Arabia, and the UAE. For example, the UAE's capital emirate, Abu Dhabi, first released its *Plan Abu Dhabi 2030: Urban Structure Framework Plan* (Abu Dhabi Urban Planning Council 2007), which was followed by the UAE-wide UAE Vision 2021, launched in 2010 (UAE 2010). Bahrain has its *Economic Vision 2030* (Kingdom of Bahrain 2010), which, like Abu Dhabi's, is essentially an urban development plan. Saudi Arabia has the most developed architecture of planning documents, providing plans for specific areas such as technology and sciences and health care, as well as a long-term national economic development strategy (Kingdom of Saudi Arabia 2004).

All of these plans aim at diversifying their economies away from hydrocarbons, developing skilled workforces (including greater participation by women), and encouraging the private sector. The results have been mixed at best, though there has been notable progress in some cases. The challenges remain formidable—according to one estimate, by 2020 the Arab economies will have to produce up to 50 million jobs to absorb new entrants into their labor markets (Kamrava 2014: 24). The challenges in the Gulf monarchies are even more acute, including moving their citizens from public to private sector work and motivating them despite rentier wealth. This level and amount of economic diversification requires deep reform across social and political institutions and structures.

> True reform would involve a decisive shift away from notions of citizens' entitlement and have profound socio-political implications for the future of redistributive states. It would also require the rebalancing of the public and private sectors, together with a fundamental reshaping of state-business relations. In addition, the measures would necessarily encompass the unbundling of the nexus of intertwined political and economic stakeholders, as embodied in the power and reach of the merchant family conglomerates. Reforms thus need interlinking with comprehensive reform of educational systems and labour markets, and the move toward incentive-based and performance-linked structures. Moreover the underlying pivot should be an acknowledgement that the value of investment in human capital is limited without contemporaneous attitudinal shifts toward more sustainable patterns of development. This is particularly important in the industrialization projects that form a pillar of economic diversification, as they have added greatly to already-overstretched demands for power and water.... (Ulrichsen 2011: 106–107).

While acknowledging that these diversification efforts have had some results, Ulrichsen concludes that they may be largely "cosmetic" if not accompanied by deeper changes in economic structures and culture.

In keeping with the development of national visions and strategies in the region cited above, the two key Qatari national strategic documents are the QNV and the QNDS. As "vision" documents, inevitably they are framed with lyrical rhetoric and uplifting aspirations (for a critique, see Al Ghanim 2012). And yet they do have the status of official steering documents, as they contain statements of current problems and future goals. We approach them in that spirit.

The QNV is the shorter of the two. It claims to have "emerged from intensive consultations across Qatari society." It poses the National Vision as "transforming Qatar into an advanced country by 2030, capable of sustaining its own development and providing for a high standard of living for all of its people for generations to come" (GSDP 2008: 2). It identifies five challenges facing Qatar:

1. Modernization and preservation of traditions.
2. The needs of this generation and the needs of coming generations.
3. Managed growth and uncontrolled expansion.
4. The size and the quality of the expatriate labor force and the selected path of development.
5. Economic growth, social development and environmental management. (GSDP 2008: 3)

These may appear as distinct challenges, but they all reflect the stresses of Qatar's rapid economic and population growth. The last three challenges are self-evidently economic, while the first two touch on culture and intergenerational equity. The document forthrightly addresses the paramount issues of population and the expatriate workforce, but it frames them exclusively in terms of resource development. It should be noted that the QNV was published in 2008, well before the December 2010 announcement that Qatar had won its bid to hold the 2022 FIFA World Cup. The QNDS, published in 2011, did mention the World Cup and some attendant development (such as the Doha Metro), but it was thought that the impacts were likely to be "modest." We return to this below.

The document then highlights four pillars to the Vision, which are grounded in the guiding principles of "the Permanent Constitution and the directions of Their Highnesses the Emir, the Heir Apparent and Sheikha Moza, as well as on extensive consultation with government institutions and local and international experts" (GSDP 2008: 10). The pillars are human development, social development, economic development, and environmental development. The key points of each pillar (stripped of rhetorical flourishes) are listed below (we only mention specific initiatives if they have substance and represent potentially accountable policy commitments).

### *Human Development*

The QNV acknowledges that hydrocarbon resources will eventually run out, and economic success will depend on the ability of Qataris to compete in the global knowledge economy. It proposes to build a "modern world-class educational system," as well as an integrated, accessible health care system. It wants to increase the "effective labor force participation" of citizens, but it acknowledges that for the foreseeable future, Qatar will have to rely on expatriate workers with the right mix of skills and will have to respect their rights and safety (GSDP 2008: 13–14). Specific initiatives include the following:

- Curricula with a "solid grounding in Qatari moral and ethical values" (GSDP 2008: 16).
- Well-developed, independent, self-managing and accountable educational institutions.
- System of scientific research funding.
- A mixed health care system (public and private institutions) operating under the direction of a national health policy that sets standards.
- Incentives for Qataris to enter professional and management roles.
- Increased opportunities and vocational support for Qatari women.
- Targeting the right mix of expatriate labor, and retaining the best among them (GSDP 2008: 16–18).

*Social Development*

The social development pillar is an incongruous mix of commitments to family and to regional and international cooperation. The emphasis (we focus here on domestic commitments) is on "preserving a strong and coherent family" but it promises that women "will assume a significant role in all spheres of life, especially through participating in economic and political decision-making" (GSDP 2008: 19).

- An effective social protection system that "ensures an adequate income to maintain a healthy and dignified life" (GSDP 2008: 22).
- Strong and active civil society organizations that, among other things, "preserve Qatar's national heritage and enhance Arab and Islamic values and identity" and "enhance women's capacities and empower them to participate fully in the political and economic spheres, especially in decision-making roles" (GSDP 2008: 22).

*Economic Development*

The awareness that Qatar's resources are finite is obvious in this pillar; it is also evident that the path forward is diversification, and the challenges are in fostering entrepreneurs and innovation in the face of inflationary risks. The specific initiatives under this pillar are the typical nostrums of low inflation and sound budgetary management, mixed with pledges to carefully and sustainably nurture the hydrocarbon sector to generate "advanced technological innovations" while ultimately moving to diversify toward a "knowledge-based economy" (GSDP 2008: 28–29).

- Enabling the private sector through training and support for entrepreneurs, and financial and other means "to help incubate and grow small and medium-scale enterprises" (GSDP 2008: 25).
- Maintaining low inflation rates in the face of rapid growth.
- Coordination with GCC states to build various economic ties.
- Measured exploitation of hydrocarbon resources, creating a balance between maintaining reserves and production.
- Sustainable economic diversification towards a knowledge-based economy (GSDP 2008: 27–29).

### Environmental Development

This pillar is the thinnest of the four. In part, this was due to the exclusion of the management of the oil and gas economy from the QNV and ultimately the QNDS. We will discuss this below, but the oil and gas sector in Qatar was at that time, and to a certain degree still is, an enclave within the state. Qatar Petroleum (QP) was and is the engine of the economy. Key decisions in the oil and gas sector continue to be very much determined and driven by QP. The preamble to this section does refer to the impact of diminishing hydrocarbon and water resources, as well as global warming. All of the initiatives associated with this pillar are relatively minor, though from the perspective of 2007, they did represent some moderately significant attempts to deal with environmental degradation and sustainability (GSDP 2008: 30–33).

### The Qatar National Development Strategy (QNDS)

The QNV was designed as the foundation for the QNDS. The development of the more detailed strategy would rely on the guidance of "Qatar's Higher Authorities" but "in consultation and in full partnership with all stakeholders, especially civil society, the private sector, ministries and government agencies" (GSDP 2008: 34). We discuss the nature and scope of those consultations in the next section, but the QNDS itself claimed that they were extensive (we quote at length because of its bearing on the next section of the chapter):

This National Development Strategy 2011–2016, Qatar's first, is the culmination of extensive stakeholder consultations, dialogues and analyses. The positive and unprecedented engagement of multiple sectoral and intersectoral stakeholders reflects a genuine desire for reform that is in the best interest of the country. The consultation process began with ministers and key leaders from government, private sector and civil society and moved out into society. Reflecting the broad reach of the Strategy, cross-sectoral task teams comprised representatives from government ministries, agencies, private companies and civil society organizations. The extensive intersectoral consultations, including interviews, discussions, debates and research, were important for building a strategy that would enjoy strong and positive public ownership from the outset.

The Strategy builds on situational analyses, diagnostics, regional and international benchmarking and detailed strategies for each of 14 sectors. The situational analyses identified priority areas using baseline analyses of Qatar's situation and benchmarking against best practices in other countries, both in the region and around the world. The 14 sector strategy reports identify the priority areas and the many transformation initiatives to support each proposed programme and project, including core requirements, responsibilities, timelines and key indicators. (GSDP 2011a: 3)

The QNDS is a long (almost 300 pages) and detailed document, and we can only touch on key points here. In essence, the strategy is devoted to diversification of the economy, coupled with sustainable development, and all its major initiatives flow from that, including the ones aimed at the social sector. Moving to the knowledge economy will depend heavily on state institutions: Enterprise Qatar, the Qatar Foundation (including the Qatar Science and Technology Park), the Qatar Financial Centre, and the Qatar Development Bank. Together, they will contribute to the target of raising Qatar's research and development expenditures to 2.8 % of government revenues. State management institutions will also be reformed in the following areas to ensure effective implementation: strategic policy and planning, budget and financial management, organizational alignment, human resources development, enabled institutional processes, and performance management. Indeed, reform of the state system itself (including ministry and agency structures and practices) was a centerpiece of the QNDS implementation plan.

Within these broad parameters are a host of projects across the four pillars (five, if one includes public sector reform). Figure 3.1 reproduces a table from the QNDS that summarizes the pillars and the main challenges in each. The summary of the programs that accompanied the QNDS

### Table 8.1 Qatar's 20 key challenges

| Qatar National Vision 2030 pillar | Major challenges | Strategic responses |
|---|---|---|
| Promoting sustainable prosperity | Ensuring sustainability in a setting where hydrocarbon resource depletion is still the dominant source of income | Establishing a hydrocarbon depletion policy; sustaining high rates of saving and making sound investments in human, capital and financial assets for the future |
| | Promoting stability in an environment where hydrocarbon price volatility creates risk and presents challenges for calibration of economic policy | Reforming budgetary and fiscal processes, public investment programming, liquidity management and domestic capital market development |
| | Enhancing efficiency in the use of all resources to support high standards of living for current and future generations | Promoting competition, trade and investment; improving regulation; strengthening demand management for water, power and fuel; reforming agriculture |
| | Diversifying the economy to create durable wealth and support wider societal viability | Bolstering enterprise creation and private sector development; improving the business climate; strengthening regional integration; reforming the labour market |
| Promoting human development | Rebalancing the healthcare system to reduce the emphasis on hospital-based care and increase integration between levels of care | Establishing an integrated healthcare system to shift the balance of care towards a patient-focused, preventive and community-based model |
| | Meeting critical needs for a high-quality workforce across the health sector (and affecting other sectors) | Developing and implementing a national workforce plan that takes a multifaceted approach and optimizes the skills mix |
| | Raising the achievement of Qatari students at all levels, especially in math, science and English and, through that, increasing educational attainment | Strengthening reforms in K–12 and higher education to ease demand and supply constraints |
| | Coordinating education and training providers and aligning with labour force needs | Addressing quality, efficiency, inclusiveness and portability across the entire education and training systems |
| | Aligning labour market composition of Qataris with the objectives of a diversified knowledge economy | Realigning demand and supply in the Qatari workforce, with an emphasis on continuously upgrading skills |
| | Reducing reliance on low-cost, low-skilled foreign labour | Reviewing the sponsorship law and identifying ways of attracting and retaining higher skilled expatriate workers |
| Taking an integrated approach to sound social development | Balancing the forces of modernization and globalization with the support of traditional Qatari family values and patterns of family formation | Implementing cross-cutting measures to strengthen family ties, values and relationships |
| | Strengthening social inclusiveness | Launching a multistakeholder programme that strengthens an inclusive social protection system |
| | Improving road safety and ending the growing epidemic of traffic accidents, particularly among youth | Introducing a holistic approach to road safety, with cross-sectoral partnerships |
| | Preserving traditional Qatari culture and Arab identity | Using culture as a platform to safeguard and develop Qatar's national heritage |
| | Encouraging a more active lifestyle for young people, to reduce the health-related risks of inactivity | Promoting local sports participation and development as part of a comprehensive, active lifestyle programme |
| Sustaining the environment for future generations | Reforming unsustainable water consumption patterns | Establishing an integrated water management plan across the value chain |
| | Encouraging sustainable urbanization and consumption patterns that reduce environmental stresses | Promoting more sustainable urbanization and a healthier living environment |
| Developing modern public sector institutions | Strengthening weak institutional capacities | Strengthening the role of central functions to support institutional development and modernization |
| | Expanding human resources capacities across the public sector | Applying policies to attract talent, including staff development programmes |
| | Establishing a centralized system for managing for results and for linking resource allocation to strategic plans | Launching a public sector performance management framework linking institutional performance to strategic plans and budgets |

**Fig. 3.1** Qatar's 20 Key Challenges (GSDP 2011a: 266)

outlined the following distribution of projects: sustainable economic prosperity (20), human development (73), social development (51), environmental development (10), and developing modern public-sector institutions (16) (GSDP 2011b). This total of 170 projects was extraordinarily ambitious, given the even larger number of specific targets associated with all these projects. The highest priority project areas were clearly in health, education, and social protection, particularly regarding the family. The scope and scale reflected transformative ambitions, but also transformative resources—there was a sense that anything was possible because of the sheer abundance of revenues.

Of course it is not the number of programs, or even their cost, that is important. At least four aspects of the QNDS deserve mention. First, it is quite realistic about key substantive and operational challenges: dependence on hydrocarbons, volatility in oil prices, population pressures, water shortages, and runaway growth, among others. Second, despite its expected rhetorical flourishes, the document builds solidly on the QNV—it extends the analysis of each of the pillars. Third, it is—at least on paper—an integrated exercise. It strives to connect the various dots and stimulate synergies among programs and sectors. Finally, it pays attention to implementation, particularly the strategic capacity of the state apparatus. This was not a document written by amateurs.

In the next section we examine the policy process involved in developing this macro-economic (and social) framework—who was involved and how. In this respect, we are examining policy-making at the "strategic national heights," focusing on cross-sectoral initiatives that address issues for the country as a whole. Other chapters in this volume focus on specific policy sectors and the dynamics therein.

## THE POLICY-MAKING SYSTEM: FORGING THE QNDS[5]

Sheikh Hamad bin Khalifa Al-Thani became Emir after a soft coup on June 27, 1995. As Heir Apparent he had chaired the Supreme Planning Council, and for the two years prior to the coup he had more or less run the government on a day-to-day basis. His father had initially been a modernizer in his own right (after taking power in his own coup in 1971), but the pace of change had slowed considerably in his later years. The new Emir quickly launched a series of modestly liberalizing political reforms, discussed in Chapters 1 and 2, culminating in a new, permanent Constitution in 2004. But the economic context was changing rapidly as well. Traditionally, despite having the ninth largest crude oil reserves in OPEC, Qatar's production was the second lowest in the group. Further, although offshore natural gas was discovered in the North Field in 1971, giving Qatar the third largest proven reserves in the world, exports of LNG did not begin until 1997. Yet under Emir Hamad's initiative, exports increased rapidly from 2000 (International Energy Agency 2009: 487–490), and by 2006, Qatar had become the world's largest LNG exporter (US Energy Information Administration 2014). While the country had been relatively wealthy because of oil, gas exports began to generate a fresh flood of revenue—World Bank data show that Qatar's GDP (in constant US dollars) grew on average by 5.7 % per year between 2000 and 2003, spiking to 19.1 % in 2004, and then averaging 16.3 % from 2005 to 2009 (World Bank 2015).

Wealth on this scale posed a challenge to the nascent policy-making apparatus: Qatar now had the necessary financial resources to develop the country dramatically, but it still needed institutional and human resources to guide the strategic planning. As the chair of the Supreme Planning Council, the Emir (then Heir Apparent) had recruited Dr. Ibrahim Ibrahim (then the senior economist at the Oxford Institute for Energy Studies) as the Council's Economic Advisor in 1988. But the Council—even after the Emir took full control of the country—remained weak. The Emir, on the advice of Dr. Ibrahim, commissioned the RAND–Qatar Policy Institute to conduct a study of the Planning Council. Its 2005 report became the basis for the creation of the GSDP.

The RAND report noted that as of 2005 the country had no national vision or development strategy. The Planning Council did not engage in large-scale, big picture planning, serving rather as a general analytic resource for parts of government, which led to an overabundance of numerous plans being developed simultaneously and without coordination across ministries and agencies. Specifically, RAND identified several significant weaknesses in the Planning Council. First, the Council combined a planning secretariat with the national statistical office, as well as a technical cooperation group to deal with international organizations. It lacked focus. Second, it had weak staff capacity. Of its 165 staff, 67 were with the statistical authority. Staff hiring and compensation were governed by civil service regulations, making it difficult to attract qualified personnel. Third, and most importantly, it did not have the necessary political standing to create an authoritative national vision. The Secretary-General of the Planning Council reported neither to the Emir or Heir Apparent, nor even to the Prime Minister, but to the Council's governing board, chaired by the Deputy Prime Minister. This removed direct access to the ruling authorities. Tellingly, the governing board of the Council had not met formally at that point for almost two years.

RAND recommended the creation of a development planning secretariat that would report directly to the Heir Apparent and be exempt from civil service hiring rules and pay scales. It suggested hiring 25–35 substantive experts, more than double that category of staff at the Planning Council at that time, along with about a dozen or more junior staff. It also recommended that the statistical authority be spun off as an independent agency. The secretariat was to be independent of the Council of Ministers or any other agencies and government. Almost all of these recommendations were accepted. The GSDP was created, reporting to the heir apparent, with Dr. Ibrahim as its Secretary-General. In order to achieve the goal of developing a national strategy or vision (what became the QNV), the GSDP required both institution building and experienced senior staff. Headhunters were hired and they recruited globally for key positions within the GSDP. Despite the global economy being on the cusp of recession (hitting hard with the financial crisis in 2008), the Qatari economy was entering its peak. Rather than being affected by the global downturn, Qatar's flood of revenues from the mid-2000s onward gave a sense that "anything was possible."

In order to develop a sense of ownership and high-level coordination behind what would become the QNV and the QNDS, a Supreme Oversight Committee was established. The Committee was above the Council of Ministers, and it consisted of the Heir Apparent (chair), the Prime Minister, Deputy Prime Minister, and Director-General and Secretary-General of the GSDP. Yet this Committee met infrequently. Thus, after the launch of the QNV, institutional machinery had to be established—slowly, since everything had to be approved by Emiri decrees—in order to prepare the QNDS. Six Executive Groups were established—one each for the economic development pillar, the social development pillar, and the environmental development pillar, and three for the human development pillar (education, health, and labor force). Each encompassed key ministers, heads of departments, and other key organizations. Fourteen Task Teams were established as well, reporting to the Executive Groups. These were lower than the ministerial level—assistant secretary or director level—and in principle had the flexibility to pull in people from different departments, agencies, and expert groups. They were tasked with developing the projects that would give substance to the QNDS. In this sense, the entire exercise was intended to be a blend of "top-down" as well as "bottom up" initiatives. The Executive Groups reported to the Oversight Committee, and the GSDP was a member of each Group, in principle insuring some horizontal coordination. Once the QNDS was released, however, implementation was left to the ministry and agency level.

The QNDS was claimed to be the result of extensive consultations with stakeholders—civil society, public sector institutions, the private sector, ministries, and agencies. As we noted above, rentier state theory assumes a high degree of insulation from social actors, if not outright complete autonomy for state authorities as part of the "ruling bargain." The case of the QNDS reveals several complications with this depiction. First, it seems that there was a genuine intention to engage participants, at least among the senior officials in the GSDP. This consultation would have reflected international best practice, and the GSDP recruitment had deliberately searched the market of international practitioners of national planning strategies. However, the very nature of a Gulf monarchy made it unlikely that the Supreme Oversight Committee or members of the royal family would be engaging in "town hall" meetings. The level of engagement was thus by default left to the Task Teams, and their approaches varied. Additionally, there was an uneven "civil society" in Qatar, with relatively few NGO actors with which to engage. In the education field, the Qatar Foundation (itself led by Sheihka Moza, the wife of then Emir Hamad) and Qatar University worked with the Supreme Education Council. The health sector had more numerous stakeholders and reflected greater activity, including local meetings.

Second, we should note the unusual role played by QP in the process. As we noted above, the oil and gas sector as a target of development, rather than the stimulus for development, was not addressed in the QNDS since that sector is very much under the control of QP, which itself was closely connected to the royal family. Up until the 2000s and the QNV, QP planning was essentially planning for the entire economy—resource extraction, processing, shipment, and hiring all the labor and resources required for these. This was underscored by the fact that the CEO of QP was, at the same time, the Minister of Energy Affairs. But the scope and extent of QP's activities is remarkable, as the company itself noted in 2011 in describing its contribution to "social development" in Qatar: "Qatar Petroleum, through a number of its service departments, implements a number of projects for various government institutions. Amongst these departments is the Technical Directorate, which implements capital projects aimed at developing infrastructure in the State of Qatar, such as Qatar Foundation for Education, Science and Community Development, the Space City project, the Qatar Museums Authority, the Supreme Education Council, and others" (QP 2011: 14). The same report also pointed out that QP is the majority (up to 70 %) owner of a variety of other companies in steel, aluminum, fertilizer, real estate, petrochemical by-products, transportation, insurance, electricity, and water. QP represents a key node of macro-economic planning within the larger policy-making and strategic planning apparatus of the government of Qatar as a whole, almost a "plan within a plan," with the CEO of QP/Minister of Energy as a member of both the QNDS National Steering Committee and the Executive Group on Economic Development.

Third, despite the Emir's backing and initiative, according to interviewees there was some initial resistance from ministries, departments, and agencies to work together. This was the first time anything on this scale had been attempted, and some were skeptical about the exercise, therefore being less than energetically engaged in the beginning. As the process unfolded and developed momentum and visibility, more top-level government players began to take a more active part.

This increased momentum did not obviate all the various constraints and liabilities embedded in the decision-making system. Interviewees highlighted a number of inter-related factors that worked against the successful implementation of the QNDS, despite the financial resources behind it.[6]

1. On paper the architecture of committees and task forces looked effective, but it depended on scarce organizational resources. There was a shortage of staff, for example, with project management and technical experience. Additionally, the architecture presumed a substantial culture of cooperation and trust, which ran up against the usual bureaucratic silos among ministries and other organizations, and to some extent lingering influences of tribal loyalties.
2. While basic management and project implementation was to take place through lead ministries and agencies, the entire initiative assumed a strong degree of centralized coordination at the top. The Supreme Oversight Committee met too infrequently to do this, so the hope was that the General Secretariat of the Council of Ministers (in effect, the cabinet office) would play this role, as it does in most

advanced industrial states seeking to develop and maintain a strategic direction. Yet the Prime Minister at the time, Sheikh Hamad bin Jassim bin Jaber bin Muhammad Al-Thani (known colloquially as HBJ)—appointed in 2007 after being Deputy Prime Minister since 2003 (Bollier 2013) and simultaneously holding the position of Foreign Minister—was not directly engaged in the QNDS, and in any case the Council of Ministers was not then (and is not now) imbued with decision-making powers. Its General Secretariat declined to take on the coordinative role for the QNDS, shifting it to the GSDP. The problem was that the GSDP was indeed simply a secretariat, and while it could convene meetings, it had little direct authority over ministers or their ministries.

3. Amplifying these problems was the sheer number of projects. Without central Council of Ministers coordination, implementation was pushed down to ministries and agencies. Prior to the mandated creation of strategy and policy units in 2014, there were few strategic policy and planning units in the ministries, compounding the problem of oversight and coordination. Without a strong planning function at the ministerial level, the personal agendas of ministers tended to dominate. Further, ministerial turnover has been high, creating ripple effects throughout the organizations, not only in agenda-setting, but also in staffing—with concurrent changes to the undersecretary, assistant undersecretaries, and sometimes even the directors. This frequent turnover compounded the existing problem of a severe shortage of qualified personnel.

4. Some of the other key elements of modern administrative practice seem to be missing in the Qatari system. Until recently, budgeting has been on a line-item basis, which makes it very difficult to determine the finances of projects as a whole, thus hindering higher-order project management and analysis of outcomes and key performance indicators. There was, until the 2013 creation of the Ministry of Administrative Development, no central government human resource management framework or ministerial entity to implement the framework, so personnel decisions varied across ministries. The management function in ministries is further affected by the absence of a deputy secretary or deputy minister position. Department heads tend to report directly to the minister, which can have contradictory effects: either reinforcing the influence of the minister or diluting and disaggregating advice.

Some of these challenges were recognized as the QNDS moved forward, and they eventually triggered a change in central government functions, spurred by the new Emir, HH Sheikh Tamim bin Hamad Al-Thani, who announced a cabinet shuffle upon assuming office in June 2013. The principal changes (for the purposes of this chapter) were (1) the consolidation of human resource management and central agency planning from the General Secretariat of the Council of Ministers, along with the transformation of the former Institute of Administrative Development into a new Ministry of Administrative Development, (2) the creation of a new Ministry of Development Planning and Statistics, combining the former GSDP and Qatar Statistics Authority (and so going back to the pre-2005 model), (3) the change of the former Supreme Council of Information and Communication Technology, or ictQATAR, into a Ministry of Information and Communications Technology, and (4) the creation of a Supreme Committee for Follow-up on NDS Implementation (which, at time of writing, has not met).

These measures certainly represent consolidation, though it is not clear how effective they will be. The GSDP had previously been a secretariat reporting to the Heir Apparent, which gave it, as we pointed out above, both some greater flexibility than a regular ministry and substantial convening power because of its direct reporting structure. Now, as part of a new ministry, it reports to a minister, who in turn reports to the Supreme Committee for Follow-up on NDS Implementation, which in turn reports to the Council of Ministers. Ultimately, this hierarchical chain may dilute the GSDP's steering role in the QNDS process. To be clear, however, the QNDS anticipated these organizational challenges in its penultimate chapter on "Developing Modern Public Sector Institutions." Its chart on drivers and levers of modern public management (Fig. 3.2) could have been drawn from any current OECD report on good governance. In fact, the report explicitly benchmarked Qatar's public sector institutions against international best practices:

> Benchmarking focused on the drivers and levers of modernization in five countries, identifying best practices in public sector performance around the world. The five were Australia, Canada, Norway and Singapore, identified for international best practices, and the United Arab Emirates, identified for regional comparison. All five have implemented structural changes in public sector organization and service delivery and greatly improved public sector performance, particularly service delivery. The benchmarking analysis iden-

POLICY-MAKING IN QATAR: THE MACRO-POLICY FRAMEWORK   85

**Figure 7.2** Performance management provides dynamic links between drivers and levers to achieve public sector excellence

**Drivers**

**Efficiency**
Increasing the ratio of outputs to inputs

**Transparency**
Exposing the actions and decisions of the government and public sector to scrutiny

**Effectiveness**
Improving the quality of the elements that convert inputs to outputs

**Engagement**
Engaging customers in public decisions and processes that affect their lives

**Value creation**
Maximizing returns on investment and long-term sustainability

**Relevance**
Linking government policy and outputs to society's needs

**Accountability**
Being answerable for the consequences of government and public sector actions

**Levers**

**Performance management**
- Visibility of performance
- Outputs measured against defined objectives and targets
- Corrective actions

**Human resources development**
- Job description and hiring
- Career planning and development
- Performance management of employees
- Performance goals
- Training and capabilities

**Policy and planning**
- Vision, leadership and culture
- Institutional mandate within legislative norms
- Strategic planning and policy (outcome based)
- Targets and goals

**Institutional processes**
- Interaction and coordination within and outside the institution with private sector, other governments and the general public
- Procedure workflows and processes
- Inclusive of stakeholders (listening, communication and marketing)
- Lean processes and process excellence

**Budget management**
- Budget planning and alignment with strategy
- Budget execution
- Monitoring of budget performance

**Procurement**
- Contracting and purchasing
- Resource optimization
- Vendor and project management
- Risk mitigation

**Organizational alignment**
- Mandates and job family design
- Responsibilities and interactions
- Decision-making
- Performance orientation and standards and culture
- Accountability and collaboration

**Information and communication technology**
- Workflow automation
- E-government
- Institutional integration
- Responsiveness

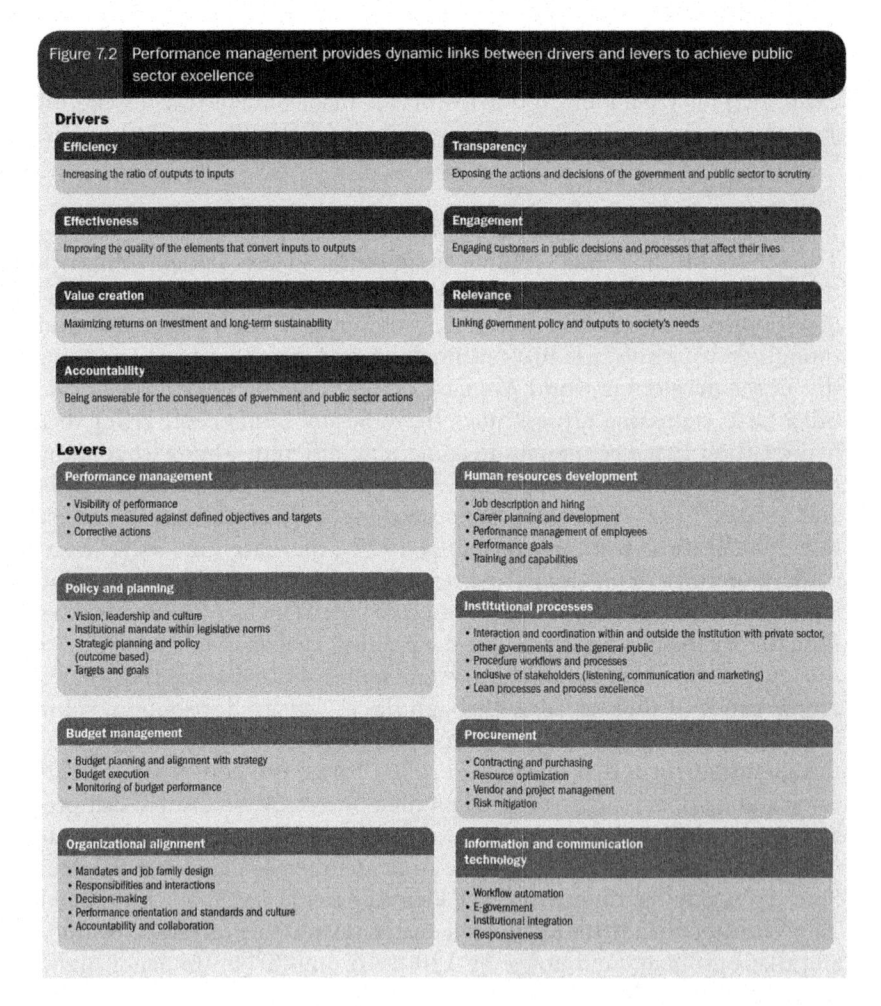

Fig. 3.2   Drivers and Levers of Public Management (GSDP 2011a: 244)

tified building blocks for Qatar's transition to modernization. The countries selected demonstrate excellence in public sector performance (government efficiency, ease of doing business, policy and regulations and delivery on promises) and institutional performance (openness and effective governance mechanisms for expenditure, dispute and regulatory management). (GSDP 2011a: 245)

The benchmarks were then used for a self-assessment exercise of public sector performance. The report noted, echoing the points made above, that "the policy planning and performance management levers stand out as requiring greatest capacity improvement" (GSDP 2011a: 249).

CONCLUSIONS

The QNV and the QNDS outline an ambition to substantially transform the economy and society of Qatar by 2030. As we note above, national development strategies are increasingly common in the developed world, though they may not use that terminology, and they have been fairly routine in the developing world. We gave current examples from some of the other GCC states that express much the same ambition of converting their hydrocarbon-based economies to something different—knowledge, tourism, global trading, and travel hub. While circumstances vary among the GCC states, most importantly between those with substantial oil and gas reserves and those without (Chaudhry 1997), they face similar challenges of development (e.g., dealing with migrant labor and, for some, creating enough well-paying jobs for nationals (see Winckler 2009)). Rentier state theory focuses principally on the political challenge of state elites (in the GCC case, ruling monarchies) retaining power by buying the political acquiescence of their citizens, through direct welfare distribution, subsidies, and large-scale public programs and projects.

Our argument is that this type of ruling bargain requires quite complicated public policy processes in designing and delivering key social programs and stimulating economic development. Of course, it is possible to simply and crudely disburse money. In September 2011, just as the Arab Spring was gaining momentum, the Heir Apparent (and now Emir) Sheikh Tamim announced that public service salaries would be increased by 60 %, and that of military and police by 120 % (Toumi 2011). In Saudi Arabia in January 2015, days after assuming power after the death of his brother, King Abdullah, King Salman announced a bonus of two-month's pay to all state employees, including pensioners, something "warmly accepted by citizens" (Decent 2015). Over the long term, however, these states have to deliver policies and programs, not simple bribery. Hence, their transformational success, not to mention their political stability, depends in large part on their policy capacities. In this regard, we believe that rentier state theory has paid insufficient attention to the administrative and policy machinery wielded by these states. This capacity should be considered as another important ingredient in survival, beyond the revenues that flow from resource and other rents.

The case of the QNV and the QNDS reveals several key features in the Qatar policy process. It is important to recall that Qatar is a monarchical state with a constitution (see Chapter 1 and Chapter 2 for detailed discussion) that gives the Emir controlling powers in all key decisions. In the Gulf context, these decisions nevertheless involve a wide royal family, as well as key members of other tribes. The distinctiveness of the system is its attempt to combine the machinery of modern state bureaucratic institutions with a personalized, familial power structure. It is tempting to think that these institutions will simply be window-dressing for the Emir's personal decisions. Yet the complexities of modern economic and social policies—from setting central bank policies to designing health services—make this kind of personalized rule risky and unsustainable, if not disastrous. Additionally, there are the pressures that come from engagement in the international system of organizations like the UN, the IMF, and the World Bank, not to mention the scrutiny of international NGOs, media, and foreign investors. Nonetheless, in this sort of system, the leadership matters even more than it does in liberal democratic regimes. In this respect, our first observation is the strategic role that Emir Hamad played in the crucial period after he took power in 1995 and as natural gas revenues ramped up. It was his decision to replace the Planning Council with a new GSDP. Added to this was the role of his key economic advisor since 1988, Dr. Ibrahim, who was the first Secretary-General of the GSDP when it was formed in 2006. As *Arabian Business* noted, "Outside the royal family, nobody has had a bigger say in the growth of Qatar," and "almost every plan and process is going through Dr. Ibrahim's desk" (Arabian Business 2012).

A second observation concerns the degree of centralization in the system. Despite the Emir's dominance and the crucial role of his key economic advisor in steering the QNDS process, that process could not be the business of only a handful of high officials. By its nature, it had to be developed by and ultimately implemented across government as a whole, across ministries and agencies. This is where, somewhat paradoxically, disaggregation of power complemented—and was in fact a function of—the centralization of power in this specific monarchical system. Key ministries are in the hands of Al-Thanis, while some others are distributed to other tribes. In the murky swirls of power in this type of system, ministers (as members of the royal clan or key tribes) have more personal power than a minister in an elected government would. Adding to that was the absence of strategic planning capacity in ministries, or even a clear channel of authority and advice up to a deputy minister. Hence, we witness the paradox of high *centralization* at the peak, in the Emir and his immediate family, and high *disaggregation* and even incoherence at the next level of ministers and their departments, impeding policy creation and implementation in ways similar to Saudi Arabia's bureaucratic "fiefdoms" described by Hertog (2010). Compounding this paradox is the absence of a functioning cabinet as a macro-policy steering mechanism. Several interviewees noted that the Council of Ministers simply ratifies decisions, but it does not serve to thrash out and shape policy. This helps explain the somewhat unusual reliance on "Supreme Councils" in the Qatari policy-making system (see Ulrichsen 2004: 84–85). The ones for health and education have been the most visible and active, and they are a way of creating what might be thought of as "super sectoral cabinets" that combine a leading role for the ruling family, key ministers, and experts and agencies. Yet these councils also create policy incoherence when they are not adequately aligned with the older and more established ministries that remain in charge of much of the day-to-day functions.

A third conclusion from this case study is the limited role of civil society and the private sector in the policy process, at least at the macro-level. The aspiration seems to have been to engage nongovernmental actors in the development of the QNDS, but in the end this was episodic at best, mirroring the government's communication and outreach problems in previous efforts, such as the K–12 reforms (Brewer et al. 2007; Mitchell 2013: 239). As we noted, this is in part because of the underdeveloped nature of civil society in Qatar. It is also the result of an inadequate enabling environment and deliberate legal restrictions (forbidding, for example, trade unions). Engaging civil society in the QNDS process was difficult for this reason, apart from some small charitable organizations and of course the large ones like the Qatar Foundation. This is part of a larger problem of accountability systems within the government structure in Qatar. Despite the ubiquity of electronic communications among the citizenry, there is relatively little effort to try to gather public opinion through social media, for example.

A fourth point that emerges in this chapter, but in others in this book as well, is the role of international consultants and advisers. In the case of the QNDS, the RAND–Qatar Policy Institute provided key advice in 2005 that led to the establishment of the GSDP. The study was, of course, commissioned by the Emir, and Dr. Ibrahim, as his advisor, played an important role in drafting it. But RAND's influence is significant, in this field as well as in others such as education reform (see Chapter 4). The design of the GSDP, for example, followed the RAND recommendations almost exactly. We should not be entirely surprised at this development. It simply reflected the lack of internal capacity at the time in Qatar to launch a major, massive initiative of this type. The dynamics of "policy transfer" were clearly evident in the sense of borrowing both expertise and international "best practice" models (Dolowitz and Marsh 1996, 2000; Pal 2014). The upshot is that ruling elites in rentier states cannot simply do whatever they wish. At the level of delivering specific development projects and important, complicated services, certain technical requirements are usually necessary if they are to be successful. Inevitably, those elites need to look outside of their own experiences and immediate circle for guidance, which allows for the possibility of external influence over domestic policy-making.

The QNDS was the first phase of the QNV development program extending to 2030. It is an open question as to whether the last decade was a unique window of opportunity for this initiative. Emir Hamad at the time had significant authority and indeed commissioned the RAND report of 2005. The GSDP was created exactly along the lines envisioned by RAND: independent, reporting directly to the Heir Apparent, and staffed by international experts. Yet as the current decade progresses, the QNV development program may be stymied by the continued lack of capacity. By 2015, the GSDP had been reabsorbed, as part of a government reorganization, into a ministry and re-joined with the Statistics Authority. At the time of writing (May 2015), the GSDP has produced an interim report assessing the first phase of the QNDS, but that report has not been released to the public. The committee to oversee the implementation of the QNDS has never met. There is no visible activity around the development of the second phase of the QNDS, 2017–2020. Ministers as well as ministerial staff have continued to change, especially after Emir Tamim's June 2013 re-organization. In short, in contrast to the early momentum around both the QNV and the QNDS, the current strategic planning machinery seems to be stuck.

There are several possible reasons for this. In Qatar's system, one always has to look to the Emir, and while Emir Tamim was nominally in charge of the QNDS, he may be more concerned about reining in the excesses of grand projects, especially with the downturn of oil prices in 2014. It was his 2013 governmental reforms that returned the GSDP to a pre-2005 configuration. Another important reason is that the QNDS and the macro-economic policy planning strategy that it represented has now possibly been eclipsed by the FIFA World Cup 2022 preparations. A successful World Cup hosting bid was not anticipated when the QNDS was first being drafted. The bid was won in December 2010, and the QNDS was published in 2011. While the QNDS referred to the World Cup, it saw the impact in 2011–2016 as "modest," though preparations would "gather momentum" in the period. Tellingly, it admitted that "public infrastructure spending will peak in 2012, though the profile of the spending pipeline will change if large new investments related to the FIFA World Cup 2022 and other initiatives are approved and commissioned prior to 2016" (GSDP 2011a: 56). In effect, at the level of economic and infrastructural development, Qatar now has two national plans. These plans would be daunting for any government, but they are especially challenging in the Qatar case where there still is a significant lack of internal governmental capacity.

And all of these developments must be set against the backdrop of lower oil and gas prices. Qatar is somewhat insulated from declining oil prices, because of its leading position in LNG. But it is possible that even a modest long-term decline in international prices will put pressure on the rentier bargain. The services, subsidies, and entitlements that Qataris now expect will be difficult to roll back. The costs of massive and almost unprecedented infrastructural development, all happening simultaneously, will be daunting—by some estimates, over $220 billion. And there will without a doubt be a post-FIFA "hangover" and the need to carefully manage subsequent steps in the QNV after the FIFA boom subsides. Navigating and managing these challenges will require considerable technical skills, as well as strategic and institutional coherence in Qatar's policy-making system. Sustainable economic growth and deep development will depend less on the country's abundance of hydrocarbon resources and more on its political and public management capacities.

## NOTES

1. Crystal (1995: 6) argues, "There are always moments when the state develops a high degree of autonomy from its social bases.... But oil-based states are unusual in that their higher degree of autonomy from other social groupings is... part of a structurally determined, ongoing process."
2. Academics have argued that the unintended consequences of both the allocation and the diversification policies of the rentier state would empower various bureaucratic or citizen groups, which would allow these groups to stymie state policy or pressure the state to accede to their demands. Richards and Waterbury (2008: 17) describe this process succinctly: "Oil rents are politically centralizing. However, as the revenues are spent, new domestic actors emerge (as contractors, agents, recipients of subsidies) who, in turn, begin to limit the freedom of maneuver of the state. This is a very typical pattern; state autonomy may rise in a particular conjuncture but then typically will decline with its exercise over time." Crystal (1995: 189) elaborates: "Oil revenues have allowed rulers to create new state institutions, but bureaucracies are never neutral: as these institutions grow in size and complexity, they are becoming less amenable to control through ruling kinship networks. The ruling houses and the state administrations, though they coexist and exercise jurisdiction over the same populations, are not identical. Bureaucrats have the potential for developing their own centers of power, social relationships, and political ideals and goals. An unintended ramification is a potential loss of control over the population by the rulers as this control is increasingly mediated by a possibly disloyal bureaucracy."
3. These surveys were made possible by two grants (UREP 12-016-5-007 and UREP 15-035-5-013) from the Qatar National Research Fund (a member of Qatar Foundation). The statements made herein are solely the responsibility of the authors.
4. The 2014 survey sampled only Qatari females (due to the nature of the research grant). The increased interest among Qatari women, relative to Qatari men, in having greater say in the educational systems also drove the result in 2013: broken down by gender, approximately 70 % of women and only 44 % of men desired more say in the K–12 reforms, with a similar (slightly lower) ratio of responses for the Qatar University reforms.
5. The following section is based in part on interviews conducted in Doha between January and March 2015. Uncited terms or quotes are from the interviews.
6. At time of writing (May 2015) the mid-term report for the QNDS has yet to be released. It will cast more light on both implementation mechanisms and actual results.

## Bibliography. Qatar: Policy Making in a Transformative State

"91.8 percent of Qatari teachers find 'HEI's List' allowed students to disrespect their teachers" [in Arabic]. 2012. Al Arab Newspaper, November 6.
Abu Dhabi Urban Planning Council. 2007. *Plan Abu Dhabi 2030: Urban Structure Framework Plan*. Abu Dhabi: Abu Dhabi Urban Planning Council. Retrieved from https://gsec.abudhabi.ae/Sites/GSEC/Content/EN/PDF/Publications/plan-abu-dhabi-full-version%2cproperty%3dpdf.pdf.
Al Ghanim, Issa bin Shaheen. 2012. The National Development Strategy of the State of Qatar, 2011–2016 [in Arabic]. In *The People Want Reform in Qatar… Too*, ed. Ali Khalifa Al-Kuwari, 109–116. Beirut: Al Maaref Forum.
Al-Khater, Maryam. 2012. Qatar University…poor planning [in Arabic]. *Al Sharq Newspaper*, May 21, p. 10.
Al-Kobaisi, Abdulla Juma. 2012. Qatar: The trends in public education and higher education [in Arabic]. In *The People Want Reform in Qatar…Too*, ed. Ali Khalifa Al-Kuwari, 60–73. Beirut: Al Maaref Forum.
Al-Kuwari, Rabia bin Sabah. 2012. The open meeting with HH Sheikha Moza at QU for developing the national university [in Arabic]. *Al Sharq Newspaper*, May 13.
Al-Saadi, Sara, Maaria Assami, and Latifa Darwish. 2012. *Bader*. Retrieved from http://www.baderfilm.com.
Al-Sulaiti, Ahmed Abdullah Ahmed. 2012. So we don't lose hope… 'Minister of Labor' [in Arabic]. *Al Watan Newspaper*, February 8, p. 6.
Arabian Business. 2012. Arabian Business Qatar Power List 2012. *Arabian Business*.
Başkan, Birol, and Steven Wright. 2011. Seeds of change: Comparing state-religion relations in Qatar and Saudi Arabia. *Arab Studies Quarterly* 33(2): 96–111.
Beetham, David. 2013. *The Legitimation of Power*, 2nd edn. New York: Palgrave Macmillan.
Ben-Gera, Michal. 2004. *Co-ordination at the Centre of Government: The Functions and Organisation of the Government Office: Comparative Analysis of OECD Countries, CEECs and Western Balkan Countries*. Sigma Papers, No. 35. Paris: OECD.
Bollier, Sam. 2013. Can Qatar replace its renaissance man? *Aljazeera*, June 26. Retrieved from http://www.aljazeera.com/indepth/features/2013/06/201362613431469150.html.
Brewer, Dominic J., Catherine H. Augustine, Gail L. Zellman, Gery Ryan, Charles A. Goldman, Cathleen Stasz, and Louay Constant. 2007. *Education for a New Era: Design and Implementation of K-12 Education Reform in Qatar*. Doha, Qatar: RAND–Qatar Policy Institute.
Center for Economic Research (Uzbekistan). 2014. *Looking Beyond the Horizon: Guidelines and Best Practices in Formulating National Visions*. Tashkent, Uzbekistan: Center for Economic Research and United Nations Development

Program. Retrieved from http://www.uz.undp.org/content/uzbekistan/en/home/library/poverty/looking-beyond-the-horizon-guidelines-and-best-practices-in-formulating-national-visions/.
Chaudhry, Kiren Aziz. 1997. *The Price of Wealth: Economics and Institutions in the Middle East*. Ithaca: Cornell University Press.
Crystal, Jill. 1995. *Oil and Politics in the Gulf: Rulers and Merchants in Kuwait and Qatar*, Rev. edn. Cambridge: Cambridge University Press.
Dahlström, Carl, B. Guy Peters, and Jon Pierre, eds. 2011. *Steering from the Centre: Strengthening Political Control in Western Democracies*. Toronto: University of Toronto Press.
Davidson, Christopher M 2012. *After the Sheikhs: The Coming Collapse of the Gulf Monarchies*. London: Hurst and Company.
Decent, Tom. 2015. Saudi Arabia's King Salman gives citizens an extra two months' salary. *Sydney Morning Herald*, January 20.
"Demands for administrative reform in QU" [in Arabic]. 2012. *Al Sharq Newspaper*, May 25, p. 11.
Dolowitz, David, and David Marsh. 1996. Who learns what from whom: A review of the policy transfer literature. *Political Studies* 44(2): 343–357.
———. 2000. Learning from abroad: The role of policy transfer in contemporary policy-making. *Governance* 13(1): 5–25.
Farha, Mark. 2015. The Arab revolts: Local, regional, and global catalysts and consequences. In *The Arab Uprisings: Catalysts, Dynamics, and Trajectories*, eds. Fahed Al-Sumait, Nele Lenze, and Michael C. Hudson, 47–68. London: Rowman and Littlefield.
Gause, F. Gregory. 1994. *Oil Monarchies: Domestic and Security Challenges in the Gulf States*. New York: Council on Foreign Relations Press.
General Secretariat for Development Planning (GSDP). 2008. *Qatar National Vision 2030*. Doha, Qatar: Qatar General Secretariat for Development Planning. Retrieved from http://www.gsdp.gov.qa/portal/page/portal/gsdp_en/knowledge_center/Tab/QNV2030_English_v2.pdf.
———. 2011a. *Qatar National Development Strategy 2011–2016: Towards Qatar National Vision 2030*. Doha, Qatar: Qatar General Secretariat for Development Planning. Retrieved from http://www.gsdp.gov.qa/gsdp_vision/docs/NDS_EN.pdf.
———. 2011b. *Qatar National Development Strategy, 2011–2016: Summary of Programmes*. Doha, Qatar: Qatar General Secretariat for Development Planning. Retrieved from http://www.gsdp.gov.qa/portal/page/portal/gsdp_en/knowledge_center/Tab/NDS_ENGLISH_SUMMARY.pdf.
———. 2012. *National Human Development Report: Expanding the Capacities of Qatari Youth: Mainstreaming Young People in Development*. Doha, Qatar: Qatar General Secretariat for Development Planning. Retrieved from http://hdr.undp.org/en/reports/national/arabstates/qatar/Qatar_NHDR_EN_2012.pdf.

Glasser, Susan B. 2003. Qatar reshapes its schools, putting English over Islam: Conservatives see reform as extension of U.S. influence in Gulf. *Washington Post*, February 2, A20.

Gray, Matthew. 2011. *A Theory of "Late Rentierism" in the Arab States of the Gulf*. Doha, Qatar: Occasional Paper No. 7. Center for International and Regional Studies. Georgetown University School of Foreign Service in Qatar.

Herb, Michael. 1999. *All in the Family: Absolutism, Revolution, and Democracy in the Middle East Monarchies*. Albany, NY: State University of New York.

Hertog, Steffen. 2010. *Princes, Brokers, and Bureaucrats: Oil and the State in Saudi Arabia*. New York: Cornell University Press.

International Energy Agency. 2009. *World Energy Outlook 2009*. Paris: International Energy Agency. Retrieved from http://www.worldenergyoutlook.org/media/weowebsite/2009/WEO2009.pdf.

Kamrava, Mehran. 2013. *Qatar: Small State, Big Politics*. Ithaca, NY: Cornell University Press.

———. 2014. The rise and fall of ruling bargains in the Middle East. In *Beyond the Arab Spring: The Evolving Ruling Bargain in the Middle East*, ed. Mehran Kamrava, 17–45. London: Hurst and Company and Centre for International and Regional Studies, School of Foreign Service in Qatar, Georgetown University.

Khatri, Shabina. 2011. During a fundraiser event in Chicago on Thursday... *Doha News*, April 16. Retrieved from http://dohanews.co/during-a-fundraising-event-in-chicago-on-thursday/.

Kingdom of Bahrain. 2010. *The Economic Vision 2030 for Bahrain*. Bahrain: Economic Development Board. Retrieved from https://www.bahrain.bh/wps/wcm/connect/38f53f2f-9ad6-423d-9c96-2dbf17810c94/Vision%2B20 30%2BEnglish%2B%28low%2Bresolution%29.pdf?MOD=AJPERES.

Kingdom of Saudi Arabia. 2004. *Long-Term Strategy for the Saudi Economy*. Riyadh, Saudi Arabia: Ministry of Economy and Planning. Retrieved from http://www.mep.gov.sa/themes/GoldenCarpet/index.jsp - 1411402481854.

Krane, Jim. 2013. *Stability versus Sustainability: Energy Policy in the Gulf Monarchies*. EPRG Working Paper 1302. Cambridge: Cambridge Working Paper in Economics. Retrieved from http://www.eprg.group.cam.ac.uk.

Lucas, Russell E. 2014. The Persian Gulf monarchies and the Arab Spring. In *Beyond the Arab Spring: The Evolving Ruling Bargain in the Middle East*, ed. Mehran Kamrava, 313–340. London: Hurst and Company and Centre for International and Regional Studies, School of Foreign Service in Qatar, Georgetown University.

Luciani, Giacomo. 1987. Allocation vs. production states: A theoretical framework. In *The Rentier State*, eds. Hazem Beblawi, and Giacomo Luciani, 63–82. London: Croom Helm.

———. 2007. Linking economic and political reform in the Middle East: The role of the bourgeoisie. In *Debating Arab Authoritarianism: Dynamics and*

*Durability in Nondemocratic Regimes*, ed. Oliver Schlumberger, 161–176. Stanford, CA: Stanford University Press.
Mahdavy, Hussein. 1970. The patterns and problems of economic development in rentier states: The case of Iran. In *Studies of Economic History of the Middle East*, ed. M.A. Cook, 428–467. London: Oxford University Press.
Mitchell, Jocelyn Sage. 2013. *Beyond Allocation: The Politics of Legitimacy in Qatar*. Ph.D., Graduate School of Arts and Science, Georgetown University.
Mitchell, Jocelyn Sage, Justin J. Gengler, Sean Burns, and Mary Dedinsky. 2013. *UREP 12-016-5-007: Qatar and the World Values Survey: Ensuring Conceptual Validity and Cross-Cultural Comparability*. Survey conducted by the Social and Economic Survey Institute, Qatar University, Doha, Qatar, January 15–February 3.
Mitchell, Jocelyn Sage, Christina Paschyn, Kirsten Pike, Tanya Kane, Justin J. Gengler, and Sadia Mir. 2014. *UREP 15-035-5-013: Qatari Women: Engagement and Empowerment*. Survey conducted by the Social and Economic Survey Institute, Qatar University, Doha, Qatar, June 10–25.
OECD. 2012. *Towards a Strategic State: Options for a Governance Contribution to the New Approach to Economic Challenges*. Meeting at the OECD Council at Ministerial Level. Paris: OECD.
Öniş, Ziya. 1991. The logic of the developmental state. *Comparative Politics* 24(1): 109–126.
Pal, Leslie A. 2014. Introduction: The OECD and policy transfer: Comparative case studies. *Journal of Comparative Policy Analysis: Research and Practice* [Special Issue: The OECD and Policy Transfer: Comparative Case Studies], 16(3): 195–200.
Peters, B. Guy, R.A.W. Rhodes, and Vincent Wright, eds. 1999. *Administering the Summit: Administration of the Core Executive in Developed Countries*. New York: St. Martin's Press.
Qatar Petroleum (QP). 2011. *Development of the Energy Sector in the State of Qatar During the Past Fifteen Years (1995–2010): Success Story*. Doha, Qatar: Qatar Petroleum. Retrieved from http://www.eisourcebook.org/cms/July 2013/Qatar, 1995 - 2010, Energy Sector Development.pdf.
"Qatari job seekers view manual labour as 'socially unacceptable'." 2012. Gulf Times Newspaper, August 9. Retrieved from http://www.thefreelibrary.com/Qatari+job+seekers+view+manual+labour+as+%27socially+unacceptable%27.-a0313938523.
Richards, Alan, and John Waterbury. 2008. *A Political Economy of the Middle East*, 3rd edn. Boulder, CO: Westview Press.
Ross, Michael L. 2001. Does oil hinder democracy? *World Politics* 53(3): 325–361.
———. 2012. *The Oil Curse: How Petroleum Wealth Shapes the Development of Nations*. Princeton, NJ: Princeton University Press.

Scott, James C. 1985. *Weapons of the Weak: Everyday Forms of Peasant Resistance*. New Haven: Yale University Press.
Seznec, Jean Francois. 2004. Democratization in the region. National Defense University Topical Symposium: "Prospects for Security in the Middle East" April 20–21, Washington, DC.
Shonfield, Andrew. 1965. *Modern Capitalism*. London: Oxford University Press.
Skocpol, Theda. 1979. *States and Social Revolutions: A Comparative Analysis of France, Russia, and China*. Cambridge: Cambridge University Press.
Toumi, Habib. 2011. Public sector in Qatar to get 60 per cent pay rise. *Gulf News*, September 7.
UAE. 2010. *UAE Vision 2021*. Abu Dhabi: UAE. Retrieved from http://www.vision2021.ae/sites/default/files/uae-vision2021-brochure-english.pdf.
Ulrichsen, Kristian Coates. 2011. *Insecure Gulf: The End of Certainty and the Transition to the Post-Oil Era*. New York: Columbia University Press.
———. 2014. *Qatar and the Arab Spring*. London: Hurst & Company.
US Energy Information Administration. 2014. *Qatar*. Washington, DC. Retrieved from http://www.eia.gov/countries/analysisbriefs/Qatar/qatar.pdf.
Weber, Max. 1958. *From Max Weber: Essays in Sociology*. Translated, edited and with an introduction by H. H. Gerth and C. Wright Mills. New York: Oxford University Press.
Winckler, Onn. 2009. Labor and liberalization: The decline of the GCC rentier system. In *Political Liberalization in the Persian Gulf*, ed. Joshua Teitelbaum, 59–85. New York: Columbia University Press.
World Bank. 2015. Data: GDP Growth (annual %). Accessed April 30. Retrieved from http://data.worldbank.org/indicator/NY.GDP.MKTP.KD.ZG?page=1.

CHAPTER 4

# Qatar's Borrowed K-12 Education Reform in Context

*Lolwah R.M. Alkhater*

In 2001 the State of Qatar decided to take the lead, in a region where education does not often make it to the top of the policy agenda, and reform its K-12 public education with the goal of building a world-class system that prepares its students to enter distinguished universities and compete in the global market. "The project...reflects the region's aspirations and its commitment to building a sustainable future for generations to come" (Brewer et al. 2007). This is how Dr. Sheikha Al-Misnad—then the president of Qatar University and a member of the Supreme Education Council, described Qatar's grand reform project, "Education for a new Era." The project had the highest political leadership in the young emirate backing it up through personal monitoring, unlimited resources, and a solid political will.

After more than 13 years after launching the reform, there is one common sentiment that underpins the reaction of the educators interviewed for this chapter: bitterness. There is bitterness about what their dream project could have achieved but hasn't, as well as bitterness about their genuine efforts and good intentions that have been misinterpreted or forgotten in the midst of the public outrage that accompanied the educational process during those years. All of the initial reform policies have been completely reversed after causing unprecedented social controversy

L.R.M. Alkhater (✉)
Qatar Foundation and RAND-Qatar Policy Institute, Doha, Qatar

© The Author(s) 2016
M.E. Tok et al. (eds.), *Policy-Making in a Transformative State*,
DOI 10.1057/978-1-137-46639-6_4

97

and after years of policy instability. Whether this policy reversal indicates the reform's failure or whether it indicates a retreat from a reform agenda, in both cases it is an indication that something went wrong at one or several points.

The chapter draws a portrait of the K-12 educational scene in Qatar and its development over the years. It then concentrates on the internal processes and governance structures of the system during the 2001–2014 period.

## K-12 Education in Qatar: A History of Reform

The inception of modern education in Qatar can be traced back to 1948/49 when the first boys' school was opened in Doha. By 1954, the government was already funding four schools, enrolling 560 boys who received education in English, Arabic, arithmetic, and geography, in addition to Islamic studies and history. In 1956, Amina Mahmoud, a pioneer Qatari woman educator, established the first school for girls, teaching a semi-modern curriculum with the consent of Sheikh Khalifa bin Haman Al-Thani, the crown prince at that time (Al-Misnad 1985: 35–36). In fact, this girls' school started in 1938, but as a Kuttab, which is a traditional form of schooling that restricts its subjects to learning about the Qur'an and reading and writing Arabic language. Katatib (plural of Kuttab) were the only form of education available in Qatar before 1948, and with a few prominent exceptions, these Katatib were mainly independent from the government. In 1957/58, the Ministry of Education[1] was established as the first ministry in the history of the young emirate (Al-Hail 2008).

From the 1960s until the 1980s, major changes and improvements occurred in the public education system in Qatar. The Ministry of Education introduced its own curriculum and textbooks in 1965, whereas before it had relied on imported material from Egypt, Saudi and other Arab countries. Qatar also became a member of a number of regional and international education-related bodies such as the ALESCO (Arab League Educational, Cultural, and Scientific Organization) in 1962 and UNESCO in 1972. This was in addition to signing a number of agreements with other Arab countries, which facilitated knowledge transfer and allowed Qatar to benefit from these countries' experiences and human resources (The Ministry of Education developed specialized schools for boys: the Industrial School, the Commercial School, and the Religious Institute. In 1984, the Ministry established two schools for students with disabilities and special needs (one for boys and one for girls)). This was in addition to improvements in the curriculum and school facilities (Ministry of Education 2005).

The past two decades were also rich in reform attempts; some were implemented and some did not see the light, and some were fundamental while others were partial. Dr. Abdullah Jum'a Al-Kubaisy is the former president of Qatar University and one of the few local scholars whose Ph.D. thesis became a classic to researchers in the history of the Qatari educational system. His paper, which attempts to reform the public education system, is the only secondary source this research could identify.[2] It documents three major reform plans that were designed in 1990, 1996, and 1997 consecutively but were never actually realized (Al-Kubaisi 1999). According to Al-Kubaisi, those plans could have elevated the K-12 educational system in Qatar had there been enough resources and a strong political will behind them.

In addition to these plans, there was a fourth reform strategy developed in 1999 under the supervision of Dr. Kafoud, the Minister of Education at the time. The only documentation of this attempt is a gray paper written in Arabic, "Qatar Education Strategy 2000–2010 Proposal"[3] (this is the author's translation of the Arabic title *Mashroo' Al-Estrateejya Al-Tarbawya li-dawlat Qatar 2000–2010*). The strategy seemed comprehensive and identified most of the weaknesses in the Qatari educational system. Dr. Kafoud was appointed in 1996, but after he left the Ministry, this 10-year strategy project was put aside. Simultaneously, another reform attempt, namely the Scientific Schools, was launched in 1999. The idea started with two segregated secondary schools—one for boys and one for girls—that were inspired by the Canadian schooling system and were designed and implemented with the help of Canadian experts (M Al-Maraghi,[4] personal communication, June 26, 2014). These were intended to provide a high-quality option for the best performing students in the public system in the hope that these schools will be a pipeline to provide students who can enroll in world leading universities (M Al-Maraghi, personal communication, June 26, 2014). In 2001, a similar idea was implemented at the elementary and then preparatory level—called the Developed Schools or *Al-Madaris Al-Mutawara*—hoping that these in turn will feed into the scientific secondary schools (S. Al-Mansoori[5], personal communication, June 11, 2014; F. Al-Kuwari[6], personal communication, June 17, 2014). These schools gained a reputation of being the most successful public schools in Qatar, yet they constituted only a small percentage of the public system, whereas the decision-makers were eager to achieve a more fundamental and widespread reform. In 2003, Shiakha Al-Mohmoud was named as the first female Minister in the history of Qatar. It was during her time that the grand reform—as this chapter describes it—namely Education for a New Era, was implemented. The design and conceptual foundation of Education for a New Era was laid by RAND Corporation in 2001 when the political leadership invited the renowned American think tank to provide recommendations to reform the public educational system. Within a year, RAND surveyed the educational landscape with the help of some locally-based experts and officials and proposed three options for reform:

Option 1 was to reform within and through the Ministry of Education by improving the curricula and teaching quality etc. Basically, this was supposed to be a modified centralized model.
Option 2 was to create a decentralized parallel system to the Ministry based on the charter schools model. This required the creation of a new regulatory body to oversee the process. This body then became the Supreme Education Council.
Option 3 was to create a voucher system which might eventually lead to privatizing the sector.

The leadership chose the second option with a belief that reforms "in which Ministry retained authority were not likely to bring about large changes" (Brewer et al. 2007: 53) given the history of the previous attempts.[7]. Furthermore, it seemed premature for "the Qatari context [to adopt the voucher system] since the country had no market for information on school performance, and the truly outstanding schools, such as Qatar Academy (a private school sponsored by Qatar Foundation) were limited in number" (Brewer et al. 2007: 57). As a result, the Supreme Education Council (SEC) was established in 2002 and a Coordination and Implementation Committee was formed to execute the implementation. The SEC and the committee consisted of political figures and local education leaders working together with experts[8] from different institutions and countries selected by a team from RAND. The first cohort of the charter schools (known in Qatar as independent schools) was launched in 2004. It took the SEC seven cohorts until all MOE schools were converted to become independent schools in 2011. Despite the Qatari decision-maker's first rejection of the voucher system option in 2001, in 2012 the SEC started implementing school vouchers. This chapter will later discuss this in detail. Today 100 % of the Qatari students are eligible for school vouchers and virtually all of them are using them[9] (Education Voucher System Law No. 7 in 2012).

Today, students in Qatar have four types of schools available to them: independent schools (the only public schools), private international schools, Arabic private schools, and community schools. Community schools are administered by foreign embassies in Qatar, primarily to serve their communities, but Qataris and other nationalities are occasionally allowed to attend. Primary education is obligatory for both girls and boys who live in Qatar until they complete middle school or reach the age of 18 (Obligatory Education Law No. 25 in 2001).

Almost 13 years have passed since Qatar launched the Education for a New Era reform of its public education; this is a good duration to pause and look back at this program to analyze it. The following sections will focus on analyzing the K-12 education reform policies that Qatar applied from 2001 until 2014. The analysis draws on the review of key reports released by the SEC and the Ministry of Education, in addition to the documentation provided by the schools whose principals participated in the 15 in-depth interviews carried out by the author between May and July 2014. Four decision-makers from the SEC and the Ministry of Education and 15 educators, including school operators/principals and school academic deputies, participated in these interviews. The selected school operators belong to different school cohorts, there are a total of seven cohorts, to cover the various stages of the reform's implementation. According to the reform model each school is operated by an operator who manages the school through a contract between him/her and the Supreme Education Council. The school operator is not necessarily the school principal; in fact, one operator can have several school principals reporting to him/her depending on the number of the contracted schools that the operator could get. The author also served as a community representative on the board of trustees of one of the independent schools for two years. This experience enabled her to have some firsthand insight.

## BORROWING AN AMERICAN MODEL

### *The Original RAND Study*[10]

A new leadership came to power in 1995, and a few years later it became clear that the then new Emir Shiekh Hamad bin Khalifa and the First Lady Shiekha Moza bint Nasser had very ambitious developmental goals (see

Chapter 3) which required a new set of skills that the educational system was not producing. Hence, RAND Corporation was invited to help in prescribing a remedy.

RAND's study (Brewer et al. 2007: 37–42) concluded that the MOE curriculum, teaching methods, and management style were obsolete, and it summarized the weaknesses of the system in 14 points, including dependence on rote memorization, unchallenging and rigid curriculum, low pay and poor incentives for teachers, and poor teacher allocation policies. Accordingly, the study proposed three reform options, and the charter school system was selected, as discussed earlier. The reformers apparently found that the name "independent schools" was more suitable than "charter schools". The latter term translates literally to *Al-Madaris Al-Ta'aqudiah* which has a commercial connotation in Arabic; this perhaps explains why the name independent schools—*Al-Madaris Al-Mustaqillah*—was used instead.

The Ministry of Education (MOE) in Qatar was administering all public schools in the State until 2004, when the first batch of independent schools was announced as part of the K-12 system reform led by the SEC.[11] Starting from 2004 there were two types of public schools, the MOE Schools and the SEC schools. This created a duality in the K-12 public educational system with two government regulators operating simultaneously until 2011, when all schools became independent schools and the SEC completely took over the Ministry. The MOE's role before the reform involved all the details of the schools' daily business, including the weekly teaching plans that the schools had to follow as well as the management of financial and human resources.

The independent school System was originally founded on four principles:

1. Autonomy: Governance is decentralized in a way so that each school manages its own finances, human resources, content, and teaching style. Each school is run by an operator who is selected through a tendering process. The selected operator then signs a contract with the SEC. The SEC provides a financial allotment to each independent school per pupil. These schools were originally designed to be for-profit entities.
2. Accountability: School operators are held accountable to the SEC, which is supposed to provide an overall governing framework. The SEC provides curriculum standards for the four core subjects: Arabic, English, mathematics, and science. All independent schools

were required to comply with these standards regardless of curriculum or learning resources. Making schools participate in standardized international and national tests is another mechanism to enforce accountability and manage the quality. This is in addition to financial audits and comprehensive school assessments that are supposed to take place every three years[12] (A. Al-Sayed[13], personal communication, May 14, 2014).
3. Choice: The core concept here is to provide parents with choice to select a "good" school for their children. This has four aspects[14]:

   (a) Good schools in theory will attract more students; hence they will have a higher financial allotment. Bad schools, on the other hand, will lose students to the good ones until the number of students, hence the finances, becomes insufficient to operate. This will lead—at least in theory—to closing down the "bad" schools or improving their performance, while the good schools will continue to flourish.
   (b) Education quality should be measured in an objective, effective, and transparent manner, and results shall be made available to parents.
   (c) Parents should be aware and engaged enough to make informed choices for their children.
   (d) There should be enough space in the good schools to accommodate the potential demand should the model work out as per the theory.

4. Variety: The "contracting Authority could provide incentives to ensure diversity or to open schools to meet particular societal demands (e.g., a school specializing in science and technology)" (Brewer et al. 2007: 59). In fact, at least in the first two cohorts, that is, the first two years of implementation, the contracted schools were supposed to work out like "magnet" schools (M Al-Dosari[15], personal communication, July 6, 2014),specializing in arts or science, for example. The variety was also supposed to be a variety in the methods and the philosophy of the offerings.[16]

These were the four principles of the reform's model which had to be translated into an implementation strategy. The following section will discuss the implementation phase.

## Between Design and Implementation

RAND's consultants worked with the Coordination Committee (representatives from the Qatari side) on developing the implementation strategy of the reform's selected model: independent schools. "Some ideas in the abstract model were redefined in this process or set aside for later consideration" (Brewer et al. 2007, p. 70). While the four principles[17] (autonomy, accountability, choice, and variety) remained the same, the disparity between the abstract model and the implementation strategy that the monograph (Brewer et al. 2007) referred to was mainly in the details which many would describe as operational. Two highlights must be made here: first, the disparity grew as the strategy was being implemented, and second, what appeared to be no more than operational details "that can be set aside or redefined" proved to be much more vital than decision-makers and consultants thought. It is interesting that the only example which the monograph gives about the ideas that were "put aside for later consideration" is related to the "hiring and firing of teachers and merit pay" (Brewer et al. 2007: 70), which proved to be very fundamental to the reform model. "These issues are complicated by the fact that teachers are civil servants" (Brewer et al. 2007: 70) and the solution was to put the issue aside, hoping it would be resolved during the implementation phase, which did not happen. In fact, the way implementation interacted with those issues[18] has somehow exacerbated them.

The total number of teachers in the public system in 2004/2005, when the first 12 independent schools were announced, was 7244[19] (Ministry of Education 2005). According to the reformers' evaluation, many teachers in the old system lacked suitable training and "are not ready to teach in schools that will be adopting curriculum standards, diversifying instructional practices and monitoring school performance at the national level" (Brewer et al. 2007: 84). The contracted schools in most cases were not newly established ones; instead, they were converted from their prior status as ministry schools to become independent schools under the SEC. In other words, the new operators who won the schools' contracts had to deal with the legacy of the former system, including the staff. In theory, an operator should have the freedom to hire and fire staff, but in practice that was complicated since they had the employment protections of public servants.[20] In reality, teachers and staff of the converted schools, at the beginning, had the option to move to other ministry schools, which seemed to be a temporary solution, although not one that was free from some frustration.

As the number of the converted schools increased and as the new system was trying to reinforce itself, decisions were made to refer hundreds of teachers and administrative staff to what was known at the time as "Al-band Al-Markazi," the Central Provision. Central Provision is a system that allows government employers to refer their Qatari national employees (without their consent) to a temporary retirement for two years to allow them to look for another job opportunity while receiving a salary. Many of the referred employees ended up as retirees under the Pension Law, while many others remained under the Central Provision for several years, as none of them—according to a declaration made by the respective Minister of the State (October 24)—were able to find an alternative job. Employers considered those referred employees as unqualified members or as a surplus. This arrangement was not exclusive to educators; it was applied across sectors and governmental entities as most sectors in Qatar were going through similar reforms and structural changes, driven by the transformative zeal described in other chapters of this book. Central Provision seemed to the government like a suitable workaround to elevate its public workforce's performance by replacing unneeded/unqualified members without causing harm to nationals or cause rage among them[21] since they are financially compensated and have the time to look for alternative employment. In 2009, however, a new Human Resources Law was announced and a decision was made to cancel the Central Provision, yet in practice it took years to completely implement the decision and contain the consequences. This was an implicit recognition that the Central Provision policy did not work, especially given press reports about misuse of the system by some employers, in addition to the societal dissatisfaction about forcing thousands of nationals to leave their jobs.

In March 2014, the SEC announced (Supreme Education Council 2014) that 805 out of 1208 teacher and administrative staff who were still subject to the canceled Central Provision would be integrated again within the educational system. One school principal commented "that some teachers who are now supposed to retire (due to age) are coming back to teach" (A. Al-Khulaifi[22], personal communication, June 17, 2014), while another principal said that "they need to rehab those employees as most of them have lost touch with teaching and with the new system for years... A lot has changed during those years" (K Al-Fidala[23], personal communication, May 28, 2014).

What went wrong with the Central Provision system? Getting rid of unqualified workers or putting some pressure on them to improve their performance without harming them financially seemed like a sound idea. It is in fact this "rational" and "abstract" analysis by the consultants and the designers that needs to be uncovered here. What rational analysis fails to capture is complex human behavior. The rational Central Provision failed to manage people's expectations about their future and about realizing themselves through having a stable decent job, especially in the context of Qatar, a rentier state in which citizens rely on their government to provide all services including decent job opportunities. Managing stakeholders' expectations through engaging them is important to policy-making, but this point apparently was not given enough attention. For example, there was no clarity about what the Central Provision was while the communication had been very poor. In fact, many employees who were referred to the Central Provision resorted to the Internet and on-line blogs to ask what that actually meant and which ministry or department they had to talk to in order to discuss the decision. In addition to managing people's expectations, the cultural dimension was partially overlooked. For example, many Qatari females choose to work in government schools because they are gender-segregated and because they find the job's nature convenient, which means they are not willing or cannot[24] look for a job outside the schooling system. This is not to imply that policies have to adhere to the status-quo. To the contrary, some policies may be designed to change the status-quo, like eradicating gender inequalities, but this requires a clarity about the objectives and a conscious interaction with the reality and the consequences of the intervention. This was not the case with educational reform. It is generally easier to make rational assumptions and design abstract models, especially if the designer comes from a different context, but this complicates the implementation process later on. More about this point is below. The rest of this section will shed more light on the implementation phase.

Independent schools reflected a world view that perceives governance to be the fundamental problem in education and believes that excessive control of centralized bureaucratic institutions must end. Accordingly, a new central office, one that is willing to relinquish some authority, had to be established: this office became the SEC. After establishing the SEC in 2002, public education for the first time in Qatar had two parallel systems operating in the same public sphere: SEC independent schools and MOE schools.

Unlike the very hierarchical structure of the old system, which was loaded with multiple layers and bureaucratic practices (Fig. 4.1), the reformed structure (Fig. 4.2) consisted of two separate offices. To avoid conflict of interest, one office within the SEC was to organize the contracting process and provide minimum academic support (the Education Institute), and one office was to monitor and evaluate the schools' performance (Evaluation Institute).

Starting from 2004, MOE schools were being converted to become independent schools. Out of tens of applicants, only 12 operators were

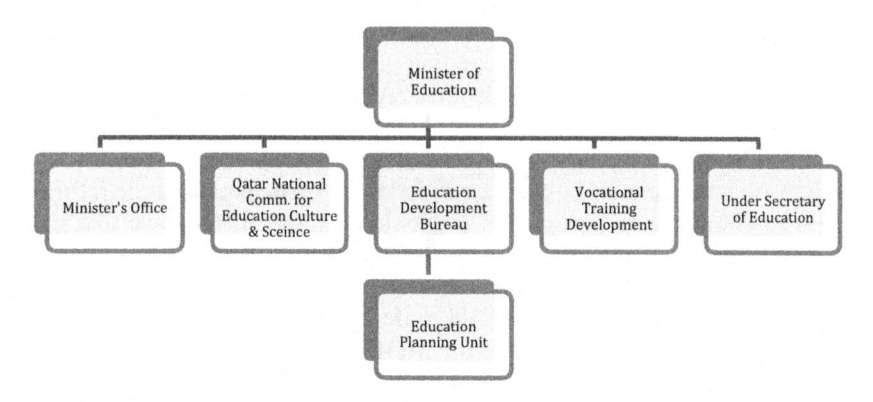

Fig. 4.1 Ministry of Education Organization Chart

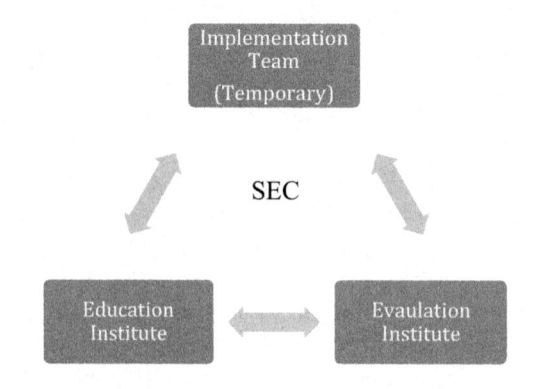

Fig. 4.2 Organizational Structure of the Reform in 2002

selected to lead the first cohort in 2004/2005. Every year more ministry schools were turned into independent schools under the SEC's management until all public schools in Qatar became part of the reformed system in 2011. Technically, this meant the end of the Ministry of Education, the oldest ministry in Qatar. While the process of selecting, contracting, planning, designing, and operating an independent school went as planned (e.g., with minimal intervention from the SEC— L. Al-Thawadi[25], personal communication, June 22, 2014; J. Al-Nu'aimi & A. Al-M'dadi[26], personal communication, June 24, 2014; A. Al-Horr, personal communication, May 13, 2014; M Al-Maraghi, personal communication, June 26, 2014)) in the first cohort, the SEC gradually acquired more authority, which required it to grow in size, role, and structure.

In addition, the SEC inherited most of the ministry's manpower, including those bureaucrats who were excluded from participating in the reform or who chose not to participate. It should be remembered here that the decision-maker during the reform's design phase chose to create the SEC instead of carrying out the reform through the MOE under the belief that the MOE was itself a part of the old, unreformed system. Despite this initial stand toward the MOE, both the MOE and Qatar University were the only local pool for educators when the reform started; therefore, the SEC capitalized (or perhaps had to capitalize) on staff mainly from the ministry to run the reform, though under a different setting. This was in addition to an arsenal of consultants that the SEC utilized. This new setting created tension and at times rivalry between the MOE and the SEC. Both entities were operating simultaneously, but the SEC was growing at the expense of the MOE as the former was taking over the latter's schools and role until the latter was completely absorbed. It is interesting to observe that many of the reform's policies have being clearly reversed as the SEC absorbed the MOE. This became very clear post-2011, when the SEC started centralizing the system again; for example, the SEC went back to the MOE practice of distributing the weekly teaching schedule to all schools. This sequence between inheriting the MOE's staff and reversing the reform policies might suggest some causality, as some analysts have observed (A. Al-Khuliafi, personal communication, June 17, 2014; L. Al-Thawadi, personal communication, June 22, 2014). This chapter, however, shall not take this last observation at face value, neither shall it attribute the policy reversal to a single factor since many other dynamics were taking place at the time. In addition, some of the reform policies were actually reversed much earlier than 2011, such as converting independent schools from being for-profit to non-profit entities in 2005/2006, only one year after implementation (Table 4.1).

Education for a New Era generated unprecedented social controversy after only a few years of implementation. Criticizing officials and ministers in the government-owned newspapers is quite rare in Qatar, yet criticizing the SEC and the Minister of Education became a favorite subject for newspapers, columnists, and social media commentators. The chief editor, at the time, of one of the main local newspapers, *Al-Watan*, was leading a bitter diatribe against the Minister Sa'ad Al-Mahmoud. In 2011, Ahmed Al-Sulaiti wrote an article titled "Oh Sa'ad, Are We Foreigners?" (Al-Sulaiti, May 15, 2011). The title is sarcastic and in the article, *Al-Watan*'s chief editor complained about the SEC's policies in general.[27] By "we," he refers to Qataris with a sense of bitterness, claiming that officials are only listening to expatriate consultants which made some Qataris feel they had become foreigners in their own country. This sense of exclusion and antagonism toward what many perceive as Westernoriented policies is not uncommon in Qatari society. The Minister in turn responded to this article with one of his own, which then triggered a reply to the Minister's response, something almost unprecedented at that level in Qatar. Faisal Al-Marzougi, a regular columnist and a famous tweeb on Twitter, is yet another example. Al-Marzougi is very critical of many aspects of the changes that took place in Qatar in the past 15 years, especially Education for a New Era. In fact, Al-Marzouqi himself was part of the team who joined the SEC as part of the reform, but he was forced to

Table 4.1   Educational statistics 2004/2005–2007/2008

|  | Public Schools 2004/2005 | Private Schools 2004/2005 | MOE Schools 2007/2008 (Public) | SEC Schools 2007/2008 (Public) | Private Schools 2007/2008 |
|---|---|---|---|---|---|
| Number of Schools | 223 | 288 | 141 | 88 | 336 |
| Number of Students | 77,394 | 62,507 | 39,115 | 41,181 | 84,533 |
| Number of Teachers | 11,167 | 4999 | 7761 | 3589 | 6029 |

*Source*: Ministry of Education 2008

retire in 2010, which might partially explain his severe critique, which a large sector of the society shared.

Besides the weak performance of the students and the low quality of teaching, which the chapter will later discuss, several reasons for this general societal dissatisfaction may be listed. For instance, the reform made hundreds of teachers and ministry employees retire or leave, as discussed earlier. Parents, on the other hand, who did not have to bother about the details of their children's schooling under the old system which was settled and pretty much mechanical, suddenly were expected to play an active role in this process, including the selection of their kids' schools. Before implementing the reform, schools and students were distributed based on geographical area, but the reform originally required admissions to be open for competition. This essentially meant that schools had the right to reject students (D. Al-Emadi,[28] personal communication, May 11, 2014), regardless of geographical proximity. It also meant that many of the nearby schools could get filled quickly, especially with the demographic influx (see Chapter 10), as many Arab expats and some other nationalities chose to enroll their children in the public system due to its low fees compared to private schools[29]. This ignited anger among parents whose children in the past were automatically assigned to the school nearest to home (A. Al-Sayed, personal communication, May 14, 2014), whereas under the reform they have to actively look for a school (S. Al-Mansoori, personal communication, June 14, 2014). This issue was addressed later on through giving students priority if they already have a sibling in the respective school or if they live close to it, as well as through increasing the maximum size of students per class (S. Al-Mansoori, personal communication, June 14, 2014). Because of these factors, the reform, which originally planned to limit the class size to 20 students (Zellman et al. 2009), led to actual class sizes of around 35 in many schools. Those changes in the admission and enrollment policy, however much they were needed to address the previously mentioned issues, partially defeated the original purpose of "competition" and "choice," two of the four principles of the reform model that were discussed earlier. This is another example[30] that illustrates that design and implementation are extremely interdependent and not totally separate phases: the reality that policy practitioners are struggling with while some policy analysts are still not paying enough attention to. There is, however, a growing literature that talks about "program theory" and "implementation theory" and how they complement each other.

Program theory deals with a given policy and its impact as a sequential process which consists of a series of cause-effect relationships, more or less like a logic model. Implementation theory, on the other hand, gets into the details of executing a policy, which means it needs to deal with a dynamic reality that includes the behaviors of the different actors and how they communicate with each other, etc. Deploying implementation theory also serves as a checkpoint to validate the cause-effect assumptions of the design. In this case, for example, the designers of the reform, as the original study reveals, relied in their recommendations on many assumptions regarding the behaviors of the school operators and the different actors, including parents. The details, nevertheless, were left for the implementers to figure out. While the implementers did not seem very faithful to the design, especially as they were reversing many policies, it is actually the design that was not very faithful to reality. The design, for instance, assumed that communicating the performance of the different schools will lead to awareness among parents, and this awareness will lead parents to make informed choices and select the good schools. In turn, this will make good schools flourish while the bad ones should diminish. The designers made these assumptions with no attempt to examine the behavior of its target population, for instance, through a survey. Are we talking about educated parents in general? For example, can they read the school reports when they are published? How engaged are the parents in their kids' education? Do they have transportation to send their kids to schools that are far away? It is this interactive nature of the implementation phase which creates a layer of complexity that the designers did not deal with during the design phase. These lines are not implying that this complexity could have been necessarily avoided, but they are trying to illustrate the importance of understanding and considering the context, and considering the context should go beyond being culturally sensitive when borrowing external solutions. It should also be about being factual and examining reality, because being culturally sensitive could mean superficially customizing a model, but being factual might imply reconsidering it altogether, or at least fundamental aspects of it.

By 2012 similar procedures and changes of many fundamental aspects resulted in reversing the reform policies started in 2001. The changes led to going back to the top-down centralized governance, but this time under the SEC's administration. The following sections will elaborate more on the internal processes that caused these changes.

## The Charter System in Context

In 2012 Routledge published its World Yearbook of Education, which discussed policy borrowing and lending in education. The volume looks at the traveling reforms in education, a phenomenon which is growing under the umbrella of "best practice," "international standards," and "evidence-based policy planning" in many cases. "Whether the educational transfer is whole, selective or eclectic, the transfer isolates education from its political, economic, and cultural context," as Gita Steiner-Khamsi (2004: 201) puts it in another book. Therefore, it is vital for this chapter to at least take a "snapshot" of the Charter system in context the lenders and the borrowers.

When RAND's consultants recommended the charter schools model to the Qatari leadership in 2001, another group of researchers in RAND published a book about voucher and charter schools in the USA The book traced the concept of those schools back to political economists like John Stuart Mill (1859), Adam Smith (1776), and Thomas Paine (1791). The concept, however, further crystalized and was popularized by the American economist Milton Friedman. In his 1955 article "The Role Of Government in Education," Friedman introduced the term "voucher" to describe his concept of allowing families to choose their children's schools through providing them with government monetary allotments. Despite Friedman's major theoretical contribution, the movement on the ground toward a less centralized system became powerful during the late 1980s and early 1990s (Murphy and Shiffman 2002). This popularity among reformers came in the context of discrediting governmental failure in repairing the system during the early 1980s through top-down methods. Thus, the remedy to those reformers was to promote more decentralization and school-based management. The first charter school opened in Minnesota in 1992, and by 2004 there were more than 2600 schools operating in 36 states. The No Child Left Behind federal act of 2001 under President Bush's administration gave the charter model a notable push (Bulkley and Wohlstetter 2004: 1). Giving low-income families a good educational alternative is a main objective that many politicians and advocates of the school-choice movement put forward in the United States.

In summary, the voucher and charter models come one way or the other in line with the philosophical, political, and economic developments in the USA,[31] unlike the case in Qatar where the Charter system runs counter to the country's historical, economic, and social context:

1. When the US federal government in the adopted the No Child Left Behind federal act to support low-income and minority families in 2001, Qatar adopted a similar model in the same year, although it is a country that had and still has one of the highest income-per-capita in the world (see Chapter 1).
2. The USA has a decentralized, federal governing system. Qatar, to the contrary, had and still has a highly centralized and hierarchical system. Therefore, applying the decentralized reform model in a highly centralized governing system had a very thin chance of survival.
3. The principles and mechanisms of a liberal market economy are deeply rooted in the American institutional and common culture, whereas the institutional environment is highly controlled in Qatar. In fact, the governance structures in Qatar give the government the privilege of monopolizing virtually all services while the public depends on the government to provide them. The transformation that the reform intended to make was not easy even for those who selected the "free-market" and choice reform model: when the independent schools were announced, entrepreneurs of all nationalities and backgrounds were allowed to apply to operate those schools; nevertheless, one year after implementation the SEC restricted the application only to Qataris who hold a degree in education.

Studying the reform model in context poses many questions about the universality of "traveling educational reforms" and "policy borrowing" in general. Normally, when the policy transfer occurs between the West and the Arab region, the complexity of the borrowing process is reduced to identity-related issues. Therefore, many foreign consultants tend to apply cosmetic changes to their best practice ready-made solutions in an attempt to be culturally sensitive, aiming to satisfy their clients. This entire chapter was an attempt to reveal some of the complex layers that surround policy borrowing, without resorting to the often misleading and superficial "identity" debate.

## Theoretical and Practical Critique

The original design of the Education for a New Era (Brewer et al. 2007; Zellman et al. 2009) reform program in 2001 was based on a number of assumptions that were not empirically tested against the reality and the local context of Qatar at the time. Most of these assumptions are related to the rational-choice and economic essence embedded in the reform model. This, on the other hand, has made the K-12 education policies vulnerable to many exogenous factors that are not intrinsically related to education itself.

The following sub-sections will work on deconstructing these assumptions and the processes resulting from them. They will illustrate the interconnectedness of design and implementation, showing that any absolute separation between the two may be a nice academic exercise, yet unrealistic at times.

### *The Rational-Choice Equilibrium: Simple Assumptions and Complex Reality*

For charter schools or independent schools to work, basic conditions need to be met. First, the different players (mainly parents and schools) need to make "rational" choices that maximize their benefits, and second, they should be able (capable, informed, and free) to make these choices. There are, however, two issues with meeting these conditions: one is both theoretical and practical, and one is simply practical. The first issue has to do with the definition of the assumed rational behavior; does each actor know all the facts he/she needs to know to make this choice? Are there other uncalculated elements that affect the actors' behaviors and choices? And lastly, is there only one way to maximize one's benefits? These questions constitute the classical critique of rational-choice theory, which the chapter will not delve into; instead, it will shed the light on part of its manifestation in the case of the discussed reform. The second issue is simply related to having the right balance of student demand and school supply.

Pertaining to the first issue, the reform assumed "that there would be enough interest among parents to enable choice among different schooling alternatives and that there would be enough parties interested in contracting with the government to run their own schools" (Brewer et al. 2007: 54). None of these assumptions made in 2001 were tested before launching the first cohort of independent schools in 2004.

Another hidden assumption of the design is the calculated behaviors by the different actors, which should collectively lead to the "good educational offerings" equilibrium. This made the entire system subject to various, newly emerging variables such as the interaction among the different actors, the formation of informed parental choice, the maintenance of transparent test-based assessments and effective communication, the efficiency and effectiveness of each single school in managing its human and financial resources, etc. This is even before the system concerns itself with the actual substance offered to students. Exposing the system to all these variables at once created a significant margin of uncertainty, which becomes particularly problematic in Qatar for several reasons:

1. The only de-facto model of governance that Qatar has ever known is a highly controlled and a very centralized one; therefore, the readiness of the legal and administrative infrastructure and the readiness of the different parties, including the decision-makers who chose the model and those who will implement it, needed to be problematized. One illustrative example is opening up the competition over school contracts to offer qualified bidders a fair chance to win a contract and run a school with no nepotism or prejudices, including those based on nationality or professional background. Only one year after implementation, restrictions were imposed and only Qatari educators became eligible to bid for a school contract (D. Al-Emadi, personal communication, May 11, 2014). Also, independent schools started as profit-making entities, and around one year later a decision was made to convert them to non-profit entities; the SEC was worried about existing and possible financial abuses by the operators (A. Al-Horr, personal communication, May 13, 2014). In fact, many teachers and workers in these reformed schools found it difficult to accept working for an independent school operator through a contract since they considered themselves employees for the government, which has many implications, including the applicability of the Retirement & Pension Law (J. Al-Nu'aimi & A. Al-M'dadi, personal communication, June 24, 2014). Many arguments may be used to justify or refute these decisions, yet what is important here is to register two observations. One is the complexity of trying to create a decentralized free-market island in a centralized and highly controlled ocean, which takes the reader back to the original point about exposing the educational system to a world of new variables

and uncertainties that don't necessarily belong to the pedagogical essence. The second observation is how these decisions have stripped the reform of its foundational premise, namely free competition, yet the decision-makers continued to add new layers of implementation instead of revisiting the entire reform model. This, the chapter claims, is one of the common characteristics of the relationship between the foreign consultant who bases his/her analysis on de jure standards instead of de-facto practices, and the local decision-maker who starts by wanting informed-decisions[32] through consultancy and ends up by uninformed implementation.

2. The uncertainty also stems from the fact that the market in Qatar already has limited choices in terms of finding qualified school operators, administrators, teachers, and pedagogy experts with virtually no local companies that can develop suitable learning resources. In fact, the reform study itself acknowledges many of these points as weaknesses of the previous system. Therefore, leaving these elements to the market and restricting the role of the government to incentivizing the good alternatives instead of developing them meant that the process of reaching the equilibrium—to use rational-choice logic—will take a very long time if it is to be reached. The chapter makes this claim given the vast challenges human capital development in Qatar experiences (also see Chapter 10). So, while the government is deliberately offering undergraduate, post-graduate, and professional programs, and while it finds the justification to do so, it might seem inherently contradictory to leave this task in K-12 education to the market dynamics.

The other practical issue that pertains to the original assumptions of the model is reaching the right balance of supply and demand. In a retrospective analysis, the founding director of the Education Institute commented that "parents cannot have a choice as long as the demand is higher than the supply and this had been the case from the very beginning" (D. Al-Emadi, personal communication, May 11, 2014). In addition, Qatar has witnessed an unprecedented demographic influx since 2001, and service-based sectors have been trying to catch up with this rapid increase. The interconnectedness of education policies with other policy areas such as demography and human development was further intertwined through the reform, yet an integrative framework has not been developed. In fact, the original study did not carry out any market research or forecasts despite the significance of the economic element to the selected reform model.

### *Procedures Versus Content*

Procedures here refer to any rules, conditions, or arrangements that regulate a process or define its territories without necessarily dealing with its substance or content. With this understanding, the discussed reform is essentially a procedural one. The idea becomes clearer when the reform is mapped out as a logic model,[33] with inputs, processes, outputs, and outcomes. Such analysis is shown in the following.

1. The inputs of the system such as the teachers, the parents, the curricula, and the school operators are dealt with as a "black box." In other words, whatever happens in this black box is not important as long as it gives the right results. Therefore, the reform did not examine factors like developing a sustainable pipeline to supply qualified teachers locally, bearing in mind that providing such teachers has been one of the fundamental challenges of Qatar's K-12 education. The reform focused, instead, on the overall results of the students as an indicator of many things including the effectiveness of teaching.
2. Organizational processes are overemphasized on the expense of the core of the enterprise, that is, the teaching content. One symptom of this attribute is the extra administrative burden educators had to undertake under the reform. All interviewees confirmed that administrative tasks leave them with little time and energy to invest in developing their educational content and classroom practices. "Documenting the work is taking more time than actually doing it," says one school principal (K Al-Fidala, personal communication, May 28, 2014). This finding is not unique to Qatar; the same complaints by educators exist in many charter schools in the United States as well. Abbey R. Weiss describes this phenomenon as the main challenge in charter schools, in a study of Massachusetts charter schools titled *Going It Alone: A Study of Massachusetts Charter Schools* (Weiss 1997).
3. Since the reformed schools needed to be "held accountable for the results that they achieve, rather than the means they use to achieve them" (Plank and Sykes 2004: 177), the model has put more weight on assessing the system's outputs. Students' performance in stan-

dardized test-based assessments is considered the main measure of system quality. Other types of assessments such as student and parent satisfaction surveys were being implemented and the results, along with other indicators about each school, were being published. Massive efforts and tremendous amount of time were put in this yearly exercise that was mostly outsourced to international experts and companies. Transparency and access to data are crucial to enable "informed choice" among parents. The society and some decision-makers, however, were not ready yet to deal with this new culture of transparency, as the founding director of the Evaluation Institute explained (A. Al-Sayed, personal communication, May 14, 2014). He also added that publishing the data—which the Institute has been doing—is one thing, while interpreting its implications to inform policy-making is another thing.

In general, the design made sure to define the reform's guiding principles and to establish the institutional setting as "the new rules of the game [needed] to be carefully designed" (Brewer et al. 2007, Page 54) Nonetheless, the details of the tools and mechanisms were left for the implementers to figure out. This in turn left an impression that the program lacked many elements and was not ready when the first cohort of independent schools was launched (M Al-Dosari, personal communication, July 6, 2014). While the chapter agrees with that impression, it makes the claim that this inherently comes from the nature of the model that aims, for better or worse, to provide more autonomy to the different parties instead of centralizing the game.

During implementation, these mechanisms and tools were being designed and constantly refined until they have actually shifted the entire system and in many cases overridden the original principles of autonomy, accountability, variety, and choice they were created to serve. This highlights a greater question about the interdependence between design and implementation in policy-making and the following example further elaborates.

The Qatar Comprehensive Educational Assessment[34] or the National Assessments—as they are called in Qatar sometimes—became a major tool to measure school performance and ensure that those who do not perform well are held accountable. This itself aimed to support the schools' autonomy as "the fundamental bargain of charter schools [hence independent schools] is the exchange of increased autonomy for enhanced accountability"(Plank and Sykes 2004: 177). Publishing the results and making them available also aimed to enable parents to make informed choices. Accordingly, these assessments were not designed to count in the student's school grades. The student's grades, on the other hand, depended entirely on the school's internal assessments, known as the Student Continuous Assessment or *Al-Taqweem Al-Mustamir Lil-Talib*. While students seemed to perform extremely well in the internal assessments, the Student National Assessments in 2010/2011 showed that only 5 % of the students in grades 4–11 met the national standards in mathematics, 12.3 % met the national standards in science, and 15.7 % and 17.9 % met the national standards in Arabic and English respectively (Evaluation Institute 2011). The scores remained generally low over the years. The Evaluation Institute, the producer of these national assessments, associated the low scores of the students with their carelessness about the tests as they did not carry any weight in the students' final grades (A. Al-Sayed, personal communication, May 14, 2014). Hence, in 2010 these assessments were made mandatory to pass and they weighed 30 % of the student's grade. This proved to be a revealing decision as it exposed how vulnerable the Student Continuous Assessment was, which schools were carrying out independently from the SEC (Fig. 4.3).

Students were passing and being promoted from one level to the next; nonetheless, right after applying the new policy, the failure rates steeply increased (A. Al-Sayed, personal communication, May 14, 2014). This was an indirect indicator of "gaming the system" as students were passing when the evaluation was left to the schools, whereas the failure rate suddenly increased when the Evaluation Institute (SEC) centrally provided the evaluation. The published failure rate[35] in 2011/2012 was 21.7 %; 8734 students passed and 2423 students did not (Al-Raya 2012). Despite complaints by school operators and principals about the pressure that external national assessments were adding, most of them believed that some schools were actually misusing the internal assessments or did not understand their purpose and hence how to properly carry them out (K. Al-Fidala, personal communication, May 28, 2014; F. Al-Kuwari, personal communication, June 17, 2014; L. Al-Thawadi, personal communication, June 22, 2014; M. Al-Maraghi, personal communication , June 26, 2014). As a result, the Education Institute started exercising more supervision to increase the schools' performance. Procedures included dedicating more hours for revising the four core academic subjects (Arabic, English, mathematics, and science) at the expense of teaching extracurricular and other subjects like arts,[36] as well as instructing schools to train their students through test

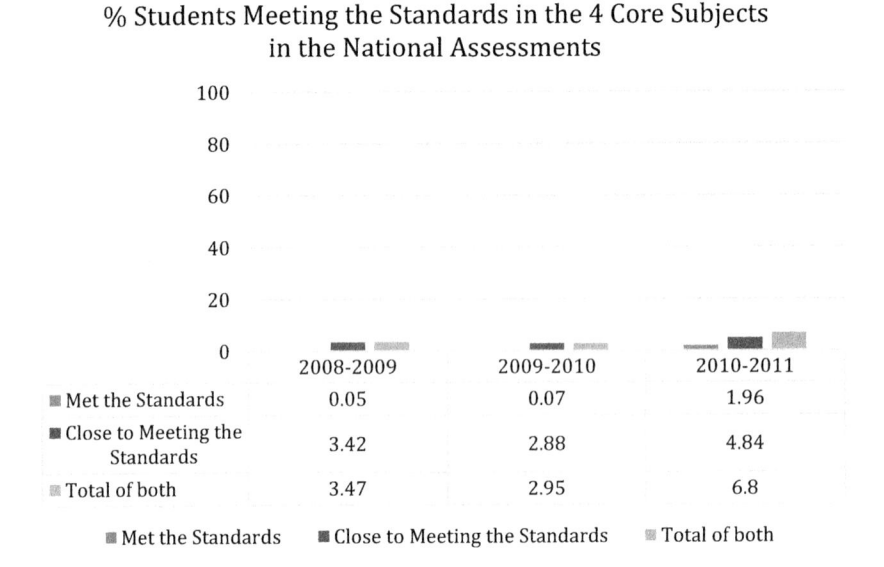

## % Students Meeting the Standards in the 4 Core Subjects in the National Assessments

|  | 2008-2009 | 2009-2010 | 2010-2011 |
|---|---|---|---|
| Met the Standards | 0.05 | 0.07 | 1.96 |
| Close to Meeting the Standards | 3.42 | 2.88 | 4.84 |
| Total of both | 3.47 | 2.95 | 6.8 |

■ Met the Standards   ■ Close to Meeting the Standards   ■ Total of both

Fig. 4.3  Student Performance: 2008 and 2011

examples. The Education Institute went as far as providing test samples and models for students to practice. The accumulation of such procedures have gradually ended up reinforcing centralization and "studying for the test" culture, whereas the National Assessments were intended to promote the opposite: a culture of autonomy and creativity. Even the "variety" principle that the SEC aimed for was overridden by its constant attempts to reduce the manipulation or uninformed school-based management through introducing more standardization. This increasing standardization was in fact eradicating the margin of variety that the old system accommodated reasonably well. For example, both the scientific schools and the specialized schools (commercial, religious, and technical) had had special budgets and sets of rules due to the nature of their mission, but those schools were struggling to keep this arrangement as they were facing the changing reality (M Al-Maraghi, personal communication, June 26, 2014; A. Shams[37], personal communication, June 30, 2014).

In his edited volume about charter schools in the United States, Bruce Fuller, professor of education and public policy at Berkley, said that "charter reformers thus far are scoring high on process and low on hardcore results" (Fuller 2002). Given the past arguments, can a similar remark be made about the education reform in Qatar thus far?

## K-12 Education in Qatar Today

All schools in the public system are still called independent schools, the name remains from the reform, though the charter model is completely abrogated and the system is totally centralized by the SEC. In 2012 the School Vouchers Law (Law No.6 2012) was issued to adopt the voucher system, one of the three reform options that RAND provided in 2001. As discussed earlier, the voucher system was not selected at the time because the government believed the system was not ready. According to the new law, every Qatari student is eligible to get a school voucher for one of the private schools approved by the SEC. In 2013, a new minister of education and new SEC leaders were appointed. Apart from the voucher policy, the attempts to improve the system and to contain the consequences of the previous policies continue, yet in an incremental way (Peter Hall 1993) compared to radical changes during the implementation of the Education for a New Era reform.

Furthermore, initiatives on the margin of the main system appeared recently, such as "Teach for Qatar," which is borrowed from "Teach for America." It attracted some media and societal attention at the beginning, but it is getting less visible overtime. The use of school vouchers, on the other hand, is growing and many private schools are being added to the SEC's approved list every year. In fact, it seems as if the SEC is betting on private education. An SEC official stated in 2015 that "tens of new private schools will open their doors for students in 2015/2016...[and] this should eliminate the students' waiting lists" (Al-Raya Newspaper, 23, March, 2015).

To summarize, there are now three policy streams in the public educational landscape:

1. Incremental changes in the main public system; public schools (independent schools).
2. Increasing dependence on privatization through providing school vouchers and through inviting and subsiding selected international schools[38] to open and operate in Qatar.

3. Out-of-the-box initiatives that exist outside the system yet attempt to influence it, like Teach for Qatar and other initiatives that aim to elevate Arabic language literacy among the public system students[39].

Many local observers are skeptical about the current "privatization" wave and are worried it will eclipse the public system. According to them, this puts the local culture and Arabic Islamic identity of the students at risk, given that most of these private schools are Western-oriented.

## Conclusions

This chapter provided a process-based evaluation of Qatar's ambitious program, Education for a New Era. which aimed to reform its K-12 education system. The analysis covers the period from 2001 until 2014. Although not officially announced, the Education for a New Era program has been technically abrogated by a series of decisions which reversed most of its policies and mechanisms. In fact, no one today, including education officials, talks about Education for a New Era, except as a part of history. Yet like any policy reversal process, the result is not going back in time to the moment that preceded the reform, as some of the reform's opponents would wish or some of the proponents would fear. There is more than 13 years of changes not only in the educational system and its personnel, but also in the society and other policy sectors that cannot be reversed. This is, of course, in addition to the legacy of the reform itself. Beyond the success/failure duality of the results-based assessment, this chapter tried to analyze the reform model and its different constituents through applying two lenses: the holistic theoretical lens and the detailed empirical lens. In doing so it shed some light on the following policy issues:

1. The complexity that surrounds educational policy borrowing, showing how much local context matters especially in transformations that deal with human subjects, such as in traveling educational reforms.
2. The interdependence between policy design and policy implementation, which is often underestimated or understudied. Policy designers resort at times to a number of "rational" assumptions about the expected or perhaps the supposed behavior of the different stakeholders, whereas the "reality" during implementation can be at odds with those assumptions.

3. The unintended consequences of the policy itself or of other related policies which lead to counterproductive results.
4. The shortage of results-based and test-based assessments which could lead to gaming the system. In general, results-based assessments are efficient mechanisms to answer the "what" question, but at the same time they lack the explanatory ability of answering the "why" question: "what is the pass rate this year?" versus "why is the pass rate so high this year?" Therefore, relying mainly or solely on test results can give a false sense of success or a sense that things are on the right track.

The chapter inductively can describe Qatar's K-12 education policies between 2001 and 2014 as genuine, creative, generous, unstable, and non-accumulative. The huge financial resources, massive foreign expertise, and unlimited political support that were made available to reform the system were unprecedented in the history of Qatar and the GCC region. There is no doubt that the reform was radically transformative and that the decision-makers were courageous enough to try new ideas. In fact, it might be this spirit that led the system into a state of instability. "The Qatari leadership was anxious to reform the system as quickly as possible and to show tangible results" (Brewer et al. 2007: 88). As showed earlier in the chapter, some decisions were canceled shortly after being issued; of course, some of these were more critical than the others. The language policy is a clear example. The reformed schools were expected to shift from teaching in Arabic to English as soon as they were selected to be part of the reform. A few years[40] later those same schools and the entire system had to shift back to Arabic. The reform, on the other hand, represented a policy break in the educational system. Through creating a new central office, appointing a team of foreign consultants and locals from outside the bureaucratic system to lead the reform and issuing a new body of policies and governing structures, the reformers apparently wanted to build a new system without dealing with the issues of the old one. Today, after dismantling the ministry (old system) and after reversing the reform policies (new system), it seems like the current educational system is going through a new learning curve and is not necessarily building on the old experiences. "There used to be an archive unit in the Ministry, where is it today? No one knows" (Abdulaziz Al-Tamimi,[41] personal communication, July 10, 2014).

There is no doubt that Education for a New Era has generated unprecedented societal controversy and at certain points has ignited anger, yet it shall be acknowledged as "the reform that succeeded in engaging Qatari parents and many sectors in the society to become active stakeholders in the educational process" (Al-Heidous,[42] personal communication, May 18, 2014). While the rentierism theory assumes that the monarch monopolizes decision-making in exchange for distributing a share of the rent to the people, the school-choice model that Qatar adopted has actually catered to a grassroots type of participation which opened a window for "policy feedback." In fact analyzing the interaction between the different actors in the Education for a New Era program shows that even in a typical rentier state such as Qatar, policy-making is not always a straight forward, top-down process. The example of forcing thousands of employees to retire under the Central Provision and reversing the same decision only after a few years is one example that was discussed in details in this chapter. Acknowledging policy feedback in the discussed reform, on the other hand, does not cancel the transformative effect that Qatar's educational policies had in the past 13 years.

While I still confirm that the rentierism theory can explain many aspects of policy-making in Qatar very effectively (e.g., distributing school vouchers to dissatisfied parents seems like a typical example), I think it stands incapable of explaining many other aspects including why the reform happened in the first place. For example, why did the reform occur at that point of time in Qatar and not in another GCC state? In fact, why did the reform occur altogether if the traditional assumption made by rentierism theorists is that the regime is only interested in retaining power backed up by the rent revenue? A closer look at the internal dynamics of the local policy-making in Qatar including the K-12 educational reform clearly shows that politicians, even in a highly controlled system, not only "power," but they also "puzzle " (More about the concept of "puzzling" in "public policy" can be found in Freeman (2006: 372–373)). In other words the blanket statements made by rentierism theorists both overlook many contextual factors including societal culture, stakeholders' behavior, and the institutional setting, and they fall short of explaining the transformations that took place in Qatar in the past 15 years.

## NOTES

1. At the time it used to be called Wizarat Al-Ma'arif. Over the years, this name has changed several times.
2. Brewer et al. (2007) mention those attempts in a couple of lines without giving any details about their content and the circumstances that surrounded them.
3. Provided during the interview with Dr. Abulaziz Al-Horr (May 13, 2014), a prominent Qatari Educator. When he participated in developing the strategy, Dr. Al-Horr was the Director of the Development Office in the Ministry of Education.
4. Principal of Omar bin Al-Khattab Educational Complex (Boys Scientific School) since 2002.
5. Principal of Moza bint Mohammed Elementary and Preparatory School for girls. Moza bint Mohammed started as a Developed School for the elementary level in 2001. Shiekha Al-Monsoori was the founding principal of the school. Later on the school was converted to become an Independent School in 2008.
6. Principal of Jo'an bin Jassim Elementary School for boys. Jo'an bin Jassim started as a Developed School in 2001 and was converted to become an Independent School later on.
7. Concluding that the previous attempts have all failed might not be very precise, especially since most of these attempts were not fully realized. The 1990, 1996, and 1997 attempts, along with the 2000 ten-year strategy, remained in the initiation/design phase, but no decision was made to allocate the necessary resources and to start implementing. The partial reform attempts like the Scientific Schools and the Developed Schools (Al-Madaris Al-Mutawara), on the other hand, started implementation in 1999 and 2001 respectively, which means it was premature to evaluate their success or failure when the Education for a New Era designers started their study in 2001. In fact these two models are still, as these lines are being written, considered among the best performing schools in the public system. This is not to suggest that prior reform attempts were necessarily going to succeed had there been enough resources and time, but rather to suggest that the conditions, tools, and criteria of "evaluation" were somehow absent when the judgment on the previous reform attempts was made.
8. Also, what was known as System Support Organizations were assigned to the reformed schools to provide support (Zellman et al. 2009).
9. The SEC provides financial allotments to independent schools (public schools) per pupil. So, if the parents decide to send their kids to an independent school instead of a private one, the financial support for which the

student is eligible goes to this independent school. On the other hand, not all private schools, at the moment, are eligible to receive SEC vouchers.
10. The descriptive part which describes the original model of the reform in this section is mainly based on RAND's monograph (Brewer et al. 2007), which describes the reform's design phase and the early period of the implementation phase between 2001 and 2004.
11. Known as Education for a New Era or the "Independent Schools System," as indicated earlier.
12. Until 2014, when I carried out the field study, after ten years of implementation, most schools did not undertake this comprehensive school assessment more than once. These assessments include assessing teachers, facilities, curricula, and finances, which make them resource-intensive. Therefore, this might have affected the newly established SEC's ability to carry them out regularly. One characteristic, which this chapter claims, of Qatar's education policies during the analyzed period is instability or "over-dynamism." "Every day there is something new," as most interlocutors explained, which makes it hard for the systems and regulations to stabilize and start accumulating. The chapter will come back to this point in its concluding section.
13. A current advisor at the office of the Minister of Education. Served as the Director of the Evaluation Institute from 2003 to 2010.
14. Those implications and what they actually meant on the ground were not necessarily clear to the designers and implementers during the design and implementation phases, as will be shown in the rest of the chapter. Please refer to the "Theoretical & Practical Critique" section.
15. An educator and a prominent "professional development" trainer. Operated one of the independent schools for five years.
16. This vision was never realized, as will be shown in the rest of the chapter.
17. When I carried out the field study in 2014, all interlocutors were referring to the principles as part of the early stages of the reform; there was a shared sense that these principles had been overridden. The chapter addresses policy reversal and counterproductive results below.
18. Teachers are fundamental to the educational process. Add to this that the reform gave more authority and freedom to the teacher to play a greater and more creative role. So in other words it was inevitable for the implementation to interact with "teachers" as a main player, whether the designers decided to remain silent about it or not.
19. The number of schools' administrative staff in the same year was 2571.
20. At the beginning, the legal status of the independent schools was yet another issue. Are they private entities owned by the operator and subsidized by the government, or are they government entities operated by individuals who don't work for the government but work with it through

a contract? (Al-Sayed, personal communication, May 14, 2014). At the early stages of the implementation this was not clearly decided. Staff of the contracted schools had to sign contracts with the new operators, which confused many teachers and caused anxiety among those who insisted that they work for the government and not for a private owner. The SEC then confirmed that teachers are public servants, yet many of the practices like signing a contract between the school operator and the teachers and allowing the former to specify salaries and benefits continued until the SEC centralized the recruitment and HR processes again by 2013/14.

21. The public sector is dominated by Qatari national employees and like most countries, discharging public servants is not easy. Add to this what the rentier state theory perceives as the role of the public sector in redistributing the country's wealth. According to this view, nationals in the public sector are receiving their portion of wealth, which is monopolized by a small unelected group, in the form of a monthly salary.

22. A school principal. Her husband Mohamed Hilal Al-Khulaifi (February 1, 2012; 21 March 2012; 11 April 2012) published a number of articles that constitute important critique of the reform and the educational system in Qatar during the early years of the reform.

23. A school principal of an elementary and a preparatory girls' school.

24. Some conservative families still don't approve of a mixed-gender (to use the Arabic expression) workplace.

25. Principal of Qatar's Education Complex, which comprises all pre-university schooling levels from K to grade 12. The school was in the first cohort of independent schools. Al-Thawadi had been in the field of education for over 30 years.

26. Jabr Al-Nu'aimi (Ph.D. in physics from Imperial College London) and Afaf Al-Mu'dadi are a husband and wife team who won the contract of one of the Independent schools in the academic year 2004/2005, but they left after a couple of years. They then decided to establish their own private school, Newton International School. Today, the school has around six branches in Qatar.

27. The Minister was heading the SEC as well, through his position as the General Secretariat of the SEC.

28. The founding director of the Education Institute for a year and a half. Witnessed the late planning phase and early implementation phase of the reform. Dr. Al-Emadi is currently the Director of the Social and Economic Survey Institute at Qatar University. He led several surveys that looked into education in Qatar and has thankfully provided the results of a couple of these surveys (Al-Emadi 2012a, b).

29. In April 2015 the SEC announced exempting non-Qatari students from paying school fees in the public system. Due to the rapid changes in the

education system in Qatar, one cannot anticipate if this decision will still be in effect after publishing this chapter.
30. Please refer to the issue of hiring and firing staff that was discussed at the beginning of this section.
31. This does not mean that the charter schools model in the USA is trouble-free. In fact many of the issues that appeared in the Qatari experience exist in the USA as well. Issues include gaming the system (Ravitch 2010), the massive administrative burden on teachers, and emphasizing the process over the content (Fuller 2002).
32. Evidence-based decision-making became one of the used terms in the policy-making circles in Qatar. For example, it was used around 17 times in the Qatar National Development Strategy 2011–2016. Also one manifestation of this "evidence-based" growing trend in Qatar's public policy is the unprecedented amount of data that the government is collecting and publishing about the different sectors.
33. "The essence of a logic model is a narrative of what the program is targeting, how it works, and what it is trying to achieve." (Pal 2014: 277)
34. Annual standards-based assessments that all public schools had to undertake under the reform. Interestingly enough, the students' performance baseline was determined in 2004 before finalizing the standards.
35. Publishing all the results is a politically charged issue. Therefore, most interlocutors believed that the failure rates were generally higher than what was published.
36. The author participated in a commissioned study in 2013 to design an arts-oriented school in Doha. The landscape survey showed that independent schools, especially starting from 2012, were receiving detailed instructions from the Education Institute, including the weekly teaching plans. This came as a reaction to the students' weak performance.
37. Principal of the technical school for boys.
38. Some examples are Qatar-Finland International School, SEK International School, Sherborne Qatar, and others.
39. It is somehow ironic that the policy instability and the system's misuse by some school operators which accompanied the reform led to problems in the students' Arabic reading and writing skills. The assessment that preceded the reform stated that the system was not producing the required English language skills, but the assessors did not seem specifically worried about the status of the students' Arabic literacy at the time.
40. There were eight years or less between the two decisions as the first batch of independent schools—reformed schools—was announced in 2004 and the decision to shift back to Arabic was made in 2012.
41. At that point, the director of the International Education Office at the Supreme Education Council. Al-Tamimi had been an educator for over 40

years and was among the first generation of Qatari teachers who have ever taught in a modern school. He graduated from *Dar Al-mo'alimeen*, the first post-secondary institute in Qatar to prepare local teachers. Later on, he became a school principal and assumed several positions after that, such as working for the Ministry of Education and the Supreme Education Council.

42. The previous director of the Education Institute. Al-Heidous served in office from 2004 to 2012; hence she oversaw most of the reform program.

## BIBLIOGRAPHY. QATAR: POLICY MAKING IN A TRANSFORMATIVE STATE

Al-Hail, Fatima. 2008. *Pedagogy, Curricula and the Education System [in Arabic]*. Cairo: Nahdat Masr For Publishing and Distribution.

Al-Kobaisi, Abdulla Juma. 1999. Attempts to Reform the Educational System [in Arabic]. *College of Education Journal in Qatar University* 15.

Al-Misnad, Sheikha. 1985. *The Development of Modern Education in the Gulf*. London: Ithaca Press.

Al-Raya. 2012. 78% have passed in the Independent Schools [in Arabic]. *Al-Raya Newspaper*, June 22. http://www.raya.com/news/pages/fc747001-45a8-4352-9826-916160b0a374.

Al-Sultaiti, Ahmed Abdullah Ahmed. 2011. Oh Sa'ad, Are We Foreigners? [in Arabic]. *Al-Watan Newspaper*, May 15. http://www.al-watan.com/viewnews.aspx?n=19894fd5-dd5e-4ad8-8a85-c7d4ef107513&d=20110515.

Brewer, Dominic J., Catherine H. AUgustine, Gail L. Zellman, Gery Ryan, Charles A. Goldman, Cathleen Stasz, and Louay Constant. 2007. *Education for a New Era: Design and Implementation of K-12 Education Reform in Qatar*. Doha, Qatar: Rand-Qatar Policy Institute.

Bulkley, Katrina E., and Priscilla Wohlstetter. 2004. Introduction. In *Taking Account of Charter Schools: What's Happened and What's Next?,*, eds. Katrina E. Bulkley, and Priscilla Wohlstetter. New York: Teachers College Press.

Evaluation Institute. 2011. *Results of the Comprehensive Educational Assessment 2010-12*. Doha: Supreme Education Council.

Freeman, R. 2006. Learning in public policy. In *The Oxford Handbook of Political Science*, eds. M. Moran, M. Rein, and R. Goodin, 367–385. Oxford: Oxford University Press.

Fuller, B. 2002. Breaking away or pulling together? Making decentralization work. In *Inside Chater Schools: The Paradox of Radical Decentralization*, ed. Bruce Fuller, 230–256. Cambridge, MA: Harvard University Press.

Hall, Peter A. 1993. Policy paradigms, social learning, and the state: The case of economic policymaking in Britain. *Comparative Politics* 25(3): 275–296.

Ministry of Education (Qatar). 2005. *Annual Statistics Report*. Doha: Retrieved from http://www.qsa.gov.qa/eng/PopulationStructure.htmMinistry of Education.

Murphy, J., and C.D. Shiffman. 2002. *Understanding and Assessing the Charter School Movement*. New York: Teachers College Press.

Plank, D.N., and G. Sykes. 2004. Lighting out for the territory: Charter schools and the school reform strategy. In *Taking Account of Charter Schools: What's Happened and What's Next?* eds. K.E. Bulkley, and P. Wohlstetter, 176–184. New York: Teachers College Press.

Ravitch, D. 2010. *The Death and Life of the Great American School System: How Testing and Choice are Undermining Education*. New York: Basic Books.

Steiner-Khamsi, Gita. 2004. *The Global Politics of Educational Borrowing and Lending*. New York: Teachers College Press.

Supreme Education Council. 2014. *Press Release: Hundreds of the Central Provision Referred Employees Come Back to Work in the Independent Schools [in Arabic]*. Doha: Supreme Education Council.

Wiess, A. 1997. *Going it Alone: A Study of Massachusetts Charter Schools*. Boston: Northeastern University.

Zellman, Gail L., Gery W. Ryan, Rita Karam, Louay Constant, Hanine Salem, Gabriella C. Gonzalez, Charles A. Goldman, Hessa Al-Thani, and Kholode Al-Obaidli. 2009. *Implementation of the K-12 Education Reform in Qatar's Schools*. Santa Monica, CA: RAND Corporation.

CHAPTER 5

# Transforming Qatar's PSE: Achievements and Concessions

*Ahmed Baghdady*

This chapter aims to provide an understanding of why and how Qatar's post-secondary education (PSE) was reformed. It contains an overview, analysis, and discussion of PSE reform policies in Qatar for the period 1998–2013, drawing on the author's experience for a decade in Qatar working on aspects of the PSE reform as well as other education and social development policies, both as a practitioner and a policy researcher. This chapter addresses a number of research questions. First, what triggered Qatar's PSE reform and what were the indigenous needs of the state? Second, how was Qatar's PSE reformed and what were the major reform policies? Third, how did the society respond to this reform? Finally, what were/are the challenges, if any, to Qatar's PSE reform?

This research was designed as a case study given the uniqueness associated with education reform and the need to understand the context in which the reform process took place and the reform policies were formulated and implemented. Case study research allows an understanding of phenomena in their original context and provides an opportunity for deep investigation of issues. The author adopted the qualitative research method to allow for in-depth understanding of the issues related to the reform and to present readers with sufficient details about the policies and

---

A. Baghdady (✉)
Qatar National Research Fund, Doha, Qatar
RAND-Qatar Policy Institute, Doha, Qatar

© The Author(s) 2016
M.E. Tok et al. (eds.), *Policy-Making in a Transformative State*,
DOI 10.1057/978-1-137-46639-6_5

processes adopted and challenges encountered during the reform process. The author reviewed documents related to PSE reform such as decrees and laws, documents related to Qatar University (QU) and the Supreme Education Council (SEC), and relevant reports published by the RAND Corporation—the research and policy analysis institution that helped the Qatari government, the Qatar Foundation for Education, Science and Community Development (QF), and QU formulate several of the reform policies.

The chapter begins with background information on PSE in Qatar and locates it within the Gulf Cooperation Council (GCC) region. It then discusses the main motives for reforming Qatar's PSE and draws on discussions of moving from a carbon-based economy to a knowledge economy in Qatar and the surrounding region. The following section provides a detailed and critical discussion of the reform process and the relevant policies. This section outlines the three main aspects of PSE reform in Qatar: (1) establishing university branch campuses and colleges; (2) reforming Qatar University; and (3) reforming the government higher education scholarship system. It also presents the institutions that were established either to lead the reform process or as a result of it. The chapter then moves to a discussion of the public reaction to the reform and the challenges encountered during the reform process. The chapter closes with a synthesis and conclusion.

## PSE in Qatar and the GCC Region

Higher education in the Middle East has changed dramatically since the late 1950s, when most Middle Eastern countries gained independence. Initially, governments established national universities as symbols of nationhood and to provide education to their citizens locally (Findlow 2005). However, in the 1990s private universities were allowed to operate (Akkari 2004). Since the 1970s the GCC states have been sponsoring their citizens to study abroad but have recently realized that they also need quality higher education programs offered locally (ibid).

Until the 1950s, Egypt, Syria, and Iraq were the centers of knowledge in the Middle East (Romani 2009), where students from most other Middle Eastern states moved to earn university degrees. Egypt's Al-Azhar University, one of the oldest and largest universities in the world, and Cairo University (established in 1908) were important destinations for many students. Syria's Damascus University was established in 1923 and was known as the Syrian University then (Damascus University 2011). Although the University of Baghdad was founded in 1957, several individual colleges were already operational and joined the new university shortly after it was established (University of Baghdad 2014).

The GCC states established national universities shortly after independence, starting with Kuwait University in 1966, King Abdulaziz University in 1971, Qatar University and the United Arab Emirates University in 1977, and Sultan Qaboos University in Oman and University of Bahrain in 1986. These higher education institutions followed the models of other well-established universities in the Middle East. In fact, some of these GCC universities were established and led by academics and administrators from Egypt, Iraq, and Syria for a number of years, until local capacity was developed to take over leadership and operations of these institutions (Romani 2009).

Around the same time that universities were being established in the GCC region, governments introduced scholarship programs to encourage their citizens to study at reputable institutions overseas. The main goal of these scholarship programs was, and still is, to prepare a cadre of qualified citizens to lead their states and utilize the wealth from natural resources to develop their countries (Stasz et al. 2007; Donn and Al Manthri 2010). These scholarships enabled thousands of GCC students to study in other Arab countries, Europe, the United States and other parts of the world (Abouammoh 2012). For example, there were almost 12,000 Saudi students studying abroad in 1982 (Saleh 1986) and 1222 Qatari students on scholarships abroad in the academic year 2001–2002 (Augustine and Krop 2008). They were mostly at universities in the US, UK, and Australia.

Higher education in the GCC states has witnessed rapid growth, development, and reforms; and higher education institutions have developed in size and increased in numbers and in program offerings (Abouammoh 2012). GCC leaders have realized the role that private higher education can play in improving education in their countries and that reliance only on state-run and funded universities will not lead to the targeted development. Therefore, toward the end of the twentieth century, private universities appeared in the GCC region, with the first one being the American University of Sharjah (AUS) in 1997, followed by the Gulf University of Science and Technology (GUST) in Kuwait in 2002.

Around the same time that private universities emerged in the region, partnerships and agreements with universities from North America, Europe, and Australia were being formed, either to help establish private universities in some states such as the case in Kuwait and Bahrain or to establish branches of universities from these regions in some GCC states, such as the case in Qatar and the UAE.

Leaders of the GCC states have realized that the quality of education is critical for economic development. Private higher education and university branch campuses provide the type and quality of education most relevant to and needed by the labor market for jobs that contribute to building a knowledge economy (Gonzalez et al. 2008). Although this type of education can be attained through student scholarships, local provision of this type of education was deemed necessary for cultural, social, and economic reasons (Willoughby 2008). Although the demand for quality higher education offered locally is high, many students in the region are not academically prepared for this rigorous education. This has created a challenge for both GCC countries and Western and local private institutions to bridge this gap (Stasz et al. 2007).

Although Qatar and the UAE have the largest concentration of branch campuses of foreign universities in the GCC region (11 and 33 respectively, C-BERT 2015) and started this initiative around the same time, they followed two different models in their endeavors to bring universities to set up campuses locally. The UAE, where most branch campuses are located mainly in Dubai, has followed a model whereby universities from around the world were encouraged to establish branch campuses in newly created hubs with flexible terms and exemption of certain obligations, such as immigration and profit repatriation, in return for rent paid to the state. The government of Dubai did not directly support the institutions financially although it has done so indirectly in a number of ways (Lane 2010).

On the other hand, the State of Qatar, through the QF[1], has covered all the start-up and infrastructure costs of the branch campuses created in Doha within its Education City[2] and contributes to the operating costs of these campuses to maintain their financial viability (Lane 2010; Altbach 2007). Qatar now has branches of seven colleges of world-class universities in Education City (in addition to four outside it), each offering mutually agreed-upon degree programs in the area(s) for which it is known (see details below). A similar approach was adopted by Abu Dhabi, the capital of the UAE, to establish campuses of world-class universities but with a slightly different flavor than Qatar. The Abu Dhabi government established branch campuses for the Paris Sorbonne and New York

University to offer a full spectrum of programs that are offered in their home campuses.

The huge spending on education, estimated at over $80 billion in 2014, is an attempt by these countries to develop their human capital and ultimately reduce reliance on income from natural resources, namely oil and gas (Alpen Capital 2014). The main driver for the GCC states in improving their higher education is moving to what has been termed "the knowledge-based economy" which, as the term suggests, refers to a state with an economy that relies on knowledge and skills, rather than natural resources that might run out in the future. This can justify the large spending that the states in this region are directing toward education in general and higher education in particular. However, there seem to be other reasons for establishing private universities and inviting reputable foreign institutions to set up presence in the region. For cultural and social reasons in the GCC region, many female students cannot live alone in a foreign country (Willoughby 2008), and it is not always easy for men with dependents to move their families to another country for a few years to obtain a university degree (Stasz et al. 2007). Having quality higher education locally through university branch campuses represented a good alternative for many citizens.

Additionally, after the 2001 terrorist attacks on the United States, many Arab students studying there returned home and many others were denied visas to go back to their study destinations in Western countries. Thus, the need to establish local branch campuses of Western universities grew (Donn and Al Manthri 2010). Furthermore, the increasing number of expatriate families living in the GCC states and contributing to the development of these states has created demand for quality higher education for the children of these families, which can be met by the Western-style education offered at the branch campuses (Willoughby 2008). For example, the population of Qatar grew from around 800,000 in 2005 to over 2 million in 2014 (QSA 2014) mostly as a result of the growing expatriate population involved in development projects.

Enrolment in private higher education is growing very rapidly in almost all the GCC states. For example, the number of students enrolled in private universities in Saudi Arabia increased sharply from 390 in 2000/2001 to 26,333 in 2008/2009. Kuwait witnessed over a 50 %increase in the number of students enrolled in private higher education institutions during the periods of 2005–2006 and 2009–2010 (Abouammoh 2012). These figures reflect the increasing demand for quality higher education and the important role private and Western universities play in the region. Efforts to reform higher education in most GCC states included allowing and encouraging the establishment of private institutions, and in some cases financially supporting them, such as the cases of Qatar and the UAE (Gonzalez et al. 2008). Some of these efforts succeeded in meeting the demand for higher education, but the quality of education offered at these institutions, accreditation of these institutions locally and internationally, and the recognition of degrees issued by these institutions are issues that continue to concern policy makers and regulators in the region. These issues are unfortunately beyond the scope of this chapter.

## WHY REFORM PSE?

Qatar is a small resource-rich country which, like most GCC states, relies heavily on importing labor to meet the increasing workforce and labor market needs for both skilled and unskilled labor (see Chapter 10). Oil and gas revenues enabled Qatar to embark on major development projects in many areas around the same time (Gonzales et al. 2008). These efforts started shortly after Shaikh Hamad Bin Khalifa Al-Thani took office in 1995, but they were more visible starting 1998 when several new government and semi-government organizations were established to lead aspects of the country's development, such as the Supreme Council for Family Affairs in 1998 and the Supreme Education Council in 2002.

The massive revenues from oil and gas are an obvious benefit but also pose challenges to the GCC states, and Qatar is no exception. Although income from oil and gas exports enables major developments, the high standard of living it provides for the small population of citizens has a negative impact on student motivation. This is clear in the lack of motivation of students at the K-12 level, as well as, though perhaps less evidently, at the higher education level (Stasz et al. 2007). The government provides guaranteed employment to citizens in addition to generous benefits including free education, health, and social services. Many secondary school graduates in Qatar join the labor force after graduating from secondary schools given the availability of jobs that provide reasonable income.

The leadership of Qatar has realized that relying heavily on income from natural resources is risky, since these resources will eventually run out. Therefore, it was necessary for Qatar to become a knowledge-based society with a knowledge-based economy. This required major reforms to both K-12 and higher education, outlined in the Qatar National Vision and the National Development Strategy. The quality of higher education in Qatar was low and the outcomes were not up to the standards that the leadership envisions. QU was a traditional institution and was not producing graduates who met the needs of the labor market. There was a clear mismatch between the skills the employers in Qatar were looking for in university graduates and what QU was producing. QU was the only higher education institution in Qatar at the time, and there were no other options for students locally. Students who wanted better quality education had to apply for scholarships through the Ministry of Education. These scholarships were not open to all students and there were conditions for qualifying for these scholarships such as a minimum score in high school exams. This had an impact on the society and the skills of the national workforce and was a challenge to both the society and leadership.

There were several economic challenges at the time when the initial reform started, including low oil prices in 1998. It was also a period of recession in the state and there was almost no development. The infrastructure was poor and many aspects of life in Qatar were not up to a good standard. However, the leadership had a vision for improving the situation at that time (Anderson et al. 2010). The decision to reform higher education was a central part of this vision, and improvements in the economic situation helped speed up the development efforts to achieve it.

## THE REFORM AND THE RELEVANT POLICIES

### *Establishing University Branch Campuses and Colleges*

In 1998, the leadership of QF decided to invite reputable universities to establish branch campuses in Qatar and to offer the programs that these universities are well-known for in Qatar's Education City (Stasz et al. 2007). This decision came at a time when the branch campus phenomenon emerged in the Middle East, especially in the GCC region (Naidoo 2009; Lane and Kinser 2009). Around the same time, the UAE started attracting institutions from around the world to establish a presence in Dubai and offer world-class university programs locally. The Dubai government established the Dubai Knowledge Village (DKV) in 2003 and later established the Dubai International Academic City (DIAC) in 2007. These education hubs in Qatar and the UAE attracted a number of universities, mostly from the USA and UK, to establish branch campuses. A few other campuses were established in other GCC states such as Kuwait,

Oman, and Bahrain in the same decade. Although the branch campus agreements and models varied from one state to the other, this chapter will only focus on the model adopted in Qatar.

A number of scholars have discussed the rationale behind inviting world-class universities to establish branch campuses locally. Some think that prestige for the host state plays an important role (Altbach 2007), while others think that an indigenous need for quality education offered locally is the main driver for this effort (Knight 2010; Willoughby 2008; Lane and Kinser 2009), especially after the challenges that many scholarship students from the Middle East faced in obtaining or renewing study visas in the USA and some European countries after 2001.

However, Qatar, as well as Dubai, embarked on this effort well before 2001 and, therefore, seem to have a different rationale for this initiative. Realizing that reliance on revenues from natural resources, namely oil and gas, is risky in the long term (Gonzalez, et al. 2008), Qatar's leadership decided to move to a knowledge-based economy and transform the society to become a knowledge-based one. One of the major steps Qatar took in this direction was setting up branch campuses of world-class universities locally at Education City in QF, which was established in 1995 by the emir and his consort at that time (QF 2015). Khodr (2011: 514) states that the main drivers behind the creation of Education City were "the region-specific tradition to import 'best practice', regional and global competition, local education reform and policies, national liberalization initiatives, and globalization, internationalization of education, and transnational education."

On the other hand, universities have motives behind venturing abroad and establishing a presence in other countries. Altbach (2009, 2010) believes that the financial gain is the major driver for these universities; while others such as Knight (2013) and Lane and Kinser (2011) argue that serving internationalization purposes and having a competitive advantage are the main drivers. Prestige was also considered one of the drivers for universities to establish branch campuses in other countries, but it can be viewed as part of their internationalization agenda. Besides these drivers, there are risks for Western universities when establishing a presence in the Middle East. Romani (2009) argues that the move toward Western higher education in the Middle East is viewed by many in the local societies as a threat to culture and religion. This can lead to resistance from the society and thus campuses not "fitting in" locally. The other risk is associated with ensuring financial viability and sustainability of the branch campuses so that they become a source of income to the home university as opposed to a burden on the already shrinking budgets of these universities.

The leadership of QF seems to have understood the motives and drivers for world-class universities to venture abroad and establish branch campuses, and therefore, QF adopted a model that ensures financial viability of the branch campuses. The foundation covered all the start-up costs of the campuses, including the infrastructure and capital equipment, and provided a legal status under the Education City entity of the foundation. The campuses are responsible for providing the agreed-upon programs and bringing in faculty from their home universities or from the region who meet the quality standards of the home universities (see the appendix for information about the branch campuses and the home-grown institutions of Education City).

Establishing the Education City as a higher education hub in Qatar changed the local and regional scenes. Qatar has become one of the most important destinations for quality Western higher education in the region and has provided opportunities for hundreds of students in the region, mostly from other GCC states, to move to Qatar to join one of the branch campuses at Education City. In the early years of Education City a large number of full and partial scholarships were offered to international and regional students to encourage them to move to Qatar. Some of these scholarships were provided in return for working at an institution in Qatar for a number of years equivalent to the time spent at the branch campus. Although small in numbers, these scholarships gave enrollment at the branch campuses a boost in the early years. In addition to full and partial scholarships for regional and international students, Qatari students who gained admission to one of the Education City branch campuses were provided full government scholarships by the Higher Education Institute of the Supreme Education Council (see below).

One of the main challenges that the leadership of QF and branch campuses face is how to work together to achieve the goals of the state as well as those of the branch campuses and their home universities. This led the QF leadership to create an umbrella entity to bring together the diverse branch campuses into one large institution with a unified goal while maintaining the uniqueness of each campus. In 2008, QF leadership brought the branch campuses together into Education City University. This model of education hubs is referred to in the recent literature as "multi-varsities" (Altbach 2010; Knight 2013) that bring branch campuses of diverse universities under one entity.

In 2011, QF established Hamad Bin Khalifa University (HBKU) as a research university to continue fulfilling QF's vision of unlocking human potential. It builds its foundation upon innovative and unique collaborations with local and international partners (the branch campuses). HBKU will deliver graduate programs through its colleges (Science, Engineering, and Technology; Humanities and Social Sciences; Law and Public Policy; Public Health; Islamic Studies) in partnership with the branch campuses or with other international institutions.

A look at HBKU and its partner institutions now reveals a great deal of progress. This is clear in the number of degree programs offered, the number of students enrolled in these degree programs, the graduates' employment status, and the partnerships and collaboration with government and industry. The branch campuses and HBKU combined offer over thirty degree programs at the undergraduate and graduate levels, spanning such areas as technology, engineering, business, information systems, medicine, arts, international relations, media, communications, archeology, and translation. These institutions now have a combined enrollment of almost 3000 students at post-secondary levels. The over 2000 graduates of these institutions (QF 2015) now hold positions in various public and private sector organizations in Qatar and the surrounding region, and a number of them moved to graduate level education mainly in the USA, UK, and Canada. However, it remains unclear whether the cost per student in Qatar is reasonable or comparable to that in other countries regionally or internationally.

### *Reforming Qatar University*

At the time branch campuses and colleges were being established in and outside of Education City, QU was due for a major reform. QU was established in 1977 as part of a wave of new universities in the GCC region established shortly after independence of these states (Findlow 2005). In fact, the College of Education was established in 1973 before the university was envisioned. The College of Education was needed to provide qualified teachers to support school education in the state. QU currently has eight colleges: Arts and Sciences; Business and Economics; Education; Engineering; Law; Pharmacy; Sharia and Islamic Studies, and Medicine, which offered its first class in September 2015. It has a student body of over 14,000 students and over 30,000 graduates (QU 2013).

QU was modeled after other government higher education institutions in the Arab World and, therefore, had faced challenges similar to those other universities in the region. The university's academic, administrative, and financial structures were marked by highly centralized decision-making processes, overly bureaucratic administrative and financial operations, and traditional pedagogy and program offerings (Moini et al. 2009). Moreover, QU had no formal faculty appraisal system; faculty and staff salaries were low compared to other universities in the region; and employers were not satisfied with the skills of most graduates. A study of QU revealed the need for broad reforms in several aspects of the University, including governance, administration, and structure, to enable the university to serve Qatar adequately in the future. Autonomy was critically needed so the university can manage its own affairs, provide a more rigorous education for its students, and enhance the quality of faculty instruction and scholarly endeavors (QU 2012).

Almost three decades after its establishment, QU was set for a major reform project mandated by the emir. This move seems to have been triggered by the establishment of branch campuses and colleges in Qatar and the need for the national university to compete in the new era of PSE in the state. Lane (2010) argues that establishing branch campuses of world-class universities in developing countries has a knock-on effect on the local institutions and usually leads to improvement in the whole system.

In 2003, QU started an ambitious reform project to increase the efficiency of its administrative and academic processes. The project started with an in-depth examination of the conditions and resources needed to turn it into a model national university. A plan was developed to improve all academic and administration aspects of the university. This plan was implemented over a number of years. The main recommendations of the Senior Reform Committee that was formed to lead the reform effort were as follows: (1) establish university autonomy by forming a Board of Regents to govern QU; (2) decentralize administrative arrangements; (3) modify the academic structure of the university; (4) institute a core curriculum; (5) introduce university-wide academic planning; (6) improve management of faculty and staff; and (7) foster and support student achievement. These recommendations were approved by the emir and were implemented over a number of years (Moini et al. 2009).

The main feature that characterized the reform of QU was the focus on quality. This is reflected in the policies that governed student admission, enrollment, and graduation, as well as faculty and staff hiring, retention, and promotion. QU leadership raised student admissions requirements by requiring the Test of English as a Foreign Language (TOEFL) examination and higher scores on the high school exit exams for direct admission into the university; otherwise, students would be required to enroll in the preparatory Foundation Program. Student retention was linked to students' maintenance of a GPA of 2.0 (as opposed to 1.5 previously). More stringent standards were set for faculty and staff hiring; and retention and promotion policies underlined the importance of efficiency and productivity, and they were linked to a newly developed performance appraisal system. These policies, in addition to the move to English as the medium of instruction for many of QU programs, faced resistance from various groups of the university community and the wider society (see discussion below).

The first outcome of the reform project was realized in 2005 when the engineering programs offered by the College of Engineering received Accreditation Board for Engineering and Technology (ABET) equivalency. Other programs offered by the university received accreditation later. In a subsequent phase of development at QU, a university-wide strategic plan was launched in 2009 incorporating key performance areas that focus on promoting quality education and efficient and effective services. The plan included revisiting the university's vision and mission, scanning the internal and external environments, and identifying key performance areas, objectives to be achieved within the plan's timeline (2010–2013), and key performance indicators to measure the success in achieving the planned objectives. The plan also placed research and community service as key priority areas in accordance with the goals outlined in the university's mission and vision (QU 2015).

*Reforming the Government Scholarship System*

The reform of PSE in Qatar was not restricted to education offered inside Qatar but was also extended to education offered to Qatari citizens overseas on government scholarships. Qatar has had a government scholarship system for higher education at the undergraduate and graduate levels since the 1970s. The system has provided scholarships to thousands of national students to study at universities in the Middle East and around the world in fields of study not available at Qatar University. This system had been managed by the Ministry of Education since its inception. In 2003, a study was commissioned to look into the weaknesses of the system and provide recommendations for improvement. Specifically, Qatar's leaders wanted the scholarship system to fulfill the following objectives: (1) satisfy workforce needs; (2) develop language, critical-thinking, and problem-solving skills; (3) prepare future leaders; (4) provide international exposure and establish ties with other countries; and (5) meet civic and cultural goals (Augustine and Krop 2008).

The study recommended developing a new scholarship system for Qatar and establishing a new entity (the Higher Education Institute—HEI) under the SEC to lead the development of this system. The SEC specified that the new scholarship system should complement and promote its national K-12 reforms, utilize the expanding high-quality postsecondary options available in the country, and meet the labor-related, civic, and cultural needs generated from Qatar's significant economic and social development (Augustine and Krop 2008).

The new system features a number of scholarship programs that support Qatari students who gain admission to highly selective universities in Qatar (the branch campuses at Education City) as well as comparable highly selective universities around the world. Through more stringent award criteria, the system encouraged students to seek admission to world-class universities in return for generous financial support. It also provided students with professional academic advising before and during their application process through a dedicated office in the HEI. One of the main features of the new system is that it limited scholarships to students who have gained unconditional admission at eligible universities; therefore, it limited the awards to students with high academic standards. The old scholarship system provided awards to students to study the English language for up to two years before they would be admitted to a degree program. Many of these students failed to gain admission at eligible universities, thus jeopardizing their scholarships.

Another important feature of the new system is that it limited scholarships to world-class, highly selective universities. Although the old scholarship system run by the Ministry of Education did not provide scholarships to students admitted to community colleges or universities that are considered "diploma mills," it allowed students to enroll at a large number of universities around the world without consideration of the quality of education offered by these universities. By contrast, the new system restricted scholarships to students who have gained admission to world-class universities through two types of scholarships: (1) emiri scholarships; and (2) national scholarships. The Emiri Scholarship Program provided generous financial support and rewards for students enrolled in one of the top 50 US universities, the top 10 UK universities, and the top five universities in other countries. The National Scholarship Program provided opportunities for students who are admitted to other highly selective universities, but with less financial support. Although the scholarship programs were restructured in 2010, they maintained the competitiveness and quality aspects of the system.

The HEI leadership established an office to examine the ranking of universities and develop and maintain a list of eligible universities where students should gain admissions in order to secure a scholarship. This was a major shift from the old scholarship system that guaranteed a scholarship for most secondary school graduates with more lenient eligibility criteria.

## Achievements of PSE Reforms

The PSE reforms in Qatar have changed the education scene in the state remarkably. Graduates of the branch campuses, QU, and other colleges in the state and internationally have become more employable than before. The caliber of university graduates has improved and most of them have developed language and other interpersonal skills. A number of university graduates have started their own businesses and many have moved on to postgraduate education. In fact, the number of postgraduate programs offered in Qatar has increased significantly as a result of the reform, from a handful in 2000 to more than 30 programs in 2013, most of them offered by QU. The increase in the number of postgraduate programs offered locally has ignited a remarkable increase in research budgets at universities and colleges in Qatar. This coincided with the establishment of the Qatar National Research Fund (QNRF) in 2006 as the main research funding body in the state. Currently, a large number of academic and professional conferences and meetings are held in Qatar regularly, and local chapters of international associations, such as Qatar TESOL, are now active in the state.

## Societal Responses to PSE Reforms

Qatar has witnessed unprecedented development and reform since 1995 in many areas and specifically in education since 1998, when the first branch campus was set up at Education City. The tightening of standards at QU, the invitation to and support of highly selective universities to set up campuses in Qatar, and the new funding criteria for scholarships have created societal "push-back." This resistance has led to the reversal of some policies introduced at the beginning of the reform effort.

It is noteworthy that the three reform initiatives (QU, foreign universities, and scholarships) were implemented almost simultaneously. Although the first branch campus was established in Education City in 1998, the majority of the campuses were established between 2002 and 2005. The reform of both QU and the government scholarship system started in 2004. Qatari students who graduated from secondary schools in 2005 had limited higher education choices. QU raised its admissions standards and included a TOEFL score requirement for direct admissions to its programs. Therefore, many students ended up in the Foundation Program, where they spent one or two years before they were admitted to degree programs.

Similarly, many secondary school graduates who applied for the Education City branch campuses did not meet the admissions requirements and, therefore, enrolled in the Academic Bridge Program where they spent one or two years of academic preparation before they were considered prepared for the rigorous Western-style education offered by the branch campuses. Those students who decided to apply for government scholarships to study in universities overseas were asked to obtain unconditional acceptance into a degree program by one of the highly selective institutions listed as eligible for government scholarships. In the early years of the scholarship system reform, funding for students with conditional acceptance or acceptance into English language and other academic preparation programs was not allowed. Those students who could not gain admission into a degree program spent a year or two at the Academic Bridge Program or enrolled in a foundation program in a university overseas at their own expense.

For students and parents, therefore, the PSE system in Qatar was transformed in a few years from a flexible system with a number of choices to a challenging one with limited feasible options. For the three decades prior to the reform, secondary school graduates were encouraged to continue their studies in higher education through flexible admission at QU and financial support to study at a wide variety of universities around the world, including those at other Arab states. Many of the universities in the Arab states had lenient admission requirements, especially for students from the GCC region who paid much higher fees than the citizens of these states. These shifts, both in scope and timing, created notable public discontent.

Societal discontent was demonstrated in a variety of ways and was reflected clearly in the media from 2004 to 2010, and less clearly thereafter. Weekly articles appeared in local newspapers expressing public discontent with the reform and the major shift toward more stringent university admissions and scholarship funding. From 2005 to 2007 there was almost a weekly article or report in the *Al-Raya* or *Al-Watan* newspapers discussing public discontent with PSE. The large number of students who decided to enter the labor market upon completing secondary education continued to represent a challenge to policy makers (Stasz et al. 2007) as the state moved to a knowledge economy. The situation continued to be challenging until 2008 when some policies were reversed and new ones were enacted.

The first major change in policies was implemented by the SEC's Executive Committee, which eased the requirements for government scholarships and allowed scholarships to some universities in the Arab states in specific majors. Students were provided with financial support to study for a foundation year before starting a degree program, and support for language study was also reintroduced. This change in policies was associated with a change in the leadership of the Higher Education Institute and in the financial packages of scholarship programs.

To address the public discontent with the tightened PSE options for students with low high school grades and to meet the needs of those who did not qualify to enroll at QU or obtain a scholarship, a community college was established in 2010. The college offers associate (two-year) degrees in arts, sciences, and applied sciences and it admitted its first cohort of students in the fall of 2010. Unlike the branch campuses, where student enrollment grew gradually over a number of years, the Community College of Qatar (CCQ) has more than doubled its student enrollment one year after its inception and maintained a steady increase of about 50 % annually in subsequent years (CCQ 2014). This major increase in student enrollment reflected the societal need for more flexible higher education offerings.

Although the Education City branch campuses were not affected by these reversed or changed policies, QU witnessed a remarkable shift back to the pre-reform years in some aspects. In 2012, QU reverted to Arabic as its primary language of instruction for undergraduate programs in business, law, social sciences, and humanities. Admission to these programs no longer requires proof of English language or mathematics competency. Science, engineering, pharmacy, and some education programs were not affected by the policy reversal. Although academics inside and outside QU expressed major concerns about these changes, there was clear public acceptance of the new policies as evidenced in the remarkable increase of student enrollment at QU for the academic year 2012–2013. Student enrollment for 2012–2013 reached 12,000 with an increase of around 4000 students over the previous year (QU Annual Report 2013).

The response to the reform of Qatar's PSE reflects the society's strong reliance on government support in the form of guaranteed university places for secondary school graduates and guaranteed employment upon graduation. The shift to quality higher education by implementing stringent university admissions and scholarship criteria conflicted with the interests of the society, mainly parents and students, who expressed strong discontent with this move. This has put pressure on policy makers to ease the situation by reverting back to old policies that represented the interests of the society.

## Challenges in Reforming Qatar's PSE

In spite of the achievements in PSE reform in Qatar and the major changes in the system, there were several obstacles and challenges in this path. First, the reform of the K-12 education did not yield the expected results in terms of student academic achievements. Consequently, students were not as prepared coming out of the K-12 system as had been hoped and expected. Second, the reform took place over a relatively short period of time and, therefore, many of the decisions created a sense of uncertainty for those involved in or affected by the reform. Finally, the enacted policies conflicted to a large extent with the interests of parents and students, thus triggering societal discontent and backlash. Below is a brief discussion of each of these challenges.

### *The Impact of the K-12 Education Reform*

Although Qatar's PSE reform resulted in a number of positive changes at QU and the government scholarship system, it was negatively affected by the less successful K-12 education reform, since the government-funded independent schools in Qatar are the main feeders of national students for PSE (see Chapter 4). In spite of all the reform efforts at the K-12 level, the wide gap between the skills secondary school graduates have and those required for university entrants still exists. The growing number of Qatari students enrolled at the Education City branch campuses can be attributed largely to the increasing number of Qatari students moving to international K-12 schools, especially after the introduction of educational vouchers for citizens. The educational voucher system allows Qatari parents to send their children to eligible international schools, known for their quality education and high student outcomes, and receive government financial support for a large portion of the fees. Although some of the independent schools are important sources of Qatari students for the branch campuses, a growing number of Qatari students come from international schools (Baghdady 2008).

*The Pace of Reform*

Like the K-12 education reform in Qatar, the PSE reform featured some bold changes in a short time with policies that affected the higher education scene dramatically. Raising the admission and graduation requirements at QU and restricting government scholarships to students accepted at highly selective universities was a major shift that was implemented in 2004–2005. This major change from a flexible, inclusive system to a more stringent system that links government support to student outcomes was implemented around the same time as the K-12 education reform. Both reform efforts featured bold changes in a short period of time, creating uncertainties and resistance within groups of the society, especially those with direct interest in the education system (mainly parents and students).

*Societal Response*

The societal response to the bold reform efforts represented a major challenge for policy makers. Although academics and some employers commended the move toward higher quality PSE, major groups in the society responded otherwise. The constant complaints about admission at QU and the higher standards for government scholarships created a negative atmosphere and led many secondary school graduates to enter the labor market instead of pursuing PSE. Societal views of the branch campuses at Education City in the early years were mostly negative. Besides being Western institutions in a conservative Muslim society[3], the branch campuses were viewed by many groups as elitist given their high admission standards. Although this view started to change gradually as more Qatari students qualified for admission at these campuses, some parents expressed major concerns in various media outlets about the higher education options available for their children locally, especially between 2004–09, until the CCQ was created and some policies were reversed.

## CONCLUSIONS

Although there seems to be a turnaround for Qatar's PSE reform, there are some positive impacts of the reform on the PSE sector. Qatar now has a much wider variety of higher education options locally. There are world-class universities with branch campuses in Qatar offering high quality education to students with high academic achievements. QU offers programs of higher quality than before as evidenced by the accreditation these programs received during the reform process. These programs target mainstream students with reasonable academic achievements and promise to produce graduates who meet the labor market needs to a large extent. There are also a number of institutions that meet specific labor market needs such as the College of the North Atlantic (offering one-year certificates and two and three-year diplomas in various technical fields), University of Calgary in Qatar (offering diplomas and bachelor and master degrees in nursing), and Stenden University (offering bachelor degrees in business and management, tourism management, and hospitality management).

These three options target secondary school graduates who wish to pursue university education and obtain BA/BSc degrees. Other graduates, usually with lower academic performance, who wish to obtain two-year associate degrees or enter the labor market directly after secondary school and study on part-time basis, have the option to enroll at CCQ. This is a sizable group of secondary school graduates given the rapidly growing enrollment at CCQ, with mostly Qatari students.

The variety of higher education options in Qatar promises to improve the quality of education with the competition element at play. The Education City branch campuses compete to attract the best secondary school graduates in Qatar while QU is improving its program offerings to stay at par with other institutions locally and regionally. All higher education institutions in Qatar need to maintain some level of quality to ensure government support and sustainability in a more competitive environment.

Sustainability of the PSE reform in Qatar is an important issue to consider. QU is the only national university and thus is ensured state funding. However, branch campuses at Education City are still foreign institutions and operate under ten-year agreements with QF. Although the agreements of some of these institutions have expired and have been renewed, there are still questions regarding the sustainability of this model in the long run. How long will QF continue to support these branch campuses the way it does now? Will Qatar, at one point in the future, look at the output of Education City institutions in terms of the number of Qatari graduates and weigh this against the investment it makes in Education City? Will the QF leadership come to a point of asking the branch campuses to change their business model from one that relies heavily on funding from the host state to a more sustainable model? These same questions, in fact, also hold for the Education City institutions. Will they be able to continue to offer their programs if the host state decides to reduce its financial support? Will they be able to recruit academically qualified and motivated students for their programs if the K-12 schools do not improve the quality of their education?

Qatar is in a stage of transformation from reliance on oil and gas revenues to a more sustainable knowledge economy. This has implications on all aspects of life in Qatar. The reform of PSE has achieved some important milestones since 1998. However, the drawbacks that resulted from changing, and in some cases reversing, some policies can negatively affect the gains achieved. Although it is difficult to fully predict what PSE will look like in the future given the recent policy changes, the move toward quality in higher education will need to strike a balance between meeting the labor market needs necessary for economic, social and human development, as set in the Qatar National Vision 2030, and at the same time respecting the interests of the society.

## Notes

1. "Qatar Foundation for Education, Science and Community Development is a private, non-profit organization that serves the people of Qatar by supporting and operating programs in three core mission areas: education, science and research, and community development. The Foundation strives to nurture the future leaders of Qatar. By example and by sharing its experience, the Foundation also contributes to human development nationally, regionally, and internationally. In all of its activities, the Foundation

promotes a culture of excellence in Qatar and furthers its role in supporting an innovative and open society that aspires to develop sustainable human capacity, social, and economic prosperity for a knowledge-based economy." (QF 2015)
2. Education City is an initiative of Qatar Foundation for Education, Science, and Community Development. It is located on the outskirts of Doha and covers 14 square kilometers. It houses educational facilities from school age to research level and branch campuses of some of the world's top universities. Education City aims to be instructing students in fields of importance to Qatar and the GCC region. It also acts a forum where universities share research and forge relationships with businesses and institutions in public and private sectors. (QF 2015)
3. Branch campuses of Western universities in the Middle East and Asia are being accused of not respecting the local culture and imposing their Western culture on their students through the curriculum, teaching methods, and adopting the co-educational model (Wang 2008; Altbach 2010; Shams and Huisman 2012).

## BIBLIOGRAPHY. QATAR: POLICY MAKING IN A TRANSFORMATIVE STATE

Abouammoh, Abdulrahman. 2012. *Higher Education in the GCC States: Reforms and Regulations.* Riyadh: http://goo.gl/4rW3V0Centre for Higher Education Research and Studies.
Akkari, Abdeljalil. 2004. Education in the Middle East and North Africa: The current situation and future challenges. *International Educational Journal* 5(2): 19–22.
Alpen Capital. 2014. *GCC Education Industry.* Dubai: Alpen Capital.
Altbach, Phillip. 2007. Twinning and branch campuses: The professional obstacle. *International Higher Education* 48(Summer): 2–3.
———. 2009. Peripheries and centers: Research universities in developing countries. *Asia Pacific Education Review* 10(1): 15–27.
———. 2010. Why branch campuses may be unsustainable. *International Higher Education* 58(Winter): 2–3.
Anderson, Margery, Tarfa Alnaimi, and Shaikha Alhajri. 2010. National student research fairs as evidence for progress in Qatar's Education for a New Era. *Improving Schools* 13(2): 235–248.
Augustine, Catherine, and Cathy Krop. 2008. *Aligning Post-Secondary Educational Choices to Societal Needs: A New Scholarship System for Qatar.* Santa Monica, CA: RAND Corporation.

Baghdady, Ahmed. 2008. *How Effective are the Marketing Methods used by Qatar's Education City Universities to Recruit Students?* Leicester, MA: University of Leicester.
Community College of Qatar. 2014. About CCQ. Accessed March 27. http://ccq.edu.qa/index.php?option=com_content&view=article&id=111&Itemid=695.
Damascus University. 2011. Historical Background. Accessed February 20, 2015. http://damasuniv.edu.sy/english/
Donn, G., and Y. Al-Manthri. 2010. *Globalization and Higher Education in the Arab Gulf States*. Oxford: Symposium Books.
Findlow, S. 2005. International networking in the United Arab Emirates higher education system: Global-local tensions. *British Association for International and Comparative Education* 35(3): 285–302.
Gonzalez, G., L. Karoly, L. Constant, H. Salem, and C. Goldman. 2008. *Facing Human Capital Challenges of the 21st Century: Education and Labor Market Initiatives in Lebanon, Oman, Qatar, and the United Arab Emirates*. Santa Monica, CA: RAND Corporation.
Khodr, Hiba. 2011. The dynamics of international education in Qatar: Exploring the policy drivers behind the development of Education City. *Journal of Emerging Trends in Educational Research and Policy Studies* 2(6): 514–525.
Knight, Jane. 2010. Higher Education Crossing Borders: A Framework and Overview of New Developments and Issues. In *Cross-border Partnerships in Higher Education: Strategies and Issues*, eds. Robin Sakamoto, and David Chapman, 16–44. New York: Routledge.
———. 2013. Cross border education in the Gulf countries: Changes and challenges. In *Education in the Broader Middle East: Borrowing a Baroque Arsenal*, eds. G. Donn, and Y. Al-Manthri. Oxford: Symposium Books.
Lane, J. 2010. Joint ventures in cross-border higher education: International branch campuses in Malaysia. In *Cross Border Collaborations in Higher Education: Partnerships Beyond the Classroom*, eds. D. Chapman, and R. Sakamoto. New York: Routledge.
Lane, J., and K. Kinser. 2009. The private nature of cross-border higher education. *International Higher Education* 53(Fall): 11–13.
———. 2011. Editors' Notes. *New Directions for Higher Education* 155(Fall 2011): 1–4.
Moini, J., T. Bikson, C.R. Neu, and L. DeSisto. 2009. *The Reform of Qatar University*. Santa Monica, CA: RAND Corporation.
Naidoo, V. 2009. Transnational higher education: A stock take of current activity. *Journal of Studies in International Education* 13(3): 310–330.
Qatar Foundation. 2015. About Qatar Foundation. Qatar Foundation. Accessed March 31. http://www.qf.org.qa/about/about

Qatar University. 2012. *The Reform Plan*. Qatar University. Accessed February 12. http://www.qu.edu.qa/theuniversity/reformproject/principles.php

———. 2013. *Undergraduate Student Catalogue 2012–2013*. Accessed February 21. http://www.qu.edu.qa/students/documents/catalog/undergraduate_catalog_2012_2013/files/assets/basic-html/page13.html

———. 2015. *QU Strategic Plan*. Qatar University. Accessed February 21. http://www.qu.edu.qa/theuniversity/strategic_plan.php

Romani, V. 2009. *The Politics of Higher Education in the Middle East: Problems and Prospects*. Waltham, MA: Brandeis University.

Saleh, M. 1986. Development of higher education in Saudi Arabia. *Higher Education* 15(1986): 17–23.

Shams, F., and J. Huisman. 2012. Managing offshore branch campuses: An analytical framework for institutional strategies. *Journal of Studies in International Education* 16(2): 206–127.

Stasz, C., Eide, E. and Martorell, F. (2007). *Post-Secondary Education in Qatar: Employer Demand, Student Choice and Options for Policy*. California: RAND Corporation.

University of Baghdad. 2014. *University History*. University of Baghdad. Accessed February 20. http://www.uobaghdad.edu.iq/PageViewer.aspx?id=44

Wang, T. 2008. Intercultural dialogue and understanding: Implications for teachers. In *Teaching in Transnational Higher Education: Enhancing Learning for Offshore International Students*, eds. L. Dunn, and M. Wallace, 57–66. New York: Routledge.

Willoughby, J. 2008. Title. Working Paper Series, Washington, DC.

CHAPTER 6

# Fragmentation and Continuity in Qatar's Urbanism: Towards a Hub Vision

*Ashraf M. Salama and Florian Wiedmann*

In the past two decades Doha has witnessed enormous urban growth driven by various projects and strategies, which were launched to realise the vision of a hub city within international networks. Successively, the increasing investments in combination with liberalisation strategies have affected the decentralisation of urban governance, while dramatically transforming Doha's urban structure and built environment. This chapter explores the recent developments in Qatar's "urbanism". The impact of large-scale investments of oil and gas revenues on urbanism in Qatar's capital city of Doha is discussed to offer insights into recent developments by adopting a multi-layered methodological approach that includes two major components. The first is a series of interviews with experts and planners working on strategies and plans within the public sector, while the second is a review of recently published data and figures regarding investments in relation to positioning Doha as future "hub city". The methodology helps identify investment strategies and aspects of decentralised urban governance within which urban development is undertaken. The chapter concludes with a brief on how a new form of urban governance may enable the effective implementation of a hub vision in the case of Qatar.

---

A.M. Salama (✉)
Department of Architecture, University of Strathclyde, Glasgow, UK

F. Wiedmann
Department of Architecture, University of Strathclyde, Glasgow, UK

© The Author(s) 2016  155
M.E. Tok et al. (eds.), *Policy-Making in a Transformative State*,
DOI 10.1057/978-1-137-46639-6_6

## INTRODUCTION

Since the middle of the twentieth century, increasing oil production has generated rapid urbanisation on the Arabian Peninsula, which has led to newly emerging cities along the Gulf coast. While the emirate of Dubai and the Kingdom of Bahrain established more diversified local economies due to their limited hydrocarbon resources, other GCC states relied extensively on oil and natural gas development after their national independence in the 1970s (Scholz 1999: 69). In the case of Qatar, a rapid transformation process was undertaken, which in turn led to extensive immigration. Subsequently, the population of its capital city, Doha, increased from less than 400,000 inhabitants in 1995 to more than 2 million today (Qatar Statistics Authority 2015).

Based on a fortunate geopolitical location between Asia, Europe, and Africa, Qatar's leadership recognised a potential to develop its capital city into a hub within regional and global business networks by investing in extensive state-of-the-art harbours and airports (Salama and Wiedmann 2013: 34). The global hub vision is rooted in the increasing competition between cities worldwide to attract the headquarters of key advanced producer services and high-tech branches (Friedmann 1986; Sassen 1996). Therefore, decision makers in emerging countries, such as Qatar, are challenged to balance between implementing consolidation strategies and reinforcing fast growth mechanisms. While the investment driven sector needs to be attracted by a deregulated and dynamic environment, other regulations have to be enforced in order to enable a more sustainable urban development attracting the long-term commitment of businesses and their highly qualified migrant workers.

Coupled with this general hub vision, different types of investments were introduced in order to accelerate Doha's urban growth. As a result, new economic sectors have emerged through joint ventures between public and private sectors, which required a new era of urban governance in Qatar. Privatisation and decentralisation have been integrated to stimulate and accelerate investment in order to realise the vision of becoming an emerging regional centre. This vision implies the development of new socio-economic realities and takes little account of existing conditions. Today, hydrocarbon wealth can still be considered the main basis of recent expectations for urban growth in Qatar (Qatar Statistics Authority 2015). The newly applied investment strategies, however, differ from the previous development model during the 1970s and 1980s of establishing a rentier state (see discussion of rentier state theory in Chapter 3). Thus, the new urban development era in Qatar and the Gulf region as a whole can be described as a decisive transition phase from oil driven urbanisation and modernization towards the creation of dynamic service hubs driven by the general vision of a shrinking dependency on fossil fuels in a post-oil future.

Despite parallels or similarities with other emerging cities, Doha should be considered a particular case, not only because of its fast urban growth in recent years, but also because of its political realities wherein traditional forms of urban governance meet a modern administration (Gardner 2014: 354). The ruling family became the visionary force introducing various strategies to transform Doha into a regional and global hub city. These strategies included a strong advocacy of investing oil and gas revenues in large-scale projects, while establishing new organisations in order to create a suitable environment for an expanding private sector. In this respect, semi-public holdings were often introduced to develop profit-oriented subsidiaries in various economic sectors, which accelerated growth by stimulating markets. Thus, it can be argued that government investments were in most cases catalysts of recent economic diversification processes, which were usually accompanied by the deregulation of markets, for example, the real estate market.

General economic visions are being put into place by adopting various strategies for investments and liberalisation policies. However, urban planning has faced the challenge of guiding the recent construction boom in Qatar into a functioning urban structure. The idea of developing the capital city of a former administrative centre of a rentier state into an emerging service hub resulted in large-scale projects and a new form of decision-making in physical planning processes. The previous centralised process of defining land use has been partially substituted by the master plans of developers for "city-within-a-city" projects, which usually occupy a large portion of new urban areas. The resulting urban structure can be described best as a patchwork of various developments connected by macro-infrastructural projects that are typically carried out by the public sector. Thus, the economic vision of creating hubs has led to a process of morphological transformation and resulted in a new city with new identities. The dynamics between investing oil and gas revenues in key development strategies and the liberalisation of local markets have changed urban governance from a centralised administration into a multi-layered cooperation between various stakeholders (Wiedmann 2012: 218).

## A METHODOLOGICAL APPROACH: EXPLORING QATAR'S URBANISM

We introduce Qatar's capital city of Doha in order to illustrate how the hub city vision is realised in the form of large-scale investments, as well as how urban governance is affected by deregulation and an emerging private and semi-public sector. Our approach seeks to offer insights into the way in which urban structure and the overall built environment have been transformed by this new way of conceiving the potential of urbanisation in Doha by various decision makers. Using a multi-layered methodology, the chapter is based on a series of face-to-face interviews with ten planning authorities involved in elaborating and implementing the new Qatar National Master Plan.

The interviews were undertaken over a concentrated period and used a matrix of a limited number of key questions (see Fig. 6.1). The ten interviewees were selected according to their role in developing and implementing strategies and plans at the Ministry of Municipalities and Urban Planning (MMUP). The major aim of the interviews was to explore various investment strategies that have been launched to transform Doha into a hub city, as well as to identify the key factors that led to a decentralised type of urban governance. Moreover, it aims at recognising the consequences of these strategies and their impact on the urban structure of the city in order to identify the key challenges for urban sustainability in the future.

The interviews were followed by a questionnaire in which the ten interviewees were asked in a second round to identify and rate the most important investments and decentralisation factors within urban governance. Additionally, they were asked to rate the most significant consequences for contemporary urban morphologies. A five-point scale was utilised in this procedure, where 1 represents least important and 5 represents most important.

## CREATING A GLOBAL HUB IN DOHA

The change in Qatar's rulership in 1995 with Sheikh Hamad bin Khalifa Al-Thani opened the door to a new path of economic development for what was a restrictive and conservative country (Scholz 1999: 185). Qatar has developed into a rising political centre in the Middle East, claiming the role as intermediator within relationships between the West and Arab

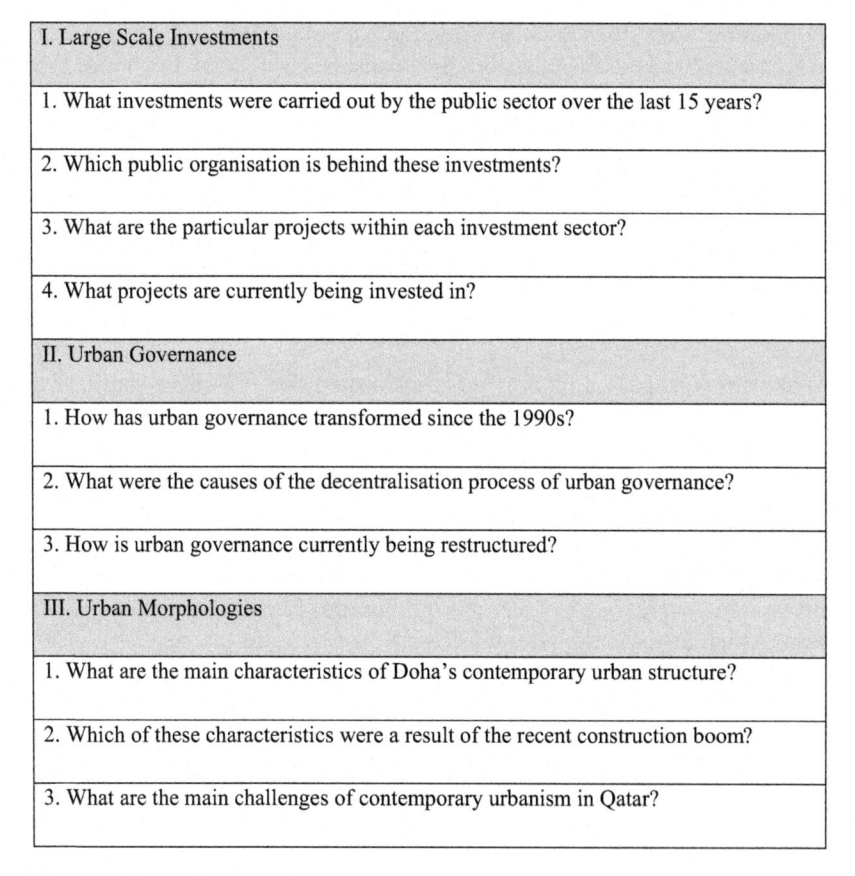

| I. Large Scale Investments |
|---|
| 1. What investments were carried out by the public sector over the last 15 years? |
| 2. Which public organisation is behind these investments? |
| 3. What are the particular projects within each investment sector? |
| 4. What projects are currently being invested in? |
| II. Urban Governance |
| 1. How has urban governance transformed since the 1990s? |
| 2. What were the causes of the decentralisation process of urban governance? |
| 3. How is urban governance currently being restructured? |
| III. Urban Morphologies |
| 1. What are the main characteristics of Doha's contemporary urban structure? |
| 2. Which of these characteristics were a result of the recent construction boom? |
| 3. What are the main challenges of contemporary urbanism in Qatar? |

**Fig. 6.1** Interview questions

World, which was, for instance, expressed in fora such as the Doha Debates (The Doha Debates 2015). Coupled with its growing political engagement, various projects were launched to develop the capital city Doha into a regional service hub. Since the mid-1990s Qatar's overall population has more than tripled to more than 2 million inhabitants, making it one of the fastest growing nations in the world.

This rate of population growth is largely due to the recent construction boom that incited the immigration of hundreds of thousands of guest workers from South Asia (Naqy 2006). Almost 90 % of Qatar's current population lives in Doha and its metropolitan area (Qatar Statistics Authority 2015). Liberalisation mechanisms have been introduced by deregulating the real estate market through the Foreign Ownership of Real Estate Law in 2004 (Colliers International 2008). However, the interest from the private sector in investing in the capital city was mainly ignited by direct investments of oil and gas revenues, which can be categorised in terms of real estate, infrastructure and services, culture and sports, education and science, and media (Fig. 6.2).

*Real Estate Investments*

While the Qatar Foundation was established for the main purpose of investing oil and gas revenues in the development of society, the Qatar Investment Authority (QIA) was founded in 2005 for the purpose of investing sovereign wealth funds in international markets as well as in local sectors such as the upcoming real estate market. The real estate boom in Qatar began in 2004 when the large-scale revenues from liquefied natural gas exports were invested in major urban developments in Doha. These investments were accompanied by the Foreign Ownership of Real Estate Law, which enabled the sale of freehold properties to international investors in designated areas (Colliers International 2008). In order to accommodate the increasing interest in real estate investment, the QIA was put in charge of the Qatari Diar Real Estate Investment Company, which was founded in 2004 as a property investment fund and is responsible for several real estate projects. It is currently in charge of the Doha Exhibition

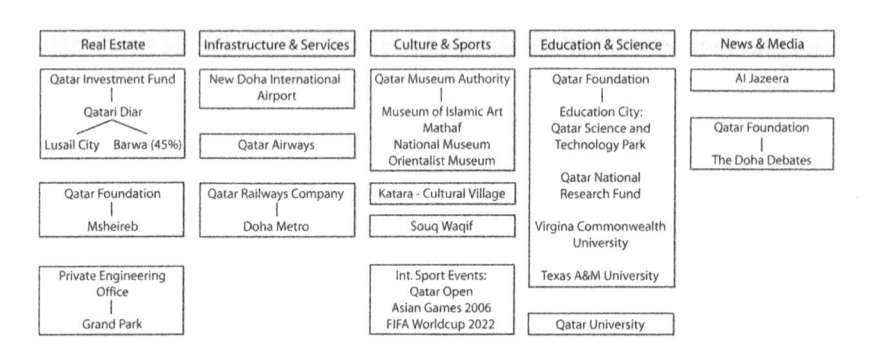

**Fig. 6.2** Five main categories of investment. *Source*: Authors

Centre and a mixed-use project in Ras Al Khor, in addition to its signature project—the Lusail City development. In addition to Qatari Diar's function of founding subsidiaries such as the Lusail Real Estate Development Company to carry out projects as master developer, it holds 45 % of the shares in Barwa, the largest listed real estate company in Qatar. The large-scale involvement of the public sector in the real estate market in the form of either Qatari Diar, a state-owned real estate investor, or as the main shareholder of other companies, has attracted the private sector to join the expanding construction business.

### *Infrastructure and Services*

In order to become a global hub, large investments were made to expand the existing airport and harbour as well as to develop new facilities. Since the end of the 1990s passenger movement has accelerated from around just 2 million to more than 15 million passengers a year at the Old Doha International Airport, which, in spite of its many extensions in recent years, was beyond the projected capacity of 12 million (Doha International Airport 2011). Thus, a new airport development project was launched in 2004, with estimated funds of over 11 billion USD, on a reclaimed area of 890 hectares to the east of the existing runways. The new Hamad International Airport was in partial operation at the end of 2013, and its first phase opened with full capacity in 2014. After the completion of its last phase in 2020, it will have reached an expected annual capacity of around 50 million passengers (Salama and Wiedmann 2013: 92).

Parallel to this large-scale investment in a new airport, Qatar Airways, one of the fastest growing airlines in the world, is directly funded by the state with the aim of becoming one of the world's leading aviation providers. Notably, these investments have turned Qatar into a serious future competitor as a transit hub for passengers and cargo beyond the Gulf region itself. In addition to aviation it has been declared that more than 100 billion USD will be invested in building an efficient local infrastructure in Doha during the next 12 years (MENANN 2011). One of the main projects in this regard is an ambitious metro project that is being developed incrementally in various phases with expected dates of completion in 2020 and 2026.

## Culture and Sports

Due to the fact that Doha was a rather insignificant settlement before oil and gas production and that its traditional buildings were replaced in the 1950s and 1960s during the first phase of modernisation, its potential for hosting international tourism has been rather low. In order to fill this gap several efforts were undertaken to attract international sporting events to Qatar such as the IAAF International Track and Field Meet, the Qatar Tennis Open and the 2006 Asian Games. While large investments in such events led to the successful bid for the 2022 FIFA World Cup, the development of cultural projects has also been important in attracting tourists, mainly transit passengers, as well as enhancing liveability in what used to be a rather monotonous urban landscape (Adham 2008: 245).

The most notable project was the redevelopment of the traditional market area, known as Souq Waqif, followed by the Museum of Islamic Art, both of which were nominated and shortlisted for the Aga Khan Award for Architecture in 2010 and became the new face of the historic city centre (Wiedmann et al. 2013). More recently, the Katara Cultural Village was built along the first public beach north of Doha in order to combine cultural and leisure facilities. In 2010 the Qatar Museum Authority opened the Arab Museum of Modern Art in Education City. In the future, while some projects were put on hold for various reasons, projects such as the new National Museum, the Orientalist Museum and the Olympic and Sports Museum will expand and diversify the collection of cultural institutions. These cultural investments should be seen as both an attempt to establish tourism as an emerging economic sector and as a branding strategy to transform the image of Doha from a stagnant city into a vibrant tourist attraction.

## Education and Science

Apart from stimulating the growth of new economic sectors by investing in infrastructure and tourism projects, the former Emir Sheikh Hamad bin Khalifa Al-Thani and his wife Sheikha Moza bint Nasser initiated the development of educational and research facilities early on in order to build a foundation for a more diversified economy and offer opportunities for international education. Thus, in 1995, the Qatar Foundation was introduced as a non-profit organisation focusing on three pillars, namely, education, science, and community development (Oxford Business Group

2009: 23). Its first project was Education City, the development of which was launched on an area of 2500 acres in the north west portion of the city in the late 1990s (Adham 2008: 243). In order to attract high-profile universities, various investments were made such as the 759 million USD in Cornell University in order to open a faculty in Doha. Science and research are promoted by the subsidiaries of the Qatar Foundation, namely, the Qatar National Research Fund and the Qatar Science and Technology Park, the tax-free environment which has attracted global corporations such as EADS, GE, and Microsoft (Qatar Science and Technology Park 2012). The multi-billion dollar investment in the Qatar Foundation and its various subsidiaries is one of the particular cornerstones of the hub city vision due to the long-term nature of its plans to develop a society for future knowledge economies and to establish higher education as an important economic sector itself.

## *News and Media*

One of the very early investment strategies to initiate the transformation of Qatar and its capital city into an emerging hub with international attention was the large-scale investment in Al Jazeera. The founding of Al Jazeera in 1996 altered the world perception of Qatar due to its role as a news provider from the Middle East. Despite the fact that the initial funds of 137 million USD were provided by the emir, Al Jazeera has always maintained that it maintains an independent editorial policy (Sakr 2001: 58). This liberalised news network has influenced an understanding of Qatar as a progressive and politically engaged country in the Gulf. The idea of investing in such a large-scale broadcasting service supports the vision of becoming a global hub by attracting world attention. Often seen as controversial, the role of Al Jazeera in regional politics has led to increasing recognition of the small country of Qatar around the world. Large amounts of investment enabled the news agency to hire various high-profile journalists and thus establish a growing level of credibility. Despite the still open question of the extent to which Al Jazeera can be considered independent, it has had a major impact on the development of the media in the Middle East as the voice of the people instead of a pure reflection of political agendas (Rinnawi 2006: 23). After all, Al Jazeera has influenced the general business climate and thus development dynamics by promoting a new image of Qatar as being liberal and open to future reforms.

| I. Large-scale investments | Which public investments had the biggest impact on urban developments over the last 15 years? | I. Large-scale investments | Which public investments had the biggest impact on urban developments in the future? |
| --- | --- | --- | --- |
| A. Real Estate | 40/50 | A. Real Estate | 31/50 |
| B. Infrastructure & Services | 31/50 | B. Infrastructure & Services | 42/50 |
| C. Cultre & Sports | 29/50 | C. Cultre & Sports | 33/50 |
| D. Education & Science | 29/50 | D. Education & Science | 38/50 |
| E. News and Media | 13/50 | E. News and Media | 13/50 |

Fig. 6.3 Questionnaire results

The analysis of the responses of the interviewee experts reveals that they have identified public engagement and investment in real estate projects as the main factors affecting the recent urban transformation process (Fig. 6.3). The subsequent construction boom has shaped contemporary Doha not only morphologically but also socio-economically due to the businesses and foreign workers that have moved there as a result. In regard to future development dynamics, the interviewees are convinced that the government investments in infrastructure projects of approximately 200 billion USD will play the most decisive role within future urban transformation processes during the next ten years (Qatar Financial Centre 2014). Large scale projects, such as Doha Metro, will continue to attract businesses, leading to a sustained growth rate. According to the interviewees the infrastructure projects are key to enhancing urban qualities and thus the general attractiveness of the city, which is key to attracting knowledge economies in the long term.

## THE NEW FORM OF URBAN GOVERNANCE

Since the 1970s Doha has grown according to master plans designed by international consultants on behalf of the urban planning department of the Ministry of Municipal Affairs and Agriculture (MMAA), and they were implemented as legal zoning plans. Although many adjustments were made to these plans in order to accommodate the unexpected speed of urban growth during the oil boom, the initial plans were followed to a large extent. They formed the basic urban structure of Doha that consists of a reclaimed Corniche and a network of ring roads around the city centre. The last master plan, known as the Physical Development Plan (PDP), was prepared during the 1990s. Although it is still used as the basis for general land use policies, its implementation in 1997 has had a rather limited impact on Doha's urban development because of the increasing influence of new public authorities and public-private partnerships (Adham 2008: 237).

This merger of the public and private sectors was the direct consequence of expanding investments and the liberalisation of markets in order to increase the urban growth rate. In order to develop Doha into a well-connected international hub, many projects were, however, initiated without being part of holistic development strategies. The resulting rapid urban growth challenged the existing administration within the public sector. Thus, urban governance was increasingly decentralised and case-by-case decision-making was followed instead of central planning (Salama and Wiedmann 2013: 114). One of the main characteristics of urban governance in Qatar is the fact that leading families own a significant share of urban areas and thus they control access to decision-making regarding new developments. The extensive investment of oil and gas revenues in local urban growth and the subsequently high population growth rate have thus led to speculative tendencies and the rapid increase of land prices, as well as large scale investments in new developments without following any regulations.

Based on the interviews with ten planners, four major factors within the public sector and its administration were identified, which drove the recent decentralisation of urban governance in Doha.

*Staff Capacity Deficits*

The new urban development strategies at the end of the 1990s and the subsequent investment pressure challenged a public administration that was not able to manage urban growth in this scale and manner. The limited staff capacity did not permit the urban planning department within the MMAA to coordinate urban developments by implementing new or adjusting existing plans in a very short period of time. In the past, staff was recruited mainly on the basis of administrative qualifications, while international consultants were engaged to develop new policies and plans for implementation. This procedure of allocating key planning responsibilities to external consultants led to capacity deficits following accelerated urban growth and pressure from investors to challenge existing plans and policies.

### Fragmented Organisational Structure

A further reason for the decentralisation of urban governance has been the absence of a coordinating and communicating central organisation, which is empowered to supervise the various departments and stakeholders on the basis of a transparent legal framework. While during the oil urbanisation developments followed a general pattern and thus governance was based on fixed procedures, the various investments in recent projects have led to an intense urban growth acceleration making developments more dynamic and complex. Many parallel developments were carried out without being centrally coordinated or assessed. Subsequently, new departments and authorities were founded, such as Ashghal (the Public Works Authority), in order to coordinate certain aspects of urban development more efficiently. The result has been a fragmented organisational structure that makes case-by-case decisions based on immediate problem resolution techniques, when what is needed is an interconnected form of governance integrating all parallel developments on the basis of one holistic vision. While key stakeholders within the semi-public and private sector have become the main drivers of many new developments, the public administration and its various authorities have been degraded to task forces reacting to new realities rather than defining them. Thus, the lack of coordination between the various task forces has increased the general problem of the missing efficient organisation in regard to responsibilities, as well as legal frameworks needed for a best-practise form of urban governance.

### Out-dated Plans and Policies

Due to the new situation of unprecedented amounts of investment being made in Doha's urban development, existing zoning plans that were developed on the basis of the Physical Development Plan during the 1990s have quickly become outmoded. Thus, existing land use and building regulations have lost the status of legally binding documents and have been treated in many cases as technical recommendations rather than development regulations. The most prominent example of this is the development of high-rise buildings in West Bay, where the original zoning plan restricted the maximum building height to eight floors. After a first adjustment to a maximum height of fifteen floors, the restriction was completely cancelled at the end of the 1990s, permitting unlimited heights (Salama and Wiedmann 2013: 82). In other cases shopping malls were built in areas allocated to low-rise residential developments. Thus, the central control of urban development using land-use plans and zoning regulations has been rather limited during the last fifteen years, and many decisions were rather isolated. These were often legalised by temporary permissions that allowed construction, and they were usually not subsequently retracted.

## *Legal Rights of Master Developers*

In addition to the fact that initial zoning plans have been bypassed in many cases, another phenomenon that decentralised governance was the rise of what is known as "megaprojects". These projects are usually connected with the investment strategies and are thus in most cases joint ventures between the private and public sectors. The main public bodies involved are the Qatar Investment Fund, the Qatar Foundation, and their subsidiaries. Other holdings are initiated as single public-private partnerships, mainly on the basis of state-owned land and private investments. For all megaprojects, one master developer is created to coordinate the development and given extensive legal rights to develop and implement master plans for their projects without major approval from the ministry and its urban planning departments. Furthermore, impact studies about the effects of projects on environment and traffic are not carried out independently, but they are instead part of the master planning process of the developer itself. Thus, these megaprojects are governed as "cities within the city", with a relatively limited relationship to their surroundings, involving mainly infrastructural concerns. Major examples of these megaprojects are Education City and Msheireb, carried out by subsidiaries of the Qatar Foundation, and Lusail City by Qatari Diar.

Most interviewees shared the opinion that an inefficient organisational structure, in combination with a *laissez faire* attitude regarding existing policies, were the main factors for the decentralisation of urban

| II. Urban Governance | What were the main causes of the decentralization of urban governance? |
|---|---|
| A. Staff Capacity | 38/50 |
| B. Organisational structure Lack of coordination | 43/50 |
| C. Master Deveopers & their legal rights | 29/50 |
| D. Laissez -faire attitude regarding existing policies | 42/50 |

**Fig. 6.4** Questionnaire Results

governance in Qatar (Fig. 6.4). Moreover, staff capacity deficits exacerbated and accelerated this process, particularly at the beginning of the construction boom. The allocation of legal rights to master developers of semi-public holdings regarding the design and development of large scale projects was, however seen, as the smallest factor in spite of its indisputable role in decentralising urban governance.

## THE IMPACT ON THE URBAN STRUCTURE AND BUILD ENVIRONMENT

The five major investment strategies, in combination with a more decentralised decision-making process, have shaped a new urban structure and built environment over the last fifteen years in Doha. The construction boom led to unprecedented urban growth, which did not follow a holistic strategic plan and transformed previous urban morphologies. In this regard, we can distinguish five main aspects regarding Doha's contemporary urbanism.

### *Fragmented Development*

The construction of large-scale projects by joint ventures between the private and public sectors has led to a focus on individual development sites of megaprojects rather than consolidation and cohesion within overall urban areas. Today, around six of these projects have been completed or are still under development, occupying more than 30 square kilometres. Despite their large size most of these projects do not serve adjacent settlement areas with services and infrastructure. This "island" approach to development has led to a general lack of land-use integration, creating long driving distances between residences and services. In addition to an absence of integration of land uses, projects have been built without taking into account their surrounding built environment or future urban areas under construction. The main reason for this lack of integration is the decision-making process itself, wherein the master plans of individual projects are approved without regulations of a central strategic plan regarding overall urban developments. Thus, many developments have been built without taking infrastructure into account and so have been completed before infrastructural networks have been established to serve them. The overall result is a rather fragmented structure of developments leading to a pattern of urban patchworks instead of cohesive and integrated urban areas (Fig. 6.5).

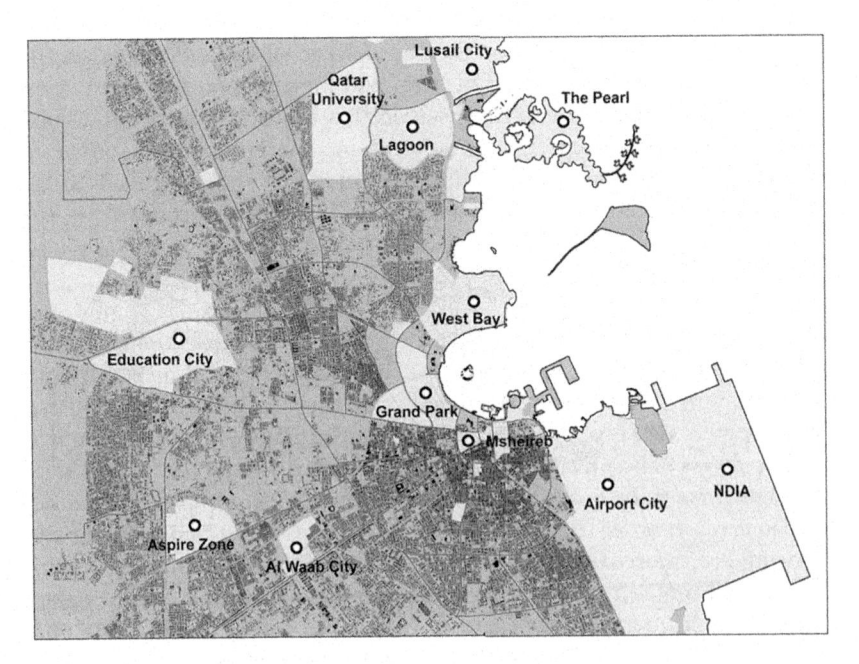

Fig. 6.5 Map of Current Megaprojects. *Source*: Authors

## The Predominance of Urban Peripheries

Another aspect of contemporary urbanism in Doha is the lack of a defined urban structure consisting of centres and sub-centres. This circumstance is rooted in the fact that Doha's urban area has been growing exponentially towards the outskirts over the last decades without the guidance of plans for developing sub-centres. The establishment of "decentralised centralisation" has been further complicated due to a lack of public transport networks and thus no major junctions that would enable higher densities of residential and commercial use. In addition, the old city centre's previous function as a centre for commercial and public activities has been increasingly undermined by new shopping mall developments and business districts along the urban periphery. Despite redevelopments of the historic centre, large parts of Doha's central urban area are occupied by high-density residential districts for low-income groups. Today, three major shopping malls in West Bay, Al Duhail and Al Aziziyah can claim to be new city centres due to their role as the biggest shopping and leisure spaces. However, their exclusive retail and entertainment facilities exclude over 70 % of Doha's population. Lower social groups would still define the historic centre as the commercial heart and meeting point for their communities. In general, it can be observed that the lack of public transport and extensive social segregation between income groups have caused an urban structure of sprawling peripheries served by shopping malls and a high-density mixed-use down town area for low income groups.

## Privatised Urban Landscapes

Another characteristic of Doha's contemporary urban development is the increasing privatisation of many urban areas due to megaproject developments by the private sector. In this regard, the Education City and Pearl developments are prominent examples of gated developments with limited public access. The privatisation of urban space is rooted in the nature of megaprojects to be exclusive entities that set themselves apart from other urban areas in order to attract attention and thus investment. Gating and fencing are, moreover, based on the assumption that future communities would prefer a secure and exclusive living environment. The Katara Cultural Village is another example of a controversial development that has introduced the first "public" beach in Doha, which again is only accessible by entering gates and paying entrance fees. Public space has become commercialised and thus filtered and limited in its function to invite all social groups to interact. The Souq Waqif, one of the most prestigious developments in Doha, appears to be a public space but is actually managed like an open-air mall with limited access for low income labourers (Neue Zuericher Zeitung 2011). Other public spaces such as Aspire Park, which is currently the biggest park in Doha, are not accessible by most inhabitants due to its remote location in a low density suburban area. Today, the Corniche can be considered to be the city's main public space in traditional terms as it constitutes an accessible central area to be used by anyone at any time. Most parts of Doha's urban area are, however, hidden behind borders in the form of walled compounds and villas in residential suburbs and by security gates and entrance fees in the case of megaprojects.

### *Emerging Contrasting Typologies*

In addition to the fact that the decentralisation of urban governance has led to the privatisation of urban areas, the previous urban morphology has been changed by higher building heights. The most prominent example is the Diplomatic District in West Bay, where more than 50 high-rise buildings have been built, of which 18 have a height of over 150 metres. This high-rise agglomeration has changed the morphology of contemporary Doha from a rather simplistic structure of a medium-high urban centre surrounded by low-rise suburbs to vertical developments with a new emphasis on the waterfront (Fig. 6.6). The high-rise waterfront at West Bay is to a large extent the product of public incentives that provided private investors with the prospects of ministries and other public or semi-public

**Fig. 6.6** Waterfront High-Rises in West Bay. *Source*: Authors

organisations occupying commercial high-rises as tenants in the future. Along the coast to the north, however, many high-rise and medium-rise developments arose out of speculation in the growing freehold-property market and the potential for selling seafront properties at higher prices. Today, although a variety of building typologies can be found along the coast and in megaprojects, in suburban residential areas the general use of low-rise buildings in developments has continued to contribute to the expansion of urban sprawl. The reasons for this are outmoded planning, cultural habits, and problems with delay in the supply of infrastructure and services in relation to increasing built densities.

## *Low Building Standards*

The construction boom in Doha has created a high contrast between masses of poorly designed projects and those of exceptional quality in a small number of representative buildings or developments. This concerns both construction and design and has three main causes, namely, a need for a rapid supply of housing in order to accommodate the fast rate of growth, a lack of restrictions in the case of building regulations, and deficient standards within the construction industry itself. One result is, therefore, catalogue designed residential typologies, mainly introduced by South-Asian and Chinese contractors, made of cement pre-fabricated elements, and assembled in a few weeks by poorly skilled construction workers with limited supervision. These instant buildings occupy large areas of newly built settlements in the outskirts of Doha, mainly in the form of compounds. A generic appearance and the need for a high level of maintenance due to low-quality finishing and utilities are two main results. However, the lack of quality is not restricted to low-profile residential and commercial developments and can also be found in cases of exclusive projects, particularly when properties are sold on paper before they are actually built. An additional problem is the common practise of choosing one major contractor and architectural consultant for an entire development complex, which can lead to monotonous and repetitive designs. Exceptions are landmarks, such as the buildings of the Qatar Foundation, and public museums, high-rise buildings, and hotel developments, which were built by experienced and internationally renowned contractors. Today, the contrast between the mass production of buildings and the state-of-the-art design of individual landmarks has become a reflection of a segregated and fragmented

| III. Urban Morphologies | What are the consequences for the current urban structures and build environment? |
|---|---|
| A. Lack of integration-fragmentation | 47/50 |
| B. No efficient structure of centres and subcentres | 37/50 |
| C. Typological contrasts–High & low rise | 25/50 |
| D. Conflict between quantities & quality – Poor construction in most cases | 35/50 |
| E. Privatised urban landscapes | 33/50 |

**Fig. 6.7** Impact of investment strategies on urbanism

urban development that is experiencing a continuous struggle to integrate quality within quantities.

The fragmentation of Doha's urban morphology has been identified by most interviewees as the main result of the recent construction boom (Fig. 6.7). Furthermore, the missing structure of interconnected centres and sub-centres and the decreasing quality of construction is seen as a major effect of the recent form of urbanism in Qatar. The contrast between vertical and low-rise developments was rated as a less important side effect of recent development tendencies.

## TOWARDS AN EFFECTIVE HUB VISION

Large-scale investments initiated by Qatar's ruling family have shaped contemporary Doha into one of the fastest growing cities in the world and a serious contender as an international hub in the region. The initial investments, however, followed no comprehensive strategy and were thus often carried out in a rather isolated manner from one another based on case-by-case decision-making. In contrast to other Gulf cities the construction boom in Doha was mainly ignited by the investment of oil and gas revenues, which led to an on-going transformation process of urban morphologies. Today, Doha is experienced as being more and more diverse and contrasted, offering a state-of-the-art waterfront and various architectural landmarks. However, the overall urban structure is more and more dominated by the fragmented clustering of single "island" developments, which have to a large extent replaced the cohesive old urban centre. The absence of coordinated planning has led to a disjointed urban landscape requiring an efficient network of centres and sub centres. Thus, the main challenges today are to reorganise urban governance by implementing holistic strategic plans in order to increase urban consolidation on the basis of large-scale investments in infrastructure.

Recently, many attempts have been made to strengthen urban governance towards more flexibility and efficiency regarding the implementation of investment strategies. In 2008 the General Secretariat of Development Planning published the Qatar National Vision (QNV), which introduced capacity development programmes for the public sector in order to achieve socio-economic development goals for 2030 (Qatar General Secretariat for Development Planning 2008). The QNV is currently being implemented via a five-year plan known as the Qatar National Development Strategy (QNDS—see Chapter 3) in order to guide socio-economic development (Qatar General Secretariat for Development Planning 2011). Due to the subsequent restructuring process of governmental institutions, the MMAA was reorganised to become the Ministry of Municipalities and Urban Planning (MMUP), and the previously founded Urban Planning Development Authority was pulled back under the umbrella of the ministry in 2009. The main reason for this move was a general attempt at minor decentralisation by avoiding institutions existing outside the ministerial structure. And, in order to diminish the negative impact of a lack of coordination in the future, the Central Planning Organisation (CPO) was established at the end of 2011 to enhance communication and coordination processes between various parties involved and to supervise the phasing of parallel infrastructural projects. In addition to this reorganisation of urban governance, physical planning is expected to evolve positively when the Qatar National Master Plan is implemented as a holistic strategic plan in accordance with the development goals of the QNDS (Fig. 6.8).

The Qatar National Master Plan addresses the particular challenges of urban development in Qatar by introducing a comprehensive set of key development objectives, strategies, and regulations. The Qatar National Master Plan is in line with the Qatar National Vision and contains two parts: the Qatar National Development Framework (QNDF) and the Municipal Spatial Development Plans (MSDP). The QNDF sets the strategic framework for sustainable development and establishes objectives, policies, and implementation actions that must be followed by all government ministries and authorities. It therefore provides a disciplined framework for making

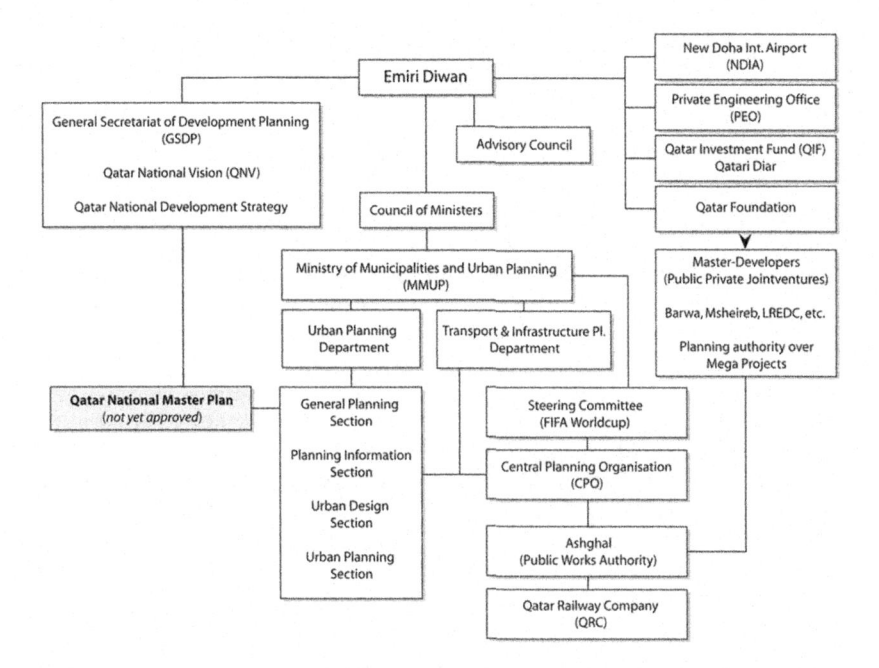

# FRAGMENTATION AND CONTINUITY IN QATAR'S URBANISM 175

**Fig. 6.8** The New Form of Urban Governance in Qatar. *Source*: Authors

spatial and land-use decisions to guide the development of Qatar until the year 2032 (Rahman 2014: 82). Its main spatial strategy is the introduction of a transit-oriented development based on a clear hierarchy of centres and sub-centres in order to reduce urban fragmentation and to integrate urban identity and diversity. The master plan has been elaborated by focusing on the macro-urban context and the main present challenge is its implementation in the case of specific areas and their development constraints. Thus, its future role in transforming Qatar's urban governance will depend greatly on the overall effectiveness, flexibility, and transparency of its comprehensive legal framework, which needs to become the new basis of every decision-making process concerning any major urban development.

**Acknowledgement** This study is developed as part of a comprehensive funded research project of the National Priorities Research Program, QNRF-Qatar National Research Fund (NPRP 09—1083—6—023). The project was concluded in May 2014.

## BIBLIOGRAPHY. QATAR: POLICY MAKING IN A TRANSFORMATIVE STATE

Adham, Khaled. 2008. Rediscovering the island: Doha's urbanity from pearls to spectacle. In *The Evolving Arab City*, ed. Yasser Elsheshtawy, 218–258. New York, NY: Routledge.
Friedmann, J. 1986. The world city hypothesis. *Development and Change* 17(1): 69–83.
Gardner, A. 2014. How the city grows: Urban growth and challenges to sustainable development in Doha, Qatar. In *Sustainable Development: An Appraisal from the Gulf Region*, ed. P. Sillitoe. New York: Berghahn Books.
General Secretariat for Development Planning (Qatar). 2008. *Qatar National Vision 2030*. Doha: Retrieved from http://www.gsdp.gov.qa/portal/page/portal/gsdp_en/knowledge_center/Tab/QNV2030_English_v2.pdfMinistry of Development Planning and Statistics (Qatar).
Naqy, S. 2006. Making room for migrants, making sense of difference: Spatial and ideological expression of social diversity in urban Qatar. *Urban Studies* 43(1): 119–137.
Neue Zuericher Zeitung. 2011. Deutscher Stahl und dunkle Schnuere. *NZZ Newspaper*, December 30.
Oxford Business Group. 2009. *The Report – Qatar 2009*. Oxford: Oxford Business Group.
Qatar Financial Centre. 2014. *Regulated Financial Services in the QFC*. Doha: Qatar Financial Centre.
Qatar Science and Technology Park. 2012. *Current Members*. Qatar Foundation Research and Development. Accessed January 8. http://www.qstp.org.qa/output/page54.asp
Qatar Statistical Authority (QSA). 2015. *Qatar Statistical Authority Database*. Doha, Qatar: Qatar Statistical Authority.
Rahman, K. 2014. The Qatar National Master Plan. In *Sustainable Development: An Appraisal from the Gulf Region*, ed. P. Sillitoe, 82–94. New York: Berghahn Books.
Rinnawi, K. 2006. *Instant Nationalism. McArabism, Al Jazeera and Transnational Media in the Arab World*. Lanham, MD: University Press of America.
Sakr, N. 2001. *Satellite Realms: Transnational Television, Globalization and the Middle East*. London: I.B.Tauris.
Salama, A.M., and F. Wiedmann. 2013b. *Demystifying Doha: On Architecture and Urbanism in an Emerging City*. Surrey, UK: Ashgate.
Sassen, S. 1996. *Metropolen des Weltmarktes: Die neue Rolle der Global Cities*. Frankfurt: Campus Verlag.
Scholz, F. 1999. *Die Kleinen Golfstaaten*. Gotha, Germany: Klett-Perthes Gotha und Stuttgart.

The Doha Debates. 2015. About the Debates. Accessed March 16. http://www.thedohadebates.com/pages/indexfb91.html?p=3259

Wiedmann, F. 2012. *Post-oil Urbanism in the Gulf.* Stuttgart, Germany: SVH Verlag.

Wiedmann, F., V. Mirincheva, and A.M. Salama. 2013. Urban reconfiguration and revitalisation: Public mega projects in Doha's historic centre. *Open House International* 38(4): 27–36.

CHAPTER 7

# Health Policy-Making in a Transformative State

*Faleh Mohamed Hussain Ali, Orsida Gjebrea, Chloe Sifton, Abdulrahman Alkuwari, and Rifat Atun*

## INTRODUCTION

Since 2000, Qatar has achieved one of the fastest economic growth rates in the world, with an average growth rate of 13.8 % per year over the past ten years.[1] Rapid economic development was accompanied by substantial improvements in population health.

---

F.M.H. Ali (✉)
Policy Affairs of the Supreme Council of Health (SCH), Doha, Qatar

O. Gjebrea
Office of the Assistant Secretary, Supreme Council of Health (SCH) Qatar, Doha, Qatar

C. Sifton
Supreme Council of Health (SCH) Qatar, Doha, Qatar

A. Alkuwari
Former Minister of Public Health, Qatar, Doha, Qatar

R. Atun
Harvard University, Cambridge, MA, USA

Harvard School of Public Health, Boston, MA, USA

© The Author(s) 2016
M.E. Tok et al. (eds.), *Policy-Making in a Transformative State*,
DOI 10.1057/978-1-137-46639-6_7

Driven primarily by reductions in all causes of mortality, between 2001 and 2012, average life expectancy at birth increased by 4.6 years to 79 years, exceeding the Gulf Cooperation Council (GCC) average of 77 years. Maternal and child mortality also declined significantly in the same period (Bener et al. 2013a, b; SCH 2015a). However, fast-paced development has also brought significant new challenges for Qatar's health system: rates of non-communicable diseases have rapidly risen, and the unprecedented population increase has placed substantial pressure on the health system's infrastructure and workforce (Ali et al. 2014).

Recognizing the importance of keeping pace with the country's rising healthcare demands and expectations, in 2008 the government made the health sector a top priority and committed itself to transforming it into a sustainable "world-class healthcare system" (GSDP 2008). To accelerate the massive reform overhaul, the Supreme Council of Health (SCH) was created in 2009, with superior decision-making resources to that of its predecessors, the National Health Authority and the Ministry of Public Health.

The aim of this chapter is to provide an overview of the Qatari health system's transformation and to assess its performance using the World Health Organization's (WHO) Health Systems Framework (WHO 2007). As shown in Fig. 7.1, in the WHO Framework a health system is conceptualized as six building blocks that include governance; financing; work-

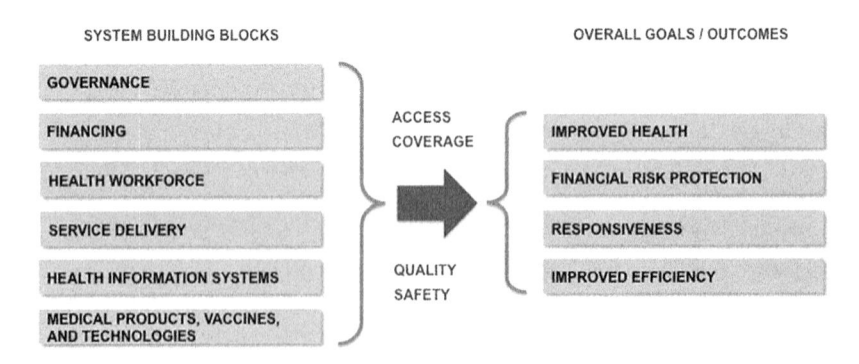

Fig. 7.1 WHO Health Systems Framework. *Source*: Adapted from WHO (2007)

force; service delivery; health information systems; and medical products, vaccines, and technologies. In a well-functioning health system, these components are effectively built to produce universal healthcare coverage that provides access to high quality and safe services to produce improved population health outcomes, financial protection against the costs of ill-health, satisfactory responsiveness to the legitimate expectations of the population, and improved efficiency throughout the health system. This chapter discusses Qatar's health system using the WHO Health Systems Framework and assesses achievements in relation to the six building blocks and system outputs.

## GOVERNANCE

Health governance refers to "a wide range of steering and rule-making related functions carried out by governments/decision-makers as they seek to achieve national health policy objectives that are conducive to universal health coverage" (WHO 2015a). This is a complex and critical building block, requiring both political and technical action to reconcile competing demands for limited resources against a backdrop of rising expectations of citizens (WHO 2007). Good health governance is characterized by "establishing effective accountability mechanisms; articulating the case for health in national development; detecting and correcting undesirable trends and distortions; maintaining the strategic direction of policy development and implementation; [and] regulating the behaviour of a wide range of actors" (WHO 2015a; Murray and Frenk 2000"collaborat[ion] with other sectors, including the private sector and civil society, to promote and maintain population health in a participatory and inclusive manner"). In addition, good health governance also involves (WHO 2015a). Good governance not only implies that citizens be able to participate in the decision-making process, but also be empowered to hold both the government and healthcare providers accountable (Fox et al. 2010; Brinkerhoff and Bossert 2008).

Between 1970 and 2005, the Ministry of Public Health (MPH) governed the country's health system and reported to the Council of Ministers (Law No. 5, 1970; Law No. 21, 2005). However, the ministry also provided primary care services and often shared leadership with the country's main hospital provider, Hamad Medical Corporation (HMC)

(Decree-Law No. 10, 1993; Decree No. 35, 1979; Al Binali 2015). While shared leadership helped optimize available resources, it also blurred the lines between the roles of regulator and provider, potentially hindering accountability and effective health governance. For this reason, in well-functioning health systems, health ministries often provide stewardship while separate bodies with different leadership manage financing and provision of health services (Boyle 2011; Anell et al. 2012).

Consequently, in 2005, the Government of Qatar established the National Health Authority (NHA) to govern the health sector as an independent organization, but it was still responsible to the Council of Ministers (Emiri Resolution No. 13, 2005). No longer responsible for primary care provision and headed by different leaders from those of HMC, the NHA's creation helped separate the roles of regulator and provider (Emiri Resolution No. 13, 2005; Resolution No. 22, 2005). Furthermore, the NHA incorporated the first departments for governing health financing, planning and assessment, e-health, and quality and research, introducing for the first time explicit accountability mechanisms for all WHO health system building blocks (Emiri Resolution No. 13, 2005; Decree-Law No. 10, 1993). Nevertheless, the extensive roles assigned to HMC upon its establishment and through subsequent legislation, including the transfer of responsibility for delivering public primary care services, eroded some of the intended split between regulator and provider (Decree No. 35, 1979; Resolution No. 22, 2005).

To further strengthen health governance, in 2009, the government established the Supreme Council of Health (SCH) to govern the health system with a unique governance model that has allowed for significant acceleration of the ambitious vision for world-class health care articulated as part of Qatar National Vision 2030, which was published in July 2008 (Emiri Decree No. 13, 2009; GSDP 2008). While the SCH continues to be responsible to the Council of Ministers, it is also vested with resources for enhanced decision-making, which is key to enabling a strong steering capacity in the face of rapid transformation. The Board was chaired by the then crown prince and now Emir of Qatar, His Highness Sheikh Tamim bin Hamad Al-Thani, until 2013, and since then it has been chaired by His Excellency the Prime Minister and Minister of Interior. Furthermore, the board Vice-Chair until 2014 was Her Highness Sheikha Moza bint Nasser, a driving force behind the country's social reforms over the last 15 years. Notably, health sector accountability and transparency has grown substantially since the SCH's establishment, with the SCH introducing SCH Annual Reports to track progress against published targets; the GCC's first National Health Accounts to track health expenditure annually; and Qatar Health Reports to monitor system inputs and outputs against policy context each year (SCH 2015a, b, c). In addition, Qatar ranks twenty-sixth out of over 170 countries in an independent transparency index for the public sector (including health), at the same level as France and higher ranked than several European countries (TI 2014).

Key to maintaining the strategic direction of health policy development, in 2010, the SCH set out to operationalize the health vision articulated in Qatar National Vision 2030. In line with participatory and inclusive health governance, SCH first identified undesirable system and population health trends and weaknesses, led by a multi-sectoral SCH committee and based on the largest stakeholder consultations in the history of Qatar's health governance (SCH 2010, 2011a). Subsequently aiming to reverse these trends, the SCH launched the country's first National Health Strategy (NHS) 2011–2016 in April 2011 (SCH 2011b). A cross-cutting plan, the National Health Strategy 2011–2016 outlined seven goals for improving all system building blocks, namely, a comprehensive world-class health system; an integrated health system; enhanced preventative health care; a skilled health workforce; a national health policy; effective, affordable, and fair financing; and enhanced research governance (SCH 2014a). The National Health Strategy was followed by the development of five specialist action plans for the priority areas of cancer, cancer research, primary care, and mental health under National Health Strategy Goal 1, and laboratory integration under National Health Strategy Goal 2, to help maintain the system's strategic direction (SCH 2011c, 2012; PHCC 2013; SCH 2013a, 2014b). Notably, in a 2013 study, Qatar was found to have the one of the most clearly articulated health visions among Australia, Brazil, England, India, South Africa, Spain, and the United States (Darzi and Parston 2013).

The inclusive and transparent governance of the National Health Strategy implementation underscores several challenges and achievements in maintaining the strategic direction of policy implementation, key to good health governance. (Panel 7.1)

*Panel 7.1 Implementation of the Qatar National Health Strategy*
The National Health Strategy was divided into 35 Projects with 203 outputs, as of 31 March 2015 (SCH 2015d). Their implementation is led by 35 dedicated project managers and governed by a monthly steering group and quarterly ministerial board (SCH 2013b). While only the largest public providers are represented in both project implementation and program governance, this is to temporarily optimize available sector policy resources. To uphold the regulator-provider split, the SCH maintains overwhelming representation, and an SCH National Health Strategy program management office provides daily monitoring of implementation, including risk monitoring (SCH 2014c). For enhanced accountability and transparency, each year since 2011, the SCH has published updated National Health Strategy plans and held dedicated events. According to surveyed attendees, over 85 % rated the 2014 annual event as good or excellent (SCH 2014d). Reflective of public perceptions that "patient voice and patient care are held at the core of the NHS," patients have also taken note of initiatives to reduce waiting times and provide excellent customer service (SCH 2014e). As of 31 December 2014, 55 % of National Health Strategy outputs were complete, up from 40 % the previous year (SCH 2015b).

As in most other developed health systems, the SCH also regulates all public, semi-public, and private providers and additionally funds and oversees Qatar's largest providers (SCH 2015b; PHCC 2014). Of note, in 2012, the Primary Health Care Corporation was established to provide public primary care independently of HMC, reducing provider/regulator overlap (Emiri Decree No. 15, 2012). While funding of public providers by the government in and of itself is not problematic as long as there is a level playing field between public and private providers (Chernichovsky 2000), private providers have claimed in National Health Strategy project stakeholder consultations that the HMC and Primary Health Care Corporation are difficult to compete with because of the government support afforded to them. Importantly, however, by 2016, as will all other healthcare service providers, HMC and Primary Health Care Corporation will be funded through the new national health insurance scheme which was first implemented in 2013, clearly delineating the roles of providers, financer, and the regulator. A key indicator for responsive and inclusive governance—patient satisfaction—is high across public and private providers, indicating effective provider regulation (SCH 2015b).

As part of its remit, the SCH also regulates providers through licensing of facilities and devices. It introduced facility accreditation standards, which it is integrating with licensing standards for a streamlined process (SCH 2014a). Notably, by the end of 2014, all but one of the country's hospitals had received international accreditation by an organization accredited by the International Society for Quality in Healthcare (SCH 2015b). In addition, SCH has introduced a medical device regulatory framework, and it is on schedule to achieve its target of 100 % device regulation by end of 2015 (SCH 2013b). Meanwhile, regulation and accreditation of health professionals was transferred to the semi-independent Qatar Council for Healthcare Practitioners, which the SCH established in 2013 to improve accountability and effectiveness (Emiri Decree No. 7, 2013; SCH 2015b). Funded by the SCH and governed by an independent board, the establishment of Qatar Council for Healthcare Practitioners is in line with international trends toward greater independence of regulatory bodies (DH 2007; CHRE 2009). Previously, and owing to limited resources, public and semi-public providers were exempted from licensing and vetted their own workforce, resulting in unstandardized regulation (Law No. 5 of 2001). By 31 December 2014, however, the Qatar Council for Healthcare Practitioners had notably engaged 100 % of its practitioners in licensing and successfully licensed 72 % of HMC practitioners, 83 % of Primary Health Care Corporation (PHCC) practitioners, and nearly 100 % of semi-public practitioners (SCH 2015b; QCHP 2015a). Since 2013, the QCHP has also introduced retrospective verification of practitioners licensed prior to 2009, to further strengthen and standardize regulation and oversight (SCH 2015b).

Importantly, to meet any vital gaps in health services and detect and correct health risks, the SCH does have the responsibility to provide a limited number of clinical services. However, in order to uphold the separation between regulator and provider, it not only outsources the delivery of these services to other healthcare service providers, but also applies the same regulatory and monitoring mechanisms as to all other providers. For example, the SCH provides most of the clinical and other screening tests (for communicable diseases) for new expatriates and persons working in high-risk professions. In addition, it provides vaccinations and immunization services, with high average population coverage rates of 96.1 %

(SCH 2015a). High immunization coverage and screening for infectious diseases has enabled Qatar to achieve one of the world's lowest communicable disease rates, despite having the world's second highest proportion of migrant population (UN 2013; SCH 2015a). In 2013, Qatar's overall communicable disease rate was 958 per 100,000 population, which represents a 46 % annual decline (SCH 2015a). Since 2012, the SCH has outsourced many of these screening services to private providers, and it has now also transferred oversight and delivery of immunization to the Primary Health Care Corporation. In 2010, it began delivering through the private sector onsite specialized healthcare services for single male laborers (SML) in higher risk occupations and communal habitation in remote areas (SCH 2015b). According to the International Labour Organization (ILO), higher risk occupations include those in construction, mining, and agriculture sectors (ILO 2004). Between 2012 and 2014, publicly provided healthcare service coverage for SML increased from 44 to 60 %, their satisfaction of health services increased from 66 to 72 % (see Fig. 7.2), and their burden of out-of-pocket health spend from household spend decreased from 1.8 to 0.5 %—proxies for effective, inclusive, and responsive governance (SCH 2013c, 2014f, 2015b).

Consistent with the need for government intervention and regulation in regards to public goods, the SCH also provides a number of non-

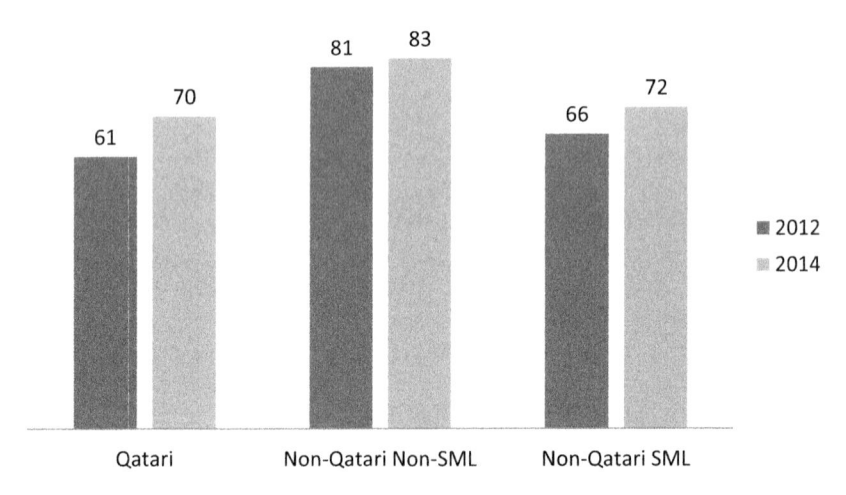

**Fig. 7.2** Patient Satisfaction, by Nationality, 2012–2014. *Source*: SCH (2013c, 2014f)

clinical services that have high social value and attract low private sector interest (Myles 1995). These services include tests for drug quality, public health, food, water, other consumables, and air quality. Notably, a separate Food Safety Authority that is estimated for completion by 2016 will help to further enhance governance and provision of services that have high social value (SCH 2013b), as the Food Safety Authority can "adopt scientific opinions free from any inappropriate influence" and provide them to decision-makers (EFSA 2015). The testing and regulation for monitoring air quality is conducted in coordination with the Ministry of Environment, resulting in some regulatory overlaps and gaps. To streamline governance, the SCH is clarifying its role and functions, sharing data with the Ministry of Environment, and monitoring implementation of environmental health initiatives through monthly steering committee meetings (SCH 2013b).

With respect to inclusiveness, a key aspect of good health governance, the SCH has developed various initiatives, including the first Patient Bill of Rights in the most common languages; a patient advocacy framework that encourages patients to exercise their rights; a national e-complaints system; the establishment of patient consultative councils; and a new website ranked highest by local civil society for connecting people with disabilities (SCH 2014g, 2015b; WHO 2007). The SCH has also created a national feedback portal called the Government Health Communication Centre to increase patient engagement, through which SCH received 210 % more feedback in 2014 than 2013 (SCH 2015b).

The noteworthy progress in Qatar's health governance in recent years has been underpinned by the development of strategic policy and its timely implementation, establishment of effective accountability mechanisms, strong independent regulation of health actors, increased transparency, and substantially improved patient involvement. This is significant as it impacts the ability of the health system to carry out its other functions and meet its objectives (Fox et al. 2010). At the same time, however, some governance challenges remain. As with all regulators, there is a need for improved coordination and alignment of roles and responsibilities across relevant stakeholders and the National Health Strategy projects (SCH 2013b), especially with regard to reforms that require policy changes that involve regulators beyond the SCH (e.g., ministries of environment, education, and labor), with whom the SCH is working to collaboratively review progress of projects.

Given the scale of the health reforms, there is a need to develop greater human resource capacity within the SCH to ensure successful and timely implementation of the National Health Strategy and other strategies (SCH 2013b). The SCH needs to recruit additional staff to develop capacity by offering competitive remuneration and professional development opportunities. Human resource issues are further discussed below in the Workforce section.

While Qatar has made substantial progress on patient involvement in recent years, the SCH should continually strive to more directly and concretely involve patients, possibly through the inclusion of patients on boards and committees that hold decision-making power for planning, financing, and provision of health services to further enhance inclusive governance.

FINANCING

A good health financing system "raises adequate funds for health, in ways that ensure people can use needed services, and are protected from financial catastrophe or impoverishment associated with having to pay for them" (WHO 2007).

Since 2005, total health expenditure (THE) in Qatar has increased fivefold over the last decade (see Fig. 7.3) (SCH 2015c). By 2013, the per capita health expenditure was US $2504 based on Qatar's total popula-

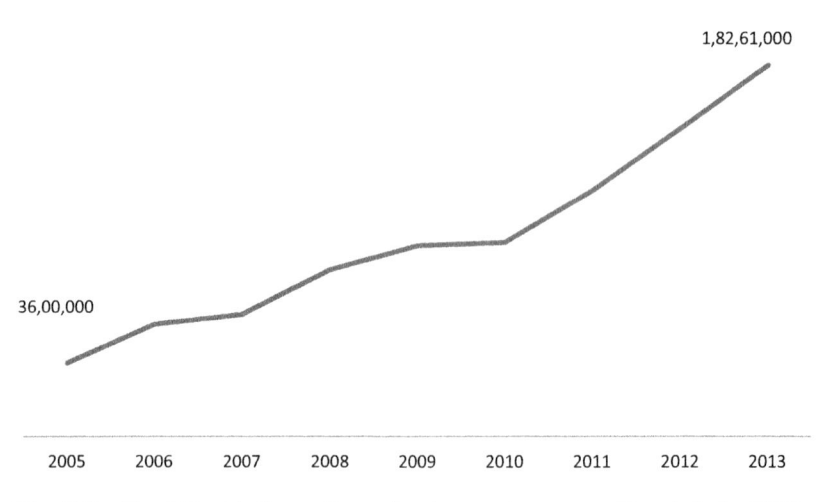

Fig. 7.3 Total Health Expenditure (in thousands, current Qatari riyals, 2005–2013. *Source*: SCH 2015c, 2014h

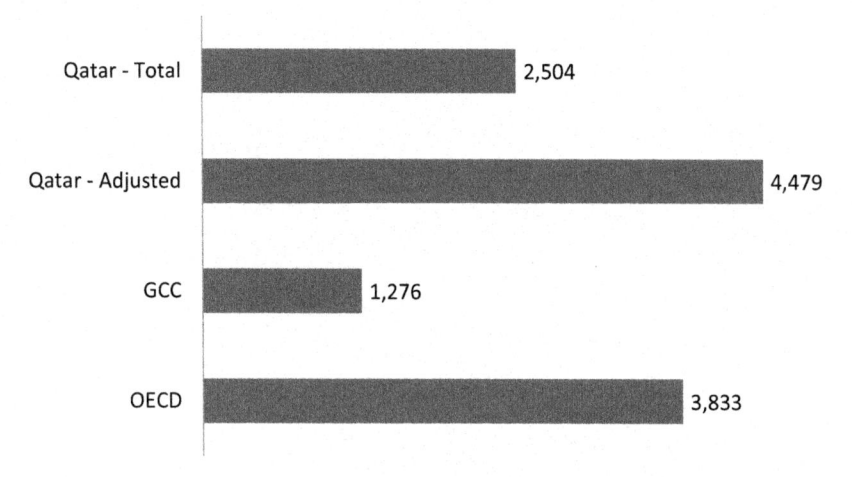

| Category | Value |
|---|---|
| Qatar - Total | 2,504 |
| Qatar - Adjusted | 4,479 |
| GCC | 1,276 |
| OECD | 3,833 |

**Fig. 7.4** THE per Capita (current US dollars at average exchange rate), 2013. Source: SCH (2015a). *Note*: OECD and GCC estimates are based on 2012 data (SCH 2015a)

tion and US $4479 after adjusting for the skewed age and sex distribution of Qatar's population (see Fig. 7.4) (SCH 2015a). This adjustment is done to account for Qatar's skewed population structure (predominantly young and male due to migrant workers) when making international comparisons, by replacing the non-national male population aged 25–60 years with the equivalent age and sex structure from five regions (i.e., Northern Africa, Asia, Eastern Europe, Latin America, and the Caribbean) for populations 30 years of age or more (1979–2008) (SCH 2011a). Notably, Qatar's adjusted THE per capita was higher than 2012 GCC and OECD averages (SCH 2015a).

Importantly, however, while Qatar has historically maintained some of the world's highest levels of financial risk protection across all socio-economic groups (see Figs. 7.5 and 7.6) and populations that do not have financial coverage can normally access public providers for essential care, voluntary public insurance coverage that has been in place since 1965 had led to fragmented coverage of health services over time due to voluntary opt-outs (SCH 2015c; Decree-Law No. 6, 1965; Law No. 7, 1996). To address fragmentation of financing and service coverage the SCH has been undertaking substantial changes to the ways revenue is collected, pooled,

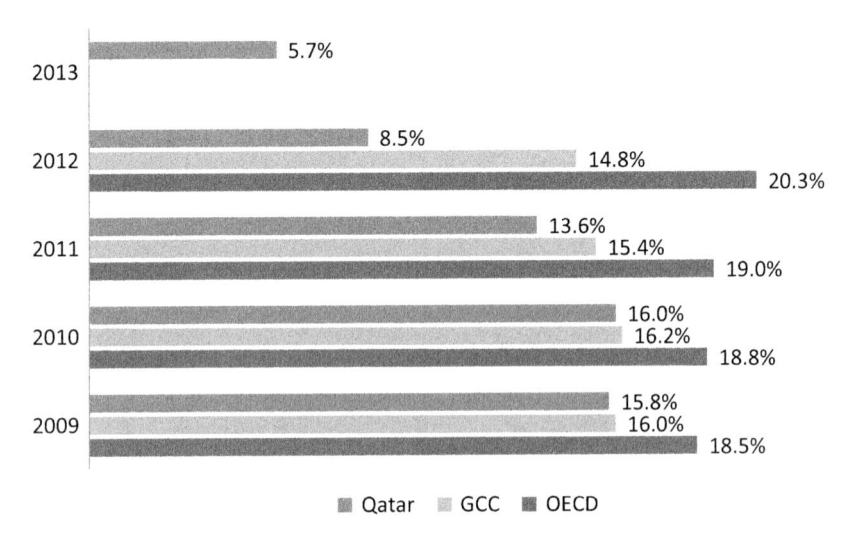

Fig. 7.5 Out-of-Pocket Health Spending as a Share of THE (%), 2009–2013. *Source*: SCH (2015c, 2014g)

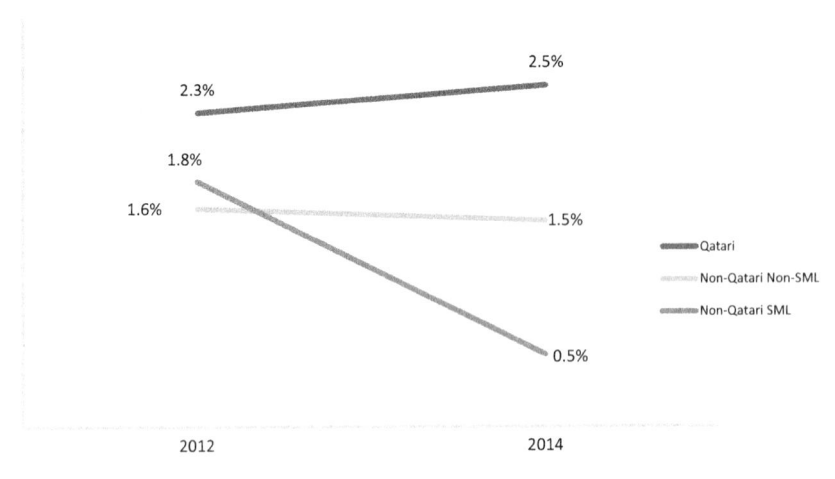

Fig. 7.6 Burden of Health Spending (% household spending), by Nationality and Occupation, 2012–2014. *Source*: SCH (2015b)

and allocated under the National Health Strategy Goal 6 that is dedicated to developing effective and affordable services with partnership of citizens in bearing part of the costs of healthcare services (SCH 2015b). Most notably, the SCH is implementing Seha, covering all nationals as part of a new Qatar's National Health Insurance Program. Under the scheme, mandatory coverage for a broad set of services across public and private providers is expected to be extended to all nationals and non-nationals by 2016 (SCH 2014a). This is consistent with the public/private mix of healthcare provision in most developed health insurance systems, in which all residents of a country have financial coverage (Busse and Blumel 2014; Chevreul et al. 2010; Ferre et al. 2014; Hofmarcher 2013). Notably, Qatar will become the first GCC country to cover all nationals and non-nationals under a single health insurance scheme, placing the country at the forefront of UN and WHO resolutions calling for universal health coverage (WHO 2011; UN 2012). Launched in July 2013, the National Health Insurance Scheme covered all the nationals by April 2014 (see Fig. 7.7), with more than 170 public and private providers joining the scheme's network in 2014, and 222 by July 2015 (SCH 2015b). It is expected to cover all non-nationals by the end of 2016.

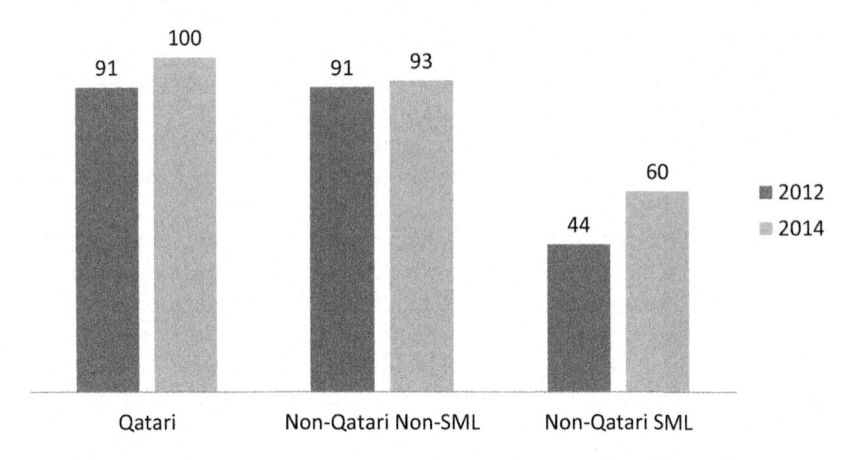

Fig. 7.7 Healthcare Coverage (%), by Nationality, 2012–2014. *Source*: SCH (2013c, 2014f)

## Collection

The majority of healthcare in Qatar is financed from general government revenues, which are largely raised through oil and gas exports. In 2013, Qatar's general government expenditure on health as a share of total health expenditure was 87.9 %, a 15.7 % increase since 2009 (SCH 2015c, 2011d). This proportion is higher than both the GCC and OECD averages of 76.0 % and 72.3 %, respectively (SCH 2015c). While the rise in government revenue contributions reflects population growth, large-scale reforms, and rising expectations, it also reflects low contributions from other actors—a situation which is unsustainable in the longer term. For instance, the funding provided by employers for healthcare services has been low and adherence to requirements laid out in the 2004 Labour Law for onsite care inconsistent through patchy adherence (Law No. 14, 2004). Under the country's new national health insurance scheme, however, the government will continue to finance health coverage for nationals, while employers will finance non-nationals (Law No. 7, 2013). This rebalancing of financing is in keeping with local expectations, as reflected in the views expressed during the National Health Insurance scheme's design phase from employers, providers, and the general public (SCH 2010). The introduction of employer contributions to public health coverage is in keeping with international best practice for cost-sharing and financial risk solidarity to uphold equity (Saltman et al. 2004). To uphold employer financial protection and to disincentivize shifting of costs to employees in the form of reduced wages, the SCH has included appropriate provisions in the law that bans such cost-shifting, and it is working to develop progressive and sustainable cost-sharing arrangements for employers in 2015 (Law No. 7, 2013; SCH 2015b).

Under the old health financing scheme, individuals made minor contributions: annual health card fees that cost US $2.75 for nationals and US $27.47 for non-nationals (HFID 2015). Social health insurance contributions are abolished under the new scheme, making Seha one of the world's most generous and equitable health benefit designs, especially considering the large expatriate population. Under the new health insurance scheme there will be nominal cost-sharing by users, though this is largely to disincentivize misuse of health services, such as for certain pharmaceuticals and cosmetic care (Thomson et al. 2010). The low levels of cost-sharing and comprehensive benefits are in keeping with international best practice, as in the United Kingdom, as high user charges can deter use of necessary care (OECD 2013; Newhouse 1993; Lohr et al. 1986; Xu et al. 2005). Notably, as shown in Figs. 7.6 and 7.7, out-of-pocket expenditure in Qatar is among the lowest in the world.

*Pooling*

Under the old health financing scheme, revenue was not pooled since it was not collected. Under Seha, however, the revenues collected from the government and employers will be centralized into a single pool, to avoid revenue fragmentation, increase finance transparency, and lower administrative costs through economies of scale and avoidance of complex and unproven risk-adjustment mechanisms (Chernichovsky and van de Ven 2003; Oliver 1999). The revenue pooling is consistent with high-performing health systems such as the United Kingdom, Sweden, Denmark, and Norway (Mossialos et al. 2015). Furthermore, the European experience suggests that risk and income solidarity in health systems contributes to social cohesion, a valuable outcome for Qatar's diverse population (Saltman et al. 2004).

*Purchasing*

Under the old health financing scheme, healthcare service purchasing was highly fragmented and inefficient. Public providers were largely paid through advance governmental block budgets, with no link to performance or market forces. Private providers were largely paid through private health insurance and out-of-pocket payments, with no link to performance or affordability. Under the new health insurance scheme, however, a single national purchaser, the National Health Insurance Company (NHIC), established by the SCH in 2013, will purchase healthcare services. This new purchasing arrangement will allow for more efficient purchasing through monopsonistic gains in negotiating service prices at a national level, and reimbursing providers following service to ensure purchasing of high-quality, medically necessary services and against the same and annually updated prices, thus incentivizing competition through quality enhancements, not pricing (Anderson et al. 2003; Figueras et al. 2005; Law No. 7, 2013). As a commercial government-owned entity with its own independent board, the creation of NHIC ensures regulator/purchaser split, while introducing private sector efficiencies in purchasing (Simonet 2011). Importantly, however, the regulatory role for defining benefits, beneficiaries, premiums, and fees remains with the SCH, while the NHIC is responsible for procurement subject to SCH approval (NHIC 2015a, b). Of note, in 2014, the NHIC incorporated fraud and abuse controls, conducted audits, and effected recoveries, and in 2015, the SCH closed the first clinic for misuse (SCH 2015b).

With regard to provider payment, providers are paid after service provision and at the same price. In addition, in line with international best practice, plans are underway to reimburse hospitals on the basis of Australian Refined Diagnosis-Related Groups (AR-DRGs)—a form of prospective, case-based payment in which hospitals are paid a flat rate for each patient they treat depending on the nature of the patient's illness (Busse et al. 2011). In order to improve quality through financial incentives, the SCH is also developing a pay-for-performance framework and measurement system in 2015 (see below under Service Delivery, Monitoring) (SCH 2015b). Given the challenges associated with financial incentives, such as gaming and improved reporting without any corresponding quality improvement, performance-linked provider payments will need to be designed carefully and closely linked to improvements in health outcomes. For example, the incentives should not be "excessively" large in size, and they may be more effective when given continuously rather than in an annual bonus (Nolte and McKee 2008).

## WORKFORCE

A well-performing health workforce "works in ways that are responsive, fair and efficient to achieve the best health outcomes possible, given available resources and circumstances (i.e. there are sufficient numbers and mix of staff, fairly distributed; they are competent, responsive, and productive)" (WHO 2007).

Qatar's health sector employs over 28,000 health professionals across nearly 250 regulated scopes of practice (SCH 2015a, e). Similar to other sectors, the health sector is dependent on an imported workforce, with non-nationals accounting for over 90 % of workers and domestic graduates totaling around 150 annually (SCH 2015f; MDPS 2014a, b). The result is a workforce more vulnerable to global shortages and regional competition (SCH 2015a, f). This shortage is further complicated by salary constraints in the public sector (over 65 % of the workforce) and resource-intensive licensing and immigration processes typical for such an international workforce (Law No. 8, 2009; SCH 2015f). With Qatar's population expected to grow considerably leading up to the 2022 World Cup, these challenges will be intensified as a larger health workforce will be needed to serve a larger population.

Despite a growth in the health workforce of more than 60 % in the past five years, workforce density, which is an important indicator of workforce availability, service coverage, and health outcomes, remains low as the population outpaces workforce gains (SCH 2011a, 2015a). In 2013, the health workforce density was 21.3 physicians, 61.8 nurses, 10.1 pharmacists and assistants, and 6.2 dentists per 10,000 population (SCH 2015a). While having higher than GCC average workforce densities, except for physicians, these figures are lower than OECD averages. When the adjusted population is used, however, Qatar's health workforce densities exceed both GCC and OECD averages (SCH 2015a). In addition, as noted previously, the health system's responsiveness, as measured by patient satisfaction, remains high across providers and nationalities (SCH 2013c, 2014f).

To achieve its goal of a skilled national workforce in line with WHO guidance, the SCH has prioritized workforce planning, recruitment and retention, education and training, and regulation (WHO 2007; SCH 2014a). As part of its efforts to build national workforce planning capacity, the SCH has completed Qatar's first National Health Workforce Plan and modeling tool (SCH 2015f). Similar to developments in OECD countries, the plan covers needed actions across major policy areas to meet health workforce gaps and to guide provider expansion (Ono et al. 2013). The tool projects workforce gaps up to 2033 for 26 categories, and it is integrated with service and facility modeling tools to synchronize national planning and decision-making. With a current overall workforce gap projection of over 30,000 by 2033, recruitment of these workers is a key challenge, which is compounded by the risk that population growth may exceed projections.

An important component of National Health Workforce Plan relates to enhancing recruitment and retention of both Qatari and non-Qatari health professionals. The SCH is also supporting staged improvements to health workforce recruitment and retention in line with international best practice and experience (Henderson and Tulloch 2008; ICN 2008). Specifically, the SCH is initially assessing current salaries to determine competitive remuneration, establishing defined career progression pathways for promotions, and creating staff exchange programs for international experience (SCH 2015b). These will first be implemented in the public sector, with the aim of expanding to the rest of the health sector.

In addition, in order to develop a more sustainable domestic workforce and reduce the country's reliance on foreign health professionals, SCH will be promoting health professional education and training within Qatar. Focusing on public campaigns to encourage youth, particularly Qatari nationals, to enter the health professions, SCH plans for this to be supported by more financial and employment assistance through sponsorship arrangements, more local education and training, and continuing professional development opportunities. In line with these priorities, Qatar University is opening a new medical school in late 2015 (Walker 2014). However, it will take time for new and existing local institutes, such as medical and pharmacy schools, to develop more local capacity. Even with the new medical school, however, the health sector will continue to rely primarily on international professionals if current population trends remain the same.

The SCH has enhanced national workforce regulation with the establishment of QCHP in 2013. Of note, the QCHP has introduced provisional licenses for all health professionals to expedite the registration and licensing process while ensuring sufficient regulation (QCHP 2015b). Despite the enhanced regulation to ensure patient safety and promote quality, there is an ongoing need to better manage and incentivize the workforce to provide more responsive and efficient services through quality improvement initiatives discussed below.

## Service Delivery

Service delivery forms the backbone of all health systems. Given that the health service delivery building block is "concerned with how inputs and services are organized and managed, to ensure access, quality, safety and continuity of care," this section focuses on service planning, organization, provision, and monitoring (WHO 2007). Several studies have shown high and similar service access between nationals and non-nationals in Qatar, such as no differences between the probability of having a usual source of care (Hussin and Ali 2010; Hussin et al. 2015).

## Planning

Qatar's health infrastructure has experienced similar population pressures to that placed on the health workforce. Due to rapid population increases, between 2005 and 2009, there was a 43 % decline in hospital bed density despite an increase in the number of hospital beds (SCH 2011a). While hospital bed density has not decreased since 2009, as a result of the addition of three new hospitals, it is still below the OECD average, and the significant amount of time and resources required for establishing hospitals and other facilities means that population growth could continue to outpace the expansion of infrastructure (SCH 2015a). This imbalance represents a critical challenge for the health system given the crucial importance of adequate infrastructure availability (WHO 2007). For example, in spite of continued investments in 2013 the number of MRI and CT scanners per one million population in Qatar were 13.0 and 7.0 respectively—lower than the corresponding OECD averages in 2012 of 13.9 and 23.7 per million population (SCH 2014i; OECD 2014).

In order to address the imbalance between population growth and the expansion of the health facilities, the SCH has developed long-term infrastructure planning based on population and health needs, to ensure an appropriate number, balance, and distribution of facilities and other infrastructure. In 2013, the SCH published the first Qatar Healthcare Facilities Master Plan (QHFMP) 2013–2033, one of the longest-term planning strategies in the world (SCH 2014i). The plan outlines the numbers, types, locations, and projected costs for required hospitals, health centers, pharmacies and major medical equipment until 2033, based on population and inpatient and outpatient service projections. The Master Plan is accompanied by a geographic information system application, which updates facility and service projections on the basis of live morbidity and mortality statistics obtained from National Health Insurance Scheme claims (SCH 2015b). Guided by the QHFMP, SCH, with HMC and PHCC, Qatar is planning to open 25 health centers, 11 hospitals, and 82 other new and refurbished facilities by 2022 (SCH 2015b). As with workforce gaps, however, there is a risk that real population growth may exceed projections, and as such, infrastructure expansion may be unable to keep pace. The SCH needs to continually enhance and refine its projection models and ensure the allocation of sufficient financial resources for infrastructure expansion projects.

## Organization

Qatar's healthcare system has been historically centered around hospital services (SCH 2011b). The population has unrestricted access to hospital specialists, unlike many countries that employ a referral process for non-emergency care, frequently making hospitals the first point of contact despite primary care often being the most appropriate setting (SCH 2011b; Saltman et al. 2006). Around 50 % of Qatar's health spending is devoted to hospital inpatient care compared with 37 % OECD average. By contrast, only 14 % is devoted to primary care and hospital outpatient services (SCH 2015c).

The SCH is trying to rebalance the distribution of healthcare services with an emphasis on more prevention and primary care, especially in light of the increase in non-communicable diseases and risk factors as the country has developed (IHME 2013; Bener et al. 2012; Mamtani et al. 2011; Bener et al. 2013a, b; Al-Thani et al. 2014). The rebalancing includes strong public health governance, and expanded health promotion activities, including launching the country's first large-scale public health campaign (Ali et al. 2014; SCH 2013d, 2015b). The National Primary Health Care Strategy 2013–2018 was also launched to establish primary care as the first point of contact, with sufficient capacity to be the foundation of care (PHCC 2013). The strategy includes 64 recommendations to achieve this, covering strengthened prevention services, specialized clinics for priority conditions, and a referral process for non-emergency care. A key part of the strategy given the importance of primary care in maternal and child health, the Primary Health Care Corporation is improving its antenatal and child health care services, piloting new care models that include additional services and checkups, disease screening, and clinical guidelines (SCH 2015b). According to the latest available estimates (2012), more than 91 % of women are seen at least once by skilled personnel during pregnancy, 85 % are seen at least four times, 100 % have a skilled attendant at delivery, and 99 % have an institutional delivery (SCH 2015a). In 2013, there were no maternal deaths recorded in Qatar, down from 8.3 deaths per 100,000 live births in 2001 (SCH 2015a). Similarly, service delivery improvements have helped to reduce child mortality from 12.1 to 7.8 deaths per 1000 live births between 2001 and 2013, (SCH 2015a).

SCH is also focusing on more specialized hospital care, which will be complemented by stronger prevention and primary care capacity in the healthcare system. Hospital services are being reconfigured to shift less specialized services to community-based and home-based care, and to centralize specialized services to retain core clinical mass based on international evidence on appropriate care settings (NHS England 2014; Medeiros et al. 2008). A continuing care strategy and pilot are being developed, which will emphasize community-based and home-based care in line with international developments (SCH 2015b; Nolte et al. 2014). The SCH has also launched a National Laboratory Integration and Standardization Strategy 2013–2018, which will support the coherent development of centralized high-quality laboratory services (SCH 2013a). As a sign of improved efficiency in delivering high-quality hospital care, the national ambulance service had surpassed 2016 response targets by 2013, with close to 90 % of calls responded to within 10 minutes (SCH 2015b).

To support the rebalancing of healthcare service provision, the SCH has developed strategies for priority conditions across the care spectrum. For example, the SCH launched the National Cancer Strategy 2011–2016 to enhance cancer services. As part of the Cancer Strategy, the first population-based national cancer screening program is being established in primary care in line with international best practice, which emphasizes the effectiveness of such programs for early detection and treatment of breast, cervical, and colorectal cancers (EC 2014). Targets were also set for timely access to cancer services in hospital care. These targets are one of the world's highest, with the aim of 80 % of patients seen by a hospital specialist within 48 hours of referral from screening and primary care, and 95 % of patients diagnosed within two weeks following referral. In 2014, adherence to these targets was close at 73 % of patients being seen by a hospital specialist with 48 hours, and 88 % diagnosed with two weeks following referral (SCH 2015b). The SCH also launched the Qatar National Mental Health Strategy 2013–2018 (QNMHS) to enhance mental health services, and it is planning a strategy for diabetes and oral health services. These strategies also build on other prevention, primary care, and hospital care reforms outlined in the NHS.

Importantly, however, full implementation of the future model of care, which calls for a shift toward more prevention and primary care as well as greater integration of care, will be challenging to achieve until primary care is fully strengthened and there is greater coordination across the health system. In particular, there is a need for the adoption of a family medicine model of care in which patients are treated more holistically by the same doctor on an ongoing basis as a family unit. Of note, the challenges associated with full strengthening of primary care are cross-cutting across health system building blocks and include having well-trained primary care professionals, sufficient health centers in place, adequate quality performance measurement, provider adaptation to new reforms, and integrated health information technology systems, which are discussed throughout the chapter. In addition, there is a risk that patients will be resistant to changes in the care delivery model and continue to seek hospital care, which can be mitigated with the introduction of a primary care gatekeeping system to reduce overreliance on specialist care. Lastly, despite the NHS' commitment to primary care, the allocation of financial resources across the care spectrum remains an important challenge. The SCH should continue to support the expansion of primary care.

*Provision*

While there is a mix of public, semi-public, and private providers in Qatar, the health system has historically been dominated by the public sector (Law No. 7, 1996). The eight public hospitals operated by HMC provide 75 % of all inpatient care, 27 % of outpatient care, and 87.4 % of hospital beds in Qatar (HMC 2015, 2014; SCH 2015a, b). The 21 health centers operated by PHCC provide 39 % of all outpatient care (SCH 2015b). The remaining services are provided by a combination of private, semi-public, and smaller public providers.

Public or private health care service provision can be used to ensure appropriate capacity as long as there is a level playing field to ensure competition, good measurement of health system performance, and suitable regulation to avoidance of private sector market niches and public sector bureaucracy (Chernichovsky 2000). The SCH is seeking to ensure these criteria are in place by moving toward the same regulatory standards and payment mechanisms across all providers. The SCH, with Primary Health Care Corporation, is also more actively encouraging the involvement of the private sector by outsourcing the operation of ten facilities to private providers through competitive processes. The new Seha network, which includes both public and private providers, is also facilitating this and is expected to increase provider responsiveness, efficiency, and quality by encouraging competition among providers, while upholding patient choice (Seha 2015). Notably, all healthcare service providers participating in the scheme have to sign a Provider Network Agreement with the NHIC and fulfill certain requirements to ensure patient safety and quality (discussed below).

In 2013, the average bed occupancy rate, an indicator of hospital efficiency, was 70.3 % overall, but as high as 96 % in one of the public hospitals and as low as 24 % in one of the private hospitals (SCH 2015a). A similar trend is seen for average length of stay, which was 4.3 days overall, 8.3 days in public hospitals, and 2.1 days in private hospitals. The uneven bed occupancy and average length of stay across hospitals suggest that there is some spare capacity, particularly in the private sector, which could be used to partly address the growing population and increasing healthcare demands with the appropriate service reconfiguration.

### *Monitoring*

Ensuring high-quality care is one of the defining components of good health service delivery (WHO 2007). Until recently, however, health providers had been largely responsible for upholding their own voluntary quality standards and identifying improvements (SCH 2013b). Providers were required to meet facility licensing requirements to operate, which the SCH enforced through announced and unannounced inspections, consistent with practices in leading regulatory agencies (SCH 2015b; FDA 2015; CQC 2015). In 2011, the SCH mandated accreditation for all private hospitals by 2015 by assessment organizations accredited by the International Society for Quality in Health Care (iSQua). By 2014, all but one private hospital had been accredited by iSQua-accredited assessment organizations (Accreditation Canada International, Australian Council of Healthcare Standards), and the remaining one was under progress. The HMC and PHCC had achieved accreditation by iSQua-accredited assessment organizations (Joint Commission International and Accreditation Canada International), and PHCC achieved platinum level in 2014

Given the need for additional guidance and oversight, the SCH is establishing national clinical guidelines, mandatory quality reporting, and accreditation standards based on international best practice as these promote improvements in care quality and safety through more robust monitoring and greater standardization of practice across providers (SCH 2013b; Nolte et al. 2014; Busse et al. 2010). By the end of 2016, the SCH will pilot national clinical guidelines focused on priority conditions, ensuring all providers have access to the best clinical evidence (SCH 2015b). In 2014, all of the major providers signed health service performance agreements with the SCH, requiring regular data submission on 25 hospital and 15 primary care quality indicators. The providers' performance will be audited based on these indicators, with the ultimate goal of linking the results to incentives at a later stage. To mitigate adaptation challenges, SCH trained providers to collect and report on the key performance indicators, and they should provide timely feedback once auditing commences. Further, providers in the Seha network must now also fulfill additional quality requirements, including the ability to capture clinical coding data and SCH minimum dataset specifications (HFID 2015). In addition, the SCH has established national facility accreditation standards, which will be integrated with the licensing process and apply to all providers, to ensure consistency in quality standards (SCH 2015b).

The available data suggest that progress is being made in. HMC, which provides over three-quarters of all hospital care in the country, has been performing well across several important patient safety indicators. HMC trauma rates for normal deliveries remained below the OECD averages in 2014, and HMC's medical reconciliation rate at admission was almost 100 % (SCH 2015b). In addition, the number of unplanned HMC readmissions after discharge from intensive care in 2014 remained low and declined by 11 % from 2013—an indication not only of improved patient safety but also greater efficiency in the use of clinical resources (SCH 2015b). Furthermore, the proportion of diabetic patients tested for glycated hemoglobin (HbA1C) as well as receiving foot and eye examinations at HMC and PHCC, which collectively account for two-thirds of all outpatient care, remained at 90–100 % in 2014, in line with international best practice (SCH 2015b).

## Information Systems

A good health information system "ensures the production, analysis, dissemination and use of reliable and timely health information by decision-makers at different levels of the health system, both on a regular basis and in emergencies" (WHO 2007). To achieve this, a health information system needs to be able to generate population and facility-based data; detect, investigate, communicate, and contain events that threaten public health when and where they occur; and synthesize information and promote its availability and application (WHO 2007).

At present, the availability of comprehensive and accurate health data in Qatar is limited given the lack of adequate data collection and management standards, the absence of a central data warehouse architecture, and the widespread use of paper-based records that are difficult to compile and analyze as well as transfer across providers (SCH 2013b). Recognizing the importance of having access to accurate data for health sector planning, quality monitoring, and measurement of population outcomes, the SCH is developing a comprehensive health data management program, which will establish data standards and management policies (SCH 2013b). As part of this initiative, a national health observatory is planned that will be custodian of all national health datasets and will enable the development of quality and outcomes measurement (SCH 2014a). The development of the national health observatory is consistent with the approaches employed in developed and developing countries, which use national health observatories for monitoring health systems, public health surveillance, evidence-based policy advice, and information and knowledge production (Public Health England 2015; WHO 2015b; Pourmalek 2012; Gattini 2009). Of note, the SCH initiated the procurement of an early-warning surveillance and tracking system that will allow for national data collection, as well as reporting and prioritization of public health threats (SCH 2015b). In addition, as part of health information technology developments for NHIC, providers are required to code each billed service according to the Australian Modification of the International Classification of Diseases, 10th revision (ICD-10-AM) mandated by the SCH for clarity and accuracy.

Furthermore, the SCH is expecting to implement an e-health strategy with the objective of creating an integrated national health information exchange system in line with developed countries including Sweden and South Korea, to increase efficiency, accuracy, and quality (Doupi et al. 2010; Ryu et al. 2013; EC 2012). Notably, HMC, PHCC, and Sidra Medical and Research Center are already introducing an electronic clinical system called Cerner that will replace paper records and allow for integration among these providers (SCH 2015b). Further work is needed to achieve data linkages across all providers and between electronic medical records and administrative data. There are also plans underway for the integrated national health information exchange system to allow full participation by all providers by 2016 (SCH 2013b). Provider adaptation to the aforementioned new standards and systems, however, is an important challenge to successful implementation, which the SCH can mitigate through provider training and scaling up of information technology resources and human resource capacity to provide technical support.

MEDICAL PRODUCTS, VACCINES, AND TECHNOLOGIES

The last defining feature of a well-functioning health system is that it "ensures equitable access to essential medical products, vaccines and technologies of assured quality, safety, efficacy and cost-effectiveness, and their scientifically sound and cost-effective use" (WHO 2007). To achieve this, countries need to have national pharmaceutical policies, guidelines, and regulations in place as well as the ability to set and negotiate prices.

Currently, new drugs are approved through the SCH Pharmacy and Drug Control Department in collaboration with the Gulf Central Committee for Drug Registration (GCC-DR), which is responsible for ensuring drug effectiveness, safety, quality, and good manufacturing practices in line with legal statutes and best practice (SCH 2015g; Al-Rubaie 2013; Law No. 3, 1983; Law No. 1, 1986; Law No. 5, 2011; Law No. 9, 1987). Importantly, however, Qatar does not have an effective system to regulate medical devices; the use of generic medicines is low because of cultural pressures to use high-cost drugs; private providers cannot purchase pharmaceuticals at the same low costs as public providers; and there is no system yet fully in place to assess the comparative and cost-effectiveness of new medicines and thereby contain costs (SCH 2013b).

Consequently, the SCH plans to regulate all new medical devices by the end of 2015 and is developing a comprehensive list of all approved medical devices and suppliers (SCH 2013b). The planned regulatory approaches are consistent with developments in the United Kingdom, though there remain important challenges internationally with regard to medical device regulation, namely monitoring real-world utilization and exchanging critical information on devices with health providers and patients (Sorenson and Drummond 2014). The SCH is also implementing a national formulary to be used by all health professionals as recommended by the WHO (2004). The Qatar National Formulary will provide comprehensive information about pharmaceuticals to providers and patients in order to promote their appropriate and safe use, including the use of generics. To complement these initiatives, NHIC is developing a Pharmaceutical Benefit Management (PBM) scheme to monitor consumption and ensure more rational distribution and utilization of medicines, and the SCH is supporting the development of community pharmacies in an effort to increase efficiency and improve access to essential medicines in line with international best practice (Seiter 2010). Further, in order to contain health expenditures, as well as to address private sector concerns that the current regulatory and supply chain system restrict commercially sustainable pharmaceutical products, one option the SCH is considering is to centralize the purchasing of drugs and medical supplies (SCH 2013b, 2014g; Seiter 2010).

## Conclusions

Qatar has significantly transformed its health system in a short period of time against a backdrop of rapid economic expansion and population growth. Since the establishment of the SCH in 2009 with enhanced decision-making resources, Qatar's health governance has improved substantially. In the last six years, the SCH has developed one of the world's clearest health visions, established effective accountability mechanisms, increased transparency, introduced strong independent regulation of health providers through the creation of the QCHP, and improved patient involvement. Enabled by these governance reforms, comprehensive health financing changes have been implemented, most notably the creation of the NHIC, the record-setting rapid rollout of a new national health insurance scheme that will cover all nationals and non-nationals by 2016, and significant purchasing reforms aimed at improving quality and safety.

To meet the country's increasing health workforce demands, the SCH has developed a national workforce plan to ensure sufficient numbers and the optimal mix of skilled health professionals, and they also revised remuneration packages and professional development opportunities to recruit and retain high-quality staff. At the same time, substantial service delivery reforms have been implemented, including significant health infrastructure planning and expansion, initiatives to shift the current model of care toward prevention and primary care while strengthening hospital and continuing care, and safety and quality improvements through increased regulation and oversight of public and private providers. Complementing this progress, SCH is also strengthening the country's health information systems through the development of a national e-health strategy, as well as improving pharmaceutical regulation and rational use of medicines.

With such rapid transformation, however, uneven development has been inevitable. While significant advancements in health insurance coverage and hospital care have been achieved, reforms relating to primary care, provider payment systems, and pharmaceutical policy are still evolving. At the same time, given the potential for unintended consequences arising from such rapid reform, it is crucial to continue strengthening the SCH's monitoring, oversight, and regulation capacity. As resources are not limitless, however, it will be increasingly important to reflect on the health system's ability to maintain high efficiency in implementing policy as well as the sustainability of the reforms underway. In the face of external pressures now and in the future, there should now be a growing focus on achieving value for money as well as making incremental but longer-term focused health system improvements. With continued support and commitment from the highest levels of government and the health sector's unique governance model, however, Qatar is well positioned to meet its growing health care demands in the coming years.

## Notes

1. http://data.worldbank.org/indicator/NY.GDP.MKTP.KD.ZG.

## Bibliography. Qatar: Policy Making in a Transformative State

Al Binali, H. (2015). Hajar Ahmed Hajar Albinali. drhajar.org. Retrieved 30 March 2015, from http://www.drhajar.org

Ali, Faleh, Zlatko Nikoloski, Husien Reka, Orisida Gjebrea, and Elias Mossialos. 2014. The diabetes-obesity-hypertension nexus in Qatar: Evidence from the World Health Survey. *Population Health Metrics* 12(1): 18.

Al-Rubaie, Mohammed. 2013. Evaluation of the Regulatory Review Process of the GCC Centralized Procedure: Development of a Model for Improving the Approval Process. Ph.D., Cardiff: Cardiff University.

Al-Thani, M., E. Sadoun, A. Al-Thani, S. Khalifa, S. Sayegh, and A. Badawi. 2014. Change in the structures, dynamics and disease-related mortality rates of the population of Qatari nationals: 2007–2011. *Journal of Epidemiology and Global Health* 4(4): 277–287.

Anderson, Gerard, Uwe Reinhardt, Peter Hussey, and Varduhi Petrosyan. 2003. It's The Prices, Stupid: Why The United States Is So Different From Other Countries. *Health Affairs* 22(3): 89–105.

Anell, Anders, Anna Glenngard, and Sherry Merkur. 2012. *Health Systems in Transition: Sweden*. Copenhagen: World Health Organization.

Bener, A., Zirie, M., Kim, E., Al Buz, R., Zaza, M., & Al-Nufal, M. et al. (2012). Measuring Burden of Diseases in a Rapidly Developing Economy: State of Qatar. *Global Journal Of Health Science, 5*(2). doi:10.5539/gjhs.v5n2p134

Bener, Abdulbari, Mahmoud Zirie, Eun-Jung Kim, Rama Al Buz, Mouayyad Zaza, Mohammed Al-Nufal, Basma Basha, Edward Hillhouse, and Elio Riboli. 2013a. "Measuring burden of diseases in a rapidly developing economy: State of Qatar." *Global Journal of Health Science* 5 (2):134-144.
Bener, Abdulbari Abdulbari, Mohammad T. Yousafzai, Shafiq ur-Rehman, and Waleed Waleed K. Abdullatef. 2013b. Trends of cause and sex-specific mortality, and its impact on the life expectancy among Qatari population. *Public Health Frontier* 2(2): 69–76.
Boyle, Seán. 2011. *Health Systems in Transition: United Kingdom (England)*. Copenhagen: World Health Organization.
Brinkerhoff, D., and T. Bossert. 2008. *Health Governance: Concepts, Experience, and Programming Options*. Washington, DC: U.S. Agency for International Development.
Busse, Reinhard, and Miriam Blumel. 2014. *Health Systems in Transition: Germany*. Copenhagen: World Health Organization.
Busse, Reinhard, Miriam Blumel, David Scheller-Kreinsen, and Annette Zentner. 2010. *Tackling Chronic Disease in Europe*. Copenhagen: World Health Organization.
Busse, Reinhard, A. Geissler, W. Quentin, and M. Wiley. 2011. *Diagnosis-Related Groups in Europe*. Maidenhead, UK: Open University Press.
Care Quality Commission. 2015. *Preparing for CQC Inspection*. London: Care Quality Commission.
Chernichovsky, D. 2000. *The Public-Private Mix in the Modern Health Care System*. Cambridge, MA: National Bureau of Economic Research.
Chernichovsky, D., and W. van de Ven. 2003. Risk adjustment in Europe. *Health Policy* 65(1): 1–3.
Chevreul, K., I. Durand-Zaleski, S. Bahrami, C. Hernandez-Quevedo, and P. Mladovsky. 2010. *Health Systems in Transition: France Health System Review*. Copenhagen: World Health Organization.
Council for Healthcare Regulatory Excellence. 2009. *Annual Report Volume II: Performance Review of Health Professional Regulatory Bodies 2008/2009*. London: The Stationery Office.
Darzi, A., and G. Parston. 2013. *Report of the Global Diffusion of Healthcare Innovation Working Group*. Doha: Qatar Foundation.
Department of Health (UK). 2007. *Trust, Assurance and Safety: The Regulation of Health Professionals in the 21st Century*. London: The Stationary Office.
Doupi, P., E. Renko, S. Giest, and J. Dumortier. 2010. *eHealth Strategies Country Brief: Sweden*. Bonn: European Commission.
Emiri Decree No. 13. 2009. Establishment of the Supreme Council of Health. *Official Gazette*.
Emiri Decree No. 15. 2012. Establishment of the Primary Health Care Corporation. *Official Gazette*.

Emiri Decree No. 7. 2013. Establishment of the Qatar Council for Healthcare Practitioners. *Official Gazette.*
Emiri Resolution No. 13. 2005. Establishing the National Health Authority. *Official Gazette.*
European Commission. 2012. *eHealth Action Plan 2012-2020: Innovative Healthcare for the 21st Century.* Brussels: European Commission.
———. 2014. *Implementation of the Communication from the Commission, from 24 June 2009, on Action Against Cancer: European Partnership [COM (2009) 291 final] and Second Implementation Report on the Council Recommendation of 2 December 2003 on cancer screening (2003/878/EC).* Brussels: European Commission.
European Food Safety Authority. 2015. EFSA: Independence. Accessed March 30. http://www.efsa.europa.eu/en/values/independence.htm
Ferre, F., A. de Belvis, L. Valerio, S. Longhi, A. Lazzari, G. Fattore, W. Ricciardi, and Anna Marresso. 2014. *Health Systems in Transition: Italy Health System Review.* Copenhagen: World Health Organization.
Figueras, J., R. Robinson, and E. Jakubowski. 2005. *Purchasing to Improve Health Systems Performance.* Maidenhead: Open University Press.
Food and Drug Administration (FDA), US. (2015). Mammography Facility Inspections - Part III: Inspections. Fda.gov. Retrieved 30 March 2015, from http://www.fda.gov/MedicalDevices/DeviceRegulationandGuidance/MedicalDeviceQualityandCompliance/ucm260273.htm
Fox, L., N. Ravishankar, J. Squires, R. Williamson, and D. Brinkerhoff. 2010. *Rwanda Health Governance Report.* Bethesda: Health Systems 20/20 Project, Abt Associates, Inc.
Gattini, C. 2009. *Implementing National Health Observatories: Operational Approach and Strategic Recommendations.* Santiago, Chile: Pan American Health Organization.
General Secretariat for Development Planning (Qatar). 2008. *Qatar National Vision 2030.* Doha: Retrieved from http://www.gsdp.gov.qa/portal/page/portal/gsdp_en/knowledge_center/Tab/QNV2030_English_v2.pdfMinistry of Development Planning and Statistics (Qatar).
General Secretariat for Development Planning (GSDP). (2008). *Qatar National Vision 2030.* Doha: General Secretariat for Development Planning.
Hamad Medical Corporation. 2014. *Annual Report 2013/14.* Doha: Hamad Medical Corporation.
———. 2015. About HMC. Accessed March 31. http://www.hamad.qa/en/hcp/about_hmc/about_hmc.aspx
Health Financing and Insurance Department, Supreme Council of Health (2015)
Henderson, L., and J. Tulloch. 2008. Incentives for retaining and motivating health workers in Pacific and Asian countries. *Human Resources For Health* 6(1): 18.

Hofmarcher, M. 2013. *Health Systems in Transition: Austria.* Copenhagen: World Health Organization.
Hussin, A. H., and F. M. H. Ali. 2010.
Hussin, A.H., F.M.H. Ali, H. Reka, and O. Gjebrea. 2015. Tracking access, utilization and health system responsiveness to inform evidence-based health care policy: the case of Qatar. *Journal of Local and Global Health Perspectives* 2015(1): 2.
Institute for Health Metrics and Evaluation. 2013. *Global Disease Burden Profile: Qatar.* Seattle: Institute for Health Metrics and Evaluation.
International Council of Nurses. 2008. *Incentive Systems for Health Care Professionals.* Geneva: International Council of Nurses.
International Labour Organization. 2004. *Towards a Fair Deal for Migrant Workers in the Global Economy.* Geneva: International Labour Organization.
Lohr, K., R. Brook, C. Kamberg, G. Goldberg, A. Leibowitz, and J. Keesey. 1986. Effect of cost-sharing on Use of medically effective and less effective care. *Medical Care* 24(Supplement): S31–S38.
Mamtani, R., M. Al-Thani, A. Al-Thani, J. Sheikh, and A. Lowenfels. 2011. Motor vehicle injuries in Qatar: Time trends in a rapidly developing Middle Eastern nation. *Injury Prevention* 18(2): 130–132. doi:10.1136/injuryprev-2011-040147.
Medeiros, H., D. McDaid, and M. Knapp. 2008. *Shifting Care From Hospital to the Community in Europe: Economic Challenges and Opportunities.* London: London School of Economics and Political Science.
Ministry of Development Planning and Statistics (Qatar). 2014a. *Labor Force Survey: Third Quarter (July-September) 2014.* Doha: Ministry of Development Planning and Statistics.
———. 2014b. *Qatar Monthly Statistics - June 2014, Qatar Monthly Statistics.* Doha: Ministry of Development Planning and Statistics.
Mossialos, E., M. Wenzl, R. Osborn, and C. Anderson. 2015. *International Profiles of Health Care Systems, 2014.* New York: The Commonwealth Fund.
Murray, C., and J. Frenk. 2000. A framework for assessing the performance of health systems. *Bulletin Of The World Health Organization* 78(6): 717–731.
Myles, G. 1995. *Public Economics.* Cambridge: Cambridge University Press.
National Health Insurance Company. 2015a. About NHIC. Accessed March 31. http://www.seha.qa/about-us-nhic.html
———. 2015b. National Health Insurance Company: About Us. Accessed March 31. http://www.nhic.qa/about-us-nhic.html
Newhouse, J. 1993. *Free for All? Lessons from the RAND Health Insurance Experiment.* Cambridge, MA: Harvard University Press.
NHS (England). 2014. *NHS Five-Year Forward View.* London: NHS England.
Nolte, E., and M. McKee. 2008. *Caring for People with Chronic Conditions.* Maidenhead, UK: Open University Press.

Nolte, E., C. Knai, and R. Saltman. 2014. *Assessing Chronic Disease Management in European Health Systems: Concepts and Approaches*, First edn. Copenhagen: World Health Organization.

OECD. 2013. *Health at a Glance 2013: OECD Indicators*. Paris: OECD.

———. 2014. OECD Health Statistics 2014: Frequently Requested Data. Organization for Economic Cooperation and Development.

Oliver, A. 1999. *Risk Adjusting Health Care Resource Allocations*. London: Office of Health Economics.

Ono, T., M. Schoenstein, and G. Lafortune. 2013. *Health Workforce Planning in OECD Countries*. OECD Health Working Papers. Paris: OECD.

Pourmalek, F. 2012. National Health Observatories: Need for stepped-up action. *The Health* 3(3): 63–64.

Primary Health Care Corporation. 2013. *National Primary Health Care Strategy 2013–2018*. Doha: Primary Health Care Corporation.

———. 2014. *Business Plan 2013–2016*. Doha: Primary Health Care Corporation.

Public Health England. 2015. The Network of Public Health Observatories. Accessed March 30. http://www.apho.org.uk

Qatar Council for Health Care Practitioners. 2015a. *Submission to Supreme Council of Health for SCH Annual Report 2014*. Doha: Qatar Council for Health Care Practitioners.

———. 2015b. *Circular No. (3/2015) Granting Provisional Licenses for all Healthcare Practitioner*. Doha: Qatar Council for Healthcare Practitioners.

Ryu, S., M. Park, J. Lee, S. Kim, B. Han, K. Mo, and H. Lee. 2013. Web-based integrated public healthcare information system of Korea: Development and performance. *Healthcare Informatics Research* 19(314–323).

Saltman, R., R. Busse, and J. Figueras. 2004. *Social Health Insurance Systems in Western Europe*. Berkshire, UK: Open University Press.

Saltman, R., A. Rico, and W. Boerma. 2006. *Primary Care in the Driver's Seat?* Maidenhead, UK: Open University Press.

Seiter, A. 2010. *A Practical Approach to Pharmaceutical Policy*. Washington, DC: World Bank.

Simonet, D. 2011. The New Public Management theory and the reform of European health care systems: An international comparative perspective. *International Journal of Public Administration* 34(12): 815–826.

Sorenson, C., and M. Drummond. 2014. Improving medical device regulation: The United States and Europe in perspective. *Milbank Quarterly* 92(1): 114–150.

Supreme Council of Health (SCH). 2010. Implementing a Social Health Insurance Scheme in Qatar Final Report. Unpublished.

———. 2011a. *Qatar Health Report 2009*. Doha: Supreme Council of Health.

———. 2011b. *National Health Strategy 2011–2016 (Original Executive Summary)*. Doha: Supreme Council of Health.

———. 2011c. *National Cancer Strategy (NCS)*. Doha: Supreme Council of Health.
———. 2011d. *Qatar National Health Accounts Years 2009 & 2010*. Doha: Supreme Council of Health.
———. 2012. *Qatar National Cancer Research Strategy (QNCRS)*. Doha: Supreme Council of Health.
———. 2013a. *National Laboratory Integration and Standardization Strategy (NLISS) 2013–2018*. Doha: Supreme Council of Health.
———. 2013b. *National Health Strategy 2011–2016: Project Implementation Plans (Update 2013)*. Doha: Supreme Council of Health.
———. 2013c. Health utilization and Expenditure Survey 2012. Unpublished.
———. 2013d. *Qatar Stepwise Report 2012*. Doha: Supreme Council of Health.
———. 2014a. *Qatar National Health Strategy 2011–2016 (2014 Update)*. Doha: Supreme Council of Health.
———. 2014b. *Qatar National Mental Health Strategy (QNMHS) 2013–2018*. Doha: Supreme Council of Health.
———. 2014c. NHS project leadership and key stakeholders overview (December 2014). Unpublished.
———. 2014d. NHS Event 2014 Survey Post Analysis. Unpublished.
———. 2014e. *Enhancing the patient journey: A key stakeholder and patient perspective Qualitative Research Report, May 2014*. Doha: Supreme Council of Health.
———. 2014f. Health Utilization and Expenditure Survey 2014. Unpublished.
———. 2014g. *SCH Annual Report 2013*. Doha: Supreme Council of Health.
———. 2014h. *Qatar National Health Accounts 2012*. Doha: Supreme Council of Health.
———. 2014i. *Qatar Healthcare Facilities Master Plan 2013–2033*. Doha: Supreme Council of Health.
———. 2015a. *Qatar Health Report 2013*. Doha: Supreme Council of Health.
———. 2015b. *SCH Annual Report 2014*. Doha: Supreme Council of Health.
———. 2015c. *Qatar National Health Accounts 2013*. Doha: Supreme Council of Health.
———. 2015d. National Health Strategy Targets (March 2015). Unpublished.
———. 2015e. Qatar Council for Healthcare Practitioners Scopes of Practice. Unpublished.
———. 2015f. SCH National Health Workforce Plan. Unpublished.
———. 2015g. SCH Pharmacy & Drug Control. Sch.gov.qa. Retrieved 31 March 2015, from http://www.sch.gov.qa/about-sch/departments/pharmacy-n-drug-control/pharmacy-n-drug-control
Thomson, S., T. Foubister, and E. Mossialos. 2010. Can user charges make health care more efficient? *BMJ* 341 (Aug 18 3):c3759–c3759.

Transparency International. 2014. *Corruption Perceptions Index 2014*. Berlin: Retrieved from https://www.transparency.org/cpi2014/resultsTransparency International.

United Nations. 2012. *United Nations General Assembly Resolution A/67/L.36: Global Health and Foreign Policy*.

———. 2013. *International Migration 2013*. New York: United Nations.

Walker, L. 2014. Amid doctor shortage, Qatar University to set up new medical school. *Doha News*. Accessed March 31, 2015.

World Health Organization. 2004. *How to Develop a National Formulary Based on the WHO Model Formulary*. Geneva: World Health Organization.

———. 2007. *Strengthening Health Systems to Improve Health Outcomes: A Framework for Action*. Geneva: World Health Organization.

———. 2011. *World Health Assembly Resolution WHA 64.9. Sustainable Health Financing Structures and Universal Coverage*. Geneva: World Health Organization.

———. 2015a. *European Observatory on Health Systems and Policies*. World Health Organization. Accessed March 30. http://www.euro.who.int/en/about-us/partners/observatory

———. 2015b. *Health Systems: Governance*. World Health Organization Accessed. March 31. http://www.who.int/healthsystems/topics/stewardship/en/

Xu, K., D. Evans, G. Carrin, and A. Aguilar-Rivera. 2005. *Designing Health Financing Systems to Reduce Catastrophic Health Expenditure. Technical Briefs for Policy-Makers, No. 2*. Geneva: World Health Organization.

CHAPTER 8

# The Qatari Family at the Intersection of Policies

*Lina M. Kassem and Esraa Al-Muftah*

Although many scholars (Cooke 2014; Foley 2010; Gray 2013) have documented the impact of oil and gas wealth in transforming Qatar from a "traditional society" into a modern one, the speed at which Qatar has developed over the past 15–20 years is still striking. Almost overnight the small state's foreign population has increased dramatically. The resulting demographic imbalance and the rapid urbanization and development have had a tremendous impact on Qatari society. The focus of this chapter is how this rapid transformation has affected the family in Qatar in general and the role of women in particular. We examine the centrality of women in state polices that attempt to address the challenges that face the family.

We begin by arguing that the state's policy toward the family, which was developed during the process of state formation, has unintentionally undermined the extended family. We examine how many, if not most, of functions of the traditional tribal extended family have been replaced by state agencies. However, the transformation of society has occurred at such a fast pace that the relevant agencies and institutions have had difficulty coping with or anticipating the new responsibilities with such a shift. This situation, we suggest, led the government to retroactively enact

---

L.M. Kassem (✉)
Department of International Affairs, Qatar University, Doha, Qatar

E. Al-Muftah
Doha Institute for Graduate Studies, Doha, Qatar

© The Author(s) 2016 213
M.E. Tok et al. (eds.), *Policy-Making in a Transformative State*,
DOI 10.1057/978-1-137-46639-6_8

policies that target issues or "problems" that have emerged in society as a result of major changes taking place in Qatar.

THE HISTORICAL DEVELOPMENT OF THE FAMILY IN QATAR

This section of the chapter traces the transformation of the Qatari social landscape over a relatively short period of time, from small traditional communities to a sprawling metropolis in Doha (Chapter 10 goes more into more detail on the demographic changes). Funded by oil and gas wealth, Qatar, like other Gulf states, has developed into an advanced welfare state that provides its citizens with free land and loans for new families, which has given rise to a growing number of nuclear family households (Foley 2010).

The tribe is the oldest social and political institution in the Arabian Gulf. Tribal allegiances existed long before the newly founded nation states, and some continue today to cross national borders. With the founding of modern nation states in the Gulf, these tribal allegiances represented a challenge to the new structures and institutions created by the states[1]. Often, states had to make allowances for these tribes who represented competition when it came to the loyalty of the citizen (Alsharekh 2007). States often give specific privileges and limited powers to tribal elders in order to co-opt them. The tribal elders in turn ensure the loyalty of the tribe to the state and its ruler.

The newly founded states found themselves needing the support of the tribe to gain legitimacy, even though the tribes represented the single most serious threat to that same legitimacy. This duality led the state to have contradictory policies toward the tribe and, by extension, the family. States introduced new legal definitions for the family that were based on the more nuclear family model with the legal authority for the family going to the husband, as opposed to the tribal elder or *sheikh* (the tribal sheikh is the head of the tribe and usually the eldest male). On the other hand, the state emphasized the role of the family, meaning the nuclear family, as the cornerstone of society. For example, Article 21 of the Qatari Constitution stipulates the following: "The family shall be the foundation of the society. Its pillars shall be religion, morals and love for the nation. The law shall organise means of protecting the family, supporting its principles, bolstering its ties, preserving ideals of matrimony, childhood and the elderly."

However, the state did not completely ignore tribes, and it continues to recognize their influence. One of the most important examples of the continued salience of the tribe is when the emir, during official celebrations and religious holidays, visits the tribal ceremonial locations (*'arda*). The *'arda* is often a very elaborate, public ritual that different tribes hold, and the emir, or his representative, will visit them around the country. Alanoud Alsharekh (2007: 14) argues, "Even though considerable independence has been achieved (by individuals), members of extended families and tribes remain connected by ties of mutual obligations and support that are often translated into political alliances and business undertakings in which kinship takes precedence over other loyalties."

This new definition of the family, based on a nuclear family, that was empowered by the state also led to another interesting dichotomy. Although some scholars have argued that this new independence from the tribe has provided more individual freedom to members of the tribe, especially women, there is evidence that the weakening of extended families has caused irreparable damage, not only to the traditional roles of the tribal elders, but more importantly to the informal networks that had ensured the protection of the more vulnerable members. Functionalist sociologists such as Young, Willmott, and Mills (1973) argue that the "modern" nuclear family has resulted in more "egalitarian marriage." However, this idea of the symmetrical family has been criticized by feminist sociologists, such as Oakley (1974). More recently, scholars have pointed out that although women in a nuclear family are more likely to work outside the home, in fact what often results is that these women end up having a "double burden" (Sullivan 2000; Stanko 2000). Working women are still expected to take on the majority of the responsibility at home, including housework and child care. However, in the new nuclear family, wives have much less support from the extended family, and as such, the pressures on them become more intense. Nuclear families are finding it difficult to deal with the dichotomy of the modern nuclear family, which in theory is supposed to promote a more egalitarian family on the one hand, as well as the traditional gender specific roles that allocate housework and childcare as the exclusive responsibility of the women.

Some scholars blame the predicament of women on patriarchal core values of tribal societies. They suggest that the solution is for the society to modernize, which can only be accomplished when the state undermines the relationship between the citizen and the traditional tribe. Alsharekh (2007) suggests that a continuation of these tribal allegiances has hindered the efforts of the state to modernize. She argues that "the major hurdle facing all GCC countries seeking to modernize the political process is ensuring that all their citizens, regardless of gender, recognize that they are just that—citizens of a state and thus part of a greater collective, and not just members of a tribe, family or ethnic group, and that they accept a new set of duties and obligations that flow from that notion of citizenship" (Alsharekh 2007:14).

Other scholars have argued that this transition from extended to nuclear family has had a negative impact, not only on the tribe, but also on the individual. Yahya El-Haddad (2003) claims that these efforts by the state to modernize have in fact created an alienated citizen. He claims that "[c]itizens have moved from living in small-size traditional communities to residing in complex cities characterized by impersonal and secondary social relationships. The structural system of the city as a whole separates the individual from the environment of local community relationships, thereby turning his life toward greater solitude" (El-Haddad 2003: 2).

The first Qatari constitution introduced what was referred to as the "Basic Law" in 1970. This law indicated that the state now had the duty to "protect" and "strengthen" the family. This would provide official justification for the intervention of the state into the family in order to protect it. One of the resulting consequences of the change in the family structure, from the extended to the nuclear, has been a change in the function of the family as well. The function of the family as the main support system was also challenged. The Basic Law mandates the state as the protector of the family. As mentioned above, the traditional extended family had its own informal network of protecting all its members, especially the most vulnerable. This traditional support system was replaced with a smaller unit wherein the husband became the legal guardian of the family, codified in the Family Law of 2006. The authority over members of individual families moved from the tribal elder or sheikh to the husband or father (Moghadam 2004).

State institutions were set up to protect members of the family from potential harm from both strangers and even their own relatives. Institutions such as the *faz'a* (internal security forces), which could be translated as "I have your back," have replaced tribal predecessors, the historical inspiration. Historically, the term *faz'a* refers to the support that members of a family receive from the rest of the clan. Whenever a tribal member is in need, the rest of the able members of the tribe are obligated, out of a sense of honor, to come to the aid of the beleaguered member of the tribe. Other institutions include the Family Consulting Center, which couples that plan on having a divorce need to go though. It is similar to the family elder, who often would have been a source of resolving conflict in the family.

Nonetheless, as Alanoud Alsharekh argues, "all the GCC countries are welfare states that at their core re-enact the traditional tribal system of allegiance for economic support. Citizens expect their rulers/governments to provide free housing, education, healthcare and a myriad of other perks and privileges without the obligation of having to pay taxes" (Alsharekh 2007: 15). As a result of these state initiatives, more and more young Qataris are able to obtain land and build houses that allow them to be relatively independent of extended family influence. Often, building a house away from the traditional family *fereej*/neighborhood[2] is not by choice but by necessity, given Doha's rapid urbanization.

Development projects have dispersed and replaced the traditional *fereej*, to make room for massive skyscrapers and modern housing complexes (see Chapter 6). Younger generations are either choosing to leave, or are being forced out of their *fereej* due to lack of space. Most end up moving into newly constructed apartment buildings where they not only do not know their neighbors, but may well find themselves as one of a handful of Qataris among many foreigners. The reason that Qatari families seem to be running out of space is due to the fact that Qataris have always lived in small villages that later expanded to be cities. Therefore, with the growth of the city, these families have found themselves struggling to remain in their traditional villages.

Interestingly, Qatar's housing policy is often described in media reports as not clearly documented or transparent (see, for example, Al-Arab 2014). Yet it is often perceived that in the past the state's distribution policies attempted to allow family members to live close to each other. However, current policy does not take the issue of proximity to the family into consideration when allocating land. This is mostly due to the fact that in most neighborhoods, it is difficult to find available land for new dwellings. A recent news article reported on this changing policy by stating that the main problem is the fact that the government now gives land directly to individuals. The article argues that previously the state would allocate land based on "an old tradition that the state practiced; it provided space to tribal leaders to enable them to house tribe members close together. With parents growing old and needing people to take care of them it is important for the families to live close to one another," unlike today where "land is distributed to the individuals and not to the tribes" (Al-Arab 2014).

## CURRENT ATTITUDES TOWARD THE FAMILY

Despite the transition from an extended family to a nuclear family, most Qataris still place strong emphasis on the extended family, even in relation to where they choose to live. For example, in a survey administered by the Social and Economic Survey Research Institute,[3] the overwhelming majority of Qatari respondents stated family is very important in their lives (99 %). However, it is not that Qataris simply value family in a general manner, but it seems they put special emphasis on the extended family in their housing decisions. When asked about the reasons for choosing to live in their current neighborhood, almost half of the respondents stated it was the proximity to their family that determined their choice (47 %), while the second most popular response was that it (house or land) was provided by the government (28 %). Interestingly, the relationship between these two choices seems to have created tension in land distribution policy. In an interview with Ahmed Al-Muhannadi, Director of the Land and Survey Department at the Ministry of Municipality and Urban Planning, the Al-Watan newspaper reported that even though land distribution policies are transparent, some individuals insist on having land near their family, which delays the process for them (Al-Watan 2014).

This inclination to live in a neighborhood close to one's family could also explain why 66 % of respondents felt they strongly agree to somewhat agree they have a lot in common with people who live in their neighborhood. Similarly, they felt the people in their neighborhood would generally be willing to help if help was needed (88 %). Hence, to a certain extent there continues to be a strong connection to the space of living and family connections, beyond those direct ones shared in the household.

Yahya El-Haddad (2003) points out that "[t]he Arab Gulf nuclear family is in a transitional stage that carries many features of both the Western model and the traditional extended family model. Hence, we are dealing with a nuclear family characterized by extended relations" (El-Haddad 2003: 2). Al-Ghanim (2013), while examining the case of Qatar specifically, similarly found that even though the nuclear family has become the dominant family structure, the extended family still plays a powerful role in people's lives.

Similarly, this strong attachment to the family raises the question of why Qatar's national vision and state policy have placed strong emphasis on "modernization" along with "protecting" family values in Qatar, indicating to a certain extent that one endangers the other.

## STATE INTERVENTIONS AND PERCEIVED THREATS TO THE QATARI FAMILY

The question of family and the role of women are inextricably combined in Qatari government policy. However, as indicated above, the balance of tradition and modernity within the family and the balance between serving the family and developing independent and autonomous roles for women are unclear. The following quotes provide a snapshot of these dilemmas:

> The State of Qatar aspires to advance and develop the social dimensions of its society by nurturing Qatari citizens capable of dealing effectively and flexibly with the requirements of the age they live in, and by preserving a strong and coherent family that enjoys support, care and social protection. Women will assume a significant role in all spheres of life, especially through participating in economic and political decision-making. (Qatar National Vision 2030, 2008: 19)

> Women are central to the evolving Qatari family. Even as they maintain an adherence to valuable traditions, women are adapting to the impacts of modernization. Through their nurturing of language, codes of ethics, behavioral patterns, value systems and religious beliefs, women play an indispensable role in upholding traditional familial and cultural values. (Qatar National Development Strategy 2011: 165)

> The State of Qatar declares that the question of the modification of "patterns" referred to in article five (a) must not be understood as encouraging women to abandon their role as mothers and their role in childrearing, thereby undermining the structure of the family. (Qatar Fourth National Human Development Report 2015: 21)

Like many other young nations, Qatar developed an interest in family and reproduction policy as its nation building efforts intensified after 1995, but there were earlier manifestations. The first constitution drafted in 1953 described the family as "the nucleus of [Qatari] society," to be protected by law. The first family-related entity, Dar Tanmiyat Al-Usra, appeared in 1996 under the Qatar Foundation for Education, Science, and Community Development, a non-profit organization headed by the former Emir's wife, Sheikha Moza bint Nasser (Al-Attiyah 2009; other organizations are listed in Table 8.1).

Nonetheless, policy targeting family and women emerged more strongly in Qatar after 1995, when Emir Hamad bin Khalifa Al-Thani took power. The new Emir had a vision to reform the country and embrace globalization and change. Within a few years, a new constitution was drafted, and the first municipal elections took place, with the involvement of women (see Chapters 2 and 3). Around the same time, in 2001, RAND was invited to assess the education system and recommend ways to reform it to meet the new needs of the country (see Chapter 4).

Recently and in light of the demographic imbalance, a new focus has been placed on population planning. It has been noted by scholars that "reproduction is fundamentally associated with identity: that of 'the nation' as the 'imagined community' that the state serves and protects, and over which it exercises authority" (Kligman 1998: 5). Therefore, nation-formation often coincides with the state's effort to codify personal status laws and other population-related policies. Sonbol (2009) notes when tracing the term *usra* that "[t]he personal status laws developed in the modernization period established a construction of the family with the father as the recognized official head of the family whose powers are legally defined and protected by the powers of the state" (Sonbol 2009: 180), which as mentioned earlier, is not necessarily the common family structure in the region. Under this new state condition, "the modern family is impotent to resist intrusions into its space: the education, health, and welfare of its individual members have been politically redefined as social issues, of public as well as private concern" (Levine 1991: 13). Therefore, it is no surprise that, since 1995, the state has established several institutions related to population planning and family support, which in turn have replaced the traditional function of the extended family.

Focusing on empowering women, institutions like Dar Tanmiyat Al-Usra have worked to enable women to "engage actively and positively in the comprehensive development momentum the nation is witnessing, while armed by her values, faith, knowledge of her culture, and experiences" (Al-Hayat Newspaper 1999). Women's empowerment policies that were seen as pivotal for the *usra* were reflected in the appointment of women in leadership positions, which encouraged women to aim for

THE QATARI FAMILY AT THE INTERSECTION OF POLICIES   221

**Table 8.1**   List of Institutions and Legislation Related to Family and Women

| Name | Year | Information |
| --- | --- | --- |
| Social Development Center | 1996 | Established by H.H. Sheikha Moza Bint Nasser to provide "guidance programs to support the family." Also creates awareness campaigns on multiple issues. The most recent one was to encourage moderate spending among families. The center also provides families in need loans with no interest if they are deemed eligible. |
| Supreme Council for Family Affairs | 1998 | The council was established by an Emiri Decree and headed by H.H. Sheikha Moza bint Nasser (she later founded the below listed centers/foundations). It played a central role in the development of legislation related to women and the family and also the establishment of most of the centers related to women that followed. Before shutting down its website it had described its aims and objectives to be as follows:<br>• "Build united and self-reliant Qatari families.<br>• Instill pride in Arabic identity and Islamic culture.<br>• Ensure the family's rights and responsibilities in Qatari society.<br>• Create family protection policies.<br>• Creating policies to assist the needs of Qatari young people<br>• Empower women and increase of their participation in social, political and economical life." |
| Family Consulting Center | 2002 | The center describes its services as aimed to "protect and maintain the cohesion of the family." It provides free counseling for Qataris and residents. Judges often refer couples who wish to divorce to the center before finalizing the divorce. The Center also provides expert reports on issues related to custody. |
| Childhood Cultural Center | 2002 | It aims to work with children under the age of 18 to "develop children's personality and talent" and also "develop respect to the child's culture and language and national values." |
| Qatar Foundation for Child and Women Protection | 2002 | The foundation offers many services to "protect target group [women and children] from deviant practices in the family setting and in society." It also houses women and children subject to violence or "deviant practices" in a temporary house until their cases are resolved. The center also provides legal support to women and children subject to domestic violence. |

(*continued*)

Table 8.1 (continued)

| Name | Year | Information |
|---|---|---|
| Qatar Foundation for the Care of Elderly | 2003 | The foundation offers housing and care for elderly that are unable to live on their own and have no family to take care of them. |
| Qatar Foundation for the Care of Orphans | 2003 | The foundation provides housing and care for the children that have been orphaned in Qatar. It is also important to point that children born to unknown parents in Qatar are considered Qataris. |
| Qatari Constitution | 2005 | Article 34: The Citizens of Qatar shall be equal in public rights and duties. Article 21: The family is the basis of the society. A Qatari family is founded on religion, ethics, and patriotism. The law shall regulate adequate means to protect the family, support its structure, strengthen its ties, and protect maternity, childhood, and old age. |
| Qatari New Citizenship Law/Law No. 38 of 2005 on the acquisition of Qatari nationality | 2005 | Article 14 maintained that nationality can only be passed down from the father not the mother as it deemed a Qatari to be "any person born in Qatar or in a foreign country to a Qatari father." |
| Law no. 22 of 2006 promulgating "the family law" | 2006 | Law clearly stipulated the role and duties of men and women in the family. They both need to be concerned for the "conservation of the family's welfare." Nonetheless Article 58 clearly stipulates that it's the woman's duty toward her husband to "take care and obey him" and "look after him and his property well," something that is not listed for men. |
| Doha International Family Institute (DIFI) | 2006 | The center was established to fulfill the outcomes of the Doha International Conference for the Family, which was held under the Supreme Council for Family Affairs. One of its goals is "making family issues a priority for policy-makers through advocacy and outreach at the national, regional and international levels, and building an international coalition of regional experts" (Doha International Family Institute 2013). |
| Ratification of the Convention on the Elimination of All Forms of Discrimination Against Women (CEDAW) | 2009 | Qatar ratified the CEDAW agreement with reservations on some clauses on the basis that they do not comply with "Shari'a law" or Qatari Constitution. Qatar's first review, where the delegation was headed by the Supreme Council for Family Affairs, was in February 2014. |

(continued)

Table 8.1 (continued)

| Name | Year | Information |
|---|---|---|
| Closure of Supreme Council for Family Affairs | 2014 | The council was suddenly closed in 2014 and it was claimed to have been reincorporated under the Ministry of Social Affairs. With its closure it can be said that the government's drive for reform regarding women has slowed down. |

**Table 8.2** Qatari Women in the Labor Force. Increasing proportion of Qatari women in the labor force working outside government sector

| Sectors | 2001 (%) | 2008 (%) | 2013 (%) |
|---|---|---|---|
| Government | 89.1 | 73.7 | 68.2 |
| Government corporation | 7.2 | 18.2 | 12.4 |
| Mixed | 1.6 | 3.2 | 4.7 |
| Private | 2.1 | 4.9 | 14.7 |
| Total | 100 | 100 | 100 |
| (Number) | 10,851 | 24,829 | 30,256 |

*Source*: Qatar's Fourth National Human Development Report. Qatari Ministry of Development Planning and Statistics, June 2015

higher positions. Previously, many women were socially restricted to working in schools or specific ministries, and their educational choices were also therefore limited. Nonetheless, gradually, women started to enter different work fields and different university specializations, though reaching top managerial positions is still a struggle (Al-Nasr 2011; Al Muftah 2010a, b).

As Table 8.2 indicates, the percentage of Qatari women working in the private sector increased from around 2 % in 2001 to almost 15 % in 2013. Even though this, along with the increase of Qatari women's participation[4] in the labor force, is due in large part to the state's empowerment policies, there continues to be some contradictory state sponsored policies.

Overall, the government continues to sense that the Qatari family is under threat, which definitely spurs policies to "preserve and protect" the Qatari family (Qatar National Development Strategy 2011). One of the oldest examples of the protection of Qatari family has been the policy to prevent and discourage marriage to non-nationals and to "manage 'single', South Asian migrant men in the city" (Buckley 2015: 134; Foley

2010).[5] These policies are coupled with policies that encourage nationals to marry within their nationality, such as the provision of marriage funds or common marriage ceremonies that can cover the marriage ceremony expenses, and they are on the rise for young couples (Rashad et al. 2005; Doha News 2012).

*The Fear of Demographic Imbalance*

This interest in increasing the population of nationals or "at least [in maintaining] it to achieve an appropriate balance among Qatar's total population" is visible in many state documents and statistics, especially Population Planning Committee (PPC) documents. In recent years, several government officials from GCC countries have been extremely apprehensive regarding the growing number of expatriate workers and their effect on the national identity of the Gulf states. In January 2008, according to an Al Arabiya news article, Bahrain's Labor Minister Dr Majid Al Alawi stated that the presence of almost 17 million foreign workers in the Gulf represented "a danger worse than the atomic bomb or an Israeli attack."[6] Miriam Cooke (2014: 23) argues that "[f]oreigners began to outnumber the native population. The stream of workers has grown exponentially and, with their exploding numbers, the fear factor ... their visibility everywhere has led to fear of their contaminating influence, and a determination to deny them the rights and entitlements of citizenship."

This is unfortunately not only a matter of state policy but is also reflected in the attitudes of Qataris ; for example, 46.5 % of Qatari respondents in the World Values Survey 2010 indicated that they would not like to have immigrant/foreign workers as neighbors.

This threat of migrant workers is compounded by the "rise in divorce rates" and "decrease in fertility among women" discussed regularly in the media. An example is Manal Abbas's (2013) report for the *Al-Raya* newspaper, a widely circulated newspaper in Qatar, on the outcomes of a state-endorsed meeting titled, "Towards achieving a balance between women's professional and family responsibilities." Abbas (2013) starts her report by pointing out that "fertility rates have dropped for working Qatari women" and states that "Sheikh Ahmad Al-Buanain, in a comment on this, calls for polygamy as a radical solution to the problem, which in turn would resolve the demographic imbalance [between nationals and expatriates] the Qatari society faces specifically, and the Gulf Cooperation Council states face in general."[7]

## Divorce Rates

The divorce rates that have raised flags are not specific to Qatar, as divorce rates have increased across the region (Rashad et al. 2005). In contrast, a report commissioned by the General Secretariat for Development Planning (responsible for the fulfillment of QNV 2030) pointed out that their estimates for 2002, 2004, and 2008, based on the Qatari population over 15 years of age,[8] show that the "trend in population adjusted divorce rate appears to be flat" (Evans et al. 2010: 16).

Nonetheless, Qatar's Permanent Population Committee (PPC) clearly states that there is a need to "encourage and facilitate marriages among persons of marriageable ages, adopt policies that will reduce delayed marriages, especially of girls, and facilitate the remarriage of divorcees and widows and reduce high divorce rates and mitigate the consequences of divorce" (Permanent Population Committee 2009: 13).

Some researchers argue that state development projects, specifically those that are geared toward empowering women by increasing their education and employment rates, are in fact the same factors that paradoxically lead to an increase in divorce rates and the breakup of the traditional family structure (see, for example, Al-Ishaq 2004). The argument is that, as more Qatari women get an education and enter the workforce, thus becoming more financially independent, the less submissive and more demanding they will become. This argument holds that these developments strain relationships that have been built on traditional notions of male dominance. Qatar government reports also commonly link the higher rate of educational attainment among Qatari women with either marrying late (at an older age when they are less fertile) or not getting married at all. According to the 2015 National Human Development Report, produced by the Ministry of Development Planning and Statistics, the average fertility rate of Qatari women "fell from 4.5 in 2000 to just 3.6 in 2012. One factor in the fall in the total fertility rate is the rising proportion of women remaining permanently unmarried" (Qatar Fourth National Human Development Report 2015). The report goes on to argue that, "In most societies lesser-educated men tend to be reluctant to marry higher educated women and vice-versa. Thus a rising gap in educational attainments between Qatari males and females is a big factor in the rising proportions of females remaining permanently unmarried." So here, the state reports highlight the issue of lower fertility rate, which is still well above the world average of 2.5, as a problem which is caused primarily by the education gap between Qatari men and women. The report, in summing up the main issues facing Qatari society, asserts that, "Social and cultural implications of lifetime singleness and declining fertility need to be a central focus for family policy" (Qatar Fourth National Human Development Report 2015: 19).

It is important to note that correlations between women's education and divorce and fertility are not consistent across the region. For example, Jordanian women are highly educated, but their fertility rates are still high (Adely 2012), which raises the question of what other factors could be leading Qatari women to delay marriage or have fewer children. Further, "even when statisticians control for factors such as income and geography, the relationship between increase in girls' education and improved health outcomes persists, although the relationship to lowered fertility rates is less consistent" (Adely 2012: 140). Therefore, if it is not the level of education that is causing women to delay their marriage, then what is? Is education interacting with another variable and resulting in women to marry late, such as the level of education of Qatari men? This is a factor that is often overlooked in state documents. Therefore, researchers and state policies should be more focused on unpacking the causes that lead women to have fewer children when they receive an education instead of framing the problem as inherent in the education they receive.

*Domestic Workers*

Another issue that frequently comes up is working mothers and their "neglect" of their households, motherhood, and caregiving duties through over-reliance on domestic help, which is also perceived to negatively affect the children's development and sense of national identity. The Qatar National Development Strategy (2011: 168) states that "[h]eavy dependence on domestic helpers is leading to weakened family ties, affecting traditional family values and child well-being. This reality raises three key impact concerns: weakened bonds between parent and child, adverse impact on child safety and development, and negative effects on Qatari heritage and culture." This negative attitude is also reflected in the high level of agreement, in the World Values Survey 2010: 79 % agreed with the statement, "when a mother works for pay, children suffer."

Hamad Al-Hajri, former secretary-general of the Supreme Council for Family Affairs,[9] stressed in a newspaper article in 2013 that the purpose of the meeting in 2013 was to discuss the status of working women to improve their performance by providing a suitable working environment that meets their needs, understands their nature, and promotes their role in the family (Abbas 2013). He also argued that there is an additional need to curb the increase in the number of domestic workers. According to Al-Hajri, excessive reliance on domestic workers can result in problems that reflect negatively on the stability of the Qatari family in particular and society in general. According to Al-Hajri, prolonged interaction between children and domestic workers will leave the children at risk of losing their identity and taking on the identity of the domestic worker. In order to avoid this potential identity crises for the future generation of Qataris, Al-Hajri recommends that mothers stay at home and raise their own children.

Those perceived threats, as voiced in the statements of a respected mosque leader and a state agency representative, are the assumed outcomes of women entering the workforce. Working mothers are therefore not bearing enough children to help narrow the demographic imbalance between nationals and expatriates, and they are not available enough in the household to play their "natural role," but they instead rely on domestic help. Again, this brings to the forefront the constant dilemma of how to "empower women" in the labor market without jeopardizing the "family cohesion" in the state. Clearly there is an apparent conflict in state policy to increase the number of women in the workforce while also expecting women to have a large number of children, while providing little if any state-sponsored daycare in the workplace. The result is a dual burden on working women, which is exacerbated in situations where these women do not have the support of an extended family (discussed further in our recommendations section).

### *Tensions in State Policy*

While these challenges are clearly listed in Qatar's national strategy, which tries to tackle some of them, we find that, in the same section where family cohesion is discussed, women's empowerment is quickly brought up. It is no surprise that women are placed at the center of Qatar's national document given "the development discourse today and the international scrutiny that has been directed toward Arab and Muslim women by the West" (Adely 2009: 105). Hence, we find that women's work or education in many instances carries important "symbolic capital" that the state mobilizes to maneuver between the sometimes incompatible demands of local and global constituents (Mazawi 2008; Mazawi 2007). Nonetheless, the Qatar National Vision 2030 (QNV 2008) has also become incorporated into school and university curricula, becoming an integral part of the state's self-image and a document for the imagined community.

Similar to development reports, such as the Arab Human Development Report 2005 (AHDR), the Qatar National Development Strategy (2011) borrows from liberal feminists and the human capabilities approach in which employment and education are "considered crucial for women's advancement and capacity to live a good life" and would "eliminate gender discrimination and oppression" (Abu-Lughod 2009: 88; Pearson and Jackson 2000: 2). Qatari scholars such as Dr. Juhaina Al Easa, former deputy director with the Supreme Council on the Family and Qatar's representative for CEDAW's 2014 review session, blame patriarchy on culture and the traditional tribal structure. She claims that the path to empowerment is through modernization and support for the modern family structure by the state. Al Easa (2012) argues in her blog that "the Qatari woman will be the first to benefit from the transition from the extended tribal family to the modern nuclear family. At least she will only be under the control of her husband, after she was controlled by every man in the family or the tribe."[10] Hence, investments in women's advancement and empowerment are assumed "to lead to many positive development outcomes and to support economic growth" (Qatar National Development Strategy 2011: 177).

Nonetheless, Qatar's interest in ranking high on sustainable development indicators is not the only factor that inspires its incorporation of policies that target women's empowerment and family cohesion. Other important factors include the overall low Qatari representation in the labor force and the demographic imbalance in the state in general, as discussed earlier. It is understood that national development needs a literate workforce, which has "led to expanding women's opportunities, despite residual understandings of women as primarily reproductive" (Abu-Lughod 2009: 93). For example, we still find in the national vision and strategy a push for the reduction of "the proportion of Qatari women who are unmarried by ages 30–34 by 15 %" (Qatar National Development Strategy 2011: 168), language that emphasizes women's reproductive roles.

## Conclusion: Where the Problem Lies

In the next section, we reiterate some of the described changes by placing them within a framework to better assess their impact on the family in Qatar.

## Continuity and Change

There is no doubt that change is inevitable. However, there seems to be an intention to allow change in some areas while maintaining continuity in others. For example, there is a willingness to promote women entering the workforce (through direct appointment of women to leadership positions); however, laws have been enacted to ensure that women maintain their gender-stereotyped roles (through the establishment of family law that clearly dictates the role of the mother). Hence, we have seen the codification of norms that were challenged by social practices in the country, yet laws have been passed to reinforce them. In addition, placing women at the heart of family policies undermines men's involvement in the family structure, maintaining a narrow patriarchal image of the family.

This continuity versus change is also demonstrated in the country's aspiration to become open and multicultural yet at the same time not allow any intrusions on what is perceived as the "Qatari identity" of the country. This can be clearly seen in the laws that make marrying outside of Qatar a challenge that requires approval from the Minister of Interior, and not allowing women to grant their children their citizenship if they marry a non-Qatari. Secondly, the changes that have occurred in the past, especially the demographic change, has not only led the government to adopt the policies to exclude others, but has also become ingrained in people's social attitudes, as indicated earlier regarding World Values Survey indicators. For example, the question of involving domestic workers is not necessarily something that should be seen in a negative light. Therefore, what has occurred is that state policy has created somewhat of a "civic ethnocracy" in which the perceived purity of individuals determines many relevant outcomes in their lives (Forstenlechner and Rutledge 2011: 38) and therefore publicly embraces "internal aspects of [the] country's past that do fit with the preferred national identity protected by its leadership" (Patrick 2009, cited in Forstenlechner and Rutledge 2011: 38).

## Institutional Instability

These different desires and wishes also seem to be reflected at the institutional level, where institutions have been established and dismantled to promote (or not) specific aspirations at different points in time. Many of the policies that have been adopted have been very sudden, and the speed at which institutions such as those shown in Table 8.3 have changed has

**Table 8.3** Institutional Changes in Family Policy

| Year | Registered changes by Decree |
| --- | --- |
| 1995 | Eliminating the Ministry of Social Affairs and Housing and redistributing its responsibilities |
| 1998 | Establishing the Supreme Council of Family Affairs |
| 1999 | Appointing a Ministry of Civil Services and Housing Affairs |
| 2002 | Reorganizing the Supreme Council of Family Affairs |
| 2007 | Eliminating the Ministry of Civil Services and Housing Affairs |
| 2007 | Establishing the Ministry of Labor and Social Affairs |
| 2008/2009 | Separating the Ministries of Labor and Social Affairs |
| 2013 | Integrating the Ministries of Labor and Social Affairs |
| 2014 | Eliminating the Supreme Council of Family Affairs |

*Source*: Alkhater 2015b. Translation by authors

negatively affected the capacities of employees working in them and the attempt to make sustainable change in areas affecting the family.

The government's reaction to these perceived threats has created a large number of associations related to the family (see Table 8.1 above); nonetheless, the speed at which these organizations have been set up has created institutional disturbances. This disruption demonstrates the speed at which changes were made to these family organizations. Alkhater (2015) states that the speed at which these organizations have been established, reshuffled, and, in some cases, suddenly closed, has demoralized them. Further, the comprehensive approach that the state adopted in dealing with the question of "family," even though it narrowly linked family to women, ended with the closure of the Supreme Council of Family Affairs and the sudden reintegration of many family institutions under governmental bodies.

### *The Authoritarian Model Versus the Laissez-Faire Model of Family Policy*

The state's policies can be mapped on a continuum of authoritarian to laissez-faire models with a clear leaning toward the authoritarian. Harding (1996: 179) defines the authoritarian model of family-state relationships as distinguished by the state's being "*dirigiste* in its approach to family life, with the clear intention of enforcing certain preferred behavior and patterns and family forms, and prohibiting others."

We see this in Qatar, where policies are very strongly *dirigiste* regarding the family structure and the responsibilities of each member. Furthermore, the state clearly has declared itself the "protector of the family" in its documents. As previously mentioned, the government has the ability to draw lines as to who may be considered part of a Qatari family and who is excluded. Both sanctions and rewards are employed to ensure the formation and maintenance of this family structure through laws that make it difficult to marry people of other nationalities or grant citizenship to children of non-Qatari fathers. There are also incentives to encourage younger men to get married, as earlier mentioned. Some state charity associations have joint marriages, which aim to decrease the costs of marriage for newlyweds (Rashad et al. 2005), and there are sanctions, such as those imposed when a Qatari student on scholarship decides to marry a non-Qatari. The marriage would not be considered for approval, and there is a clear risk of the loss of scholarship funding and their marriage deemed as null.

Every family policy has clear negative and positive aspects. Many of the state policies, as earlier demonstrated (e.g., housing policies) have affected the family even if the effects were unintentional . However, policies such as encouraging Qataris "to change their attitudes towards housing" and to "adapt to small and medium-sized accommodation housing units" (Permanent Population Committee 2009: 17) all play a role in what the family structure might be in the future.

Therefore, it seems that there is a need for better family policy that is conscious of how it implicitly or explicitly affects the family and not only considers the well-being of the essentialized image of the family, but also pays clear attention to different types of family households and how it influences the well-being of the individuals that comprise them.

The policy should consider people's situations and not just "snapshot figures." The working mother's well-being should be considered, enabling her to live in a dignified house setting that does not sanction her work outside of the household, or even the child's well-being as a result of living with a divorced family rather than trying to maintain a broken home that looks good on government indicators regarding the family. In addition, instead of emphasizing having larger families to narrow the demographic imbalance, policymakers should consider the fact that larger households, with seven or more children, have higher rates of poverty (45 %; Evans et al. 2010). Yet, having multiple earners in the household, meaning, in many cases, a working mother, reduces the risk of poverty.

Therefore, first, we need to pay attention to the social stigma that we are falsely attaching to working mothers who "abandon their children with nannies" or even the social stigma regarding divorce, which further stigmatizes divorced women rather than helping them deal with poverty. While the number of poor children living in divorced households is only 5.8 % (Evans et al. 2010), there is still a relationship between divorce and an increased risk of poverty. This definitely requires policies to tackle such problems that might arise.

Second, so far, the emphasis on women in family policies has meant that very little interest has been directed toward fathers' roles and responsibilities. Therefore, there is an important need to reassess what is expected of the father. For example, Mitchell, et al. (2015) rightly point out that this constant worry that women are not finding a perfect match hardly ever looks at ways of encouraging men to attain higher degrees, yet it is just focused on how women are too educated to get married.

*Recommendations*

We end this chapter by making policy recommendations that address some of the issues and concerns we have highlighted. It can be noted from the earlier discussion that the subject of family crosscuts a wide range public policies. Hence, there is a need to adopt a "family perspective on policy," where there is sensitivity by policy makers to the ways in which family impacts and is impacted by different policies, either intentionally or unintentionally (Harding 1996: 144–5). In the following recommendations, we address a variety of topics, but we hope to emphasize the need to address issues more holistically.

*The Education Gap and Marriage Barriers* With Qatari men leaving the education ladder early to get jobs created by the push for Qatarization, an increasing disparity has become visible between men's and women's education levels. Among Qataris in tertiary education the ratio of females to males is 2 to 1 (Qatar Fourth National Human Development Report 2015). As previously mentioned, this education gap may be a barrier to marriage and could lead to marital conflict. This possible factor is supported by the negative attitude Qataris hold toward women having a higher income than their husbands (35 % agree it is a problem) (Social and Economic Survey Research Institute 2012). The Qatari government has so far worked on easing monetary constraints to enable young couples to get married, but minimal efforts have focused on changing negative attitudes toward educated working women. If anything, it seems there is a continuous negative media campaign against working mothers in state-sanction newspapers. Similarly, preliminary research has indicated that the outdated marriage practices have not changed amid drastic changes occurring across the country (Al-Nasr 2011). More research can be conducted on the social barriers that prevent men and women from being more involved in the selection of their partners, to help address this challenge.

Finally, it is important to note that selection of a marriage partner outside of one's nationality, as earlier pointed out, limits Qatari women's marriage choices. For example, the restriction on women to transfer their citizenship (as in the case of Qatari men) to their partners and offspring is hardly ever mentioned when concerns of the demographic imbalance (between national and non-nationals) is brought up in state documents. This is again associated with negative attitudes toward foreign interference to what is deemed purely "Qatari." More efforts could be focused on public campaigns that demonstrate the diversity among Qatari families' lifestyles instead of promoting a limiting ideal image of what the "Qatari family" should like.

*Domestic Help and Childcare* To encourage families to rely less on domestic help, the state needs to review parental leave and childcare policies in place. While Qatar's labor law ensures women have a six-month maternity leave, support for working mothers needs improvement. State policies should consider subsidizing or requiring workplace daycare for working mothers. Other policies that support working mothers include subsidized nurseries, pre-school programs, daycare, and paternal leave. These policies may encourage families to have more children and enable them to cope without the need to rely on domestic helpers. However, for this to happen, some amendments to the gender stereotypical roles in Qatar's family law needs to be addressed. Additionally, Qatar can possibly implement media campaigns that address marriage and child upbringing as a partnership instead of being solely the responsibility of mothers. Having state policies of this sort would be even more beneficial for low-income families and mothers that might have not been able to enter the workforce due to the lack of domestic help available at home.

Finally, extended families play an important role in ensuring a strong and stable family life as well. A grandmother, aunt, etc. can help in providing care for young children while their parents/mothers are away. Of course for this to work, the extended family needs to live in close proximity to make the arrangement feasible. Therefore, the state has to rethink its policy in order to ensure that families remain as geographically close as possible. This would allow parents to rely less on domestic helpers to be in charge of caregiving for young children. As in the case of a majority of households in Qatar, few of these domestic workers are actually hired as nannies or have the required qualifications. More often than not, these women are actually hired as maids, and they end up being the primary caregiver to young children. Dr. Maria Kristiansen has pointed out that often "in the Gulf [that] these women are first hired as maids for cooking and cleaning, then a child is put into their care like a new task …as that was not her primary job. They will be more engaged in keeping the house neat and tidy while the kids are left on their own, because she has enough to do already" (Oliveira 2014). A policy recommendation that could help deal with this issue would be to subsidize extended family housing. Helping families live in close proximity to each other will allow working parents a familial support system that they could rely on.

## Notes

1. Literature on the tribe has also argued that some aspects of the tribal culture offer a source of legitimacy, when they symbolize national identity, for the current state leaders;therefore, only some aspects of it are seen as a threat to the state. This would also explain why the government clearly notes that as part of its preservation of family values in face of modernization, it intends to maintain the "inherited status and prestige of the leading families" (Qatar National Development Strategy 2011–2016, 2011: 20). For examples of this literature, see Layne (1989) and Gengler (2013).
2. Law and Underwood (2012: 147) define *fereej* as "the building block of a traditional Arab settlement where family homes and extended family quarters are interconnected and grew in an apparent organic form over time. The *fereej* embodies the family-based social structure and it expresses the collective identity of the clan network as well as individual family lineage within it." Therefore, it is no wonder that today there are still areas in Doha named after the families that inhabited them; an example is Fereej Bin Mahmoud, in central Doha.
3. The survey "From Fareej to Metropolis: A Social Capital Survey of Qatar" interviewed Qataris and non-Qataris from across Doha. In our analysis of the data, we only reflect on the 800 Qatari respondents' data made available to us by the Social and Economic Survey Research Institute (SESRI) (2012).

4. Qatari women's participation (age 15 and above) in the labour force has increased from 27.4 % in 2001 to 34.7 % in 2013, according to the Qatar's Fourth National Human Development Report. Qatari Ministry of Development Planning and Statistics, June 2015.
5. For example, a ban on marriage while studying abroad was stipulated in the Qatari 1989 law, which regulates marriages to foreigners. Other restrictions for citizens in general can be seen in the full text in English, accessible at the following link: http://www.almeezan.qa/LawArticles.aspx?LawTreeSectionID=8702&lawId=2555&language=en
6. "Asians worse than Israeli attack: Bahrain MP." Al Arabiya News, January 28, 2008
7. Even though there is a certain level of naivety in the argument that polygamy would resolve the demographic imbalance in the country, it is worth noting that the government has done nothing to discourage polygamy; instead, it was incorporated in the 2006 family law. A recent study in Malaysia has documented the negative impact of polygamy not only on the wives but also on children. Again, the state is permitting policies that are even more anti-child than they are anti-woman.
8. It is important to note that Qatar's 2006 family law makes marriage legal for women at 15 years of age and at 18 years for men.
9. Interestingly, the Family Supreme Council was dismantled in 2014, after the presentation of the first state report in the 2014 CEDAW review. This could be read as a step back for women given that the Family Supreme Council has been responsible for publishing research on many family-related issues and reforming state policy that touches on the family in general and women specifically (see Table 8.1).
10. http://bintsultan1.blogspot.com/2012/09/blog-post_26.html

فتمثل الأسرة الحديثة تهديدا للنظام الأبوي التقليدي بالنظر للتحولات التي تحدثها في مكانة المرأة ووضعها الاجتماعيين، حيث أن المستفيد الأول من وضعية التحول من نمط العائلة الممتدة والقبيلة إلى شكل الأسرة الحديثة هي المرأة. فهي على الأقل تصبح تحت سلطة زوجها فقط بعد أن كانت تحت سلطة كل رجال العائلة/العشيرة أ والقبيلة.

## BIBLIOGRAPHY. QATAR: POLICY MAKING IN A TRANSFORMATIVE STATE

Abbas, Manal. 2013. The decline of working Qatari women's fertility rate [in Arabic]. *Al-Raya Newspaper*, April 16. http://www.raya.com/home/print/f6451603-4dff-4ca1-9c10-122741d17432/a02798c6-3ac7-41a6-8960-4afacbb39fa6.

Abu-Lughod, Lila. 2009. Dialects of women's empowerment: The international circuitry of the Arab human development report 2005. *International Journal of Middle East Studies* 41(1): 83–103.

Adely, Fida. 2009. Education women for development: The Arab Human Development Report 2005 and the problem with women's choices. *International Journal of Middle East Studies* 41(1): 105–122.

Al Easa J., 2012. Dawr al-Mara' Fi Al-Usra min Khilal Amaliyat AlTamkeen [Women's role in the family through the process of empowerment]. *Juhaina's Blog*. 26 September, Available at: http://bintsultan1.blogspot.ca/2012/09/blog-post_26.html [Accessed August 2015].

Al Muftah, Hend. 2010a. How do Qatari females make it to the top? An examination of the organizational constraints to the advancement. *Hawwa* 8(2): 97–119.

———. 2010b. *Human Capital Formation in Qatar: A Story of Oil and Gas-based Industries*. Saarbrücken, Germany: VDM Publishing.

Al-Arab. 2014. Al-ma'yer almutaba' litawzea' alaradhi tuther jadal.. wal dahabibiya wa naqs alshafafiya dahira tahtaj ila ta'del [The standards followed for land distribution lead to controversy.. and the ambiguity and lack of transparency surrounding them needs resolving]. *Al-Arab Newspaper*, August 3. http://goo.gl/XKbU9M.

Al-Attiyah, Asma. 2009. The Role of Women in Sustainable Development in the Gulf Cooperation Council for the Arab Gulf States. The Cooperation Council for the Arab States of the Gulf.

Al-Ghanim, Kaltham. 2013. The hierarchy of authority based on kinship, age, and gender in the extended family in the Arab Gulf states. *International Journal of the Jurisprudence of the Family* 3: 329–360.

Al-Ishaq, Moza. 2004. *Social Change and the Divorce Phenomenon in the Qatari Society [in Arabic]*. Tanta, Egypt: University of Tanta.

Alkhater, Khalid Rashid. 2015a. *The Challenges of Collapsing Oil Prices and Economic Diversification in the GCC countries*. Doha: Arab Center for Research and Policy Studies.

Alkhater, Lolwah. 2015b. Siyasat al'usra al-Qatariya bayn almubadara alshmela wa alta'qloum almufaje' [Family policies in Qatar: Between the comprehensive initiative and the partial adaptation]. Doha International Family Institute (DIFI) Annual Conference on Family Research and Policy: The Arab Family in an Age of Transition: Challenge and Resilience, Doha, May 3–4.

Al-Makki, Mohammed Ahmed. 1999. Zawjat amir Qatar taftatih haflat ishahar "dar tanmiyat alusra" wa ma'rathan khayriyan [Qatar's Emir's wife attends the initialization of the "family development center" and two charity exhibition]. *Al-Hayat*, April 11. http://daharchives.alhayat.com/issue_archive/Hayat INT/1999/4/11/زوج-ة-ريم-ا-يمطق-رتفتحت-ح-ةلش-ا-رهاد-ر-تنمي-ة-الس-رق-ومعرض-يريخ.html.

Al-Nasr, Tofol Jassim. 2011. Gulf Cooperation Council (GCC) women and Misyar marriage: Evolution and progress in the Arabian Gulf. *Journal of International Women's Studies* 12(3): 43–57 .http://vc.bridgew.edu/cgi/viewcontent.cgi?a rticle=1112&context=jiws

Alsharekh, Alanoud. 2007. Introduction. In *In The Gulf Family: Kinship Policies and Modernity*, ed. Alanoud Alsharekh. London: Saqi Books.

Al-Watan. 2014. Al-Muhandai: tawze'a (7782) kasemat ardh sakniyah al-muwatneen hatha al'am alkhitwa alkabeera min nawe'ha [Al-Muhanadi: Distribution of (7782) housing vouchers for nationals this year, a big step of its kind]. *Al Watan Newspaper.* https://www.facebook.com/AlWatanQatar/posts/494194930701387.

Buckley, M. 2015. Construction work, 'bachelor' builders and the intersectional politics of urbanisation in Dubai. In *Transit States: Labour, Migration and Citizenship in the Gulf*, eds. A. Khalaf, O. Alshehabi, and A. Hanieh. London: Pluto Press.

Cooke, M. 2014. *Tribal Modern: Branding New Nations in the Arab Gulf.* Berkeley: University of California Press.

Doha International Family Institute. 2013. Mission & Vision. http://www.difi.org.qa/about/mission-and-vision

Doha News Team. 2012. High cost of Qatari weddings blamed for rising rates of "spinsterhood". *Doha News,* January 31. http://dohanews.co/high-cost-of-qatari-weddings-blamed-for-rising-rates-of/

El-Haddad, Yahya. 2003. *Major Trends Affecting Families in the Gulf Countries.* New York: United Nations Department of Economic and Social Affairs.

Evans, M., P. Powell-Davies, and T. P. Chung. 2010. *Child Well-being in Qatar.* General Secretariat for Development Planning.

Foley, S. 2010. *The Arab Gulf States: Beyond Oil and Islam.* Boulder, CO: Lynne Rienner Publishers.

Forstenlechner, I., and E.J. Rutledge. 2011. The GCC's "demographic imbalance": Perceptions, realities and policy options. *Middle East Policy* 18(4): 25–43.

General Secretariat for Development Planning (Qatar). 2008. *Qatar National Vision 2030.* Doha: Retrieved from http://www.gsdp.gov.qa/portal/page/portal/gsdp_en/knowledge_center/Tab/QNV2030_English_v2.pdfMinistry of Development Planning and Statistics (Qatar).

———. 2011. *Qatar National Development Strategy 2011–2016: Towards Qatar National Vision 2030.* Ministry of Development Planning and Statistics (Qatar): Retrieved from http://www.gsdp.gov.qa/gsdp_vision/docs/NDS_EN.pdf Doha.

Gengler, J 2013. Political segmentation and diversification in the rentier Arab Gulf. Fourth Gulf Research Meeting, Cambridge, July 1–5.

Gray, Matthew. 2013. *Qatar: Politics and the Challenges of Development*. Boulder, CO: Lynne Rienner Publishers.
Harding, L. 1996. Family, State and Social Policy. Houndmills Basingstoke: Palgrave Macmillan.
Kligman, G. 1998. *The Politics of Duplicity: Controlling Reproduction in Ceausescu's Romania*. Berkeley, CA: University of California Press.
Law, R., and K. Underwood. 2012. Msheireb Heart of Doha: An alternative approach to urbanism in the Gulf region. *International Journal of Islamic Architecture* 1(1): 131–147.
Layne, L. 1989. The dialogues of tribal self-representation in Jordan. *American Ethnologist* 16(1): 24–39.
Levine, D. 1991. Punctuated equilibirum: the modernization of the proletarian family in the age of ascendant capitalism. *International Labor and Working-Class History* 39(Spring): 3–20.
Mazawi, A. 2007. Besieging the king's tower? En/gendering academic opportunities in the Gulf Arab states. In *Aspects of Education in the Middle East and North Africa*, eds. Colin Brock, and L.Z. Levers, 77–97. Oxford: Symposium Books.
Mazawi, A. 2008. Policy politics of higher education in the Gulf Cooperation Council member states: Intersections of globality, regionalism and locality. In *Higher Education in the Gulf States: Shaping Economies, Politics and Culture*, eds. C. Davidson, and P.M. Smith, 59–72. London: Saqi Books.
Ministry of Development Planning and Statistics (Qatar). 2015. *Qatar Fourth National Human Development Report*. Doha: Ministry of Development Planning and Statistics.
Mitchell, J. S., C. Paschyn, S. Mir, K. Pike, and T. Kane. 2015. In Majlis Al-Hareem: The Complex Professional and Personal Choices of Qatari Women. Doha International Family Institute (DIFI) Annual Conference on Family Research and Policy: The Arab Family in an Age of Transition: Challenge and Resilience, May 3–4, Doha.
Moghadam, V.M. 2004. Patriarchy in transition: Women and the changing family in the Middle East. *Journal of Comparative Family Studies* 35(2): 137–162.
Oliveira, Cassey. 2014. The nanny dilemma: Dealing with the 'third' parent. *Just Here*, March 23. http://www.justhere.qa/2014/03/nanny-dilemma-dealing-third-parent/
Oakley, A. 1974. The Sociology of Housework. London: Robertson.
Partrick, Neil. 2009. *Nationalism in the Gulf States*. London: Centre for the Study of Global Governance. Retrieved from http://www.lse.ac.uk/middleEastCentre/kuwait/documents/NeilPartrick.pdf
Pearson, R., and C. Jackson. 2000. Interrogating development: Feminism, gender and policy. In *Feminist Visions of Development: Gender, Analysis and Policy*, eds. R. Pearson and C. Jackson, 1–16. London: Routledge.

Permanent Population Committee. 2009. The Population of the State of Qatar 2009. Permanent Population Committee.

Rasha, H., M. Osman, and F. Roudi-Fahimi. 2005. *Marriage in the Arab World.* Retreived from: http://www.prb.org/pdf05/marriageinarabworld_eng.pdf

Social and Economic Survey Research Institute (Qatar University). 2012. From Fareej to metropolis: A social capital survey of Qatar. Available at: http://sesri.qu.edu.qa/From-Fareej-to-Metropolis-2012.

Sonbol, A. 2009. The genesis of family law: How Shari'ah, custom and colonial laws influenced the development of personal status codes. In *Wanted: Equality and Justice in the Muslim Family*, ed. Zainah Anwar. Selangor: Musawah.

Stanko, E. 2000. Rethinking violence, rethinking social policy. In *Rethinking Social Policy*, ed. G. Lewis, 245–258. London: Sage.

Sullivan, O. 2000. The division of domestic labour: Twenty years of change? *Sociology* 34(3): 437–456.

Young, M.D., P. Willmott, and R. Mills. 1973. *The Symmetrical Family: A Study of Work and Leisure in the London Region.* London: Routledge & Kegan Paul.

CHAPTER 9

# Public Policy and Identity

*Amal Mohammed Al-Malki*

The debate over identity in general, and national identity specifically, has become the cornerstone of Qatar's private and public debates recently. Identity is a topic that pertains to culture, economics, politics, language, education, and many other civic and official and unofficial domains. Most discussion, whether private or public, refers to the Qatari national identity as a fixed form of reference that supersedes spatial and temporal changes. It is represented as a homogenous construction, one that reflects a social and cultural cohesion and a unified society, upon which the stability and continuity of the society is dependent. Several factors considered threats to this "imagined" form of identity are identified; these include globalization and multiculturalism that entail a degree of openness to world cultures and, possibly, adaptation to and appropriation of new/foreign values and ways of living, as well as increasing numbers of immigrants, mixed marriages, and Western education, amongst other factors.

Measures to protect the national identity are institutionalized and communicated to the society through national policies that protect nationals' rights. If we consider national laws relating to education, the workforce, and health services, these give apparent privileges and favour nationals over non-nationals; one example would be the Qatarization programme (see Chapter 10) that sets quotas for Qataris in the private and public

---

A.M. Al-Malki (✉)
College of Humanities and Social Sciences,
Hamad bin Khalifa University-Qatar Foundation, Doha, Qatar

© The Author(s) 2016
M.E. Tok et al. (eds.), *Policy-Making in a Transformative State*,
DOI 10.1057/978-1-137-46639-6_9

sectors. As mentioned above, debates about identity revolve around a fixed perception of identity, the threats it is facing, and how to protect it. Few are the voices that consider identity a dynamic and fluid construct of changing realities.

National identity in Qatar has been subject to several historical framings in the era after the discovery of oil, moving from "Arab identity" to "Gulf identity" to "Qatari identity." As for most Gulf states in the pre-oil era, the national identity of Qatar was based mainly on its Arabic and Islamic roots, emphasizing Arab nationalism. At the heart of Arab nationalism is the concept of Arab unity and the Palestinian cause. The collective pan-Arab identity has been a stepping-stone for Qatar as a newly-emerging state on the path of defining its own history and national identity during the initial stages of nation-building.

Like most of the Gulf states, Qatar was not colonized but was under British protection from 1916. The lack of a local history of independence struggles in the Arabian Peninsula created a desire for association through a shared language, culture, and past. This resulted in a generation of Arab nationalists, activists, and intelligentsia in Qatar who, as in the other Gulf states, subscribed wholeheartedly to Arab nationalism, which still survives along with the 1960s generation. However, the Arabian Peninsula as an economic entity has begun to attract interest and resentment, as it has become the main employer of other Arab nationalities. The shared interests of the Gulf states, amongst other factors, led them to form the Gulf Cooperation Council (GCC) in 1981, based on "[d]eep religious and cultural ties … and strong kin relations," as well as factors of geographical proximity that "facilitated contacts and interaction among them, and created homogeneous values and characteristics" (GCC "Foundations and Objectives," (n.d.): par.1). This, however, did not mean total harmony amongst these states, especially around issues concerning sovereignty and borders. Meanwhile, "Arab nationalism was weakened by a number of factors in the late 1960s and early 1970s, including the growing economic inequality among Arab states after the 1973 oil boom as well as the failure of two Arab unity experiments and the Arab defeat in the 1967 war with Israel" (Kinninmont 2013: p. 49).

The political upheavals in the Middle East during the last quarter of the twentieth century affected the romanticized image of Arab nationalism. The Gulf states faced a series of challenges that gave rise to "the notion of haweeya Khaleeji[ya] (Gulf identity) as a conscious alternative to the delegitimizing radical Islamism of the newly born Iranian Republic and of the rival resurgent assertions of Arab nationalism being expressed by Iraq as a tool of its own interests" (Patrick 2009: 31). The first direct challenge that faced the GCC was the Iraqi invasion of Kuwait in 1990. The Gulf states felt that they were in an alliance of their own, and they felt the urge to further protect their shared interests, their royal families, and their people. The emphasis thus moved to a "Gulf identity," downplaying the differences between these states in terms of their diverse histories and origins of their peoples.

Fractures in this "Gulf Identity" discourse soon appeared. The attempted counter-coup by Khalifa bin Hamad in 1997 to regain power from his son, Shiekh Hamad bin Khalif and new emir, was backed by some Gulf states, and hence there was an attack on one of their own members, Qatar. With the establishment of Al-Jazeera, for the first time in the history of the Gulf media, a news channel belonging to one of the GCC states criticized other Gulf states, entirely against the traditional code of these countries and their council's agreements! Al-Jazeera's coverage has led to the closure of many of its offices in the Gulf states and many high-level discussions about the agenda of the news channel. In 2002, for example, a diplomatic rift occurred between Qatar on the one side, and Saudi Arabia, Bahrain, and Kuwait on the other, due to reporting by Al-Jazeera (Hassan 2015).

The terrorist attacks of 9/11, the surfacing of Al-Qaeda and the violent version of Islam that was promoted, along with the subsequent Islamophobia generated around the world, have all pushed the Gulf states to confront issues in their representation and their internal policies. The 2011 Arab revolutions caused further divisions between Qatar and the other Gulf states, as well as amongst and within the other states. The most obvious of these was the leading role played by Qatar in the revolutions in Libya, Egypt, and Syria, a role that was not supported by the other Gulf states. These divisions intensified with the resurgence of the Muslim Brotherhood (MB) as a political entity in Egypt.

The constantly complicated international and regional political climate and the divided loyalties, along with the growing importance of the Gulf states as emerging political and economic powers, have led to the need for a redefinition of identities. This has involved a growing sense of pride in local identities, distinct heritage, and policies to protect nationals. The emphasis has shifted to the distinct cultural and national identities of each of these states. Thus, national projects began that reimagined the traditions and rewrote the histories of these nations to legitimize and ensure the sustainability of these newly established national communities.

Qatar has followed two incompatible approaches over the past two decades: outward and inward. The more Qatar has opened up to the world, the more urgent the need to define itself on a local/internal level. Qatar as a global player (see Chapter 13) has had to construct an identity that is compatible with its international image yet preserves its authenticity and locality. The Qatar of the new millennium publically declares its close ties with the United States, maintained friendly relations with Iran until the Syrian crisis started in 2011, and builds allegiances with Turkey. It has gained diplomatic status by playing a major role in many peace accords in the region, particularly during the Arab revolutions, as well as media status through Al-Jazeera. Moreover, the Father Emir, Sheikh Hamad bin Khalifa, has played a significant role, mimicking Al-Jazeera's symbolic "regional" role in being the voice of all Arabs. His approach has conjured up images of Jamal Abdul Nasser and the golden era of Arab nationalism, as he presented himself as the saviour of the people and, as Kamrava (2013) puts it, Qatar's role has become that of defining and leading "both symbolically and factually, what Arabism means in the twenty-first century" (Kamrava 2013: 42). However, Qatar's international image did not necessarily correspond with its internal image. The outward approach of representation and profile-building called for an equally important inward approach to attempt to redefine Qatar as a modern nation, not to the outside world but to its own people, and in terms that were more understandable locally.

## Qatari National Identity: Ethnicity and Nationalism

To better understand the characteristics of the Qatari national identity, we need to consider the interconnections between ethnicity and nationalism in shaping this identity. This chapter adopts the social anthropological approach that looks at ethnicity in terms of "aspects of relationships between groups which consider themselves, and are regarded by others, as being culturally distinctive" (Eriksen 2005: 136). Ethnicity here is more about ethnic tendencies in the preservation of a unified national identity, rather than about the demographics of the Qatari population and its status as minority or majority. And, as Eriksen (2005) suggests, "majorities and dominant peoples are no less 'ethnic' than minorities" (Eriksen 2005: 136); therefore, ethnicity in this context is not the paradigm that covers minority issues or issues of inferior groups in the nation but, rather, the opposite.

Through considering national identity in Qatar within the context of the interplay between ethnicity and nationalism, one understands the weight that is placed on shared history and culture. Eriksen (2005) states that "nationalism stresses the cultural similarities of its adherents and, by implication, it draws boundaries vis-à-vis others, who thereby become outsiders" (Eriksen 2005: 138). This type of ethnic nationalism states clearly the boundaries between the "self"—the national—and "the other"—the outsider, or foreigner. This dichotomy plays a major role in defining the roles of each in the nation, as well as the privileges and the power relationships. A clear distinction exists between Qataris and non-Qataris and even has existential implications, the most obvious being the kafala—sponsorship—system. The kafala system is merely a way to regulate the influx of incomers to the country and, were this system to be modified or even abolished, there remain other issues that are tackled less frequently, such as those of "belonging" and also citizenship rights for a large percentage of long-term residents in Qatar.

However, defining the self here is more problematic. The self—the Qatari identity—is one that is not related to passport or documentation, the very basis of citizenship, but instead to ethnic allegiances. Emphasis on shared "culture" and social cohesion are invested techniques to create a sense of belonging that can be inherited. As an ethnic nationalism, the state with its invested power enforces a nationalist ideology and employs all its institutions to realize that ideology.

### *Citizenship Versus National Identity*

A national identity in specific is a construct of necessity and its formation is as important to a nation as it is to individuals; national identities are highly shaped and reshaped by politics and the state. However, the most straightforward representation is citizenship. "Citizenship is usually defined as a form of membership in a political and geographical community. It can be disaggregated into four dimensions: legal status, rights, political and other forms of participation in society, and a sense of belonging" (Bloemraad et al. 2008: 154). These four dimensions can intersect, challenging the meaning of belonging in some cases and rights in others.

The general identity of the population officially distinguishes between citizens and residents, making citizenship a marker of the few who hold Qatari passports. Citizenship marks the differences before addressing the commonalities. Therefore, citizenship, or membership of the Qatari community, becomes an exclusive right, a main determinant of a bundle of privileges and, moreover, a cornerstone of an invented national identity. Exclusiveness and inclusiveness as binaries become important in the preservation of identity—an identity in this case that is under threat. Eriksen (2005) explains that the "[p]roblem of identity and problems of boundary maintenance have usually been studied in relation to minorities or otherwise 'threatened' or 'weak' groups, or in situations of rapid change" (Eriksen 2005: 140). This is obviously applicable to Qatar, where rapid growth has serious implications for cultural and social cohesion, turning the national identity into a "threatened" identity in need of preservation.

The biggest challenge that Qatar faces is the demographic imbalance. With a growing number of expatriates, the proportion of the national population has shrunk drastically, generating an anxiety over the national identity. Qatar has passed through phases of constructing a national identity since its independence in 1971, and the "continuous presence of a large number of foreigners has reinforced citizens' sense of the distinct Qatari-ness, and shaped a sense of nationality along clear lines of cultural belonging" (Babar 2014: 404). The first stage of constructing a national identity was to distinguish Qataris from non-Qataris, the foreigners, the migrants—those who, no matter how long they spend in Qatar, will eventually leave. Exclusiveness is, in fact, reflected in the stringent naturalization and citizenship laws that do not grant membership to the Qatari community on permanent basis. Thus, the sponsorship system stands as a binary law that "ensures the transience of the expatriate labour force" (Al-Nakib 2015: 6).

Qatar has a restrictive citizenship law that makes the Qatari passport an exclusive product. As Babar (2014) explains, "the processes of constructing citizenship have been strongly state-derived and state-driven over the past four decades" (Babar 2014: 403–4). The exclusive system of citizenship in Qatar poses a conundrum for those who live long-term in Qatar but are not eligible for citizenship in terms of the meaning and degree of their membership to the Qatari community. A large proportion of Arabs residing in Qatar face a serious identity crisis, causing a mismatch between their sense of belonging and their actual nationality/passport. They consider Qatar—the land they have lived in for most of their lives—

their homeland, yet they are not entitled to the nationality and are not considered a part of the national identity. Some of these Arabs are Qataris by virtue of their dialect, cultural norms, customs, and values; some are woven within the fabric of the Qatari culture and its traditional nuances such that they cannot be distinguished from other Qataris, or be defined as anything other than Qatari. Yet these people are Qataris in soul but not in documentation and include, for example, the children of Qatari mothers born and raised in Qatar (see below), the non-nationals (bidoun) carriers of the Qatari "travel document," and some long-term Arab national residents who have lived for decades in Qatar, where they have established their livelihoods.

However, citizenship is still not represented by a direct correlation between passport and national identity, as there are different layers of citizenship that attract different levels of economic and political privileges. Furthermore, as Patrick (2009) puts it, "holding the jinsia [passport] of a given country does not necessarily translate into being a full 'citizen' and, even where it does, there are concerns about equality in terms of political and economic opportunities" (Patrick 2009: 20). In Qatar there are two classes of citizenship: the "native" Qataris and the so-called "naturalized" Qataris, who represent an estimated two-thirds of the population and are judged to have settled in the country since 1930. The naturalized Qataris differ from native Qataris in that they have no automatic right to be candidates to vote in municipal or prospective national legislative elections (Patrick 2009: 20–1). The naturalization legislation, as Babar (2014) puts it, "has developed tiered access to citizenship benefits, so that citizens are not eligible for the same level of rights as original citizens, a reflection of the way in which the state protects the domain of citizenship against encroachment and negotiates around existing pressures" (Babar 2014: 406).

To consider the passport as the main determinant of national identity proves to be problematic as it raises issues of marginalization and minorities. The Qatari national identity is in no way a homogenous one, but one that in theory needs to capture the many layers of citizenship and the somewhat competing ethnic and, to a lesser degree, sectarian backgrounds of its population. This also leads to an ambivalent sense of national consciousness at the expense of the sub-identities, affecting first and foremost the sense of belonging to a nation. As Patrick (2009: 21) explains, "[t]he issue of national belonging is plainly distorted by these other perceptions of belonging, while legal measures effectively enforcing inequality suggest that the state itself is not based on a conception of national inclusion."

## Women as Second-Class Citizens

As citizens of their nations, women in the Gulf states have benefitted immensely from economic growth through access to education, health services, and employment. However, citizenship in the Gulf states seems to be gender-based, and women are in some cases denied their constitutional rights. Certain biases and prejudices that are entrenched in the political and legal systems deny women their citizenship rights, preventing them from participating fully and fulfilling their responsibilities towards their countries. Although Art. 34 of the Qatari Constitution states that men and women are equal in their public rights and duties, Qatari women cannot pass on their nationality to their children. "In most GCC countries, citizenship is passed through the father, meaning women who marry foreigners are penalized by seeing their children unable to benefit from the free schools, healthcare and, later, job opportunities reserved for nationals" (Kinninmont 2013: 52). Children of Qatari women receive in theory equal benefits as Qataris in education and health care, but in reality their benefits are limited and in no way equal. Some of the major challenges they face are sponsorship, limited job opportunities, and work compensations that are based on their status as "local foreigners," putting them at disadvantage in terms of allowances and benefits. The author has launched a twitter campaign under the hash-tag "#ImHalfQatari" in June 2014 that has led to a public debate on social media and has exposed some of the unknown issues this growing sector are facing; from social acceptance and identity crisis, to rigid inheritance laws that deprive them of their mother's inheritance, to their deportation after her death.

A lack of recent statistics and reliable data plays against women, as does a lack of women rights' associations, whether they're governmental or from NGOs (see Chapter 1 for more information about NGOs). However, a report conducted in 2006 by the Supreme Council of Family Affairs stated that in 2004 a total of 350 Qatari women living in Qatar were married to non-Qataris, that is, 1.2 % of the Qatari female population at the time. Of this number, 138 had a university degree, including eight with an MA or PhD; and 226 of them (64.4 %) worked (Women's Research and Studies Center 2013: 16). However, such statistics do not reveal the number of children resulting from these marriages. Any local observer can testify that the number of Qatari women marrying non-Qataris has increased considerably and, consequently, so too has the number of children deprived of their mothers' nationality, who will thus be considered "foreigners" and outside the membership of the national community.

Gendered citizenship is not the only hurdle depriving women of equal rights of citizenship. Yuval-Davis argues that we should go beyond making comparisons with men and their rights as citizens, "but also in relation to women's affiliation to dominant or subordinate groups, their ethnicity, origin and urban or rural residence" (Yuval-Davis 1997: 5). Women's job and promotion opportunities are contingent in many cases on their tribal and sectarian memberships. Furthermore, women in general face multiple layers of institutionalized discrimination on several counts and also suffer from a lack of laws and regulations that protect their existing rights, for example, gendered leadership positions and glass ceilings preventing women from reaching decision-making positions, lack of sexual harassment laws in the workplace, and unequal pay and governmental benefits.

## QATARI NATIONAL IDENTITY: STATE DISCOURSE

To define the identity of a nation is to attempt to capture the way in which the nation represents itself through its public discourse on identity and the means whereby it employs different tools to promote this discourse. We need to identify the representational elements that the nation prefers to present as opposed to the equally important elements it may repress, as well as the challenges faced by the nation in achieving the ideal or promoted identity. Clearly, to cover all aspects would be impossible, and the aim here is to draw attention to the main trends in the reimagining of a new national identity through an examination of state discourse. This discourse has helped to shape a unified narrative of Qatar's aspirations, as well as its opportunities and challenges. The state discourse on identity is important because it becomes the foundation for other discourses, a dominant narrative that shapes future narratives.

The state discourse on identity that was articulated in the Qatar National Vision 2030 (QNV2030) published in 2008 is considered here. The vision's strategic objective "aims at transforming Qatar into an advanced country by 2030, capable of sustaining its own development and providing for a high standard of living for all of its people for generations to come" (GSDP, Qatar 2008: 2). His Highness, Sheikh Tamim bin Hamad, the current Emir who was at the time the Heir Apparent, wrote the forward to the QNV2030. In language that is both authoritative and paternal, he uses the inclusive pronoun "we" to establish both familiarity and intimacy based on kinship and communal identity; and he uses the possessive pronoun "our" to connote a shared present, an interest in as well as an obligation to the community, as apparent in phrases such as "we need to galvanize our collective energies," and "[t]he welfare of our children, and of our children yet to be born" (GSDP, Qatar 2008: Forward).

The QNV2030 identifies the main challenges that the nation faces and presents "modernization and preservation of traditions" as the first of five. Although no specific definitions are provided, there is a linguistic binary that sets certain values and practices in opposition to each other: "old" versus "new"; "modern work patterns" versus "traditional relationships"; and "greater freedoms and wider choices" versus "deep-rooted social values." The vision is to mould "modernization around local culture and traditions" and to "balance the old and the new" (GSDP, Qatar 2008: 4).

The human development and social development pillars, two of four pillars of the QNV2030, make reference to national identity within the desired outcomes. The "human development outcome—an "educated population" is included with the aim to develop generations with solid grounding in Qatari moral and ethical values, traditions and cultural heritage" as well as a "strong sense of belonging and citizenship" (GSDP, Qatar 2011: 16). The "social development outcome—a sound social structure" refers to public institutions and civil society organizations that "[p]reserve Qatar's national heritage and enhance Arab and Islamic values and identity" (GSDP, Qatar 2011: 22).

The Qatar National Development Strategy 2011–2016 (QNDS; see Chapter 3) is the roadmap or action plan for QNV2030 and is a richer document that also refers to "tradition" and "culture" in multiple instances, especially in terms of family values, emphasizing the importance of the family as the core of the society. When breaking down the challenge of "[p]reserving and leveraging Qatar's heritage and culture," the document states that despite rapid changes "Qatari society has maintained the essence of its culture and continuity with the past" (GSDP, Qatar 2011: 20). This has been achieved through "observing the fundamental principles of Islam, maintaining the inherited status and prestige of the leading families and preserving the family unit as the core of society" (GSDP, Qatar 2011: 20). Nevertheless, the challenge remains of striking the balance between "modern life and the country's cultural and traditional values" (GSDP, Qatar 2011: 20). The document identifies the efforts being

PUBLIC POLICY AND IDENTITY 251

undertaken to achieve this balance, all of which revolve around promoting cultural exchanges, sport, and arts. The obvious ambiguity concerning what modernity actually is and what it entails is met with a similarly confusing description of culture and cultural identity by focusing on heritage and the past. The document states that "Qatar is also increasing attention to its own history through enhanced preservation of heritage sites and an ongoing commitment of resources to new museums and education programmes" (GSDP, Qatar 2011: 20).

The balancing formula is described as follows:

> By thoroughly embracing its cultural identity in the context of its diverse population, Qatar will be well positioned to protect its unique character while continuing to foster a creative and exceptional society. The National Development Strategy 2011–2016 will enable the cultural growth of Qatar's people and forge new international relationships, while solidifying Qatar's standing as a centre of Arab culture through its own distinctive national identity (GSDP, Qatar 2011: 20).

In summary, when looking at both QNV2030 and QNDS 2011–2016, an obvious question is, why was the national identity not given a richer space and a clearer roadmap? A simple reason is that the discourse on identity remains immature and lacks a deep understanding of what constitutes national identity, whereas other forms of sub-identities, such as communal identity, historical identity, cultural identity and Islamic and Arabic identity find their way into the documents. However, we can see two underlying factors in the shaping of the new Qatari national identity, these being traditions and modernity. Balancing traditions and modernity has become a recurrent discourse, adopted by the private and the public sector, as well as the alignment of other key players' strategies with QNV2030. The discourse can be seen as dynamic and transformative in the sense that it is self-evolving. As terms like "tradition" and "modernity" are not defined but used arbitrarily, civil actors can engage and recreate new meanings towards achieving the desired balance.

The main messages on identity as embedded in QNV2030 were reiterated by the Emir, Tamim bin Hamad, in 2015 when speaking about cultural identity, connecting it to the Gulf, Arab, and Islamic identities, and furthermore emphasizing that the Qatari identity is "also a part of humanity and the international community" (His Highness Sheikh Tamim Bin Hamad Al-Thani, (n.d.): par. 2). He gives an account of balancing tradition and modernity by stating that "we believe that integrated and balanced development is the key to establishing a modern state responsive to the needs of today … without abandoning our authentic Qatari Arab heritage and our most tolerant Islamic faith" (His Highness Sheikh Tamim Bin Hamad Al-Thani, (n.d.): par. 2). Of course, the context in which the discourse is embedded has further implications and agendas and corresponds to a different audience, yet the message is consistent even seven years after the writing of the forward for QNV2030.

National identity in Qatar has been reshaped recently by the state discourse, which in turn has been influenced by several factors, including the recent historical turns in Qatar's history. One of the main historical turns in the recent history of Qatar is the change of Independence Day to National Day. The date of 3 September 1971 had been celebrated as Qatar's national day, commemorating Qatar's independence; although Qatar was not formally colonized, it nonetheless observed the end of British protection (1916–1971). Stirring multiple sub-identities into a state-building era, the date became a national signifier and had symbolic value and importance. "Independence defined Qatar's place in the family of nations, giving it international status and recognition, providing the amir [Khalifa bin Hamad (1972, 1995)] with the most overt trappings of state, augmenting his meager cache of inherited symbols with new ones: flags, coins and anthems" (Crystal 1995: 162). However, in 2007 the Emir decreed that Independence Day would be replaced by the National Day of 18 December, the day in 1878 when Sheikh Jassim bin Mohammed bin Thani founded Qatar by uniting the Qatari tribes. This National Day embedded the revival of legends and events and the reintroduction of national symbols within a new historical context; for example, it has complemented the new anthem that was introduced in 1996 after Sheikh Hamad bin Khalifa's accession of the throne. National Day represents a new national marker for the national narrative, and its significance is projected in the extravagant associated festivities and the many means by which people strive to show and assert their patriotism.

National Day celebrates the founding of Qatar, but also and more specifically it celebrates the history of the royal family. The state history thus becomes the dominant one, yet it is not the one that resonates with popular memory.

The two dominant historical narratives of Qatar have always been the desert and the sea, recounting the histories of two people: the transient and the permanent, the nomads and the coastal. Both narratives are rich in symbols, references, oral traditions, local sayings and adverbs, local names and titles, local objectives and physical heritage, as well as allegiances and attitudes. Both construct two sub-identities, the *badou* and *hadar*, or *ahl al bar* and *ahl al bahar*. Symbols connoting fishing and pearling are imbued with national pride and have contributed immensely to the national imagination and national cohesion in Qatar. Physical monuments of pearls, dhows, and other symbols of the past are scattered all over the city of Doha and stand as a tribute to this version of the people's history. However, this historical turn has played a major role in reviving the Bedouin traditions, customs and dialect, and emphasizing specific signifiers like the tribe, desert, falcon, and so on. Hence the promotion of the Bedouin narrative has caused an elevation of tribal identity over other sub-identities and, as Cooke (2014) argues, "authenticity" becomes synonymous with the tribal and "shapes a distinctive national brand" (Cooke 2014: 13). This plays out in the educational field.

A state project has initiated the rewriting of Qatar's history and introducing it in schools as early as kindergarten. New learning outcomes have been established and Qatari history has been reintroduced in the context of developing well-rounded citizens who are proud of their Islamic, Arabic, and Qatari identity and are informed about their local history. Since 2012, the history of Qatar has also become a mandatory subject in all private schools; Qatar Academy, for example, has created a Qatari Heritage curriculum for its schools within and outside Doha.

On the one hand, it may be argued that the different ethnicities and different histories were erased in favour of a pure ethnic "tribal" identity. The fact is that the state certainly promotes one version of history, yet without denying other versions. Oral histories present comparable and in some cases competing accounts to those of the history textbooks and state narrative. A growing field of study and investigation is the oral history of Qatar. Locally, there are serious attempts being made to record the oral traditions, including folktales and historical narratives. There are also attempts to teach oral history as a subject, across disciplines, by both Arabic and Western instructors in schools and universities. Local oral historians have been encouraged and promoted, as local "memory banks," by bringing their historical versions into the mainstream and allowing for their circulation. Employment as an oral historian has become a recognized occupation in Qatar, and oral historians are encouraged to record and publish their narratives of the past. Khalifa Al-Sayyed Al-Malki, for example, is a popular heritage researcher who is the author of 13 books, has written four plays and many articles, several TV and radio shows, and is also actively involved in public speaking on Qatari heritage.

## BETWEEN TRADITION AND MODERNITY: IS THERE A MODERN QATARI NATIONAL IDENTITY?

Considering Qatar in its context as a transformational state raises the question of how Qatar is planning to consolidate the different elements that would "transform" it into a modern nation, when these elements do not necessarily complement the fixed traditional structures that have been drawn on to refer to Qatar's national identity.

During the reign of the Father Emir, Qatar went through an intensive project of modernization, which brought Qatar up to the ranks of modern nations in a very short period of time. Kamrava borrows the term "high modernism" to describe the modernization efforts that were carried out, yet simultaneously balances this with "a vibrant contrived heritage industry" (Kamrava 2013: 155). As we saw, the call for striking a balance between tradition and modernity is a significant component of the discourse on national identity in Qatar, this being a common approach within post-colonial societies who have faced political as well as cultural colonialism. These newly-independent nations attempted to fuse the modern ways that they inherited from the colonizer, including practices, language, and even values, with a revived version of their history that could be inclusive and act as a basis for a newly-emerging national identity.

Qatar's history differs significantly in the sense that it was not colonized in the conventional, political sense, but rather, it was a British protectorate from 1916 to 1971. The British presence was predominantly in and around the oil fields and did not drastically alter the cultural context of the nation. Other contemporary factors, such as foreign workers, satellite and the internet, and Western education have played a more significant role in altering the traditional structure of Qatar through forcefully diversifying its culture.

Far from finding a middle ground in the forced marriage between modernity and traditionalism, this relationship cannot be consolidated. Modernity is perceived as an external phenomenon that is imposed on the local community, and the resistance of the local community stems from its anxieties about the unknown and fear of the loss of its traditional identity to be replaced by one that is foreign. Modernity also entails a shift in the power base that is better maintained within the traditional structures underpinning society and inherited within the state model of citizenship and nationalism. Qatari writer Abdulaziz Al Khater, who has written extensively on issues of identity, suggests that the dichotomy of modernity and traditionalism is better reflected in the dichotomy between the two types of culture: the local culture and the culture of the incomers. "The culture of the incomers that is associated with the expatriates reflects the diversity of this category and its self-interest, while the local culture is described by its insistence on preserving its heritage through reviving it, and it is state endorsed and promoted by the media—albeit without a clear plan" (Al Khater 2014: par. 7).

## Main Players Promoting the New Modern/ Traditional Qatari Identity

The formation of a national identity concerns a significant proportion of public policies and is thus implemented by state actors. As Al-Nakib (2015) suggests, "theoretical and practical conceptualizations of citizenship and identity are the result of an intricate interplay between state-building, power preservation, rentierism and culture" (Al-Nakib 2015: 4).

Here, I investigate the impact of the institutionalized discourse of Qatari identity as delivered through public education, the media, and the state's cultural projects (heritage preservation and revival). My approach is necessarily selective and attempts only to shed light on current approaches and trends, rather than providing comprehensive coverage of all phases of identity formation, all facets of national identity, all actors participating in institutionalizing the identity, and all challenges faced. There remains the need for thorough empirical studies of the impact of state actors in the shaping of the individual as well as the collective identities of the nation to underpin a comprehensive set of recommendations.

### *K-12 Education Reform and Higher Education*

Modernity as a transformative state project has not only been about material infrastructure, but has been accompanied by attempts to build the modern individual who will not only appreciate but also help in sustaining the various reforms undertaken into the future. Education is a key tool in implementing the state agenda of both seeking modernity and preserving culture and traditions.

Qatar's education reform of K-12 of 2004 adopted a global approach (with independent systems promoting English and science; see Chapter 4) then ended in an almost complete reversal (implementing a national curriculum and selecting Arabic as the language of instruction). The Qatar Foundation and the collage of branches of international world-class universities represent an example of what a balance between modernity and traditionalism can be. Through the introduction of American and western higher education and allowing both sexes to obtain multiple degrees, including medicine, engineering, journalism, and political and social sciences, the younger generation has been able to obtain degrees from the best universities in the world, yet without leaving the country. Qatari males and females mix in a semi-controlled setting, at the same time mixing freely and equally with other students, whether Qatari residents or international. Graduates of Education City are equipped through their education with the tools needed in any democratic setting, but they are then confronted with a rigid traditional system that favours collectivism over individualism and uniformity over pluralism. The QNV provides (2008) provides a clear road map for the human transformation that would complement and lead towards an advanced state and the building of knowledge-based economy. However, for Qataris, construction of the collective identity is a priority over that of the individual. Individualism is particularly appreciated only when it serves the community and abides by the prevailing boundaries and restrictions, whether social, cultural, or even personal. Individual expression outside the generic traditional representation is highly frowned upon and in many cases rejected. This is not to say that Qatari society is homogenous; on the contrary, Qatari society is both diverse and dynamic. However, there are different communities of thoughts and values, and individuals within these communities are better protected and also cherished; lone voices are unwanted voices until they have sufficient grounds and followers to make them legitimate.

Al-Nakib (2015) considers citizenship and national identity in education in Kuwait. She makes references applicable to the situation in Qatar about the unattainability of a state policy directed at building a knowledge-based economy when the rigid framework of citizenship and national identity requires democratization in favour of a more inclusive form. Al-Nakib also points out the tendency to conflate citizenship and nationalism, looking at both from a fixed lens (Al-Nakib 2015: 5). The national curriculum embraces the state agenda in promoting a cohesive national identity that relies on a shared past and culture. Although the building of a national identity that is reflective of all these layers is certainly challenging, exclusion of any of them will only create more complicated challenges in the long run.

## *Qatar TV and Al-Rayyan TV*

The broadcast media play a major role in circulating the state's narrative on identity, promoting two opposite agendas: modernity and traditionalism. Local media, owned and controlled by the government, engage directly with the state's objectives regarding preserving and reviving the Qatari heritage and reflecting a unified cultural identity. The main outlets of Qatari media comprise broadcast, print, and new (social) media. Qatar TV, the national channel, was launched in 1970 but had a major facelift in December 2012, aimed at modernizing the channel to better reflect current Qatari society and its people. Although it projects a modern technological image, the approach of Qatar TV is still traditional—standing at the borderline between tradition and modernity. While there is little innovative news editing or reporting, the first round of variety programmes on Qatar TV were innovative, modern, and unorthodox. For the first time, young entrepreneurs, students and artists were presenting "reality show" types of programmes. Two specific programmes were notable: the reality show *Waad Show* in which a young designer appeared, and *We Try for You*, a reality show based on three young Qatari men experimenting with different professions. Other shows that captured and celebrated the multiculturalism of Qatari society included *Min Albidaya—From the Start*, a programme that profiled pioneers from different nationalities who contributed to the building of the Qatar in the 50s, 60s, and 70s; and filler programmes such as *Regular Faces*, which profiled working people regardless of their nationalities.

These modern approaches to broadcasting and programming were a reflection of a clear vision to present the young Qatari culture, through capturing their voices, their interests, and their new lifestyles. These programmes were excellent reflections of the negotiation between modernity and traditions within the youth culture. While adopting a progressive approach, Qatar TV, as the national television station, had to retain certain traditional elements that would distinguish it and define it as national, including a focus on Qatari presenters wearing conservative national attire to maintain a certain national appearance. Shows about heritage were presented within a historical context that defined the heritage as the ways of the past without imposing these on the present. Some shows took a didactic approach, aiming at introducing youth to different versions of Qatar's history through autobiographical episodes with Qatari pioneers of the state-building generation. The programme *Albirwaz* (*The Frame*) presents the diversity and richness of Qatar's history, by profiling different Qatari personalities belonging to different backgrounds and origins.

While Qatar TV could be described, to borrow Cook's definition, as the "traditional modern," Al-Rayyan TV stands at the opposite end of the spectrum. Unlike Qatar TV, Al-Rayyan, which was launched in 2012 and is targeted towards a Qatari audience, promotes a distinctive Qatari identity—a tribal one. The channel's website states that the channel "targets the Qatari society and takes into account the [particularity] of its national identity and aspirations" through intensive coverage of the "local culture" by locals, and "highlighting the national identity" (Al Rayyan TV, (n.d.): par. 1).

This Qatari-led/Qatari-targeted channel clearly delivers its message through the careful selection of phrases like "[particularity] of society's rhetoric, customs and traditions" to present itself as "the Qatari culture guardian," promoting an exclusive rather inclusive version of identity. Al-Rayyan TV is gaining an audience and endorsements from the community, while Qatar TV has been criticized for its progressive approach. The new look of Qatar TV was orchestrated by a young, well-educated and progressive management led by Tala al-Attiyah, Secretary General of TV Support and Development Committee, and Maryam al-Subai, Director of Programs and Creations.

Local state-controlled media play an important role in shaping attitudes, building allegiances, and promoting certain terms and notions that represent the state's definition of patriotism and citizenship. The growing attention given to tribal, religious, and nationalistic discourses causes an imbalanced representation. Arguably tending towards propaganda, the Qatari print media, especially, are generally promoting traditionalism in all its forms, and there seems to be a heightened sense of fear of loss of identity; most modern values (e.g., English language instruction, co-education, employment of women, mixed marriages) are dealt with as being either threats or potential threats to the cultural cohesion of the community.

The representation of modernity within the context of "anxiety and threat," and traditionalism within the context of "preservation," has shaped their audience's perception of both as being irreconcilable. The individual, the consumer of the media's narrative on tradition and modernity, falls victim to having to choose one over the other. Al-Khater (2014) asserts that the Qatari media have contributed to an identity crisis amongst youth, where some have been affected by the intensive heritage revival campaigns and the state discourse on the "authentic" Qatari identity and have started rejecting any values outside the traditional structure, dismissing them as "foreign" and "modern," and turning instead to the tribal practices that have survived through a process of exclusion and reinvention. Modernity for these individuals has become the custom of "others" and they define themselves as opposite to the "others," along with the foreign culture they attempt to impose. The Qatari media, Al-Khater argues, have misled youth, while at the same time the state heritage projects have attracted a large percentage of the Qatari youth without realizing that these projects clash directly with the version of modernity the state itself has adopted. In other words, Qatari youth—consumers of state owned media—have subscribed to the media's selective and idolized version of traditionalism, including a shared past and a cohesive culture, over the selective physical components of modernity that these media presented as being threatening. The didactic role of the media is completely absent here, whereby its responsibility is to promote the values of diversity, democracy, equality, and freedom.

The established Qatari media lack the tools for objective in-depth investigation and need to evolve critically and independently of the state's agenda and institutionalized discourses in order to be able to compete with other emerging on-line media outlets, and to gain credibility with the younger bilingual generation who is not only the recipient of the news, but also has become a participant in the making of the news. A new generation of Qataris have become dependent on social media for their news, which have provided them with platforms for engaging actively with local issues. Qataris not only utilize social media to voice their opinions but also as an avenue for negotiating their own identities, for attempting to engage others in the process of deconstructing certain misconceptions about Qataris and Qatari culture, and for reconstructing new frameworks that embrace the different modern representations of who Qataris are. This approach of "identity negotiation" corresponds with the identity-related motives defined by Swan and Bosson: "agency (which encompasses feelings of autonomy and competence), communion (which encompasses feelings of belonging and interpersonal connectedness), and psychological coherence (which encompasses feelings of regularity, predictability, and control" (Swann and Bosson 2008: 452).

In the absence of an active civil society in Qatar, social media have become the main platform upon which virtual civil movements exercise their freedom of expression. Many use social media to experiment with the limitations and to push the boundaries of the traditional structures. In this way, an alternative discourse has emerged to challenge the state's discourse on identity. Qatari bloggers are questioning notions of a shared history and a common origin, critiquing the tiered citizenship model and its limitations in building a national population with a national identity that is based on equality and inclusiveness. For example, Al-Naama (2013) exposes the inherent internal hierarchy amongst Qatari citizens, stating that "[t]ribalism is an inextricable facet of Qatari society, which doesn't just affect the way we value ourselves within the tribal hierarchy, but also affects us in a multitude of other ways, influencing decisions and choices in our everyday lives" (Al-Naama 2013: par. 2). Tribalism, he continues, affects career opportunities, marriage options and, moreover, citizenship rights. He presents tribal identity as a hindrance to building a national identity and argues that "as a nation state evolves, to continue to adhere to tribalism at the cost of national interests would only create divisiveness" (Al-Naama 2013: par. 5). However controversial the topic, it needs to be exposed in this blunt manner. Al-Naama was criticized harshly and his family's origins were brought into question, confirming the very claim that he made—tribalism is entrenched in Qatari society and, by presenting it as the "authentic" one, a sub-identity is given preference over other identities. Others who have discussed issues of "bidoun" on Twitter have attracted as many sympathetic as racist remarks.

Social media have also offered Qatari women a platform to discuss their citizenship rights and what it means to be a Qatari citizen. Social media have also helped women to engage actively in national issues—issues previously considered to be within the male's realm of responsibilities. Qatari women bloggers have broken many barriers by dealing with issues considered taboo. Maryam Al-Subai in her blog *Mimiz Blog—Diary of a Qatari Girl*, questioned issues such as arranged marriages, labour workers, Qatarization, and gender discrimination. She was cyber-bullied and, unfortunately, chose to stop blogging, although she left her blog active. Al-Dosari, Fatima. (2014) writes about discriminatory practices based on traditional customs when she was denied entry to a jazz event because she was a Qatari woman. In my own blog, *amalalmalki.com*, I have tackled issues including self-presentation, identity crisis, the challenges faced by Qatari women, stereotypes about Qataris, and national attire for Qatari women. Twitter campaigns have flourished recently, with a consequent impact on the social and cultural life in Qatar. The #ImHalfQatari hashtag had a domino effect and has led to a wide scale dialogue on the citizenship right of a Qatari woman to pass on her nationality to her children. Recently, a thesis titled *"minna wa feena"* (*One of Us*) written by a Qatar University senior and covering the legal standing and identity issues faced by children born to Qatari mothers, was met with a positive reaction from officials, media personalities, and the general public. These alternative narratives on identity and what it means to be part of the national identity raises the need for an open national dialogue beyond the state narrative and state media outlets.

## *Cultural Identity Makeover and Heritage Projects*

Besides education and the media, Qatar's cultural projects employ different state actors to deliver the state narrative of national identity. Culture is "a series of codes, symbols, forms of knowledge, and strategies for survival related to location and common values" (Jenkins 2008: 3). As a discourse and a state-driven project, cultural identity construction is "an object of power" to define the truth (Wikan 2002: 86 as cited in Dervin 2011: 183). "Heritage" becomes a key instrument in constructing a "modern" national cultural identity. It mobilizes memories and traditions as "resources for the present" (Graham 2002: 1003). The Gulf states have commissioned all of their state actors to plan and execute a cultural project that has led to a heritage boom, taking at its heart heritage revival more so than preservation. The heritage boom was mainly state-driven as an important component of the state-building era, and it has been transformed into a national identity-building functionality. Exell and Rico state that "[t]he nation-states of the Arabian Peninsula are now becoming openly and aggressively involved in the preservation, representation and invention of their own individual and distinct tangible national culture and heritage" (Exell and Rico 2013: 675).

Qatari heritage constitutes a large proportion of Qatar's current culture, one that is represented as "modern." There have been several attempts to emphasize a homogeneous cultural identity through processes of selecting, reviving, and inventing. Here, I will consider two interrelated aspects, heritage preservation and revival, which have contributed to the reconstruction of the new modern cultural identity (also see Chapter 6).

The heritage revival projects across Qatar were primarily state-led projects as a part of the nation-building stage and retain a prominent status in the governmental agenda in the transformative stages that Qatar is witnessing currently. Projects that thrived in the 1980s continue to the present day and are playing another major role in the reconstruction of a modern national identity. A selection of both soft and hard elements of the heritage is being reshaped and repackaged to fit the modern cultural context of Qatar. Physical representations are the obvious and most successfully achieved reflection of the fusion between modernity and traditionalism, as well as the most readily described. Here, we will look at Qatar as a city and its physical elements, the archaeology, the historical sites, and the construction of museums. "As with cultural identity, the vernacular architecture of Qatar was deemed under threat from rapid urban development and the reshaping of the city" (Exell and Rico 2013: 677). Urban heritage preservation started through restoration projects that worked on mosques, forts, old souqs, and other heritage sites.

The visualized/architectural identity of the transformative state of Qatar and its urbanization has become a reflection of a hybrid identity. Modern Doha is reflected in a hybrid landscape that includes the skyscrapers and state-of-the-art buildings, while other areas of Doha city have been restructured to reflect a traditional identity. A simple contrast between the skyline of the Corniche and Souq Waqif demonstrates this point perfectly. Following a practice of demolition of the old to make space for the new in the 1970s, Qatar is now witnessing a reversal of this approach, whereby new urban constructions are based on traditional designs. The Katara and Msheireb urban generation projects are reimagined spaces of the old and the traditional. The Msheireb development, for example, comprises traditionally-driven architecture and the aim "is to initiate large-scale, inner-city regeneration that will create a modern Qatari homeland rooted in traditions and to renew a piece of the city where global cultures meet but not melt" (Gharib and Salama 2014: 4). Furthermore, the restoration in 2004 of Souq Waqif behind its original façade is an example of the old made anew, through modernizing its functionality, presenting it as a tourist attraction and utilizing its strategic location.

The heritage boom at a tangible level created a cultural movement that not only focused on archaeology and historical sites, but also museums and exhibitions—the physical representations of historical/cultural identities. Since the early 1970s, the focus on archaeological studies and museum buildings as a physical representation of the past have been major steps taken in all Gulf states towards building a national identity. In 1973, Sheikh Khalifa bin Hamad commissioned a British archaeological study in Qatar in preparation for founding a national museum that was established in 1975. The museum focused then on recording "the ancient and recent past side by side" (Exell and Rico 2013: p. 675), with an emphasis on the historical legacy of the Al-Thani tribe. The museum was a part of a careful nation-building project that included promoting the Al-Thani monarch as a political and historical reference for the nation. And it also served two other important purposes: "to construct a distinct national identity linked to the past and to preserve a changing lifestyle," striving in the process "to pin down a cultural identity that was evolving out of all recognition" (Exell and Rico 2013: 677). In 2009, almost three and a half decades later, the Qatar Museum Authority was established and is chaired by al-Mayassa bint Hamad, who is Sheikh Khalifa bin Hamad's granddaughter and is overseeing the establishment of all museums in Qatar.

As a cultural player in the reconstruction of the Qatari cultural identity, museums of the new modern era have to reflect the dynamics of the era. We can observe this in both the physical and the symbolic facets of the building of the Museum of Islamic Art (MIA) and the new National Museum of Qatar. MIA, opened in 2008, "is a stunning hybrid of cubism and Islamic motifs that the Chinese-American architect I.M. Pei derived from iconic buildings in North Africa and Islamic Spain" (Cooke 2014: 78). It stands on an artificial island on the Corniche as a tribute to Qatar's Arabic and Islamic roots. The new National Museum of Qatar designed by French architect Jean Nouvel is due to open in 2016. Cooke (2014) considers that Nouvel's version of the desert rose caravanserai "will reflect 'the vanishing Bedouin cultures of Qatar in an effort to embrace the realities of a rapidly urbanizing society, and maintain a connection to this fading world in which the country sprang'" (Cooke 2014): 81–82). As the national museum, it bears the responsibility of reflecting a strong national identity in both past and current definitions. The museum is set to "give voice to Qatar's heritage whilst celebrating its future." (National Museum of Qatar, (n.d.): par. 1).

Heritage revival also covers intangible culture, such as the traditions and customs of the past, including traditional sports. Qatar will be hosting the FIFA World Cup in 2022, an event that has thrust Qatar into prime international media coverage. The FIFA announcement, although celebrated nationally, still raises questions regarding the value that such an event will bring to the country besides international recognition. Also, the rapid building of infrastructure, the construction of nine new stadiums and restoration of three others, has been criticized for serving specific agendas. Interestingly, at the same time, greater attention is being paid to the revival of traditional sports. These have always been celebrated seasonally, yet they recently have witnessed a significant boom in that their volume has doubled and their importance boosted through elevation into national competition. For example, between November 2014 and April 2015, Qatar held the Fourth Traditional Dhow Festival (November 2014); the Sixth Qatar International Falcon Hunting Festival (January 2015); the Annual Arabian Camel Festival (January–February 2015); the H.H. The Emir 24th International Equestrian Sword Festival (February 2015); and the Senyar (Marine) Championship (April 2015). All of these traditional sports have heritage revival as their common message and objective.

Heritage is clearly a state project, and thus a process of legitimization of its narrative on identity. The two main state players in this context are the Ministry of Culture, Arts, and Heritage and the Katara Cultural Village. The former, as the main state custodian of heritage sites, states that one of its objectives is "documenting and archiving popular heritage, organizing and animating heritage events and celebrations" (Ministry of Culture, Arts and Heritage, (n.d.): par. 7). The Ministry's heritage department is in charge of preserving the "Qatari Arab Islamic heritage" through collecting oral histories (the Ministry has hundreds of recordings), creating a national archive, and reviving popular heritage through events held all year round. The ministry, as its name entails, focuses on creating a vibrant cultural setting in Qatar, whereby the focus is divided between "supporting the cultural and artistic movement in Qatar" and preserving and reviving popular heritage—the intangible culture of the past.

The Katara Cultural Village is another major cultural player that is gaining importance. There are obvious commonalities in vision and scope between Katara and the Ministry of Culture, Arts, and Heritage. Asserting itself to be "the largest and most multidimensional cultural project in Qatar," Katara is set to become "the guardian to the heritage and traditions of Qatar," and still fuses the local and the global and promotes multiculturalism through scheduled cultural and artistic activities and events (About Us—Katara, (n.d.): par. 3). Katara is creating a new cultural scene, one that blends international and popular performances, yet its heritage-promoting agenda cannot be denied.

The cultural setting in Qatar is heavily loaded and shaped by the state's framing of a shared history and a common traditional culture. The cultural project and the heritage boom led to the articulation of a national identity that has a uniform past and a cohesive present. However, the reality is otherwise. If there is one word that can describe the population structure of Qatari society it is diversity; the identities of the individuals living in the state of Qatar are, without question, widely diverse.

In cultural terms, the multiculturalism that describes the atmosphere of Qatar implies a state of influx and fusion of many cultures that co-exist on the basis of respect and tolerance. It also implies a state that will ensure the rights of the minorities belonging to the different cultures inhabiting it. However, the reality is complex. Qatar is a country of multiple nationalities, some of whom form sub-communities with distinctive cultural identities on the basis of a shared language, religion, and cultural practices. Hence, the cultural picture in Qatar comprises different colour patches that do not necessarily complement each other; multiculturalism as a term can describe the situation in Qatar, without implying a false sense of harmony.

Heterogeneous as the cultural situation may be, the significance of different cultures varies according to their percentage of the total population in Qatar and level of income. However, the Qatari culture remains the dominant culture by default, as the native culture and the one both promoted and preserved through public policy. Moreover, Qatar has low tolerance for the promotion of other cultures, unlike the tolerance of differences and the representation of diversity in its different forms (physical and conceptual) that is typical in larger cosmopolitan cities or modern metropolises. Different cultural actors, whether state or civil, fall into the trap of promoting one "imagined" form of identification over others, favouring inclusiveness over multiculturalism, and this is clearly reflected in the controlled cultural life and careful cultural exchanges between the different cultural communities in Qatar.

Social media provide new outlets for the promotion of heritage and traditional identity, contributing in shaping certain attitudes and building specific loyalties. Virtual cultural actors in Qatar can be divided into promoters of multiculturalism and consumers and circulators of the state narrative. Civil initiatives like "See My Culture," "I Love Qatar," and "Embrace Doha" aim to establish connections between the different cultural communities and the Qatari cultural community. The "See My Culture" initiative states that its main goal "is to build bridges between locals and the international community" (Seemyculture, (n.d.): par. 1). It organizes different cultural activities that open up exclusive Qatari cultural practices to others, reintroducing the culture to them by including them as participants. "Embrace Doha" states that it aims "to become the primary cultural resource for anyone interested in learning more about our fascinating country" (Cultural Awareness Training, (n.d.): par.1). Similarly, "I Love Qatar" presents itself as an online guide to Qatar and Qatari culture. With its growing base of followers, the popularity of this initiative comes from the inclusive and international approach it takes, distinct from idolizing or romanticizing the culture. The key factor that makes both initiatives successful is their attempts at "integration," without any forced sense of assimilation. Other civil actors engage with the state narrative and utilize social media in circulating and promoting Qatar's heritage and its role in the reshaping the modern Qatari identity. Some online initiatives take a didactic approach and are set to promote Qatari heritage and culture to Arabs, Westerners, or even Qataris. The Instagram account "Turath_Lawal," for example, states that it is the first Qatari heritage account.

Certain cultural campaigns seem to be rather more reactionary movements that call for uniformity and total assimilation into Qatar's culture and its value system. An anxiety is generated amongst the Qatari community concerning the loss of the Qatari culture and, as a result, many cultural grassroots campaigns have been initiated and carried out on a voluntarily basis. Some of these campaigns call on "foreigners" to respect the conservative traditional culture, to abide by the conservative dress code, and to respect the privacy of the culture. Certain campaigns carry, as their main aim, "identity preservation," seeking to confront the many attacks faced by the Qatari community. The value-based campaigns that seek to establish a better understanding amongst the population seem more popular than those seeking to enforce particular customs and behaviours. Qatari culture, therefore, has dual representation—modern, in the sense that it is open to dialogue with other cultures with reduced anxiety levels, and a traditional culture that is conservative and calls for uniformity and focuses on manners and codes of conduct. Certain customs and behaviours are being imposed in an attempt to make the cultural look of the country uniform. To say the least, these "native" attempts seem reactionary to the influx of foreigners to Qatar, and they reflect a fear of losing the vital essence that has kept Qatar distinctive compared with neighbouring cities, such as Dubai.

## Conclusions

The question of national identity is raised when there is a need for redefinition, and now that Qatar is embracing a new era, the need becomes imperative. The current citizenship model was comparatively effective during the nation-building stage in creating legitimate national "communities" within the bigger, more established regional and national identities. However, a new historical era calls for a new form of citizenship that is inclusive and sustainable. Ultimately, investing in human capital is the way in which Qatar's economy can be transformed into a knowledge-based one. The generosity of the state towards citizens and non-citizens is unquestionable; however, to ensure returns on investments, Qatar needs to retain a proportion of its graduates and workers across the different sectors according to a systematic, institutionalized citizenship law. The building of a strong citizenry with a unified national identity is to promote inclusiveness and pluralism, to eradicate discrimination within the existing citizenship model, and to embrace previously marginalized identities. A national identity should trump all other forms of sub-identity, especially tribal identity. All citizens should have a claim over their country, regardless of ethnicity, gender, or sectarian background. At the same time, it should be emphasized that a national identity is as fluid as the identities of its people, and that "[i]dentity isn't given once and for all: it is built up and changes throughout a person's lifetime" (Maaolouf 2000: 20).

### Bibliography. Qatar: Policy Making in a Transformative State

Al-Dosari, Fatima. 2014. *No entry for Qatari women: The day I was banned from jazz.* Doha, Qatar: Last Modified April 3, 2014. http://www.justhere. qa/2014/04/entry-qatari-women-day-banned-jazz/Just Here Qatar.

Al Khater, Abdulaziz Mohamed. 2014. Title. *Abdazizbn Mohammed Al Khater: Citizen who carries the concerns of his homeland and nation*, December 29, 2014. http://azizalkhater.blogspot.com/2014/12/blog-post_29.html

Al-Naama, Nasser. 2013. In Qatar, tentacles of tribalism hold back national aspirations. Just Here Qatar. Last Modified July 17, 2013. http://www.justhere. qa/2013/07/in-qatar-tentacles-of-tribalism-hold-back-national-aspirations/

Al-Nakib, Ranla. 2015. *Education and Democratic Development in Kuwait: Citizens in Waiting.* London: Last Modified March 1. http://www.chathamhouse.org/publication/education-and-democratic-development-kuwait-citizens-waiting Chatham House, the Royal Institute of International Affairs.

Babar, Zahra. 2014. The cost of belonging: Citizenship construction in the State of Qatar. *Middle East Journal* 68(3): 403–420.
Bloemraad, Irene, Anna Korteweg, and Gökçe Yurdakul. 2008. Citizenship and immigration: Multiculturalism, assimilation, and challenges to the nation-state. *Sociology* 34(1): 153–179.
Cooke, M. 2014. *Tribal Modern: Branding New Nations in the Arab Gulf*. Berkeley: University of California Press.
Crystal, Jill. 1995. *Oil and Politics in the Gulf: Rulers and Merchants in Kuwait and Qatar*, Rev. edn. Cambridge: Cambridge University Press.
Dervin, F. 2011. Cultural identity, representation and othering. In *The Routledge Handbook of Language and Intercultural Communication*, ed. Jane Jackson, 181–194. Abingdon, UK: Routledge.
Eriksen, T. 2005. Ethnicity and nationalism. In *Nations and Nationalism: A Reader*, eds. P. Spencer, and H. Wollman, 136–140. New Brunswick, N.J.: Rutgers University Press.
Exell, K., and T. Rico. 2013. 'There is No Heritage in Qatar': Orientalism, colonialism and other problematic histories. *World Archaeology* 45(4): 670–685.
General Secretariat for Development Planning (Qatar). 2008. *Qatar National Vision 2030*. Doha: Retrieved from http://www.gsdp.gov.qa/portal/page/portal/gsdp_en/knowledge_center/Tab/QNV2030_English_v2.pdfMinistry of Development Planning and Statistics (Qatar).
———. 2011. *Qatar National Development Strategy 2011–2016: Towards Qatar National Vision 2030*. Ministry of Development Planning and Statistics (Qatar): Retrieved from http://www.gsdp.gov.qa/gsdp_vision/docs/NDS_EN.pdfDoha.
Gharib, R.Y., and A.M. Salama. 2014. Nature of urban interventions in changing the old center of a globalizing Doha. *Frontiers of Architectural Research* 3(4): 468–476.
Graham, B. 2002. Heritage as knowledge: Capital or culture? *Urban Studies* 39(5–6): 1003–1017.
Hassan, I.K. 2015. *Gulf-Gulf Conflicts: The Reasons, the Issues, and the Solution Mechanisms (in Arabic)*. Doha: Retrieved from http://studies.aljazeera.net/files/gccpath/2015/01/2015114125342702598.htmlAljazeera Center for Studies.
Jerkins, Gwynn. 2008. *Contested Space: Cultural Heritage and Identity Reconstructions: Conservation Strategies within a Developing Asian City*. Münster: LIT Verlag.
Kamrava, Mehran. 2013. *Qatar: Small State, Big Politics*. Ithaca, NY: Cornell University Press.
Kinninmont, J. 2013. Citizenship in the Gulf. In *The Gulf States and Arab Uprisings*, ed. A. Echagüe, 47–58. Madrid: FRIDE.
Maalouf, A. 2000. *On Identity*. London: Harvill.

Patrick, N. 2009. *Nationalism in the Gulf States*. London: LSE Centre for for the Study of Global Governance..

Swann, W.B. Jr., and J.K. Bosson. 2008. Identity negotiation: A theory of self and social interaction. In *Handbook of Personality: Theory and Research*, eds. O. John, R. Robins, and L. Pervin, 448–471. New York: Guilford Press.

Women's Research and Studies Center. 2013. ghyr almwaṭn bdwl mjls alt'awn alkhlyjy: ḥqwq w ḥlwl [National Women married to Non-nationals in the GCC countries: Rights and Solutions], Kuwait, May 22.

Yuval-Davis, N. 1997. Women, citizenship and difference. *Feminist Review* 57(Autumn): 4–27.

CHAPTER 10

# Demographic Policies and Human Capital Challenges

## Hend Al Muftah

The difficult economic situation of many Arab and Southeast Asian countries in the last few decades has made labour emigration an attractive option for citizens of these states. Such emigration has generally been supported by their governments to ease labour market pressures, reduce unemployment, and accelerate development. The migration of the workforce has become one of the most dynamic economic factors in the Middle Eastern and North African (MENA) countries; remittances from migrant labour exceed the value of regional trade in goods as well as official capital flows (Nassar and Ghoneim 2002). One of the largest markets for Arab and Asian job seekers has been that of the states in the Gulf Cooperation Council (GCC), including Qatar. Since the discovery of oil and gas, Qatar has had to supplement a tiny local workforce with large amounts of expatriate labour.

This process has had a significant impact on Qatar's economy, politics, and the social structure. It has allowed for a rapid development of Qatar economically, but at the same time involved the Qatari government and society in various foreign affairs developments and brought a number of negative cultural and socio-economic consequences. Although foreigners in Qatar have not created problems of the magnitude of those found in other immigrant countries of the world, different economic and political

H. Al Muftah (✉)
Doha Institute for Graduate Studies, Doha, Qatar

© The Author(s) 2016
M.E. Tok et al. (eds.), *Policy-Making in a Transformative State*,
DOI 10.1057/978-1-137-46639-6_10

interests of governments and individuals have brought numerous tensions and conflicts, such as the recent focus on workers' human rights which intensified after Qatar won its bid to host the 2022 FIFA World Cup.

This chapter analyzes Qatar's population dilemmas as well as their effects on the labour force structure. In particular, it discusses such issues as the heterogeneity of the local populations, the composition of the national and foreign workforce, the segmentation of the labour market, and the localization of the workforce.

## Demographic Trends

Since the discovery of oil and gas, the GCC states are transforming themselves from desert sheikhdoms into modern states. This process has been accompanied by rapid population growth. Qatar, as some other Gulf countries, is endowed with tremendous reserves of oil and natural gas, but with a small population of nationals. As a result, over the last decades, Qatar has depended on the exploitation of natural resources, rather than on its human capital, for its wealth. In doing so, it has relied on a large influx of foreign workers. This approach has resulted in greater wealth in the short-term, which in turn led to substantial improvements in living standards through infrastructure, social services, and employment, ultimately improving measures of human development,[1] but this has not provided for sustainable long-term social and economic development. Access to foreign labour has supported rapid growth in the non-oil sector and price stability in Qatar. At the same time, the government has increased public-sector employment and has helped raise living standards. The employment of a large number of foreign nationals in Qatar has also resulted in large remittance outflows. However, this growth model has involved costs: the public-sector wage bill is relatively high due to the over employment of nationals compared to their limited employment in the private sector, due to the domination of expatriates, low pay-scales, and other reasons. In turn, this also resulted in an increasing imbalance of Qatar's population and labour market structures, which might pose two major challenges in the near future: adequate social services to meet the increased population and job creation for nationals.

As noted in earlier chapters, Qatar's development strategy recognizes that a key ingredient of a knowledge-based economy is a skilled and intellectually capable workforce, rather than relying on natural resources. Qatar's Third National Human Development Report in 2012, however, recognizes the lack of knowledge capital as one of the main challenges facing Qatar in the long run. In addition to the main human capital challenge in Qatar, the unique position of Qatar—where only about 13 % of the total population are Qataris and only 70,000 native Qataris are in the national workforce (and often lack the required training)—poses yet another set of interrelated issues (Qatar Statistics, E-Census Registry 2010). To overcome this disparity between Qatar's vision to become a knowledge society by 2030 and the current size and capabilities of its local workforce, relying on expatriate manpower was the available option. As a result, the population grew from 614,000 to 1,715,000 in the 2000–2010 period (Qatar Social Trends 1998–2010, 2011). In 2011, expatriates constituted nearly 94.2 % of the workforce and the vast majority of the population, while statistics show a clear imbalance between the numbers of males and females—a ratio of 3:1 (Oxford Business Group 2012).

It is clear that the increase in Qatar's population has not been caused primarily by a natural growth of indigenous population, but by the influx of foreign workers. The employment of large numbers of foreigners has been a structural imperative in Qatar, as the oil-related and construction development, Education City, the Pearl, Lusial, Qatar Rail, and FIFA 2022 depend on the importation of foreign technologies and require knowledge and skills. In consequence, unlike other countries where expatriates have only complemented the national workforce, usually by filling lower-status jobs, in Qatar they have become the primary, dominant labour force in most sectors of the economy and the government bureaucracy. Infrastructure in service jobs simply cannot be filled by nationals (Rees et al. 2007; Aly-Waqfi and Forstenlechner 2010). The current demographic reality has many policy implications that go beyond the economic forces that helped formulate it in the first place. The unprecedented population growth demanding access to quality education, health, and housing alternatives has put extra pressure on the country's infrastructure. The readiness of the country's laws and systems to address the social, cultural, and political implications of hosting non-citizen residents that make up the majority of the population is another complex issue (see Chapter 9).

The modern population imbalance in Qatar is actually not new (see Table 10.1). In 1908, the total population was estimated at 27,000 people, with non-Qataris accounting for 22.2 %. In 1939, the total population continued to increase and reached 28,000, out of which 39.3 % were non-Qatari, and it then grew to a total of 111,133 in 1970, with 59.5 % being non-Qatari (Al Muftah 2010: 62). In 1997, the total population was

**Table 10.1** Population growth in Qatar, 1908–2014

| Year | Total | Non-Qatari | % of Non-Qatari |
|---|---|---|---|
| 1908a | 27,000 | 6000 | 22.2 |
| 1930a | 28,000 | 11,000 | 39.3 |
| 1955a | 40,000 | – | – |
| 1970a | 111,133 | 66,094 | 59.5 |
| 1981b | 256,000 | 161,000 | 63 |
| 1986c | 369,079 | – | – |
| 1997c | 522,023 | – | – |
| 2011 | 1,624,761 | – | – |
| 2012 | 1,8,00,00 | – | – |
| 2014 | 2,174,035 | – | – |

522,023; however, the expatriate population has shown particularly strong growth since 1997, and in March 1999, at the time of the first municipal council election, Qatar's total population was estimated at 566,000 (ELU 2010). The country's ratio of expatriates to nationals is one of the most imbalanced in the world, and most certainly within the GCC. According to the Qatar 4th National Human Development Report, 2015 (2014), nationals only make up 12 % of the Qatari population compared to 24 % in 2004. The population has quadrupled since 1990, when the 2010 census estimated the population at 422,834 (Qatar Statistical Authority 2010). The population had grown to approximately 616,000 by 2000 (ibid.), and it doubled by 2007, when the population was estimated at 1,226,000 people (ibid.). Specifically, during past last four decades, Qatar's population multiplied 15 times (1970–2011), from 111,000 to 1,624,761 in July 2011 (Permanent Population Committee 2011). More specifically, the total number of foreign workers in Qatar increased during the period 2004–2014, from 400,000 to 1,400,000, with an annual growth rate of 14.7 %: 89 % are male workers, 70 % are semi/unskilled workers in the private sector (4th Qatar Human Development Report 2015: 48).

In terms of population growth and according to mid-year population estimates of 2012, there were 1.8 million inhabitants in mid-2012 with an annual population growth rate estimated at 5.8 in 2012 (Qatar Social Statistics 2014: 7). However, in 2014, the total population of Qatar was estimated at 2.2 million (Ministry of Development Planning and Statistics 2015a: 28) and reached 2.88.929 as per August 2015 statistics (Ministry of Development Planning and Statistics 2015b).

Although the number of births increased during the period 2003–2011, the crude birth rate (the number of live births per 1000 population in a given year) tended to fall gradually, from 18.3 % in 2003 to 11.3 % 2009 with a slight increase by 11.9 % in 2011. The fertility rate in Qatar gradually increased between 2006 and 2012, whereby 1.4 live births per woman of childbearing age were recorded in 2006, while 3.4 was the average in 2012 (Sustainable Development Indicators in the State of Qatar 2013: 17). However, the fertility rate in Qatar is considered to be relatively high compared to other countries, with more developed countries maintaining a rate of 1.7 and less developed countries maintaining an average of 2.6 (ibid.).

It is expected that the population of Qatar will continue to grow rapidly to 2020, due to the enormous augmentation of the non-national labour force. Additionally, there has been a disproportionate growth in the male population compared to the female population. In 1990, 138,000 (32 %) of the total population of 422,834 were female. That proportion dropped to 29 % in 2007, and in 2014 it was down to 25 % (Qatar Statistical Authority 2010). The influx of expatriate labour has also affected the age profile of the country, making it younger than many of its neighbours. The percentage of working-age population (15–60 years) increased from 73 % in 2003 to 93 % in 2012. The percentage of population in the age group 0–14 has declined from 24.9 % in 2003 to 14.2 % in 2014 (Qatar Monthly Statistics, June 2014: 6). The percentage of elderly (65+) ranged between 0.9 % (Qatar Social Statistics 2014: 7) in 2003 and 1.06 in 2014 (Qatar Monthly Statistics, June 2014: 6).

Based on the above, it is clear that key changes in Qatar's demographics are due to recruiting a large expatriate labour force, mostly male and concentrated in the 15–64 age group. This situation has posed security, economic, social, and cultural threats to the local population. As a consequence, to maintain the highly privileged position of nationals, the government has imposed numerous restrictions on expatriates, such as required visa sponsorships by employers and limited work stays (or rotations). However, many of these measures have not brought the expected results, especially the planned rotation of the workforce, which has proved impossible to achieve (more on this below). The free market economy has been more powerful than the policies the authorities have tried to implement. The majority of expatriates have stayed beyond the term of their original contracts, since employers usually prefer to keep workers who have already gained some local experience rather than bring in new ones.

Moreover, importing a new worker involves additional costs to employers. As a result, the average period of time that foreign workers spend in Qatar continues to extend, and the number of "almost permanent" foreign workers has increased, albeit not formally. According to Qatar's 4th National Human Development Report, the 2010 census indicated that about 11 % of the total foreign workforce in Qatar lived with their families for more than 10 years (2015: 29).

Generally speaking, every nation's population consists of its indigenous citizens and expatriate immigrants who either eventually return to their home countries once their employment contract is done or who become citizens in turn. However, this is not the situation in Qatar. The majority of expatriates remain in the country for a long time, but only very few ever become citizens. Most keep moving in the labour market, hence remaining longer in the country. This creates a segregated society economically, socially, and even legally between nationals and expatriates. While not fully integrated into Qatari society, expatriates contribute to the growing population imbalance and place pressures on social services.

National policy discussions addressing such population imbalances have included possible adjustments to labour market quotas, employment restrictions in some job categories, revised labour laws and the nationalization law, and changes in education, health, and even pension and fiscal systems. How can the government deal with such an imbalanced population structure, in terms of nationality, gender, and age and in terms of regenerating the labour force and providing pensions, education, health care, and other social services while ensuring that inter-generational transfers do not disadvantage the young? In Qatar, where non-nationals represent over 94 % of the total active population, the issue is no longer quantitative, but rather an essential and economic pillar of the Qatari society. Foreigners have become an integral part that cannot be ignored in formulating future development policies and vision, yet the challenge needs to be managed wisely. Over the last decades, this issue has received considerable and growing attention associated with the transformation of the Qatari economy, society, and institutions, and it has led to a new phase of considering expatriates as a determinant part of the country's facts and reality. This is well represented in the new regulatory frameworks such as the Qatar National Vision 2030 and the Qatar National Development Strategy (see Chapter 3). These were followed by the establishment of national institutions in charge of planning, monitoring, and controlling the recruiting and residence of expatriates, including visa and work permits and transfer, as well as identifying the legislative and legal frameworks to reconcile local and international practices. A brief discussion of such legislative policies and frameworks is presented later in this chapter.

## Demographic Challenges

At the beginning of the oil era in the 1940s and 1950s, the majority of the workforce migrating to Qatar came from neighbouring Arab states, whether searching for employment opportunities or compelled to leave their home countries as a result of the domestic political situation. In addition, Indian, Pakistani, and Iranian traders and labourers went to Qatar as a result of ties their countries had maintained with the region (developed especially during the British presence in the Indian subcontinent). A new phase in migration started with the post-1973 economic boom. With the upsurge in oil revenues, Qatar made development efforts on an unprecedented scale. A massive labour emigration consequently followed. Initially, Arab workers were particularly welcomed. Their linguistic, cultural, and religious compatibility with the local population made them more attractive to nationals than other immigrants. The migrant Arabs set up a familiar Arab-type government administration and educational facilities, helped to develop health and social services, and worked in the oil industry. Nevertheless, relatively quickly, the preference of the government changed, and it began to be more open to Asian and Western workers.

The employment of foreign workers is both profitable and costly for receiving countries. The benefits of importing foreign labour are clear: foreigners provide a basic workforce as well as specialists to compensate for the limited number of nationals with required skills and knowledge, stimulate the domestic consumption of goods supplied by local merchants, and boost local property markets. The costs, although more difficult to estimate, consist of salaries, as well as the increased spending required to expand the educational and health services, housing, roads, communications, and other elements of infrastructure. Moreover, Qatar's foreign labour force is a substantial drain of the country's hard currency earnings, with remittances to migrants' home countries amounting to US $4.5 billion in 2011 (Seshan 2012). Economically, this money, if spent locally, would have a positive multiplier effect and consequently generate non-oil employment. On the other hand, foreigners benefit from their employment in Qatar. They are usually able to find better paid jobs than they would have at home, enjoy a higher standard of living, and often have a chance for quick career advancement. In particular, they are able to save large sums of money and, through remittances, often significantly stimulate their home economies.

The massive influx of foreign workers brings an influx of foreign cultures, with attendant risks for nationals and the Qatari culture (see Chapter 9) (Al-Kuwari 2008). Recent concerns have been developed strongly in the country regarding the cultural impacts of such a large expatriate workforce on the local identity and culture. For many, the presence of a large number of expatriates constitutes a major threat to the stability of Qatari society. It leads to such sentiments as, "We should save future generations from having their culture lost," and that although "we are not against the foreign population and labour" at the same time "we do not want these workers to become citizens of our country" and hence "we are proposing and preferring that for security reasons, the period a foreigner can work in Qatar should not exceed 10 years."[2]

Expatriates have often been perceived by nationals as disloyal to their hosts, and even as potentially dangerous political agents (focus group by the author) for the benefit of foreign powers. Although expatriate communities do not usually have any formal rights in the political process, they can influence their host countries' foreign policy via the local media and their connections to their governments and international agencies. The Philippines and India, for example, have become involved directly in the recruitment and placement of their nationals, facilitating their smooth flow to Qatar through efficient formal recruiting agencies that ensure their basic human and legal rights. Expatriates also exert influence through their informal access to top-ranking nationals, which some of them enjoy, and through the their involvement in the overall functioning of the state. According to al-Alkim, "the expatriate community, though without citizenship ... exerts more real political influence than most local citizens, and in many ways is considered to be crucial to the relatively smooth functioning of the political process" (Al-Alkim 1994: 49).

In 2005, low-paid Asian workers staged protests, some of them violent, in Kuwait, Bahrain, and Qatar for not receiving salaries on time. In March 2006, hundreds of mostly South Asian construction workers stopped work and went on a rampage in Dubai to protest their harsh working conditions, low or delayed pay, and the general lack of rights. Such incidents demonstrate the tense relations that have developed between nationals and expatriates in some cases. However, along with the very ambitious development projects associated with Qatar's hosting the 2022 FIFA World Cup, the desire to invest in and build infrastructure for the country has and will continue to increase. The challenge, though, has been the relatively small-size population, which possesses limited technical skill sets, and is highly selective of its role in infrastructure development (Al-Waqfi and Forstenlechner 2010; Mellahi and Al-Hinai 2000). This has contributed in no small way to the current liberal rules around the importation of foreign workers (Al-Waqfi and Forstenlechner 2010; Kapiszewski 2007). However, this reliance on expatriates will continue to put pressure on the country's infrastructure and other social services, mainly education and health.

## Labour Market Trends

The labour market in Qatar has faced stresses due to the influx of foreign labour, especially unskilled labour, into the region and the resultant population imbalances as discussed above (Al-Waqfi and Forstenlechner 2010; Madhi and Barrientos 2003; Mellahi 2000). Various imbalances in the region's health and education sectors have been noted (Gonzalez et al. 2008), as well as imbalances between the private and public sectors—Qatar has a high number of nationals employed in the public sector, leaving the private sector relatively devoid of nationals, at around 9 % in 2012 (Ministry of Planning Development and Statistics, May 2013).

Accordingly, the labour market in Qatar is segmented between the public and the private sectors (Fig. 10.1), between indigenous and expatriate workers, between females and males, and between skilled and unskilled workers. This segmentation is also evident in the wage and non-wage benefits between the public and the private sector, with higher pay for nationals in the public sector and higher pay for expatriates in the private sector, even when applicants (nationals and/or expatriates) have comparable qualifications and skills. The labour force in Qatar in 2012 increased 5 % on an annual basis to reach 1.3 million economically active persons, most of whom were male, and out of which 172,000 were female (Ministry of Planning Development and Statistics, May 2013: 11). The 2012 survey estimated that the Qatari labour force grew by 10 % annually to reach 85,000, while the non-Qatar labour force grew by 5 % annually during 2008–2012. Despite a lower growth rate, non-Qatari labour represented 94 % of the total labour force in 2012. In effect, for every economically

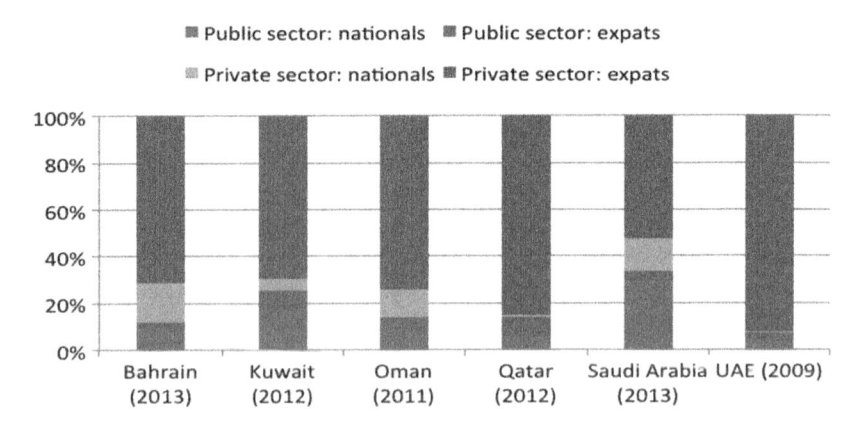

**Fig. 10.1** Distribution of Employment by Nationality in the GCC

active Qatari, there were 15 economically active non-Qataris. For every female Qatari of working age, there were five female non-Qataris.

Expatriates' employment continues to be employer-led, simply reacting to local businesses' applications for work visas, which, although controlled and not granted in all cases, are granted liberally enough to lead to continued rapid expansion of the foreign work force. Expatriate employees are attractive because they are cheap and because they are more easily controlled and, in some cases, exploited (Hertog 2014). The sponsorship system, while relaxed in some cases, continues to prevent most foreigners in Qatar from moving to a new employer without the consent of their present one. This system, which covers even long-term foreign residents, leads to artificial rigidities in the labour market, misallocation of labour, and over-importation of new foreign workers due to the weak or absent local market for foreign talent.

As a result of this situation, a further segmentation in the labour market has been created in other areas, whereby Qataris occupy highly specialized technical, managerial, and professional positions, specifically in the government, oil and gas, and banking, and non-Qataris are predominantly in low or limited-skilled manual jobs, mainly in the construction industry or services (Harry 2007). A 2012 survey showed that 83 % of the Qatari labour force worked in public administration, education, health, and mining, compared to only 9 % working in the private sector, where 74 % of Qatari males and 72 % of Qatari females occupied senior positions (Ministry of Planning Development and Statistics, May 2013: 13). Moreover, three of every four Qataris work in the public sector (General Secretarial for Development Planning, November 2012: 22). The over-employment of Qataris in the public sector is due to superior pay scales and job security, while the private sector is dominated by expatriates. It should be mentioned that labour force participation rates for Qatari men remained stable between 2001 and 2011, but with earlier retirement from the labour force than in most other countries. Labour force participation rates for Qatari females have increased over time, consistent with their rising educational qualifications and the ready availability of low-cost domestic help to take care of their households and children (ibid.).

One of the largest changes in Qatar's employment situation is in the employment of Qatari women. Qatari female participation in the local labour force increased from 27.4 % in 2004 to 34.7 % in 2013 and to 53 % in 2014 (4th Qatar 4th National Human Development Report, 2015, 2015: 35 and 58). In terms of Qatari females' unemployment, it was indicated in 2001 that about 22 % were unemployed. By 2009, this had declined to 1.9 %, with only 2400 females unemployed (Donn & Al Manthri:156). However, Qatari females' unemployment rate remains high compared to their counterparts Qatari males, and particularly amongst young women aged 20–24 and high school graduates (ibid: 32).

Generally speaking, Qatari females' participation in the labour market increased over the last decades, where they represent 68 % of workers in the government sector, 52 % are occupying professional jobs (ibid: 58). This can likely be explained by the higher achievement of females in education, increase in female role models in Qatar, and a subsequent rise in workforce participation. This may be also the result of cultural factors, as women are traditionally placed in roles such as teaching or clerical work, where they are not exposed to mature males. In turn, this may also be attributed in part to the "equal pay for equal work" in the Qatari Constitution. However, although the gap in wages between Qatari women and males decrease over time, it is still existing amongst some professional and managerial positions (4th Qatar 4th National Human Development Report 2015, 2015: 35).

## Private Sector Challenge

The under-employment of Qataris in the private sector has generated concern about losing "ownership" of the national private sector by expatriates, although the actual ownership of private businesses is largely in national hands. However, in a departure from other studies on nationals' attitudes towards private sector employment (Al-Lamki 1998; Harry 2007; Rees et al. 2007), almost 50 % of Qataris indicate that they would be willing to take a private sector position if offered one (Qatar Statistics Labour Force Survey 2010). The other 50 % indicate that they would not be willing to take a job in the private sector due to the perception of lower wages and, perhaps most surprisingly, the low-social status associated with such jobs (ibid.). This supports the available literature on the perceptions of work, status, and employment in much of the Gulf (Achoui 2009; Harry 2007; Forstenlechner and Rutledge 2010; Radwan et al. 1995). Generally, it is preferable amongst Qataris to remain unemployed than to take up undesirable employment in the private sector, where positions have traditionally been looked at as low status and low paying, and are generally avoided by nationals.[3] Like the rest of the GCC, the cultural distaste for low status jobs is also prevalent in Qatar, where there are rising career aspirations amongst young Qataris (Stasz et al. 2007).

On the other hand, the domestic labour force in low status positions such as maids and drivers is increasing in Qatar. Between 2008 and 2009, the number of non-Qatari females in the workforce with domestic positions increased from 58.6 % to 60 % (Qatar Statistics Labour Force Survey 2010). Moreover, the non-Qatari labour force working in the private sector had limited skills, while most of the Qatari labour force in the private sector had high skills (Ministry of Planning Development and Statistics, May 2013:13). However, it is argued by Hertog (2014) that gaps in labour rights—dismissal and pensions—and labour prices between nationals and migrant workers are the main causes explaining the low participation of GCC citizens in the region's private labour markets. To date, the drive to nationalize the workforce in Qatar has had limited success. Efforts to replace expatriates are complicated by the fact that privately owned businesses tend to prefer expatriates as they are cheaper, better qualified, and easier to dismiss. According to Rees et al. (2007), the way that countries in the GCC deal with large expatriate populations and nationalization issues will, to a large extent, determine their survival. Different policies were taken at the macro-level for the sake of improving recruitment policies in Qatar in line with a knowledge-based economy.

To strengthen the Qatarization process, for example, in the banking and insurance sector, the government sets quotas for the minimum level those institutions must employ. However, as yet, the government has not penalized any private companies for non-compliance. Given the inability of the public sector to directly stimulate real non-oil output, it will be the private sector that plays a pivotal role in creating more jobs. However, many private companies believe that the Qatarization process could reduce their competitiveness and actually make it harder for them to do business. Imposing job quotas and having a top-down approach may deter foreign direct investment, without which it will be even more difficult to create new jobs. It would be more effective if Qatar's nationalization policies provided incentives to private businesses, as opposed to imposing restrictions and quotas. Another beneficial step would be to separate the additional benefits of public sector jobs from the wages they provide. Providing all nationals, regardless of whether they work in the public or private sector, with the same benefits would undoubtedly make private sector employment more attractive and make the employment of nationals more attractive to the private sector.

### *Qatarization Challenge*

Qatarization refers to the government's efforts to create sufficient employment opportunities for nationals and to limit the dependence on expatriate labour. Efforts began earlier in the 1970s and were led primarily by the oil and gas industry. The purpose of the policy is to ensure workforce participation of nationals, mainly through a quota system and education and training. Other measures include reserving some professions "for nationals only" and wage subsidies and state retirement plans for nationals in the private sector, accompanied by fees and charges on foreign labour.

At the government level, the Qatarization programme was introduced formally by the Emir in 2000 in much the same manner as the localization movement in the rest of the GCC, that is, through political, legal, and quantitative methods (Forstenlechner 2010). This implementation was through a combination of quotas and government incentives (preferential treatment of Qataris). This is, for example, stipulated in Qatar's Ministry of Interior (2004), where Qatarization and the preferential employment of Qataris is a legal requirement for businesses. More specifically, the Qatar Ministry of Labour issued Labour Law No. 14 (2004), stipulating the hiring of skilled foreign workers who can contribute in the training of Qataris. The law had intended that 20 % of private sector jobs be Qatarized.[4] For Qatarization purposes, Law No. 4 (2009) was also issued to organize the entry, exit, residence, and sponsorship of expatriates: skilled foreign workers in Qatar benefit from attractive residency provisions for immediate family members.[5]

The Qatarization programme originally proposed a quota of 50 % Qataris in key positions in the oil and gas industry and 100 % in all non-specialist positions in government (Kamrava 2009). However, this was not achieved, and the goals were determined to be unrealistic (ibid.). Many organizations in Qatar are hopeful about their progress, and some have claimed to have achieved levels of Qatarization as high as 85 % for senior positions.[6] Private companies meeting quota requirements have been rewarded in public tenders. Moreover, large efforts have been made to improve the education and training of nationals. Nevertheless, all these measures have so far brought only limited results. Only the public sector has become successfully nationalized. In the private sector, the Qatarization rate is still very low as indicated above, with Qataris accounting for less than 10 % of the total workforce. In addition to the reasons mentioned above regarding Qataris' view of their employment in the private sector (low-wages and status), a forceful approach to Qatarization, like the quota system, has encountered strong opposition from local businessmen, as potentially harmful and adversely affecting productivity and profitability of firms (focus group).

In this regard, a 2012 report by Qatargas indicated that the attrition rate for nationals was below 2 %, which was attributed to the careful monitoring of Qataris, including career progression and training, and development programmes. This is a similar percentage to that of the Qatar National Bank, which reported achieving 49 % Qatarization in 2008. However, both organizations could not reach the 50 % target. Certainly, a key component of successful Qatarization is the implementation of effective human resources strategies to support the process (Middle East Company 2009). As Forstenlechner (2010: 136) points out, "... the political, legal and quantitative approaches to localization are only as effective as the implementation." Thus, Qatarization appears to be achieved most effectively through training programmes, human resources practices such as career planning that monitors and provides guidance to nationals, and a high level of job security (ibid.). Despite the optimistic outlook, the original goals of Qatarization have not been achieved, and even Qatar Petroleum and its subsidiaries have only achieved 28 % Qatarization (The EIU ViewsWire 2010). There is now evidence that there will be a more aggressive stance by the government to ensure that Qatarization goals are met (ibid.). This may, in fact, be driven by the perception by many nationals that Qatarization is not working (Shediac and Samman 2010). There appears to be an increasing animosity between nationals and expatriates, fueled in part by a perception of inequality by nationals (Slackman 2010). Many Qatari nationals believe that expatriates are prejudiced against them, which helps to undermine the Qatarization programme. This has further led to a deep sense of angst amongst nationals concerning their position in society (ibid.; The Economist 2010).

Attention is increasingly focusing on the private sector. It is predicted that imposing employment quotas on certain sectors of the private economy ensures that businesses will act proactively to develop training courses and provide incentives to attract nationals, as opposed to simply stating that locals are not interested and lack the necessary skills. The gradual replacement of expatriates with nationals is a prudent economic strategy, particularly because of the country's demographics, but it will not be successful if it focuses on job substitution at the expense of job creation. Neither will it be successful if it results in making private sector companies less competitive or deters foreign direct investment. As has been pointed out by Harry (2007), Godwin (2006), Mellahi (2007), and Rees et al. (2007), nationalization in the Middle East is of increasing concern for the region. Demographics shifts—including increasing unemployment, increasing overemployment in the public sector, rising costs, higher educational attainment, and the expectations of nationals—coupled with the ever-increasing numbers of expatriates will lead to significant, ongoing challenges to the area. Qatarization will need to become more than simply a numbers game; it will require a strategic, long-term investment that ensures the effective participation of nationals in the knowledge economy, as well as a review of national policies associated with education and labour force participation.

## *Unemployment Challenge*

Unlike many other GCC countries, Qatar has an extremely low unemployment rate for nationals. The unemployment rate has decreased dramatically since 2001, from approximately 4 to virtually zero in 2009. The total number of unemployed nationals in 2009 was only 4000 (Qatar Statistics 2009), while it reached 6000 in 2012 (Ministry of Planning Development and Statistics, May 2013: 21). In 2013, it was indicated that unemployment rate amongst Qatar males over 25 years of age accounted for 6 % while it accounted for 1.6 % for Qatar females (4th Qatar Human National Development Report 2015: 35). However, it is important to note that Qatari nationals only make up 8 % of the national workforce, and only 1 % of the private sector (State of Qatar 2009), thus the unemployment rate is quite reasonable. Interestingly, the Qatar trend is not consistent with the rest of the GCC, where unemployment amongst young, educated nationals has been growing (Forstenlechner 2010; Harry 2007). Although education appears to be a challenge in much of the GCC, contrary to the claims of Karoly et al. (2008), this does not appear to be the case in Qatar, at least from the results of the 2013 Labour Force Survey. About 32.7 % of unemployed nationals have secondary-level education, while 40 % had a university diploma or higher (Ministry of Planning Development and Statistics, May 2013:22). Thus, a lack of education does not appear to be a key factor in unemployment in Qatar. In addition, over 69 % of unemployed Qataris had applied for a job through the Ministry of Labour and other specialized offices. However, in line with the work of Forstenlechner and Rutledge (2010), Harry (2007), and Rees et al. (2007), the *type* of education may be more important than the *level* of education. Education that is market-driven and based on the requirements of the employer, rather than what is traditionally offered to nationals (such as cultural studies), is vital for integration (see Chapters 4 and 5).

While unemployment in Qatar is much lower than in the rest of the GCC, the issue is no less pressing, especially with the existence of phantom employment amongst Qataris. Evidence, particularly in the local media, of increased frustration amongst nationals, especially the educated nationals, is important and must be recognized. It is for this reason that further policies are required regarding the motivation of nationals and the articulation of human resources management practices in Qatar that support cultural aspirations, as well as counter traditional practices that hinder nationals employment in the private sector and women employment in some male-dominated professions, and reduce barriers to Qatarization.

## Public Policy

There are four kinds of policies that have a substantial impact on population and employment: immigration, education, labour, and social. Immigration policies help fill essential gaps in the labour market, education policies provide the necessary skills for workers, labour policies provide incentives, and social policies provide a safety net for those who want, but are unable, to participate in the workforce. All are essential for using the population and labour more effectively. Education policy (as discussed in Chapters 4 and 5) has yielded disappointing results to date, despite the great efforts in reforming the system, starting at the grade school level.[7]

With regard to labour policies, and as discussed above, given the small population and shortages of skilled nationals, many of the jobs that were created ended up in the hands of foreign workers. These foreign workers have today become a significant majority in Qatar, with accompanying threats to social stability and cultural identity as discussed above. Accordingly, Qatar has responded with some measures, policies, and programmes to reduce the number of foreign workers, where possible, and support labour nationalization.

1. Legal restrictions on foreign workers through various quota measures: restricting expatriates to government and non-government sectors, reserving particular job categories (e.g., administrative) and economic sectors (e.g., government) for nationals, and specifying the number of nationals in other sectors.
2. Wage supports: Financial incentives for the private sector to hire nationals and to provide benefits equal to those available in the public sector, in addition to the inclusion of Qataris working in the private sector into the pension system.
3. Increased employment opportunities for nationals through taxes: Worker visas, work permit fees, and other taxes that are mainly shouldered by employers.
4. Ad-hoc measures: Labour mobility restrictions on expatriate labour and their dependents.

Qatar has sought to establish an integrated legal system to deal with the presence of foreign workers in the country. Legislation that governs expatriates' residency, employment, and related issues rests on combination of international and national legal instruments and measures.

## International Legislation

As a member of the International Labour Organization and the United Nations, Qatar is party to a number of international conventions regarding employment and the protection of migrant labour: the Forced Labour Convention in 1998, the Labour Inspection Convention in 1976, the Abolition of Forced Labour Convention in 2007, the Discrimination (Employment and Occupation) Convention in 1976, the Minimum Age Convention in 2006, and Worst Form of Child Labour in 2000 (Permanent Population Committee 2011).

## National Legislation

The most important national legislation is Labour Law No. 4 (2009) and No.14 (2004), as well as Qatari National Law No. 38 (2005). Labour law No. 4 (2009) was issued to control and regulate expatriates' entry, exit, residence, and sponsorship. In terms of sponsorship, policies based on quotas and prohibitions have had limited success. Mandatory percentages of local employment and the limitation of specific jobs to nationals have led to an uneven distribution of cost across sectors. They have been difficult to monitor, leading to evasion and in some cases corruption between businesses and the labour administration (focus group interview by the author). Some forms of "phantom employment" of nationals are widespread across the government sector, and quotas have probably increased the informal employment of foreigners who do not officially appear on companies' payroll. Indeed–and due to the sponsorship system–a large black market in labour was created especially in the industrial and commercial sectors, where some individuals act as informal "brokers" for foreign labour, either selling it to other employers or extracting payments from workers in return for releasing them onto a large market for self-employed informal labour. Accordingly, it is very clear that as long as cheap foreign labour is amply available, it will find its way and outcompete nationals, whether formally or informally (focus group).

The entry, residence, and exit of expatriate workers are regulated through the General Directorate of the Borders Passport and Expatriates Affairs. In terms of expatriates' employment, the Department of Recruitment, Department of Legal Affairs, Department of Labour

Relations, and the Department of Labour Inspection in the Ministry of Labour were established in order to monitor labour recruitment and meet national and international legal criteria. In doing so, the Ministry of Labour issued Law No. 4 (2009) to regulate expatriates' entry, exit, residence, and sponsorship, and Labour Law No. 14 (2004) was issued to regulate labour relations in various economic activities. In addition, and in order to ensure legal protection to expatriates, the Ministry of Interior established the Department of Human Rights, while the Ministry of Foreign Affairs established the Bureau of Human Rights. Moreover, another governmental body was established to serve the same group: Qatar Foundation for Combating Trafficking and the National Human Rights Committee.

Qatar is currently discussing minimum wages for foreigners, but it has not taken any action on this front (Ministry of Labour, November 2014). Minimum wages can be difficult to implement and might require comprehensive administrative monitoring through an arrangement such as the wage protection systems in the UAE and, more recently, Saudi Arabia. Such monitoring systems, however, are arguably necessary in any case, as many labour market policies require micro-level information about wages.

However, these measures have done little to curb labour market imbalances in Qatar. The government is hampered by a lack of reliable data, by ineffective coordination between government and private institutions on immigration law, and by the absence of a national workforce development strategy, particularly for Qatarization. For the most part, these measures have sought to influence employers' decisions without introducing greater incentives for national employees. Additionally, the stigma surrounding "low status" occupations, including positions in customer service, is still challenging amongst nationals, which in turn increased labour market segmentation. To fill the expertise gap, the flow of skilled expatriate professionals and technicians has continued, and it will do so at least for the coming decade. With no social safety nets (e.g., unemployment benefits) to rely on, and with immigration rules compounding the problem (Qatar is lenient about entering and exiting, but rigid about allowing full-time residency), many expatriates have begun to fear for their economic prospects. This is raising questions about the stability of labour systems across Qatar.

## The Way Forward

From the preceding discussion, it is obvious that Qatar faces a growing population imbalance, which may threaten the country's economic, political, and social stability. There is no single solution. However, Qatar may work on some structural reforms in immigration, the economy, labour market, and education, and all must be addressed as part of a holistic strategy rather than sectorally.

### *Immigration Policy*

Immigration policies and regulations such as employment visas and sponsorship should be more controlled and targeted towards real and urgent labour market requirements that are oriented towards knowledge economy. This means, on the one hand, making it easy for companies to fill short- and medium-term labour shortages with expatriates within Qatar and, on the other hand, putting in place policies that attract only highly skilled foreigners to knowledge-based industries that Qatar has identified as strategic.

### *Labour Market Policy*

Labour market reforms will over time require enhancements to the macroeconomic policy toolkit. Reducing the reliance on foreign labour could reduce flexibility in the labour market and its ability to respond effectively to movements in the terms of economy. Although several labour market reforms are underway, more are needed.

- Reducing the availability and attractiveness of public-sector employment will be critical to create incentives for nationals to seek private sector jobs, and it will contain future growth in the relatively high public-sector wage bill.
- Liberalizing the domestic mobility of the large foreign workforce could boost productivity by boosting labour market flows, while wage subsidies could help narrow the wage differential between nationals and foreign workers.
- An increased focus on hiring skilled foreign workers can help support higher productivity, while less reliance on low-skilled foreign workers may increase wages and make employment more attractive for less-educated nationals.

## Educational Policy

Continuous education reform is critical. The following areas must be addressed to successfully link reform with national capacity building:

- Set education strategies based on carefully considered socioeconomic goals, including the labour market. This means more communication and coordination amongst stakeholders—the business community, local community groups, human capital development organizations, private and public universities, and government agencies. It can be done through formal organizations that can help establish or develop job-matching and career-building institutions (such as the Labour Department–Ministry of Labour and Career Fair Institution) that should be more oriented towards helping the private sector and the government.
- Upgrade vocational education and training in order to ensure that students are exposed at an early stage to vocational and technical skills.

## Economic Policy

Qatar's strategy must incorporate two critical steps to identify and develop the economic sectors that are likely to maximize value-added jobs for nationals:

- Develop competitive sectors. To create job opportunities for Qataris and help reduce the dependence on expatriates and reduce the gaps between the educational outcomes and the market demands, Qatar needs to formulate a clear economic development strategy, building on the current one, and determine specific measures and indicators to implement that strategy. This may require, for example, supporting immigration and labour market policies and supporting special economic zones and economic cities apart from Doha, as well as a knowledge-based infrastructure (e.g., vocational education and training centres and R&D centres), especially in cities other than Doha.
- Promote entrepreneurship. Although entrepreneurship has been growing recently in terms of culture and practices, it still needs to be fostered, to engender a culture of corporate governance and disclo-

sure and to build up an infrastructure for private business (including entrepreneurial programmes and a more competitive financial sector). More entrepreneurship will strengthen the base of small and medium-sized enterprises in Qatar.

Notes

1. Qatar ranked no. 31 in the Human Development Report of 2014. For further information about the HD index, refer to HDR, 2014, UNDP.
2. The author conducted personal interviews with 39 senior officials in different sectors during the period of June–October 2014.
3. Focus Group Interview by the author.
4. Article 27 states, "the employer who employs foreign experts or technicians shall train an appropriate number of Qatari workers to be nominated by the department on the work carried out by the experts and technicians or employ assistant Qatari workers for them for purpose of training and gaining expertise."
5. As stated in Article 16, "Residence permits shall be granted to the spouse of the person granted a Residence permit and to his/her male children who have not completed their university study up to the age of 25 years and to his/her unmarried daughters. Subject to the consent of the Minister or his nominee at his sole discretion, the parents of the person granted a residence permit may also be granted residence permits." (The Minister identifies the granting of these permits to expatriates with high level of expertise).
6. In this regard, the 2012 survey results showed that there were 47 % of Qatari males and 72 % of Qatari females in senior positions (Ministry of Development Planning and Statistics, May 2013: 14).
7. Qatar ranked low (number 50) on the 2011 Education Development Index (EDI), indicating that much progress is still required for Qatar. (http://www.unesco.org/new/en/education/themes/leading-the-international agenda/efareport/statistics/efa-development-index/).

Bibliography. Qatar: Policy Making in a Transformative State

Achoui, Mustapha. 2009. Human resource development in Gulf countries: An analysis of the trends and challenges facing Saudi Arabia. *Human Resource Development International* 12(1): 35–46.

Al-Alkim, Hassan Hamdan. 1994. *The GCC States in an Unstable World: Foreign Policy Dilemmas of Small states*. London: Saqi Books.

Al-Kuwari, Ali. (2008). *The Demographic Imbalance is a Violation of the Citizen's Right (in Arabic)*. London: Al-Quds Al-Arabi Newspaper . URL: http://www.alquds.co.uk/pdfarchives/2008/04/04-22/qmd.pdf

Al-Lamki, Salma. 1998. Barriers to Omanization in the private sector: The perceptions of Omani graduates. *The International Journal of Human Resource Management* 9(2): 377–400.

Al Muftah, Hend, (2010), *Human capital Formation in Qatar: A story of Oil and gas-based industries*, VDM Publishing House Ltd., USA

Al-Waqfi, Mohammed, and Ingo Forstenlechner. 2010. Stereotyping of citizens in an expatriate dominated labour market: Implications for workforce 'localization' policy. *Employee Relations* 32(4): 364–381.

Donn, G. & Al Manthri, Y. 2013. Education in the Broader Middle East: borrowing a baroque arsenal. Oxford: Symposium Books Ltd.

Forstenlechner, Ingo. 2010. Workforce localization in emerging Gulf economies: The need to fine-tune HRM. *Personnel Review* 39(1): 135–152.

Forstenlechner, Ingo, and Emilie Rutledge. 2010. Unemployment in the Gulf: Time to update the "Social Contract". *Middle East Policy* 17(2): 38–51.

Godwin, Stewart M. 2006. Globalization, education and emiratization: A case study of the United Arab Emirates. *The Electronic Journal of Information Systems in Developing Countries* 27(1): 1–14.

Gonzalez, G., L. Karoly, L. Constant, H. Salem, and C. Goldman. 2008. *Facing Human Capital Challenges of the 21st Century: Education and Labor Market Initiatives in Lebanon, Oman, Qatar, and the United Arab Emirates*. Santa Monica, CA: RAND Corporation.

Harry, Wes. 2007. Employment creation and localization: The crucial human resource issues for the GCC. *The International Journal of Human Resource Management* 18(1): 132–146.

Hertog, Steffen. 2014. *Arab Gulf States: An Assessment of Nationalisation Policies*, Gulf Labour Market and Migration Series. San Domenico di Fiesole, Italy: European University Institute.

Kamrava, Mehran. 2009. Royal factionalism and political liberalization in Qatar. *Middle East Journal* 63(3): 401–420.

Kapiszewski, Andrzej. 2007. De-Arabization in the Gulf: Foreign labor and the struggle for local culture. *Georgetown Journal of International Affairs* 8(2): 81–88.

Karoly, L. (2010), The Role of Education in Preparing Graduates for the Labour Markets in the GCC Countries, City of Publication, Chicago, IL.

Madhi, Salah T., and Armando Barrientos. 2003. Saudisation and employment in Saudi Arabia. *Career Development International* 8(2): 70–77.

Mellahi, K. 2000. Globalisation and employment of local workers in Gulf co-operation countries. *Management Research News* 23(24): 70–72.

Mellahi, K. 2007. The effect of regulations on HRM: Private sector firms in Saudi Arabia. *International Journal of Human Resource Management* 18(1): 85–99.

Mellahi, K., and S. Al-Hinai. 2000. Local workers in Gulf co-operation countries: Assets or liabilities? *Middle Eastern Studies* 3(3): 177–190.

Middle East Company News. 2009. Qatar gas CEO urges nationals to make best use of opportunities. *The Middle East Company News*, June 11. Accessed July 10, 2014.

Ministry of Development Planning and Statistics. 2013. Labour Force Sample Survey 2012, State of Qatar.

Ministry of Development Planning and Statistics (Qatar). 2015a. Monthly Figures on Total Population in Qatar. Ministry of Planning and Statistics.

———. 2015b. *Qatar Fourth National Human Development Report*. Doha: Ministry of Development Planning and Statistics.

Nassar, Heba, and Ahmed Ghoneim. 2002. *Trade and Migration, Are they Complements or Substitutes?: A Review of Four MENA Countries*. Cairo, Eygpt: Economic Research Forum.

Oxford Business Group. 2009. *The Report – Qatar 2009*. Oxford: Oxford Business Group.

Permanent Population Committee, (2011), Integrating Foreign Workers Issues into Qatar Strategies and Policies. Available at: http://www.gsdp.gov.qa/portal/page/portal/ppc/PPC_home/PPC_Publications/studies/Integrating%20Foreign%20Workers%20Issues.pdf (accessed April 2016).

Qatar Statistics Authority. Labor Force Sample Survey 2009. Available at: http://www.qix.gov.qa/portal/page/portal/QIXPOC/Documents/QIX%20Knowledge%20Base/Publication/Labor%20Force%20Researches/labor%20force%20sample%20survey/Source_QSA/Labor_Force_QSA_AnBu_AE_2009.pdf (accessed April 2016).

Qatar social Statistics, 2014 Ministry of Planning and statistics, Qatar Monthly Statistics, June, 2014.

Qatar Statistics Authority. 2010. E-Census Registry 2010. State of Qatar. Available at: http://www.gsdp.gov.qa/portal/page/portal/gsdp_en/statistics_en/Census_en_2 [accessed April 2016].

Rees, C.J., A. Mamman, and A.B. Braik. 2007. Emiritization as a strategic HRM change initiative: case study evidence from a UAE petroleum company. *International Journal of Human Resource Management* 18(1): 33–53.

Seshan, Genesh. 2012. Migration in Qatar: A socio-economic profile. *Journal of Arabian Studie* 2(2): 157–171.

Shediac, Richard, and Hatem Samman. 2010. *Meeting the Employment Challenge in the GCC: The Need for a Holistic Strategy*. Dubai: Booz & Company.

Slackman, M. 2010. "Affluent Qataris seek what money cannot buy." New York Times, May 13. http://www.nytimes.com/2010/05/14/world/middleeast/14qatar.html?scp%C2%BC1&sq%C2%BCAffluentpercent20Qatarisperscent20seekpercent20whatpercent20moneypercent20cannotpercent20buy&st%C2%BCcse&_r=0

CHAPTER 11

# Integrated Water, Energy, and Food Governance: A Qatari Perspective

*Rabi H. Mohtar*

This chapter describes opportunities and challenges for Qatar achieving water, energy, and food security. It also describes the environmental issues in the state of Qatar and the current governance structure for these vital resources. It provides a case study of food security and the benefits of an integrated governance of the food system and its inter-relationship with water and energy resources, outlining implementation gaps for an integrated resources management and governance. Due to the country's size, uniformity in ecological and sociopolitical governance, as well as its political governance structure, the chapter ends by suggesting an opportunity for Qatar to lead global efforts in implementing a holistic governance structure of water, food, and energy security that recognizes the interdependencies of these resources and the strong interlinkages that they exhibit.

INTRODUCTION

Between 2000 and 2010, the GCC countries as a whole exhibited excessive energy consumption that drained fuel resources and wealth at rates higher than production. While oil production rates increased at 20 %,

R.H. Mohtar (✉)
Texas AM University, College Station, TX, USA
Qatar Environment and Energy Research Institute (QEERI), Qatar Foundation, Ar-Rayyan, Qatar

© The Author(s) 2016
M.E. Tok et al. (eds.), *Policy-Making in a Transformative State*,
DOI 10.1057/978-1-137-46639-6_11

energy consumption rates did so at 120 % (Darwish and Mohtar 2013a). Following the trend in other GCC countries, the state of Qatar has also seen unprecedented growth and development since the late 1990s, with population doubling three times during this period. Such significant growth imposes stresses on the country's physical infrastructure as well as on the water, energy, and food securities. These challenges were highlighted recently by Mohtar (2015) and BQ Doha (2015). Qatar, its predominant hydrocarbon wealth notwithstanding, lacks abundant water resources, a fact which seriously impacts the nation's food security.

The renewable water resources map in the GCC, as compared to other countries in the region, shows that the water withdrawal rates clearly exceed the renewable water resources in each of the GCC countries (Darwish and Mohtar 2013). Sea water desalination has been used as a main source to bridge the water gap. About 60 % of the current world's desalination capacity is located in the GCC region (Darwish and Mohtar 2013). Desalination on the other hand, is a major consumer of prime energy in the region. Due to this severe lack of water resources, the GCC countries import the majority of their food: overall 80–90 % of the food needs in the GCC is imported from other countries (FAO 2014).

Achieving water and food security is high on the agenda of Qatari decision-makers. The purpose of this chapter is to analyze the current status of water, energy, and food resources in Qatar and then to propose an integrated governance/policy structure that will ensure an informed tradeoff of water, energy and food resources, thus allowing appropriate water and food security policies and enabling sound, interdependent management.

Qatar's water scarcity is a result of the country's geography. Located in the Arabian Peninsula and classified as hyper-arid, Qatar is among the driest regions of the world. Qatar has undergone unprecedented growth in terms of population, economic, and infrastructure development over the last 20 years. According to Qatar Demographics (2013), the country's population increased from 0.6 million in 2001 to over 2.3 million in early 2015. The majority of this population is expatriate workers, divided into working class (mainly from Asia) and management or executive staff (largely from the Middle East, North America, and Europe) (Fromherz 2012). Real GDP growth rates have averaged about 6 % in the past three years, and even the decline in oil prices in 2015 did not immediately threaten growth (see Chapter 1 for details).

Qatar is a unique case study for analyses on issues of environmental governance, partly due to its breakneck growth, its heavy reliance on hydrocarbons, and its attempts to transform its economy and society. Despite its hydrocarbon reserves, the future economic development of the country will be determined by its water, energy, and food security measures. The question posed in this chapter is whether a highly centralized form of rule can develop an integrated policy to effectively manage these three crucial natural resources (water, energy, and food) and, thereby, maintain Qatar's economic growth.

## QATAR'S CURRENT AND FUTURE ENVIRONMENTAL CHALLENGES

Sheikh Tamim bin Hamad Al-Thani not only inherited the world's richest country, he also faces severe challenges that carry the potential to threaten future economic development. Qatari nationals, as well as its foreign labor force, require affordable food, water, and energy resources if they are to continue working and living in the Gulf. While its environmental challenges are not phenomena unique to Qatar, but rather are prevalent around the world, given the geographical characteristics of a hyper-arid country, the challenges play out in a very distinct manner in Qatar.

### *Qatar's Water Challenge*

The total renewable natural water resources in Qatar are 58M m³, with a yearly average of 33 m³ per capita (y.ca) in 2010. Due to population growth, this is expected to be reduced to 22 m³/y.ca by 2050. The GCC average in 2010 was 92 m³/y.ca (Sadik 2012). Water withdrawal, as a percent of annual fresh water resources, is about 700 %: this means that in the case of ground water resources, Qatar is over pumping beyond the recharge ability of its aquifers. Water table drawdown, salinity, and seawater intrusion are typical scenarios to be expected. Most of Qatar's fresh water withdrawals are from groundwater, and the majority of that withdrawal is used for agriculture, about 60 %, which should be compared with the global average of about 72 % (FAO 2011). As in most countries of the world, the value of this scarce resource is not signaled to consumers: this leads to water wastage. Qatar's domestic water use is among the highest in the world and policies toward water conservation have yet to be agreed upon or implemented. This over-exploitation of groundwater resources has led to increased salinity of the groundwater, due to sea water intrusion and lowered fresh water levels. A large part of the problem must be attributed to agricultural production, which has caused groundwater salinity to increase as fresh water is withdrawn for the irrigation of crops. By 2004, there were 1192 farms in Qatar, though only 945 were actually operative (United Nations, Food and Agriculture Organization 2008). It is expected that many of these farms will close down as a result of water table drawdown and high salinity in the aquifers.

While the impact of climate change on future water availability is yet neither well understood nor documented on the local scale by policy-makers, there is an intrinsic threat that sea water levels may rise, making dust bowl scenarios a future reality. Except for Iraq, Morocco, Lebanon, Oman, Tunisia, Algeria, and Syria, the rest of the Arab world's water withdrawals (the amount of fresh water extracted from surface and groundwater) exceeds the quantities of naturally renewable water. In all the GCC, and Qatar is no exception, this freshwater deficit is addressed by using desalinated water to provide the required water. While in theory, desalination appears to be a good idea, these plants have high energy demand and produce high $CO_2$ emissions. This prevailing condition of supply side expansion, such as the construction of expanded water infrastructure, rather than a focus on introducing conservation measures, results in increased discharge of brine from desalination plants and the consequent intensification of the salinity level in the Persian Gulf. This impacts ecological habitats, in both marine and terrestrial systems, increasing the vulnerability of the ecosystem biodiversity, particularly mangrove and tidal salt marshes.

### *Qatar's Energy Challenge*

Similar to its exceptionally high consumption of water, Qatar is also among the highest per capita energy users in the world. In the decade of 2000–2010, oil production in Qatar increased from 757,000 bbl/day to 1,569,000 bbl/day or by 107 %. In the same period, oil consumption grew from 60,000 bbl/day to 220,000 bbl/ay: a 220 % increase (Sadik 2012). Natural gas production in Qatar, during the same decade, grew by nearly 400 %: from 23.7 to 116.7 billion cubic meters (BCM), and natural gas consumption increased 110 %, from 9.7 to 20.4 BCM (Sadik 2012). Except for Qatar, all GCC countries have, or will have, shortages in NG and have begun importing this resource from Qatar. According to Lahn and Stevens (2011), Saudi Arabia's oil production will only meet local consumption, and exports will cease to exist should this "business as usual" scenario continue.

Qatar's $CO_2$ emissions are significantly above the world average. Although Qatar continues to enhance its very high per capita energy consumption and improve its industrial efficiency, much of the high emissions rate is due to the high oil and natural gas production coupled with the low population density in Qatar. As in the United States, Qatar's energy conservation policies are in the infancy stage of development. The Boston Consulting Group predicts the energy efficiency market to reach double-digit growth rates around the world only in the coming decade. Decision-makers across the globe will need to be convinced of the perks of an energy efficiency market. Still, water waste in Qatar comes at a very high cost for the energy sector, which emits substantial amounts of $CO_2$ into the atmosphere, resulting in even higher air pollution, already high due to gas and oil production and high-density traffic. Although it is well known that air pollution negatively impacts human health, no rigid epidemiological studies have so far been conducted to assess this crucial challenge. Air pollution has additional decisive environmental costs that also impact the third challenge: food.

### *Qatar's Food Challenge*

Qatar imports 100 % of its wheat, rice, flour, and potatoes; 93 % of its maize; 98 % of its barley; 86 % of its vegetables; 77 % of its fruits; 98 % of its meat; 36 % of its fish; 63 % of its eggs; and 93 % of its milk and dairy needs. The bulk of Qatar's imports are from within the GCC region, particularly the fresh, perishable commodities. Domestic food production is negatively impacted by several factors. Much of Qatar's soil is of high salinity, unsuitable for agriculture without reclamation: an outcome of high pollution and desertification resulting from the combination of urban sprawl and over-exploitation of natural resources. The lack of fertile soil for local food production limits any hope for future agriculture production, despite the possibility of availability of desalinated water. These man-made challenges add to the existing nature-made challenges that result from the prevailing sand storms which lead, naturally, to soil loss from wind erosion. The sandstorms are expected to increase as climate change further aggravated by heavy construction and the lack of effective soil conservation measures. In a nutshell, Qatar, as most economies of the world, needs to better understand the potential of policies that address these challenges interdependently through integrated management.

## The Need for Integrated Policy

The interconnectedness of the water, energy, and food securities has been highlighted by the World Economic Forum since 2005, where a conceptual water-energy food (WEF) nexus was first introduced. This framework calls for an integrated management, allocation, and policy to address current and projected demands for these vital resources.

However, despite the enormous and interconnected water, energy, food, and environmental challenges outlined above, efforts to address them are not integrated. The challenges are highly complex in nature and constitute scenarios that can only be addressed in an integrated manner. The need for integrated planning and management of natural resources has been understood by a number of global initiatives. The nexus idea has been significantly promoted by multinational companies dealing with food, energy, and water in their supply chains on a daily basis. In particular, Coca Cola, Nestle, SAB Miller, Pepsi, and Unilever have promoted the nexus concept under the roof of the World Economic Forum in an effort to develop integrated approaches to the management of water, energy, and food security. However, given the importance of global food, water, and energy security, particularly in developing countries, the nexus concept has also been taken up by donor governments, such as the United States and Germany, in an effort to promote integrated development policies around the world (Jobbins and Pillot 2013).

The nexus concept stresses that twenty-first century environmental governance depends on understanding that resources are highly interlinked, as well as dependent on climatic, socio-political, economic, and demographic changes. In order to meet the challenges in every economy of the world, barriers to sustainable resource management, such as policies and low public engagement, must be fully explored. This requires a better understanding of the full life-cycle footprint of food, water, and energy resources and their products and services. It is evident that changes across nearly all sectors of the economy are expected as a result of these resource shortages. However, despite the evidence of inter-linkages between these key natural resources, "silo thinking" prevails worldwide.

The need for integrated resource management is now more important than ever. In the Qatari case, this need for integrated policy is especially evident, because it will impact the next phase of the nation's economic growth. Only if resources are managed interdependently can the Qatari growth model, heavily dependent upon foreign labor, be sustained. Implementation depends on the quantification of resources for improved and integrated management by decision-makers charged with oversight of the water, energy, and food resources. Mohtar and Daher (2014) outlined one example of these integrated resource management challenges surrounding food security that involves an inclusive, multi-stakeholder, multi-scale approach considering holistic and system level thinking.

## State of the Art Natural Resources Policy

In order to achieve the goal of integrated policy-making, decision-makers must be equipped with quantitative frameworks to both understand the challenges and then to effectively implement the appropriate policies to address those challenges. Several tools have been developed to address integrated planning of the resources nexus, = and some have been used in the Qatari sustainability context, such as the WEF Nexus Tool 2.0 (http://www.wefnexustool.org/login.php) (Mohtar and Daher (2014). This is an example of a resource nexus tool developed to identify, quantitatively, the inter-linkages among the energy, water, and food systems at multiple levels (international, national, regional, watershed, etc.) and to provide sustainable resource management strategies that are informed by a scenario-based WEF nexus framework. The goal is to conduct research to define and quantify these inter-linkages between water, energy, and food resources and then to develop and apply a framework that integrates water, energy, and food resource planning.

The tool assesses scenarios, and reflects various resource allocation strategies for each scenario, by quantifying the resource requirements (water, energy, land, financial requirements, and environmental impacts) for each scenario. The WEF Nexus Tool 2.0 also offers a dynamic model that enables decision-makers to systematically integrate policy preferences and to compare possible outcome scenarios, with the respective resource requirements for each. Informed policy-making depends upon the level of resolution of the data. The tool helps address the challenges of data collection by offering options that will produce actual numbers for each given scenario, allowing comparison and cost-benefit analyses. Only a decision-making tool such as the WEF Nexus Tool 2.0 can enable decision-makers to understand how they can move away from the globally prevailing "silo mode" in policy-making (Mohtar and Daher 2012).

*Case Study on Qatar Food Security Plan*

This section describes a case study on resource nexus governance inspired by the Qatari food security plan. (http://portal.www.gov.qa/wps/portal/topics/Environment+and+Natural+Resources/National+Food+Security+Program) Since 2009, Qatar has begun to address the nexus and its governance in practice. An example of such was the establishment of an integrated plan for food security. This is reflected in the establishment of the Qatar National Food Security Program (QNSFP) and the follow up implementation plan. The key strength of the Qatar food security plan is a vision based on the inclusion of the water, energy, and food resources as an interconnected nexus of resources. This is a pioneering vision, globally, in its integrated and interconnected resource planning, where managing any one of these three resources does not compromise the integrity of the other two. This plan is also consistent with the Qatar National Development Strategy 2020 where water and food security are prominent. Likewise, it is consistent with Kahramaa's (the Qatar General Electricity and Water Corporation) plans to have the country's water secure by increasing the fresh water supply through surface and subsurface storage. The food security plan has envisaged producing 60–70 % of Qatar's food domestically, without compromising natural resources management. A key factor for the attainment of this goal is seen in dryland farming, an agricultural technique for non-irrigated crop cultivation that promotes the careful husbandry of soils to ensure a holistic, integrated planning approach. Three crucial factors for the success of the food security plan include the promotion of technology, research, and development and integrated policy that address the full food supply chain, from producer to consumer, in an effort to decrease the use of energy and water. Another aspirational and internationally unique goal is the inception of policies that address the full supply chain, such as the food security plan collaboration, with local food retailers to decrease food waste in Qatar through improved efficiencies in supermarkets.

This visionary plan has gained global recognition, particularly in dry zones around the world. Instead of taking an isolationist focus, the food security plan has deliberately reached out to other countries affected by dry climates in an effort to share learning experiences and generate a global vision for the nexus in drylands. This policy choice was underlined by the establishment of the Global Alliance for Drylands, now chaired by the former general director of the United Nations Economic and Social Commission for West Asia in Beirut. By developing a road map for the nexus implementation on food security, Qatar can be a leader with a global following by offering a successful case study to lead other nations. Despite the fact that the duties of the office of the Qatar National Food Security Program were in developing the plan and it no longer functions as an implementing body, the integrated view of the food system, its interconnectedness with other vital resources (energy and water), and its environmental and socio-economic consequences carry over into the implementation of the plan. Various entities of the current public agencies carry various elements of the plan, including the ministry of the environment, Kahramaa, the ministry of foreign affairs, among others.

## IMPLEMENTATION GAPS

Implementing these holistic, aspirational approaches has been hindered by many factors for Qatar and worldwide. Despite governments all over the world are recognizing the importance of the holistic nature of resource governance, there are several limitations to implementing such an integrated plan. This section identifies some of these gaps. The major decisions surrounding the governance of natural resources have been driven by economic factors. The economics of the system have been over emphasized and must be combined with broader sustainability measures, including but not limited to social, political, environmental, and economic. Much of the implementation gap is due to the fact that the nexus topic is still in its infancy in terms of policy perception. In most affluent economies in the world, water, food, and energy security has long been a topic of minor significance, due to the cheap availability of food on the world market. The food price spikes of 2007–2008 and of 2010–2011 made global food commodity markets highly volatile and began to effect changes in the perception of decision-makers that food is abundantly available for rich economies. World commodity markets have since calmed, and with that relaxation, the existential need to act has lessened. However, this perceived, but artificial, security is highly dangerous. As researchers from Chatham House (Bailey 2012) aptly stressed, "the world is only one or two bad harvests away from a major food crisis."

At the same time, "green perceptions" have long been associated with a left-wing, Western-based middle class. Climate change is beginning to be felt gradually by most economies in the world, but paradigm changes take time to reach the minds and hearts of politicians and people. The exemplary case study of the Qatar Food Security vision may be too radical, at this point in history. Nevertheless, the example this plan has initiated in Qatar is unlikely to disappear. The advent of China's food policy that is going global will see further pressures on the global food commodity markets. China has begun to invest in food companies around the world in an effort to meet its growing demand, particularly for low-value staple food crops (GRAIN 2014). Despite Qatar's impressive success story, it is unlikely that an economy of two million people will be able to compete with the global population elephant that is China. Meanwhile, another significant bottleneck to the implementation of food security plans is capacity building. The transformation from a gas- and oil-centered economy into an economy that takes a holistic natural resources approach requires time. One important issue to address will be the development of a growing agricultural sector, and the extension service of the USA's Land Grant system offers a good success story and one that could be adopted in Qatar to train a new generation of food, water, and energy security experts. Doing so will depend crucially on the development of environmental governance in Qatar. Finally, where most of our governance has focused on single resource issues—water or food—the nexus calls for governance of issues that cuts across all of these resources and a platform to interconnect them. This platform allows for shared decision-making, an issue difficult to accomplish in the current mindset of governance.

## Environmental Governance

Addressing the outlined bottlenecks requires successful implementation of a political will to set these policies into action. This requires a reformed governance structure: one that moves away from the "silo approach," common not only to Qatar, but to the vast majority of countries in the world. Traditionally, water, energy, and food are governed by separate ministries, which often have little or no collaboration with one other. For example, while agriculture is a major contributor to water use in Qatar, it is governed under the Ministry of Environment; water management is split over various bodies, including Kahramma, Ashghal (Public Works Authority), and the Ministry of Energy and Industries. Addressing these three vital resources requires an integrated approach that identifies tradeoffs through technology implementation, aided by research and development, and sound environmental policy governed in a coordinated fashion. A major criterion for the implementation of the nexus is an "inter-governance" unit that bridges the different ministries and that understands and implements the cross cutting and integrative nature of the nexus. A suggested structure is shown in Fig. 11.1. Such governance structure is, to a degree, now governing the food security implementation where the overarching responsibility lies under the office of the prime minister, and other units are responsible for other elements of the plan. However, a deliberate integration of resources management and allocation is not in place.

Fig. 11.1 Example environmental governance

This horizontal platform of decision-makers working across units and portfolios must be supported by the highest level of decision-making. This platform would be equipped with the data generated by tools such as the WEF Nexus Tool 2.0 and applied to different scenario outcomes to generate the information necessary for effective policy. This policy would, inevitably, affect wider sectors than water, energy, and food, including construction, conservation, trade, and even foreign affairs. It is fully understood by the author of this paper that this requires a bold approach by the decision-making elite. If translated into practice, it would mean a complete overhaul of long-established governance structures where some parties would have to surrender privileges and influence for the greater well-being. Nevertheless, doing so would enable Qatar to enter a new phase of economic prosperity, as is outlined in the Qatar National Vision 2030.

CONCLUSIONS

This chapter defines a critical question about the Qatar resource nexus and its governance. It outlines opportunities and challenges surrounding the sustainable management of these interconnected resources. It describes the food security system as a case study. We wish to conclude with the question about which forms of political rule are better stewards of natural resources. The author of this paper is convinced that very few countries in the world, apart from Qatar, have the combination of vision and strong central government leadership which would allow taking such a bold approach as introduced above. Qatar has shown the world, in stunning fashion, how to transform an economy, once dependent on pearl fishing, into the prosperous leading economy that it is today. The internal discourse among Qatari elites allowed Sheikh Hamad to transform his country in less than 20 years. This transformation has sufficiently impressed the world to cause Qatar to be viewed with great empathy and respect, particularly by developing countries. The task of Emir Tamim bin Hamad Al-Thani is even greater than his father's was. Once again, he has to transform his country and demonstrate to the world the capacity of the Qataris for change. This time, however, a different type change is required: Qatar will lead into the future through a "green change" that has the potential to bring about sustainable economic prosperity and guide other nations of the world through a greater understanding of the water-energy-food nexus, the most crucial cornerstone to green change.

**Acknowledgement** The author wishes to thank the contributions of the Texas Nexus Team, namely, Mary Schweitzer and Martin Keulertz for their insightful contributions to this chapter.

## BIBLIOGRAPHY. QATAR: POLICY MAKING IN A TRANSFORMATIVE STATE

Bailey, Rob. 2012. Are we facing another global food price crisis?
Embrace Doha. 2015. What is Embrace Doha?. *Embrace Doha*. http://www.embracedoha.com/eglit.html
Food and Agriculture Organization of the United Nations. 2008. Qatar. Available at: http://www.fao.org/nr/water/aquastat/countries_regions/qat/index.stm
———. 2011. AQUASTAT on-line.
———. 2014. FAOSTAT Database.
Fromherz, Allen J. 2012. *Qatar: A Modern History*. London: I.B. Tauris.
GRAIN. 2012. *Who Will Feed China: Agribusiness or its own Farmers?* Barcelona: GRAIN.
Jobbins, G., and D. Pillot. 2013. EU and IFAD Review of CGIAR Research Programme 7: Climate Change, Agriculture and Food Security (CCAFS).
Lahn, Glada, and Paul Stevens. 2011. *Burning Oil to Keep Cool: The Hidden Energy Crisis in Saudi Arabia*. London: Chatham House.
Mohtar, Rabi H. 2015. Opportunities and challenges for innovations in Qatar. *The Muslim World* 105(1): 46–57.
Mohtar, R., and B. Dahar. 2012. Water, energy, and food: The ultimate nexus. In *Encyclopedia of Agricultural, Food, and Biological Engineering*, eds. Dennis R. Heldman, and Carmen I. Moraru. London: Taylor and Francis.
Mohtar, Rabi H., and Bassel Daher. 2014. *A Platform for Trade-off Analysis and Resource Allocation: The Water-Energy-Food Nexus Tool and its Application to Qatar's Food Security*. London: Chatham House.
Sadik, Abdul-Karim. 2012. Food security and agricultural sustainability. In *Arab Environment: Survival Options - Ecological Footprint of Arab countries*, ed. Najib Saab, 37–68. Beirut: Arab Forum for Environment and Development.

CHAPTER 12

# Macroeconomic Stabilization Policies and Sustainable Growth in Qatar

*Khalid Rashid Alkhater*

The Qatari economy has evolved through four main development stages since the discovery of oil in the late 1930s:

1. Pre-independence oil economy, spanning from the beginning of oil exports in 1949 to the declaration of independence in 1971. Through this phase the country went through a gradual process of transformation from poverty to relatively improved living standards and social services, slowly moving to a new long era to come of high oil dependency.
2. Early post-independence oil economy, from 1971 to early 1980s. This period witnessed the first major oil shock in 1973 and marked the actual beginning of building the modern state of Qatar.

---

This chapter benefitted from extensive discussion with the former Chief Economist at Qatar Central Bank (QCB), Dr. Elsayed Elsamadisy, over the past few years and from helpful recent comments. The chapter was written with a non-specialist audience in mind. Those interested in a more technical treatment may consult Alkhater and Basher (2015), Elsamadisy, Alkhater, and Basher (2014), and Alkhater (2015, 2012b). The views expressed here are those of the author and do not represent those of QCB.

K.R. Alkhater (✉)
Department of Research and Monetary Policy, Qatar Central Bank (QCB), Doha, Qatar

© The Author(s) 2016
M.E. Tok et al. (eds.), *Policy-Making in a Transformative State*,
DOI 10.1057/978-1-137-46639-6_12

3. A slow growth period following the oil price collapse of the 1980s–1990s.
4. The resource boom and rapid expansion period: 2002–present.

The purpose of this chapter is to review the macroeconomic stabilization policies in Qatar and the GCC countries, in the context of attaining economic stability and sustainable growth. While concentrating on the current development phase, a brief review of the historical development stages is helpful to track the development path of the economy and to conduct parallel assessment of the development of the macroeconomic management framework (MMF).

## QATAR'S DEVELOPMENT PATH, 1949 TO THE PRESENT

### The Pre-Independence Oil Economy: 1949–1971

Oil was discovered in Qatar in 1938, but export was delayed until 1949 due to WWII (Metz 1993). Oil had a tremendous impact in transforming Qatar from impoverishment and underdevelopment, after the collapse of the local pearling industry in the 1920s, into modernity, economic prosperity, and social progress under a new age of high oil dependency for years to come. Export of crude oil in 1949 was followed in 1950 by the first government budget and the first GDP statistics on record, estimated to be $763 million (Maddison 2001). In 1950, the Eastern Bank (British) was established as the first bank to operate in the country, and in 1965, Qatar National Bank was established to be the first national bank (Qatar Monetary Authority 1985).

The economy then was basically a single sector resource-based economy dominated by foreign trade and operated by foreign companies. There was no national currency and no monetary authority. The financial sector was underdeveloped and not integrated with the outside world, and there was no capital market.

### The Early Post-Independence Oil Economy: 1971–1980

Shortly after independence in 1971, particularly after the first major oil shock in 1973, the economy started to embark rapidly on early stages of development supported by substantial increases in oil revenues, as a result of higher prices. These developments were reflected in higher GDP growth rates and development of infrastructure and state institutions. In 1973, the Qatar Monetary Agency was established to be the first sovereign monetary authority in the country's modern history with the Qatari riyal (QR) as the first national currency. The riyal was (de facto) pegged to the US dollar (USD) in order to import monetary policy credibility with low inflation rates, and to stabilize government oil revenues (generated in USD), which were channeled to the domestic economy through government fiscal expenditure mechanism. With a pegged exchange rate regime, the MMF was essentially stripped of two important policy instruments, monetary policy and exchange rate policy, and left with only one policy instrument to manage the economic cycle, namely fiscal policy.[1] Furthermore, in Qatar, as well as in other GCC states, only one-sided fiscal policy is used—fiscal spending—and essentially no tax policy is utilized.[2] However, this simple single-instrument (fiscal policy), single-tool (fiscal spending) macroeconomic policy framework worked fairly well for the economy in the earlier stages of development.

### *The Slow Growth Period: 1980s–1990s*

By the mid-1980s, oil prices fell by more than 60 %, only to recover a decade and half later in the early 2000s. Substantial decreases in oil revenues had a tremendous economic impact and led to major cutbacks in public spending. The country went through a period of recession, where the economy basically stabilized on a steady-low growth path—very moderate growth in GDP and the trade sector, with not much development in money, credit, or financial markets (see Figs. 12.1 and 12.2).

### *The Rapid Economic Expansion Period: 2002 to Present*

At the turn of the century, two related fundamental changes started to emerge, externally and internally. Externally, there was a structural shift in the global economy toward a multi-polar system, particularly with the rise of China. Parallel to this, oil prices started to take a new course by 2002, re-bounding from low levels to a new era of high prices, mainly driven by growth in China, India, and other East Asian countries. These external developments were reflected internally by an unprecedented growth-resource boom driven by higher oil prices and expansion of the liquefied natural gas (LNG) industry in Qatar. Over a period of a decade or so, the

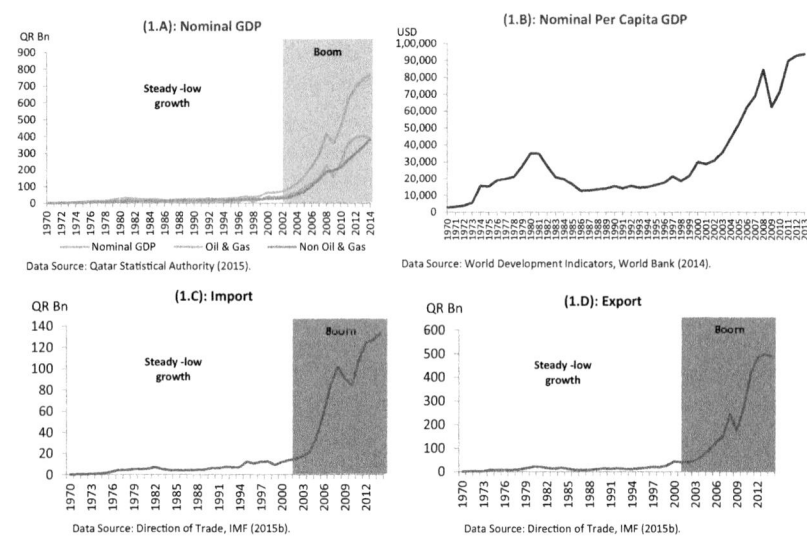

**Fig. 12.1** Real Sector (GDP and Trade)

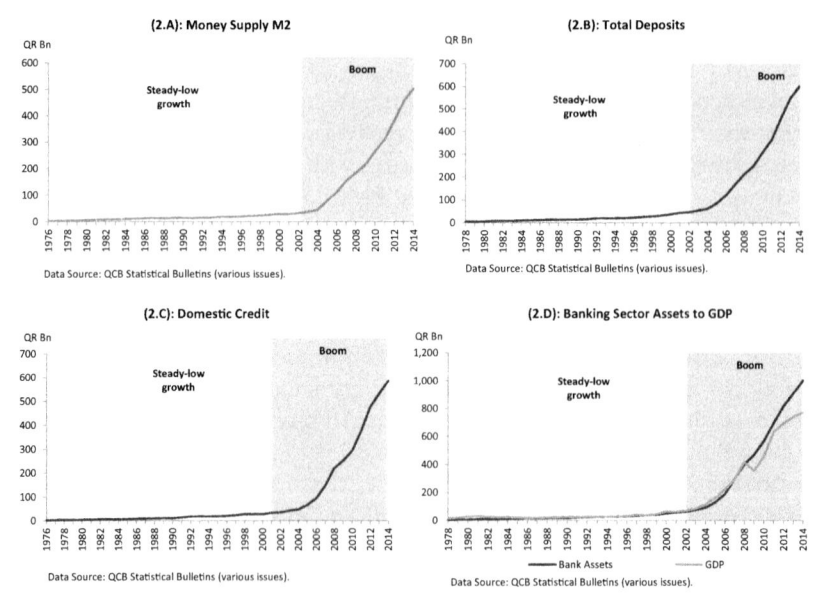

**Fig. 12.2** Financial Sector

Qatari economy went through tremendous transformation, reflected in strong growth in all sectors of the economy.

By the end of the decade, the Qatari economy emerged as one of the fastest growing emerging economies, with the highest per capita GDP globally and sophisticated money, capital, and financial markets that are integrated with the outside world. Its main indicators increased dramatically over the recent decade. For instance, Qatar's nominal GDP reached $212 billion in 2014, a 300-fold increase over its level in 1970, while per capita GDP was, globally, the highest at $93,714 in 2013, 34 times its level in 1970.[3] Exports and imports rose 315- and 199-fold respectively, relative to their levels in 1972. Money supply, domestic credit, total deposits, and the ratio of bank assets to GDP increased by 122, 203, 148, and 3.9 times respectively, relative to their levels in 1978, while government expenditure increased by 21 times relative to its level in 1980 (see Figs. 12.1, 12.2, and 12.3)

With endogeneity of population growth to economic growth, due to open labor migration, rapid economic expansion also means rapid population growth. In a matter of four years at the peak of the boom cycle, the population of the country more than doubled from 800,000 in 2005 to 1.6 million in 2009. By March 2015, the population reached 2.35 million, relative to 109,000 in 1970. This phenomenal population growth over a

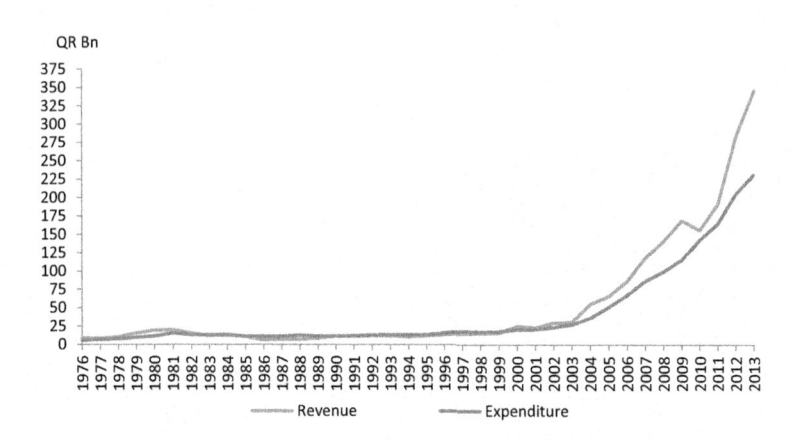

Fig. 12.3 Government Revenue and Expenditure. *Source*: Qatar Statistical Authority

short period put tremendous pressure on infrastructure, social services, and housing units.

So far, Qatar's successful growth story has made Qatar a star player, since 2008, particularly at a time of global recession. Hence, it attracted the attention of many observers and ambitious investors from around the globe. However, we need to pause for a moment and ask whether this impressive growth can be sustainable!

The answer comes from within the growth story itself. In this respect, two different incidents that took place over the previous decade and half can be identified. The first is the boom experienced during the previous decade, which culminated in a bust in 2008—with the highest inflation rate on record, bubbles bursting in asset markets, and speculative attacks on the domestic currency (see Fig. 12.4 for the historical development of inflation in Qatar). The second incident is the current oil prices collapse, which brings to mind the 1980s experience, and it can potentially pose real challenges to the current growth model in the GCC countries. These incidents, as will be shown in this chapter, prove that the resource-dependent growth model under the current MMF is not sustainable. The first incident shows the need to reform the more than four decades old macroeconomic policy framework centered around the USD peg to better guard economic stability, while the second reaffirms the long-overdue diversification of the economy away from the hydrocarbon sector to

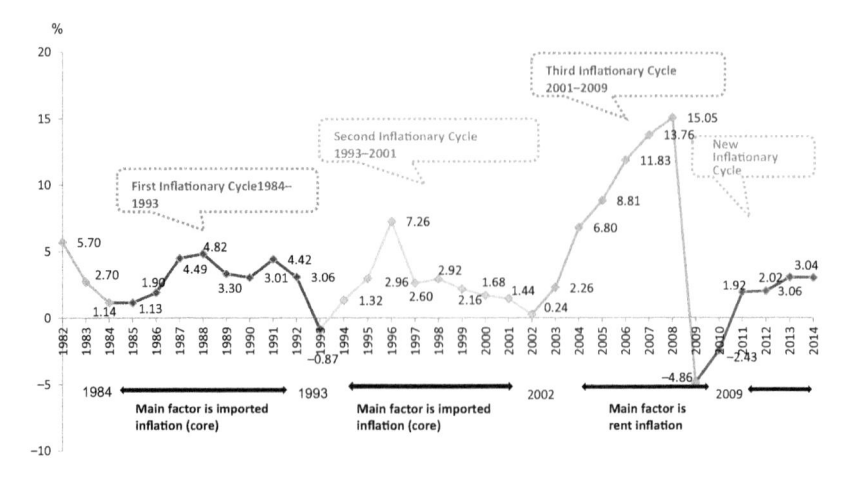

**Fig. 12.4** Annual inflation in Qatar. *Source*: World Economic Outlook, IMF, April 2015. Author's calculation and analysis

avoid dependency on volatile oil markets. Sustainability of the growth and development of the economy over the next few decades requires the fulfillment of two conditions: economic stability over the short- to medium-run and economic diversification over the long run.

The purpose of this chapter is to address the stability of the Qatari economy (the next section), which calls for the need to rethink the long standing USD hard peg and to reform the MMF or, in other words, the aggregate demand management policy instruments arsenal—fiscal policy, monetary policy, and exchange rate policy. Alternatively, these policies can also be called the macroeconomic stabilization policies. These policies should be better aligned to manage the domestic economic cycle. The USD peg started to destabilize the GCC economies in the middle of the previous decade. The reform should aim at ensuring economic stability, in the short to medium run, and improving competitiveness and supporting the diversification process in the long run. This is important, among other things, to create an attractive environment for long-term investments. Otherwise, how feasible is an investment that starts with a cost of $5 billion, for instance, and ends up costing $15 billion, mainly or partly, due to rising inflation, in which the imported easy monetary policy from the USA at the peak of a boom cycle and an overheating economy was a significant contributing factor? Higher inflation rates mean higher development costs, which in turn can hinder the diversification process and forgo the chance to diversify at a time of plenty. Escalating costs of many projects have been widely noticed over the oil boom period, partly or mainly due to higher inflation rates. The diversification issue is beyond the scope of this chapter, due to space limitations. Briefly, however, successful economic diversification requires reform to the supply side policies, particularly the following:

1. The development of human capital accumulation, to build up the required minimum-base (critical mass) of human capital stock to set the stage for a successful diversification process. However, development of human capital is often constrained from the demand side rather than from the supply side, due to weak incentives associated with expected low returns on quality education, acquiring knowledge, and capacity building.[4] Thus, the recent emphasis of the GCC states on the supply side of human capital development alone (e.g., competing to attract world class academic institutions, with luxury campuses and generous spending, etc.) is doomed to fail, if the

demand side issue is not properly addressed. This calls for reform to the sources of demand on national human capital in both the public and private sectors.
2. Reform the public sector to improve efficiency and productivity, and strengthen governance with more emphasis on the competency of the leaderships of public institutions. This is important to send the right signals to the younger generations and create the incentive among them to develop their human capital skills and capacity building.
3. Reform the private sector to limit concentrations of markets across the economy and wealth across society, hence to support creating a dynamic and competitive private sector, away from rent cycling and patronage, in which the sector can actively participate in diversification, technological development, and a knowledge-based economy. This generates employment opportunities for citizens.
4. Finally, building an industrial base to support the diversification process and help to develop an export tradable sector (see Alkhater 2015).

Throughout my discussion in this chapter, I will frequently refer to the boom-bust experience of the previous decade, as well as the current low oil prices and their potential implications for the sustainability of growth and development, to draw lessons and demonstrate by real examples the need for the required reforms.

## MACROECONOMIC STABILIZATION POLICIES AND SUSTAINABLE GROWTH

Before we further proceed, it might be helpful first to review the main stylized facts of the Qatari economy to help us understand how this economy functions.

### *Stylized Facts of the Qatari Economy*

1. Small open economy
    The Qatari economy is small in the sense that economic agents are price takers in the international markets. It is open in the sense that only minor restrictions and very low custom duties are imposed

on the trade account, and there are no restrictions on income nor on the financial and capital accounts of the balance of payments. Foreign trade constituted about 80 % of GDP over the last five years. Qatar, like other GCC countries, exports oil and gas and imports almost everything else—from consumer to capital goods, to labor. This subjects the economy to imported inflation and exchange rate pass-through under the USD hard peg.

2. Narrow and undiversified production base

   In Qatar, as well as in other GCC countries, production is concentrated in hydrocarbon and non-tradable sectors. There has been considerable success in diversifying within the hydrocarbon sector or what is called vertical diversification, but not beyond that to the export tradable sector. As such, the economy remains highly dependent on hydrocarbons, which constituted about 55 % of GDP, 79 % of exports, and 84 % of government revenues over the past ten years. Such high concentration of exports and government revenues subject the economy to volatility in the global energy market and undermine growth sustainability. The incentive structure in the economy is heavily biased toward concentration in non-tradables with the objective to maximize short-term profit from extracting rent from a combination of two factors: fiscal spending (particularly rising with oil booms) and the abundant supply of cheap, low-skill foreign labor. As such, a small resource-abundant economy with a narrow production-base can offer only limited real investment channels and can be subject to supply bottlenecks and associated symptoms of an overheating economy, particularly during resource-boom periods. Thus, substantial amounts of rent generated from the resource boom find a way to asset markets, leading to unnecessarily rapid expansion in non-tradables (construction and real estate), and fueling asset price inflation while crowding out the tradable sector.

3. Flexible labor supply

   Due to the small native population, foreign labor dominates the labor market and constitutes more than 70 % of the labor force in the GCC, reflecting a phenomenon of open labour immigration that is globally unique to the region. The size of the labor force is demand-driven and positively correlated with economic activity. The private sector constitutes about 80 % of the labor force in the GCC, but most of it (about 90 %) is low-skilled (Murphy 2011; and Hertog 2013; also see Chapter 10). The flexible labor supply has the advantage that it acts as an automatic adjustment mechanism to adverse economic shocks via contraction of the labor supply under downward wage rigidity, at periods of severe downturn. The disadvantage, however, is that the abundant supply of cheap, low-skilled labor obviates the need to invest in technological improvement and enhance the productivity of the existing workforce. It rather tends to concentrate efforts on low productivity, low technology activities in an effort to maximize short-term profit, from activities such as construction and trade imports (domestically marketing for imported goods though the monopolistic commercial agency system). However, this does not support the claim of building human capital and a knowledge-based economy, in addition to the leakage abroad it causes to national income.

More seriously, there are the demographic and social implications of the strong growth and seemingly uncontrolled expansion with a huge influx of foreign labor to the region. In GCC countries like Qatar, UAE, Kuwait, and Bahrain, citizens became minorities in their homelands, which is a serious threat of altering the demographic and social structures, losing national identities, social values, and culture, as well as potential future political consequences (see Chapter 9 for a discussion). The proportions of nationals to the total populations were as follows: 14.3 % in Qatar, 11.5 % in the UAE, 30.8 % in Kuwait, and 48 % in Bahrain.[5] Indeed, one would be tempted to wonder, are the major challenges outlined in the Qatar National Vision 2030 still kept at a balance or will they be kept at balance in the future, at the current rapid pace of expansion?[6]

4. Fiscal expenditure is the main mechanism of channeling resource revenues to the economy and is the main engine of growth.

This is natural consequence of direct state control over resource rents and their distribution in a rentier state (Alkhater 2012a). The implications of this under the current macroeconomic policy model are as follows:

(i) Pro-cyclical fiscal stance.
(ii) Pro-cyclical monetary expansion. Under pegged exchange rate arrangements, the central bank inelastically supplies local currency upon demand.
(iii) Counter–cyclical public debt management. Governments in the GCC typically tend to borrow (from local banks) during recessions and pay back during boom periods. This pattern of

public debt management tends to aggravate the recession through financially crowding out private investors, and complicating liquidity management during the boom period, particularly in case of mismatched economic cycles between the USA and Qatar.

5. Pro-cyclical population growth

In a typical Gulf model (see Box 12.1), growth is reliant on a combination of two important factors: strong fiscal spending and intensity of factor input, particularly labor. Strong fiscal spending during an oil boom period leads to rapid labor force expansion through elastic supply of foreign labor. In a small population country, this causes rapid population growth with a strong impact on the population size.[7] In Qatar, the population more than doubled from 800,000 in 2005 to 1,600,000 in 2009. This created significant excess demand and exerted tremendous pressures on housing units, infrastructure, and social services, feeding into strong inflationary pressures.

*Box 12.1 GCC Economic Model*

In a typical GCC growth model, growth is reliant on extracting resources (oil) and redistributing rents, through the government expenditure mechanism. A large part of this expenditure is current spending on public sector wages and benefits, and the other part is capital spending on infrastructure, real estate, and other development projects. The former constitutes citizens' incomes, while the latter forms demand in the private sector and constitutes its procurement contracts and income. In such a rentier growth model, there is room for taxation. Citizens are employed by the state, and everyone is dependent on the state. According to the rentier state literature, patronage of citizens on the state is actually encouraged; see Alkhater (2012a) for a review of such literature. Furthermore, taxation might entail political accountability, which might not be desirable, given the readily abundant resources. The most popular, and perhaps the most important, mechanism of patronage and rent distribution in a rentier state is through creating a huge, but not necessarily productive, public sector where citizens can be hired by the state.

In the GCC countries, production is concentrated in hydrocarbon and non-tradable sectors (construction, real estate, and services), and the GCC countries essentially export hydrocarbon and import almost everything else they need—from consumer to capital goods, and even labor—from abroad. The activities of the private sector, even after more than four decades of benefiting from oil export, are still concentrated in two sectors: non-tradables and trade import (domestically, marketing for foreign imported goods through the commercial agency system). The objective of the private sector is to maximize short-term profit from extracting rent from a combination of two important factors: (a) generous government spending (particularly rising with the oil boom) and (b) intensity of factor inputs, particularly an infinite supply of low-cost, low-skill labor from nearby regions, in addition to capital and energy inputs. With oil booms and rising capital spending, a significant share of the wealth generated from the booms finds its way to the non-tradable sector, feeding into the rapid expansion of construction and real estate activities (e.g., luxury villages, towers, shopping centers, and sometimes even overspending on infrastructure) and fueling asset price inflation. Such rapid expansion of real estate activities, while it crowds out export tradable sector, contributes little or nothing to export diversification and sustainable growth.

The most important elements of sustainable growth and development are the accumulation of human capital, technological development, and innovation. In the GCC model, however, growth is dependent on capitalizing on cheap, low-skilled labor, which obviates the need to invest in technological development and enhance the productivity of the existing labor force. It rather tends to concentrate on low productivity, low technology activity in an effort to maximize short-term rent extraction from oil booms (and associated rise in government spending) and non-tradable (construction) activities. The main outcome of such a growth model is a construction boom accompanied by explosive population growth, due to open labor immigration. If and when the boom ended up in a bust, the recovery is likely to take a prolonged period (the 1980s experience), until the next oil boom takes place. However, such a growth model does not support the claims (in the GCC national development plans) of building human capital and developing a diversified, knowledge-based economy that is less dependent on oil, with a dynamic and competitive private sector that can actively participate in technological development, economic diversification, and generate employment opportunities for citizens.

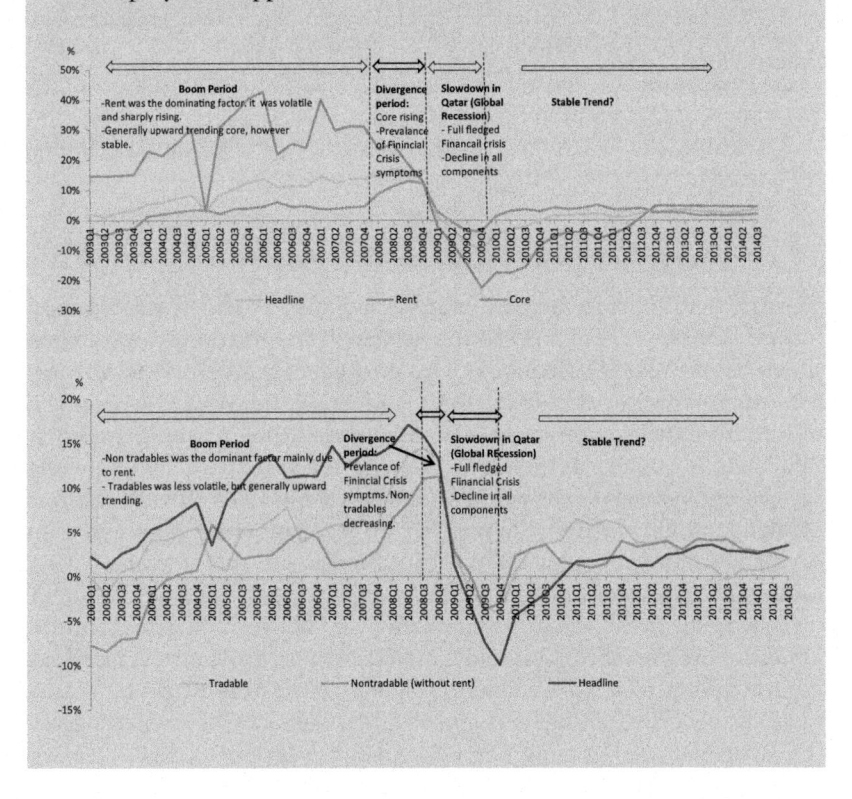

The overall implications of the above stylized facts are (i) pro-oil cycle aggregate demand, and (ii) pro-oil cycle GDP growth. Thus, the monetary policy strategy of targeting the exchange rate via pegging to the USD was a feasible policy choice to relatively stabilize government oil revenues and provide the nominal anchor to import monetary policy credibility with low and stable inflation from the USA. Indeed, such arguments hold valid as long as the economic cycles in the USA and Qatar are in tandem.

Hence, one can argue that these objectives had been accomplished, and the current MMF has served the economy fairly well until the beginning of the previous decade. However, since the economic cycles in the USA and Qatar have been unrelated, targeting the exchange rate subjected the economy to exchange rate-pass through via the following:

1. Volatility and deterioration of USD exchange rate against the currencies of Qatar's major import trading partners.
2. Passing the US Federal Reserve Bank (Fed) monetary stance (policy rate) to Qatar's policy rate.
3. Passing the US money market rates to Qatar's domestic money market.

*Structural Shift in the Global Economy and Policy Divergence*

The last decade had witnessed a structural shift in the world economy toward a multi-polar global economic system. In this context, researchers show that the World's Economic Center of Gravity (WECG) or activities is moving eastward. According to Quah (2011), the WECG has actually moved from its location in the mid-Atlantic in 1980, reaching Turkey in 2008, and is to arrive in India and China by the year 2050. Consequently, the center of gravity of the world's demand for oil is also moving eastward (Alkhater 2012b).[8] Before the year 2000, the US economy was leading the oil market; however, after 2000, China, India, and the other East Asian economies have been leading it.[9] The evidence emerging from the literature suggests a weakening of the relationship between oil prices and the US economy over the past decade, indicating a permanent structural shift in growth of petroleum demand to originate more from emerging economies.[10] The US economy and global oil markets desynchronized: while the oil market was booming, the US economy was slowing down (see Fig. 12.5a). Consequently, Qatar was desynchronized from the USA. So, while the Qatari economy expands with higher oil prices, its policy and money market rates decrease with the slowdown in the US economy, because the US Fed cuts policy rates to stimulate growth in the US economy. The obvious implication of such a situation is a policy conflict. Formal evidence in support of the desynchronization discussion above comes from Alkhater and Basher (2015). In that paper, empirically shown that that there was a pronounced desynchronization of economic cycles between Qatar and the USA during the period of 2001–2010. We observe a clear divergence

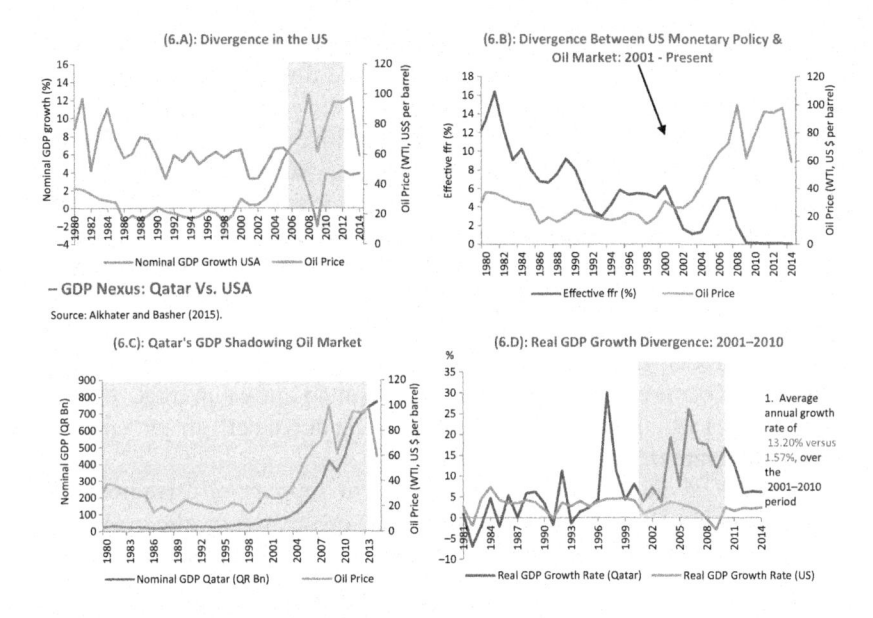

Fig. 12.5 Oil-GDP Nexus: Qatar versus USA

in macroeconomic variables between Qatar and the USA, when GDP and inflation in Qatar were both much higher in levels and volatility over the previous decade compared with those of the USA, and compared with the 1980s and 1990s. We further find that demand disturbances are highly negatively correlated between the two countries. This result finds support also in Cevik (2011), who reports weakening of the correlation between Qatar's real non-oil GDP and the USA's real GDP during the previous decade, against parallel strengthening of the correlation with Asia and the euro zone over the same period. The above two studies cast doubt on the validity of the USD pegged riyal exchange rate arrangement and suggest that Qatar should strive for an independent monetary policy to deal with its own demand shocks.

When the US economy was driving global demand, commodity markets, and consequently commodity prices, it made sense from a macroeconomic management perspective to peg to the USD. The US monetary stance was suitable for the Qatari economy. However, this is no longer the case. It is the de-synchronization between the oil price cycle and the USA's economic cycle against strengthening of the synchronization between the oil price cycle and the emerging Asian economies and other economies that delinked the cycles between the USA and Qatar and other GCC states. Figure 12.5 presents graphical evidence of the diverging cycles between Qatar and the US. In Fig. 12.5a divergence between development in the US nominal GDP and oil market started by 2003. This was reflected by the parallel divergence between the US monetary stance and oil prices (see Fig. 12.5b). In contrast, development in Qatar's nominal GDP and oil prices are almost the mirror image of each other (Fig. 12.5c). The divergence between US nominal GDP and the oil market, on one hand, and the strong correlation between development of Qatar's nominal GDP and the oil market, on the other hand, were naturally reflected in divergence between the two countries' real GDP growth rates over the past decade, where the Qatari economy was booming with an annual average growth rate of over 13 %; the US economy was slowing down with an annual average growth rate of 1.57 % (Fig. 12.5d).

Figure 12.6 illustrates further evidence in support of asymmetry of demand shocks between Qatar and the US. In this figure, the evolution of the dynamics of Qatar's foreign trade over the recent decades clearly shows East Asia emerging as Qatar's dominant export trading partners, exposing it to demand shocks originating from outside the USA.

Finally, importing the USA's easy monetary stance through the USD peg while the Qatari economy was booming with divergence of the two countries' real economic performance contributed to inflation divergence

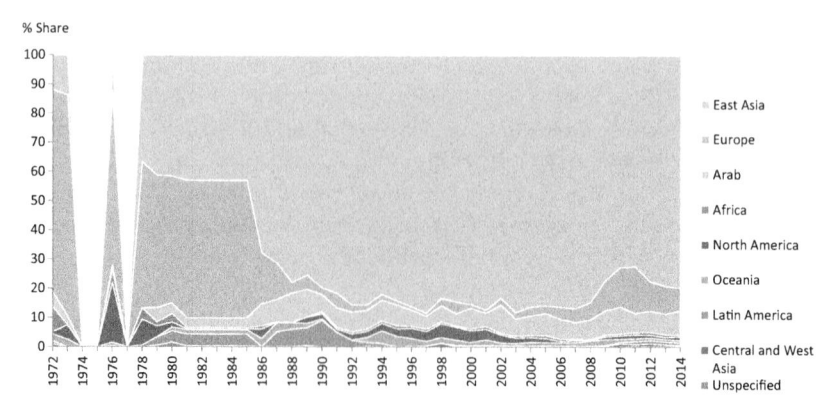

Fig. 12.6 Share of Country Groups in Qatar's Exports. Indicator of the asymmetry of demand shocks between Qatar and the US. East Asia becoming our dominant export trading partners and we are becoming subject to demand shocks originating outside the US. *Source*: Direction of Trade, IMF (2015b).

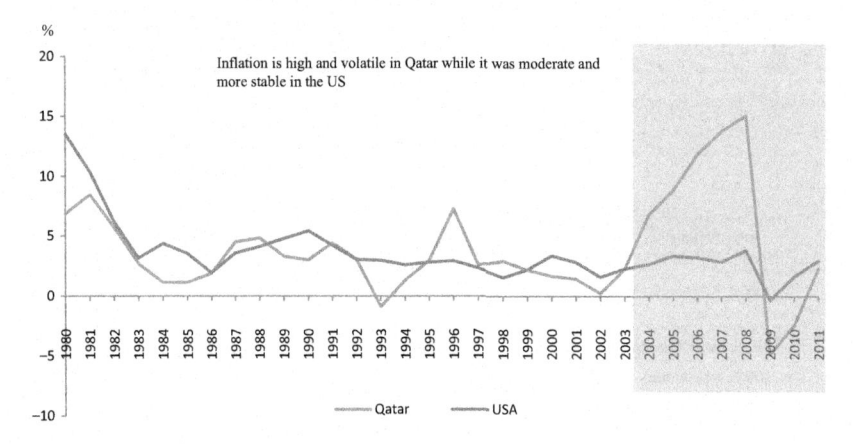

Fig. 12.7 Inflation Rate Divergence: 2001–2011. *Source*: Alkhater and Basher (2015).

between the two countries over most of the previous decade. As depicted in Fig. 12.7, while inflation in Qatar was volatile and shooting up, reaching 17 % by mid-2008, it was generally low and stable in the USA. This is the period when the USD peg started to destabilize the GCC economies. Failure to satisfy the conditions of the optimum currency area (OCA) while forcefully trying to maintain the union (the peg) can lead to policy conflict between the two countries (Mundell 1961).[11]

Economic policies needed at boom periods differ from those appropriate for slowdown or recession. Attempting to maintain identical monetary policies between the two sides at a time of conflict can be very costly and destabilizing to the economy of the pegging country.

However, rather than pursuing contractionary policies over the previous boom-cycle (2001–2008), all central banks in the GCC adopted a highly expansionary monetary policy stance, mandatorily imported through the USD peg.[12] The implications of which were overheating economies with structural liquidity surplus (SLS) building up in the banking system and near-zero lower bound (ZLB) money market rates, excessive money and credit growth, higher inflation rates, bubbles bursting in asset markets (stock markets in 2006 and 2008, and the real estate market in 2008), and speculative attacks on GCC's domestic currencies. To this end, it might be instructive to demonstrate the growth and inflationary generating process under the current MMF as we had witnessed them in Qatar over the previous boom cycle (2001–2008). This is introduced in Box 12.2.

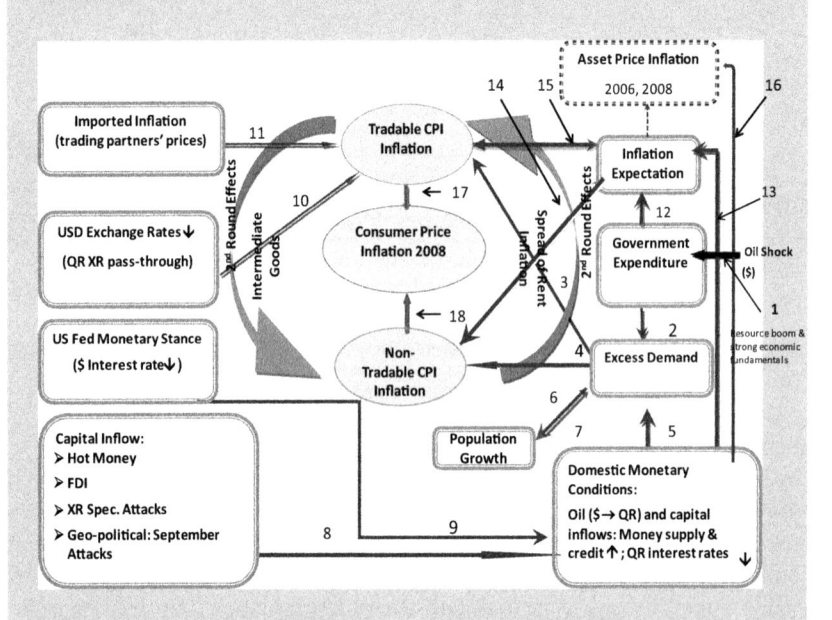

Box 12.2 Growth and Policy Model, and Inflationary Channels in Qatar

[Figure: Diagram showing inflationary channels with boxes labeled: Asset Price Inflation (2006, 2008); Imported Inflation (trading partners' prices); Tradable CPI Inflation; Inflation Expectation; USD Exchange Rates↓ (QR XR pass-through); Consumer Price Inflation 2008; Government Expenditure; Oil Shock ($); US Fed Monetary Stance ($ Interest rate↓); Non-Tradable CPI Inflation; Excess Demand; Resource boom & strong economic fundamentals; Capital Inflow: Hot Money, FDI, XR Spec. Attacks, Geo-political: September Attacks; Population Growth; Domestic Monetary Conditions: Oil ($→ QR) and capital inflows: Money supply & credit↑; QR interest rates↓. Arrows numbered 1–18 connect these elements with labels "2nd Round Effects", "Intermediate Goods", "Spread of Rent Inflation".]

In Figure above, if we start with Arrow 1, higher oil revenues are transmitted to the domestic economy via higher government expenditure—current spending on public sector wages and benefits and capital spending on infrastructure, real estate, and other development projects (Arrow 2). This in turn generates demand pressures, which feed into inflationary pressures in the tradable goods sector (goods that can be imported from, and exported to, overseas) and the non-tradable goods sector (goods that cannot exported to, or imported from overseas, such as real estate and many types of the services) (Arrows 3 and 4) Higher government spending generates immediate monetary expansion, through conversion the dollar-oil revenues into local currency. This monetary expansion impact creates further demand pressure (Arrow 5), generating a second round of inflationary pressures in both tradable and non-tradable sectors. Persistently high demand pressures lead to population growth through the expansion of the labor force, via importing labor to participate in economic activities (in public and private sectors) during periods of economic expansion (Arrow 6). The population growth, in turn, creates a new round of higher demand pressures, on consumption goods (tradables), housing, infrastructure, and public services (non-tradables) (Arrow 7) There were also capital inflows due to various reasons, leading to further monetary and credit expansion (Arrow 8). These include the following:

1. Hot money speculating in asset markets (stock and real estate).
2. Foreign direct investment attracted by strong economic fundamentals and growth prospects, particularly in the LNG sector.
3. Speculative attacks on the QR in expectations of currency revaluation.
4. National capital (Qatari and GCC's) fleeing back home due to elevated risks surrounding Arab investments in Western countries, particularly in the USA after the September 11 attack (for a good review of these capital inflow channels, see Elsamadisy et al. 2014).

Another important channel was the imported easy US monetary stance (Arrow 9). The US Fed pursued an easy monetary policy for about a decade and half prior to the global financial crisis (the Great Moderation Era), where the policy rate was kept fairly low for most of the period. The Fed further eased the monetary stance after the financial crisis, where the policy rate was further pushed down to the zero lower bound (ZLB), along with adopting a quantitative easing program to pump massive liquidity in the ailing US economy. QCB had no choice prior to the global financial crisis but to match the US Fed policy rate cuts by parallel cuts in its policy rates, although the Qatari economy was at the peak of overheating—see Fig. 12.8. The policy rate cuts exerted further downward pressure on the QR interest rates, fueling excessive monetary and credit growth, as well as further demand and inflationary pressures (Arrow 9). Another direct consequence of the USD peg was that the deterioration of the USD against major currencies was translated into equal deterioration of QR against the currencies of our major import trading partners. This translates into higher prices of imported goods that feed into inflationary pressures in the tradable sector (Arrow 10). Imported inflation via higher prices in our import trading partners feeds into inflationary pressure in the tradable sector (Arrow 11). Fiscal and monetary expansions also feed into inflation expectation (Arrows 12 and 13), which in turn feed into higher consumer (tradables) and asset (non-tradables) prices. In addition, there are feed and feedback effects between inflation and inflation expectation (Arrows 14 and 15). This is particularly the case with asset prices. This process might end up with a bubble bursting, which was the case with the Doha Securities Market in 2006 and 2008 (Arrow No 16), and to a lesser extent in the real estate market in 2008 (In this context, historically, most financial crises were preceded by asset price inflation and excessive credit growth). In addition, the above-mentioned factors interact with each other through what are called second round effects. For instance, rent inflation spreads through the tradable sector and from there to the rest of the economy. Likewise, tradable (or imported) inflation spreads into the non-tradable sector through imported intermediate (consumer and capital) goods and from there to the rest of the economy—see Figs. B and C for information on the development of core and rent inflation, as well as tradable and non-tradable inflation in Qatar from the previous inflationary episode to the present. All of the above factors and channels and their interaction with each other through the second round effects were at work over the boom period (2001–2008), contributing to higher headline consumer price inflation (Arrows 17 and 18) and causing the economy to overheat with the usual associated symptoms of buildup of liquidity surplus, excessive money and credit growth, unanchored inflation expectation, consumer and asset price inflation, and bubble busting in asset markets with headline CPI reaching 17 % by mid-2008.

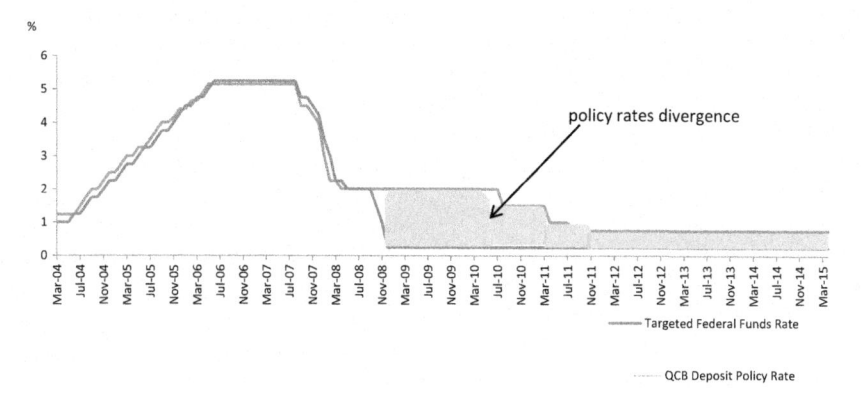

Fig. 12.8 Policy Divergence. *Source*: QCB Statistical Bulletin (Various Issues), Federal Reserve Bank Website.

## *Monetary Policy Crisis Approach in Qatar*

As a blind consequence of the USD peg, all GCC central banks followed the footsteps of the Fed when they adopted its ultra-easy monetary policy approach to the crisis, pushing the policy rates to the ZLB.[13] The only exception was the QCB adopting an independent monetary policy over the crisis period. According to the policy trilemma, or the impossible trinity, developed by Mundell (1961), no country can simultaneously pursue more than a combination of two of three possible policy options: capital mobility, fixed exchange rates, and an independent monetary policy. So, if free capital mobility with a fixed exchange rate is favored, the tradeoff is a loss of monetary policy independence. This was clearly the situation prior to the global financial crisis. However, the freeze in international capital mobility at the crisis period is equivalent to a complete shutdown of the capital account, hence neutralizing any potential capital flow pressures on the Qatari riyal exchange rate.

Early realization of the breakdown of the impossible trinity, due to a freeze of cross-border capital mobility under crisis conditions, allowed the QCB to isolate itself from the Fed's easy monetary stance.[14] First, partial policy rate separation was initiated in May 2007 by lowering only the QCB deposit policy rate (QCBDR) and keeping the QCB lending policy rate (QCBLR) fixed at 5.5 %; then, full policy rate separation was decided in October 2008 by keeping the QCBDR fixed at 2 % for two years thereafter (until August 2010), while the Fed continued to cut its rate until it

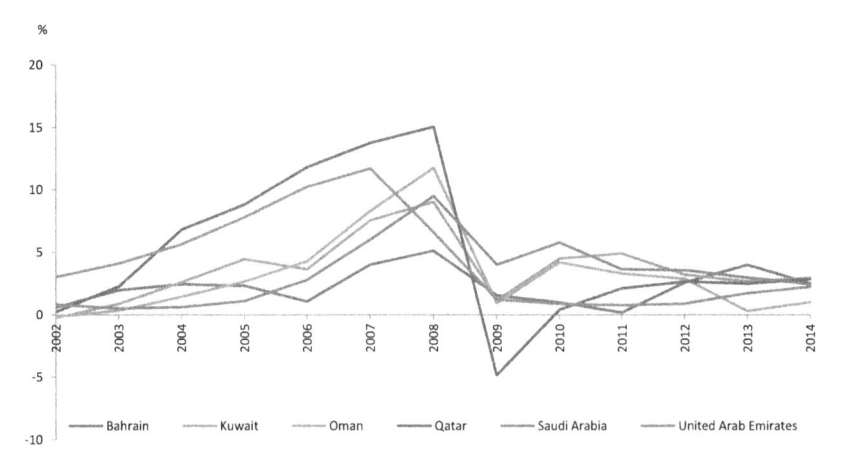

Fig. 12.9 Inflation Rates in GCC Countries. *Source*: World Economic Outlook, IMF (2015a).

reached the ZLB and then started quantitative easing programs to rescue the financial sector and revive economic growth (see Fig. 12.8).

This was a historical moment that should have been seized to temper high inflation and ride the next economic cycle with the lowest inflation rate possible. This was particularly true in the case of Qatar, which was coming to a decade of a rigidly expansionary fiscal stance due to its commitments to organizing the 2022 FIFA World Cup and meeting the development and diversification targets of the Qatar Vision 2030. In fact, in a matter of a year, the inflation rate in Qatar came down from the highest in the GCC states, at 15.05 % at year-end 2008, to the lowest, at—4.9 % in 2009 (see Fig. 12.9).

Though it is true that correction in real estate markets and the significant decline in rent inflation were major contributors to the decline of headline inflation, tightening the monetary stance was a significant contributor also. Maintaining the QCB nominal (policy) interest rate fixed at a significantly higher rate than the US Fed's rate (ranging from 175 to 200 basis points), along with a significant decline in the inflation rate, raised the real interest rate in Qatar from the negative region to a higher positive rate. Tightening the monetary stance contributed to drying up the liquidity surplus and raising Qatar's money market rate, leading to a smooth stabilization around the targeted QCBDR (2 %) after it was col-

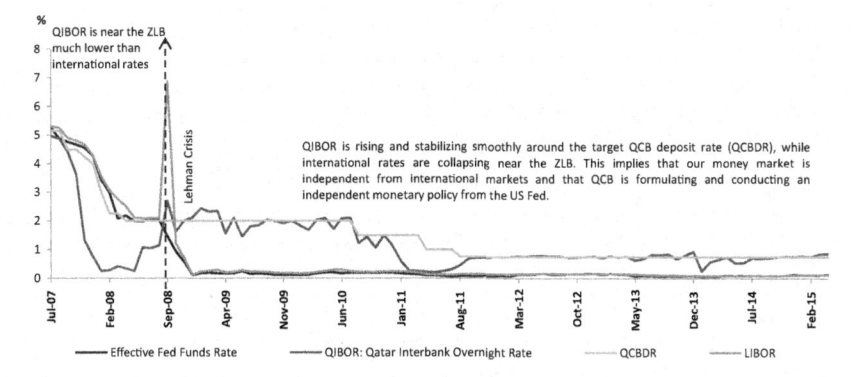

**Fig. 12.10** Qatar's Policy and Money Market Rates. *Source*: *QCB Statistical Bulletins* (various issues) and Thomson Datastream

lapsing near the ZLB prior to the crisis, much lower than the QCB policy rate and the international money market rates. Since the crisis, the international money market rates have been collapsing near the ZLB, while Qatar's money market rate has been stabilizing nicely around QCBDR to the present. This is evidence that QCB was formulating and conducting an independent monetary policy from the US Fed, thanks to the freeze of cross-border capital mobility (see Fig. 12.10). The QCB's globally unique experience had attracted the attention of many observers and was commended at the time by the IMF Mission to Qatar.

In August 2010, the QCB cut its policy rate (by 50 basis points) for the first time since the eruption of financial crisis in 2008. Further rate cuts were introduced through 2011 to reduce QCBDR to 0.75 % since August 2011 to date; this is still much higher than the Fed policy rate. Qatar's experience shows that it is possible to neutralize the unwanted negative effect of the USD peg. It also shows positive results from pursuing a monetary policy independent from the easy Fed monetary stance, though temporary. In this author's opinion, however, this temporary independent monetary policy experience was prematurely halted, and it could have been pursued for longer period. The major justification for the first rate cut was that Qatar faced a deflationary threat. However, this claim was not accurate (Alkhater 2010). The deflation was benign, meaning good deflation in the sense that it was due to positive supply shocks. Could Qatar have "bad" or "ugly" deflation with low or no unemployment, with real GDP growth of around 12 % (one of the highest in the world in 2009), while most advanced and emerging market economies were swamped in deep recession?[15] It was not due to slackening demand either; rather, it was a correction to a previous buildup of imbalances, particularly in real estate markets. Whoever was thinking or claiming that Qatar had deflation because of the negative inflation figures was mistaken. Furthermore, the capital inflows witnessed later in 2009 and 2010 were not genuine.[16] Rather than changing the monetary policy stance altogether, these capital inflows could have been effectively controlled through strict implementation of the QCB prudential measures regulating foreign borrowing, which requires local banks to maintain a minimum ratio of 100 % of foreign currency assets to foreign currency liabilities at all times. Ideally, a tight monetary stance could have been complemented by implementation of some measures of capital flow management, such as increasing the reserve requirements on Central Bank' riyal and USD positions, capital control, a minimum holding period, and limits on foreign borrowing. The last measure indeed is used in Qatar; however, it could be more strictly implemented.

Yet, Qatar still has relative or partial monetary policy independence from the US Fed. Its deposit policy rate is currently 0.75 %, while the Fed policy rate is much lower—ranging between 0.15 % and 0.25 %. Qatar's money market is stable with its rate still smoothly stabilized around the central bank's targeted policy rate at 0.75 %. That is more than six times higher than the Federal Fund effective rate and the LIBOR, both of which are still collapsing near the ZLB.

### *Low Oil Prices and Economic Stabilization Policies*

Oil prices fell by more than 50 % since mid-2014 to lower than $50 a barrel by early 2015, and they are expected to remain in the range of $70–$80 a barrel over the medium term through 2019, with the OPEC oil price being on its floor and the shale oil price being on the ceiling in the wider rage (Alkhater 2015b). The fiscal break-even prices for GCC budgets currently range from $89 a barrel in Oman and Bahrain, to around $80 in Saudi Arabia, and they are $50–$60 in Qatar and Kuwait.[17] Low oil prices can impact Qatar and GCC countries through three main channels:

1. Income and spending channel;[18]
2. The economic cycle and policies channel; and
3. The exchange rate channel.

### The Income Channel

This is the ordinary direct channel. If oil prices stay around $60 for a prolonged period of time it can potentially have adverse impacts on GCC economies, however, with varying degrees depending on the share of the oil sector in their GDPs and government revenues, their fiscal break-even prices, and the size of their foreign reserves. Basically, if oil prices stay below the fiscal break-even prices for GCC budgets, it can put pressure on the fiscal and current accounts, mainly in the form of budget deficits.

Given the USD hard peg, Qatar and the GCC countries are stripped of two important macroeconomic stabilization policy instruments—monetary policy and exchange rate policy. The only remaining macro instrument is a one-sided fiscal spending policy, with no tax policy instrument.[19] Thus, GCC countries cannot use an appropriate policy mix to reduce the adverse impact of lower oil prices. In particular, a balanced and counter-cyclical fiscal-monetary policy mix that is consistent with growth and price and financial stability is essential to minimize the costs of adverse shocks on the real economy. GCC central banks, however, remain tied to a monetary stance counter to the US economic cycle.[20] However, with the desynchronization of the cycles with the US, the Fed monetary policy is a rather pro-GCC economic cycle.

Luckily, Qatar and other GCC countries are highly efficient producers and, ceteris paribus, should be able to adapt to an environment with such low oil prices. Therefore, in the absence of monetary and exchange rate policies, in addition to absence of tax policy, those countries that accumulated sizable reserves in stability or sovereign wealth funds in a higher oil price period can tolerate budget deficits and finance the deficits from the stability funds, for a certain period. For those with inadequate amounts of reserves, they either can finance their deficits by borrowing, or cut back spending, which may not be popular particularly during heightened political instabilities in the Arab world. However, if low oil prices persist in the long run, that can present real challenges to fiscal sustainability in the GCC countries and can put pressures on many spending programs, including social spending programs that were adopted in the wake of the Arab Spring.

Lower oil prices, however, might have a positive side. It underlines the need for structural adjustments and reforms in different areas. It can discipline public expenditure and limit wasteful spending, leading to a more efficient utilization of exhaustible resources and their revenues. It can also force and expedite diversification by necessity. Furthermore, it can put pressure for reform not only in economic domains, but also in political domains.

### The Economic Cycle Channel

Persistently low oil prices, particularly if combined with rising shale fuel production in the USA, can potentially place the GCC economies on the downward side of the cycle vis-à-vis the expanding US economy–opposite to the previous boom cycle (2001–2010). While it is true that low oil prices can also adversely affect the USA's shale oil producers, the overall impact on the US economy is expected to be positive. After all, there are 42 consuming states versus eight oil and gas producing states in the USA (Plumer 2014). A potential implication would be, again, a policy conflict reinforcing the slowdown in the GCC.[21] The potential trend of the cycles and the intensity of the divergence between the two sides, however, will depend on how persistent low oil prices can be in the future, and on the pace of economic recovery in the US.[22] Low enough oil prices (below the break-even prices for GCC budgets) for a long enough period (spanning over the medium term through 2017 or beyond) can aggravate the status of the cycles between the two sides, that is, widen the gap. As the US economy expands, the Fed may potentially start to raise its policy rate sometime in 2015 and exit the unconventional monetary policy it adopted after the financial crisis in 2008. The risk is that, regardless of the status of the cycle between the GCC countries and the USA, the GCC central banks are likely to follow their faith in the Fed anyway and under any scenario (e.g., plummeting oil prices), as they have always done historically, whence monetary policy was never used proactively as a macro-management instrument (e.g., to lower the adverse impact of economic shocks or oil prices volatility; save Qatar's experience of temporary independent monetary policy from the Fed to contain high inflation over the crisis period during the period of 2008–2010). The GCC countries have often resorted to a reactionary fiscal spending policy to deal with oil price cycles.[23] Yet, this more than four decades old single-instrument, single-tool macro-management framework, in this author's opinion, is no longer suitable to manage the economic cycle in today's GCC economies.

## The Exchange Rate Channel: Why and Why Not Peg to the USD?

**A. Why?** The two main logical justifications for the GCC countries to peg their currencies to the USD were to achieve price stability and income stability.

1. Price Stability

It has been argued that a credible currency peg would deliver price stability. From this perspective, pegging to the USD would provide the GCC countries with a nominal anchor to import monetary policy credibility with low and stable inflation. Indeed, the USD peg did serve this purpose fairly well over the earlier stages of development, and it thus was justifiably credible. This is particularly the case over the 1980s and 1990s, when the US economy drove global demand and commodity markets and consequently drove commodity prices, including oil prices. Therefore, from a macroeconomic management perspective, it made sense then for Qatar and the GCC states to peg their currencies to the USD. The Fed's monetary stance that was suitable for the US economy was also deemed suitable for the GCC economies. But this is no longer the case. The situation started to change at the turn of the century, and the credibility of the imported monetary policy started to erode gradually.

2. Oil Revenue Stability

The rising oil prices over the previous decade had been marked by a heightened negative correlation with the USD exchange rate against major currencies. As the prices of oil increase, the USD becomes weaker against other currencies and against commodities. The usual rhetoric often states that since oil is priced in USD, pegging the currencies of oil exporters to the USD would reduce the volatility of oil revenues and ensure a stable stream of income to their governments. This logic is, however, fatally flawed as large swings in the USD price of oil are automatically transmitted into large swings in government oil export revenues.

**B. Why Not?**

1. A seemingly eroded Fed credibility[24]

The Fed was credible in achieving its objectives (low unemployment and stable prices) prior to the eruption of the global financial crisis in 2008. However, this credibility apparently has eroded since then. The Fed had relentlessly deployed all instruments in its arsenal to stimulate growth and avoid recession, from conventional to unconventional monetary policy instruments. The already low interest rates were further pushed down to ZLB and that was not enough, and the Fed had to engage in what is called a balance sheet expansion policy to pump massive and unprecedented liquidity to rescue the financial sector and revive growth in the ailing US economy. Yet, after six years, now there is no clear sign of recovery, or at best, there is a weak recovery. In fact, some observers have not ruled out a deflationary threat. In addition to this, there is a potential risk of long-run adverse consequences associated with a prolonged ultra-easy monetary policy that the Fed has been pursuing since 2008 (see, for instance, White 2013). Arguably, it is the easy monetary policy that the Fed had pursued over a decade and half prior to the global financial crisis in 2008 that led to the crisis to begin with.[25] However, with the imminent meltdown of the financial sector and a recession, the Fed's policy makers found themselves in a situation where they had no choice but to deal with an urging crisis with the very same policy mistake that had led to it in the first place. Hence, the credibility apparently has been lost in its homeland in the USA. Credibility of the imported monetary policy from the USA to the GCC countries has also been lost. It is true that inflation rates were more stable and generally low in the USA during most of the previous decade. However, adopting the USA's monetary stance by the GCC central banks, under a situation of diverging economic cycles that started to take place shortly after the turn of the century, led to higher inflation rates in the GCC countries.[26]

2. A seemingly eroded peg credibility

The high inflation rates were also associated at their peak in 2007–2008 with speculative attacks on the GCC currencies, since markets' confidence in the credibility of the USD peg had significantly weakened. In other words, the markets' confidence in the ability of the GCC central banks to maintain the fixed exchange rate at the pegged values in the future under higher inflation rates had come under considerable uncertainty. The markets were suspecting that the high inflation rates would eventually force the GCC central banks to either revalue their currencies or abandon the

USD peg altogether. However, as the financial crisis intensified during by mid-September 2008, speculative capital flows on GCC currencies started to flee. Hence, in this case, what is left of the credibility in the imported monetary policy? If credibility practically means monetary and financial stability, what happened was exactly the opposite. Three main channels can be conducive to economic instability in the future in relation to the USD hard peg:

(i) Interest rates channel under desynchronization of the cycles, through which the USA's monetary stance is passed to the GCC economies.
(ii) Exchange rate channel which fully transmits oil price volatility to the GCC economies through the hard USD peg.
(iii) The USD exchange rate volatility against other currencies.

3. The exchange rate is an important stabilization policy instrument

It is imperative to activate such instrument for an optimal policy mix to minimize the cost of adverse shocks on the economy. For instance, in the case of elevated risks of imported inflation and exchange rate pass-through, an appreciation of the value of local currency against major trading partners' currencies can be effective to contain imported inflation. By contrast, depreciation of the local currency can be effective to improve competitiveness and promote exports. This will be more needed as the economy progressively advances through the diversification process. Consistent with this logic, there could be a clear advantage of pegging to oil prices. Under a hard peg, the exchange rate is targeted. Therefore, external shocks—whether due to oil price volatility or USD exchange rate volatility—are fully transmitted to the domestic economy. The exchange rate cannot be used as an adjustment mechanism to absorb such shocks, or to reduce their impacts on the domestic economy. Thus, lower USD oil revenues mean an equal reduction in Qatari riyal oil revenues.

4. A superior arrangement

As advocated by Frankel (2005), and demonstrated by Setser (2007), the right way to deal with the dollar-induced volatility is to allow the revenue stream from oil to rise and fall with oil prices so that revenues from oil exports in the oil-exporting economy's own currency becomes

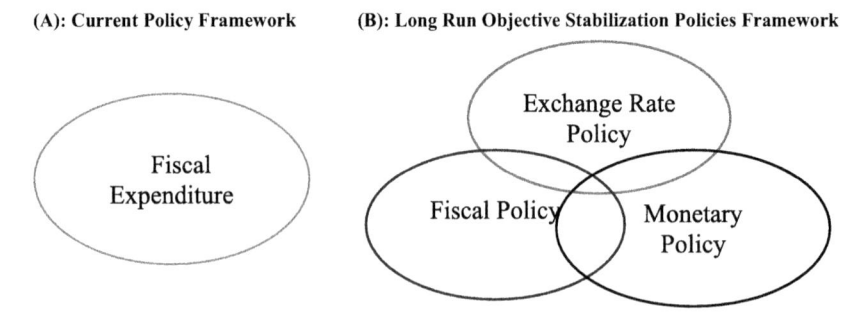

(A): Current Policy Framework  (B): Long Run Objective Stabilization Policies Framework

Fig. 12.11 Current versus Long-Run Macro-policy Frameworks

less volatile. Under this arrangement the currencies of the GCC countries would have appreciated during the oil boom period (2001–2010) and depreciated during the current low oil prices period. Currency depreciation during a low oil price period means relatively higher oil revenues available in terms of local currency, allowing for a higher ceiling of government spending than otherwise.[27] This is what is exactly needed at a period of contraction to stimulate economic growth. The exchange rate depreciation has, however, to be balanced against imported inflation. But a precise approach (in terms of timing and extent) to depreciating the value of the local currency can have positive outcomes. More often, oil prices fall with global recession, and generally falling international prices, where the risk of imported inflation is considerably low. Currency appreciation during an oil boom period would help GCC central banks to partially contain imported inflation, preserve the external purchasing power of local currencies, and better anchor inflation expectations, which are all needed during overheating periods. In retrospect, fixed exchange rate regimes can be harmful, since they can deliver micro gains (e.g., firms and investors do not need to worry about exchange rate risks) at the expenses of macro costs (e.g., inflation and more volatility in economic performance).

In a nutshell, instead of being targeted, which strips the central bank arsenal of the exchange rate and the monetary policy instruments, the exchange rate itself can be utilized and monetary policy can be set free, to assume its role as macro-management instruments (Fig. 12.11). A superior exchange rate arrangement that will deliver a higher level of price and revenue stabilities to the GCC countries would be to peg to a basket of currencies of major trading and financial partners, in addition to oil prices.[28]

## Macroeconomic Stabilization Policies in Qatar: Present through 2022

Qatar's current fiscal break-even price places it in a relatively comfortable fiscal position. Moreover, the authorities had actually anticipated fiscal challenges long before oil prices started their downslide in September 2014. It was evident as early as 2013 that the fiscal space for Qatar would decrease by 2016–2017, due to escalating expenditure profiles on one hand and diminishing revenues on account of maturing oil fields and natural gas production reaching planned capacity on the other. Any likely budgetary deficit, however, can be financed through drawing upon the country's huge reserves. The government has large net balances with local banks which can help to finance local currency spending, while its very large foreign exchange reserves can be used to finance foreign payments and bridge any deficit gap.

The issue of greater concern, however, is that fiscal policy in Qatar is becoming rigidly expansionary due to international commitments to organize the FIFA World Cup 2022 and related infrastructure to meet diversification targets in the Qatar Vision 2030. With that, the only remaining instrument of macroeconomic management has been practically lost. Monetary and exchange rate policies are already stripped from the policy makers' tool-kit, due to the longstanding USD peg.

The Qatari government's commitment to finance an ambitious infrastructure target and the resulting loss of discretionary power over fiscal policy implies that a counter-cyclical fiscal policy cannot be used in an environment of an overheated economy.[29] This presents a unique challenge for policy makers. On the one hand, monetary policy is constrained by the fixed dollar peg; on the other hand, fiscal policy is now much less flexible and may not be able to adjust in response to changes in economic conditions. The loss of both fiscal and monetary policy tools may expose the economy to the vagaries of internal and external shocks. It is at this juncture where the need arises to re-think the long-standing USD peg in order to attain more monetary policy independence that is oriented toward domestic objectives. A proactive monetary policy is also a necessary condition to offset any unwanted effects of an expansionary fiscal policy on the economy. Moreover, financial deepening and greater access to financial services have increased the relevance of monetary policy for non-oil economic activity in Qatar.

In addition, Qatar is the largest natural gas exporter in the world, and as a result, its GDP growth is highly pro-cyclical with global growth and energy demand, particularly in China. This has increased the trade links with the rising East Asian countries, and at the same, it has time weakened them with the US. The US shale gas revolution may further be a key contributor in the diverging cycles between the two countries. Therefore, on one hand, Qatar will be facing rising competition in global gas markets and might have to accept a more competitive price for its LNG that might fall below the current oil-indexed prices, which might have a considerable impact on its natural gas industry. On the other hand, Qatar is potentially facing a diverging cycle with the USA at a time when it lost discretionary power over its fiscal policy. Another concern related to rapid economic expansion and over-optimism is the chronic oversupply of real estate in several segments. There is a concern that overoptimism in the market might in the end lead to a bubble bursting sometime in the future.

CONCLUSIONS

To summarize, the objectives of monetary policies between the GCC countries and the USA were consistent over the earlier decades of development when the cycles between the two sides were synchronized. However, by the beginning of the previous decades the cycles between the two sides started to diverge, leading to A policy conflict between them with the implications of macroeconomic instability in the GCC states. Desynchronization of the cycles between the GCC countries and the USA implies that the current single-instrument, single-tool macroeconomic policy framework that was adopted by the GCC countries more than four decades ago is no longer suitable to manage the economic cycle in today's GCC economies. Potentially, the GCC countries may keep missing the cycle with the USA. The imported monetary policy to the GCC countries is not consistent with their own domestic economic cycle. It is designed for a different economy that is going through a different cycle. This signifies changes in economic fundamentals. Evidently, this simple MMF (centralized around fiscal spending and the USD peg) was suitable for the earlier stages of development when the GCC economies were relatively simple and less developed, and when the cycle with the USA was more synchronized and the relationship between oil prices and the USD was more stable. These conditions, however, no longer hold, and the USD peg started to destabilize the GCC economies by the middle of the previous decade. On the one hand, the GCC economies now are more equipped with more sophisticated money, capital, and financial markets that are more integrated with the global economy; there are also more independent monetary policies that can be conducted. On the other hand, a structural shift in global economic powers that emerged by the beginning of the previous decade led to a widening of the cycles between the GCC economies and the US economy.

To conclude, the continuously evolving nature of economic dynamics—globally and domestically, consequently—as evident by the emerging structural shift in global economic powers at the turn of the century and its potent impact on the Qatari economy (as witnessed over the previous boom cycle and with the potential implications of the current oil price collapse), however, necessitates rethinking the more than four decades old current macroeconomic policy framework, centered around the hard USD peg. To this end, a noticeable shortcoming of the Qatar national development plan is that it neglects the (past and potential future) implications of the USD peg on domestic economic performance and management.

## Notes

1. The macroeconomic management framework can be thought of as a set of economic policies that can be used as instruments to manage the macroeconomy, such as fiscal policy (and public debt policy), monetary policy, exchange rate policy, and trade policy. Our focus in this chapter will be on the three main macroeconomic stabilization policies, namely, fiscal policy, monetary policy, and exchange rate policy.
2. In the GCC states, no income tax is levied on citizens.
3. Per capita GDP is taken from World Bank, World Development Indicators Database (2014).
4. The weak incentives could be stemming from (a) limited economic opportunities and the weak role of the private sector in development or (b) a huge, saturated, and unproductive public sector—that suffers from results of the rentier economy such as disguised unemployment, rent-seeking, conflict over rent distribution, interest group competition, favoritism and loyalty, corruption, weak governance and mismanagement, etc.
5. The above statistics are obtained from Gulf Labor Markets and Migration's (GLMM) Database and refer to the periods of April 2010 for Qatar, mid 2014 for Bahrain, the end of March 2015 for Kuwait, and mid-2010 for UAE (GLMM 2015).
6. Of these major challenges are, in particular, (i) modernization versus preservation of traditions, (ii) managed growth versus uncontrolled expansion,

and (iii) the size and quality of the expatriate labor force and the selected path of development (GSDP 2008).
7. Population growth is strongly correlated with growth in the labor force, which in turn is strongly correlated with fiscal spending and economic growth.
8. This in turn has weakened the historical relation between the oil prices cycle and the US economic cycle, making the oil prices cycle more correlated with the rising East Asian economies, consequently delinking the cycles between the GCC economies and the US economy.
9. Since 2001, the Chinese economy has grown at an annual rate of about 10 % with a voracious appetite for oil compared with an annual average growth rate of less than 1.5 % in the USA. Over the period of 200–2009, the compound annual growth rate of petroleum consumption in China was 6.7 %, compared with falling demand growth in the US (-0.5 %). Along with China, much of the world's demand for oil has originated from Asian economies.
10. See, for instance, Hughes et al. (2008) and Hamilton (2009).
11. Pegging one county's currency to another country's currency is equivalent to establishing a monetary union or area between them. For that to be successful (i.e., to minimize the cost of maintaining the union and preserve its stability), it is necessary that (a) the economic cycles in the two countries are synchronized or (b) the two economies are subject to symmetric shocks.
12. During the boom, what is needed is a contractionary monetary policy to stabilize the economy—anchor expectations, combat inflationary pressure, and prevent the economy from overheating. The double-digit nominal and real GDP growth rates in Qatar, along with the high inflation rate during the boom cycle, did not seem to be logically consistent with an exceptionally low interest rate imported from the USA, and they defy the very basic lesson of standard economic textbooks, which advise fiscal and/or monetary authorities to pursue contractionary policies at a period of an overheating economy.
13. There could have been more than one way to still maintain the peg and in the meantime neutralize its unwanted effect on monetary management and the economy at large. This could be possible, for instance, through implementing a variant of capital flow management. Historically, none of the GCC central banks had tried any. They rather had taken the peg as exogenously given.
14. This decision was made by the QCB Monetary Policy Committee based on a study conducted by the Department of Research and Monetary Policy after a long and debatable discussion among the committee members.
15. Three types of deflation are identified in the literature: benign, which means it is good or desirable deflation (due to market correction or positive supply shocks), and in which output growth remains strong; bad deflation, usually

associated with slackened demand and mild recession; and ugly, which is the most severe case of deflation, typically associated with wage rigidity, high unemployment, and deep recession (White 2006).
16. These capital flows were mainly due to carry trade conducted by local banks (in violation of the regulations) taking arbitrage opportunities—see IMF (2012) and Westelius (2013).
17. Global Risk Advisors (2014).
18. The GCC countries are still highly dependent on oil. For the GCC countries as a group, oil constituted 69 % of the total exports, 84 % of government revenues, and 33 % of their GDPs in 2014 (IIF 2014). In addition to high concentration of government revenues and exports in oil, growth in the non-oil sector, which although might have witnessed increase in its relative share in GDP over the recent years, is still highly correlated (directly or indirectly) with growth in the oil sector and the oil prices cycle, through the government fiscal spending channel.
19. This is the case since under the hard pegged exchange rate system the exchange rate is kept fixed at the pegged value against the pegging currency; additionally, monetary policy is entirely subdued to achieve that purpose and maintain the exchange rate at the pegged value at all times. Both policy instruments, therefore, cannot be used for any other purposes.
20. The USA follows a counter-cyclical monetary policy, where interest rates are raised during the expansionary cycle and lowered during economic contractions.
21. Other things being equal, persistently low oil prices can also adversely affect the shale oil production; see Alkhater (2015).
22. This will consequently also depend on the pace of tightening the monetary stance by the Fed.
23. In this context, we find in Alkhater and Basher (2015) that Qatar is subject to a higher level of volatility and slower speed of adjustment to economic shocks relative to the USA, and Koren and Tenreyro (2011) find the same results hold for the GCC countries. These findings are not surprising given the fact that the GCC countries have historically used pro-cyclical fiscal policy and inflexible monetary policy.
24. "Seemingly" is used here since some may argue that the easy monetary policy that the Fed had pursued for about a decade and a half prior to the global financial crisis, during the Great Moderation Era, was a key contributor in the crisis that followed it.
25. The Fed had unnecessarily eased monetary policy for a prolonged period, regardless of the fact that the low inflation was mainly due to positive global supply shocks rather than a fall in demand.
26. Inflation rates peaked in 2007–2008 and ranged between 10 % and 17 % in most of the GCC countries, according to official statistics. In Qatar, inflation reached a record level at 17 % by mid-2008.

27. In this case, it might be argued that Russia has relative advantage over GCC countries due to the flexible exchange rate of the Russian ruble, despite its rapid depreciation since oil prices started their downslide last September.
28. At one level, this reform to the exchange rate policy can be accomplished through the future Gulf Central Bank, if the planned GCC monetary union is to materialize any time in the near future. Otherwise, if a clear plan is set to launch the Gulf single currency over the remaining half of this decade, further delay beyond that may make it feasible to act at the individual country's level. Kuwait already went a step forward in that direction.
29. Deloitte (Dubai PR Network 2013) estimates that Qatar plans to spend over $200 billion on the 2022 World Cup-related construction projects. To put the figure in a different perspective, this is an amount almost equivalent to Qatar's GDP in 2014, and it represents $100,000 per capita for Qatar, compared to $350 per capita for the 2014 Winter Olympics in Russia, $73 per capita for the 2014 FIFA World Cup in Brazil, and $54 per capita for the 2010 FIFA World Cup in South Africa. Gregory (2013) estimates that Qatar will spend 1852 times more per capita to stage the same event that South Africa did in 2010. It might be argued that the comparison here is not accurate due to the small population of Qatar relative to these countries. The point to emphasize here, however, is the size of the economic impact of the event on Qatar.

## Bibliography. Qatar: Policy Making in a Transformative State

Alkhater, Khalid Rashid. 2010. *Are We in a Deflationary Period, and What is Next?* Technical Note No. 1/2010. Doha, Qatar: Department of Research and Monetary Policy, Qatar Central Bank.

Alkhater, K. (2012a), "The Rentier Predatory State Hypothesis: An Empirical Explanation of the Resource Curse," *Journal of Economic Development*, 37(4): 29–60..

Alkhater, K. (2012b), The Monetary Union of the Gulf Cooperation Council and Structural Shift in the Global Economy: Aspirations, Challenges, and long-term Strategic Gains. *Arab Center for Research and Policy studies*, Doha, Qatar.

Alkhater, K. (2015), The challenges of collapsing oil prices and economic diversification in the GCC countries. *Arab Center for Research and Policy studies*, Doha, Qatar.

Alkhater, Khalid Rashid, and S. Basher. 2015, forthcoming. The oil cycle, the federal reserve, and the monetary and exchange rate policies of Qatar. *Middle East Development Journal*.

Çevik, S. 2011. *Desynchronized: The Co-Movement of Non-Hydrocarbon Business Cycles in the GCC*. Working Papers 11/286. Washington, DC: International Monetary Fund.

Elsamadisy, E., K. Alkhater; and S. Basher (2014), Pre-Versus Post-Crisis Central Banking in Qatar. *Journal of Policy Modeling*, 36(2):330–52

Frankel, J. 2005. Peg the export price index: A proposed monetary regime for small countries. *Journal of Policy Modeling* 27: 495–508.

General Secretariat for Development Planning (Qatar). 2008. *Qatar National Vision 2030*. Doha: Retrieved from http://www.gsdp.gov.qa/portal/page/portal/gsdp_en/knowledge_center/Tab/QNV2030_English_v2.pdf Ministry of Development Planning and Statistics (Qatar).

GLMM. 2015. Gulf Labor Markets and Migration's Database.

Gregory, S. 2013. Why Qatar is spending $200 billion on soccer. *Time*, July 11.

Hamilton, J.D. 2009. Understanding crude oil price. *Energy Journal* 30: 179–206.

Hertog, Steffen. 2013. *The Private Sector and Reform in the Gulf Cooperation Council*. Kuwait: Research Paper. Kuwait Program on Development, Governance and Globalization in the Gulf States.

Hughes, J.E., C.R. Knittel, and D. Sperling. 2008. Evidence of a shift in the short-run price elasticity of gasoline demand. *Energy Journal* 29: 113–134.

Institute of International Finance (IIF). 2014. *GCC: Strong Diversified Growth, Limited Risk*. In *IIF Regional Review*. Washington, DC: Institute of International Finance.

International Monetary Fund (IMF). 2012. *Qatar: 2012 Article IV Consultations*, IMF Country Report No. 12/18. Washington, DC: International Monetary Fund.

Koren, M., and S. Tenreyro. 2011. Volatility, diversification and development in the Gulf Cooperation Council countries. In *The Transformation of the Gulf: Politics, Economics, and the Global Order*, eds. David Held, and Kristian Ulrichsen, 188–217. London: Routlege.

Maddison, Angus. 2001. *The World Economy: A Millenial Perspective*. Paris: OECD.

Metz, H. 1993. *Persian Gulf States: A Country Study*. Washington, D.C.: Library of Congress, Federal Research Division.

Mundell, R.A. 1961. A theory of optimum currency areas. *American Economic Review* 51: 657–665.

Murphy, C. 2011. *Saudi Arabia's Youth and the Kingdom's Future*. Washington, DC: Middle East Program, Woodrow Wilson Center for Scholars.

Plumer, B. 2014. Why oil prices keep falling—and throwing the world into turmoil.

Qatar Monetary Agency. 1985. *The Banking and Financial System in the State of Qatar*. Doha: Department of Research and Statistics, Qatar Monetary Agency.

Quah, D. 2011. The global economy's shifting centre of gravity. *Global Policy* 2(1): 3–9.

Setser, B. 2007. *The Case for Exchange Rate Flexibility in Oil-Exporting Economies.* Peterson Institute for International Economics Policy Brief 07-8. Washington, DC.

Westelius, N. 2013. *Moving Toward Market Based Liquidity Management in Qatar.* Qatar: Selected Issues. IMF Country Report No. 13/15. Washington, DC: International Monetary Fund.

White, W. 2006. *Is Price Stability Enough? BIS Working Papers.* Washington, DC: Bank for International Settlements.

White, W 2013. The Short and Long Term Effects of Ultra Easy Monetary Policy. A Changing Role for Central Banks, 41st Economics Conference Publication, Oesterreichische National Bank.

CHAPTER 13

# Qatar's Global-Local Nexus: From Soft to Nested Power?

*Abdulaziz Al Horr, Ghalia Al Thani, M. Evren Tok,*
*Hany Besada, Ben O'Bright, and Jason McSparren*

Qatar is emerging as a significant regional and global actor, symbolized by its airline, its mediation role in conflict zones in the Middle East and North

A. Al Horr (✉)
Qatar Finance and Business Academy (QFBA), Doha, Qatar

G. Al Thani
International Cooperation Department, National Human Rights Committee of Qatar, Doha, Qatar

M.E. Tok
Public Policy in Islam Program, Qatar Faculty of Islamic Studies, Hamad bin Khalifa University, Doha, Qatar

H. Besada
African Mineral Development Centre (AMDC), United Nations University Institute for Natural Resources in Africa, Ottawa, ON, Canada
Economic Commission for Africa (UNECA), United Nations University Institute for Natural Resources in Africa, Ottawa, ON, Canada
Institute of African Studies, Carleton University, Ottawa, ON, Canada
Centre on Governance, University of Ottawa, Ottawa, ON, Canada

B. O'Bright
Centre on Governance, University of Ottawa, Ottawa, ON, Canada

J. McSparren
Global Governance & Human Security McCormack Graduate School of Policy and Governance University of Massachusetts, Boston

© The Author(s) 2016
M.E. Tok et al. (eds.), *Policy-Making in a Transformative State*,
DOI 10.1057/978-1-137-46639-6_13

Africa, and its hosting of media-giant Al Jazeera and world events like FIFA 2022 (Cooper and Momani 2012), in a region in flux without a history of strong regional architecture (Legrenzi and Momani 2011). Qatar learned to adapt to unexpected changes in the global natural gas market in the advent of new technologies and supplies in the USA amidst Asian, Australian, and African competition as liquefied natural gas became essential to consumers. At the same time, its investment overseas has brought Qatar onto the political stage, especially seen in the recent Libyan and Syrian interventions. This implies that Qatar's interests are more than economic and that Qatar wants to project itself as a promoter of peace, security, and prosperity in the region and beyond. It appears that from Qatar's multi-order engagement in politics and business both internationally and nationally, Doha has carefully played the wider field with a strategic plan, to learn and grow through its economic investments. Many lessons have been learned from its greater political interventions in fragile states in the region, and Qatar continues to develop a strategic focus for the future.

This chapter proposes that the existing literature and discussions pertaining to Qatar's international visibility, impact, and image fail to take into consideration the "nested" nature of its power. In this chapter, we define "nested power" and use it as a calculated approach to international relations, using multiple levels of interactions. The nature of nested power refers to the ability of a state to use various tools and resources, at the domestic, regional, and international levels, in order to manipulate them for the desired effect. The state is able to act in a multi-dimensional manner that allows it to be defined in various ways, having strongholds and influence in various industries and among different alliances, which all contribute to its foreign policy agenda. In this sense, how does nested power operate? Although it seems that Qatar's nested power approach is well orchestrated by the existing leadership, the question remains, is this approach a systematic one? Does it cascade down to second and third generations of potential political leaders? Is there any link between Qatar's nested power practice and the National Vision? Is there a plan for sustainability? Is this practice of nested power a high or a low maintenance approach? What are the limitations? What are the constraints?

These levels are embedded into one another, making a complex formula. According to nested power, a player navigates through the multiple levels of nesting according to its best interest. Some of these levels are independent and some of them are interdependent. This chapter initially lays out the existing discussions pertaining to the concept of power and discusses the existing literature which mostly focuses on manifestations of power, that is, "soft power," "subtle power," and "smart power." This section is followed by the concept of nested power and the task at hand will be to delineate and characterize the nature of "nestedness." Then, we will offer a nested power diagram and visualize the mental mapping behind the concept of nestedness. This section will also entail critical reflections and suggestions that will help policy makers and the policy community in Qatar and in the region.

## Soft Power and Policy Implications for Small States

The concept of soft power was devised to conceptualize state capabilities beyond military force or other means of coercion. It is "the ability to get what you want through attraction rather than coercion or payment" (Nye 2004: x). These attractive forces can be "culture, values and foreign policies" (ibid: 11). Cooper and Shaw (2009) consider the level of vulnerability or resilience small states embody. Qatar has to consider its security as paramount in its international relations. Natural resource wealth could be a source of "vulnerability" because larger powers may attempt to annex its resources through coercion. Qatar has utilized its non-threatening stature to protect itself by optimizing its agency in two specific ways: hedging its relations with multiple powers, often powers at odds with one another and secondly, making itself available as a mediator, projecting the image of an impartial actor on the global stage.

Qatar is an example of a resilient small state demonstrated by its emergence as a significant regional and global actor. Despite its obvious vulnerabilities, Qatar has "operationalized resilience" (Cooper and Shaw 2009: 22) displaying agency at a level of a "middle" power through its mediation roles and interventionist practices. Kamrava (2013: 45) has described this agency as subtle power—"the ability to exert influence from behind the scenes. ... [It] revolves around the ability to influence outcomes to one's advantage through a combination of bringing resources to bear, enjoying international prestige derived from a commensurate with norm-entrepreneurship, and being positioned in such a way as to manipulate circumstances and the weaknesses of others to one's advantage."

Over a period of time, Qatar has emerged as a middle power in the Gulf region. As a middle power, Qatar's foreign policy is seen as a stabilizing force and has helped legitimize the global order, typically through multilateral and cooperative initiatives. The previous Emir of Qatar, Sheikh Hamad bin Khalifa (see Chapter 3), had undertaken several projects to capitalize on Qatar's hydrocarbon resources, improve educational opportunities for Qatari citizens, and pursue economic diversification. While emerging, traditional middle powers can be distinguished in terms of their mutually influencing constitutive and behavioral differences. In order to be regionally influential, Qatar plays a unique role. For example, as part of Qatar's liberalization experiment, the Qatari monarchy founded Al Jazeera, the first home-grown, all-news Arabic language satellite television network, in 1996. The network has proven influential since its establishment, especially during recent unrest in the Arab world. In an April 2003 referendum, Qatari voters approved a new constitution that officially granted women the right to vote and run for national office. Since 2000, Qatar projected itself as wealthy and stable, and it has constructed an identity distinct from powerful states in the region.

In 1995, Sheikh Hamad bin Khalifa Al-Thani became the emir of Qatar, after deposing his father in a bloodless coup. His assumption of power was predicated on the promise of introducing extensive political reforms. Pronouncements of reforms and the developments that followed were widely touted in the global media because observers were interested to witness the democratic transformation of the emirate. Commentators have claimed that the reforms were a means by which the Al-Thani's appealed to the broader base of Qataris during a period where the new emir's power was tentative; also, it was a way to assert autonomy and distinctiveness from its Gulf Cooperation Council (GCC) neighbors, especially Saudi Arabia, as well as gain favor from the international community, primarily the United States. Beginning in the late 1990s the new regime began an ambitious program of modernization that was facilitated by steadily rising oil prices and increases in the demand for natural gas. "Liberalization promises were meant to complement—if not altogether replace—traditional sources of legitimacy within the ruling family with legitimacy derived from a loosely defined sense of "political modernity," (Kamrava 2009: 79) but, "Sheikh patterns of rule" continued to dominate, which include, "centralized, often personalized, decision-making, the lack of accountability and transparency, and a reliance on patronage networks" (Kamrava 2009).

Qatar's foreign policy strategy has drawn attention because, although it is a small state in terms of population and military might, the state has been able to utilize its strategic capabilities to an advantage that has allowed the state access to important forums and therefore, create opportunities to exact influence within them. Cooper and Shaw (2009) consider the level of vulnerability or resilience embodied in small states at the beginning of the new millennium. Qatar is an exceptional breed of "resilient" small state as it employs its capabilities within the international system. Emir Sheikh Hamad had been able to consolidate his power domestically; moreover, he had been able to exercise a foreign policy strategy that exploited the unique circumstances of Qatar in order to play a more prominent role in the region. This ability to exercise and maintain influence at the domestic, regional, and international level in turn reflects Qatar's ability to move beyond maintaining soft or hard power and instead, reflects what we will define as nested power.

Small states such as Qatar are traditionally viewed as vulnerable actors in the international system, but at times they can capitalize on their "unique vantage point in regional and international politics to make a noticeable impact in world affairs" (Cooper and Momani 2013: 12). Qatar's foreign policy strategy and broad use of soft or subtle power has allowed it to stand out within a volatile region where competition for hegemony is constant. In recent history, Qatar has projected itself into numerous regional conflicts in three capacities: as mediator, financial supporter, and as military intervener. Qatar's foreign policy exemplifies the execution of agency, finding the room to operate as an actor within the anarchic world system.

There is no agreed upon definition of a "small state," but Vital (1971) has classified large states or "great powers" as being in the 10–15 million population range, medium states or "medium powers" as being located between large states, and small states or "small powers" as having a population in the 1–1.5 million range; finally, "microstates" are those with populations below that the small state range. Vital points out that "small states could not simply assume that their sovereignty or independence would be respected by the great powers, especially if those greater powers saw strategic relevance in either interfering with the smaller states domestic policies or even, sometimes, in violating their territorial integrity" (Vital 1971: 253). This impression of vulnerability is increased when a small state was situated within the sphere of influence of the greater power (Mathisen 1971).

Qatar's foreign policy under Sheik Hamad bin Khalifa al-Thani has been cleverly developed and managed, assisted largely by the great wealth possessed by the hydrocarbon exporting nation. It is not wealth alone that has garnered Qatar the reputation of "punching above its weight," but also its calculated exploitation of regional politics driven by the desire to join the league of developed nations by the year 2030. Through its striving for international recognition, Qatar has been able to uplift its stature from vulnerable to resilient, although vulnerabilities persist and the nation has taken some criticism. When analyzing the Qatari investment portfolio and the different steps Qatar has taken to diversify its wealth and economy, it becomes clear how Qatar has used soft/subtle power tool to create a prestigious brand for itself that is respected and enhances the state's reputation globally.

An examination of Qatar's investment patterns across the globe reveals that Qatar is heavily invested in North America and Europe and is increasingly cultivating ties in Asia, especially with China. The Economist Intelligence Unit expects Asia to be the most important emerging-market region for the GCC states due to the demand for oil (Economist Intelligence Unit 2011: 10–16) (EIU). It can be surmised that Qatar's deepening relationship with Asia, China especially, reflects its hedging strategy. Certainly, Qatar is investing for the purpose of increasing the nation's wealth, but economics is only part of the strategy. Qatar's foreign policy has been to maneuver between competitors and make itself useful to powerful states. The EIU also reports that GCC trade with Africa has been increasing (ibid: 17–25), but Qatar itself has a smaller footprint than other GCC states in Africa.

A major mechanism for Qatari economic diversification and long-term wealth management of oil and gas surpluses is the Qatar Investment Authority (QIA), which manages the sovereign wealth fund (SWF). Qatar's SWF holds an estimated $256 billion USD in assets and comprises five subsidiaries: Qatar Holding LLC, which is the prime vehicle for strategic and direct investments by the state; Delta Two LTD, which is a secondary investment vehicle of QIA; Qatari Diar, which is a real estate and development company; Hassad Food, which is a farm and agricultural investment company; and Qatar Sports Investments, which concentrates on investing in sports and leisure industries (SWF Institute 2015). The state-owned enterprises that are of interest for this chapter are Qatar Holding, Hassad Food, and Qatar Petroleum International. Qatari state-owned enterprises (SOEs) are minimally transparent about their strategies, contracts, and operations.

The QIA portfolio includes what has been considered "showcase investments" in the West. The financial sector is a major focus of QIA holding stakes in European banks, Credit Suisse Group AG, and Barclays Plc, plus Agricultural Bank of China, Banco Santander Brasil, and the London Stock Exchange. Real estate development led by Qatari Diar also is a substantial component of the group's strategy; it owns London's Shard building,

Chelsea Barracks, and the historic Le Lido at the Champs Elysees in Paris; it also owns the City Center DC in Washington, D.C., which is believed to be the largest downtown development currently underway in any US city, as well as the London Olympic Village. Retail businesses are also part of the portfolio. The group purchased the famed Harrods department store for $413 million USD, QIA owns only shares in Tiffany, LVMH and Sainsbury's. Unlike Harrod's which is owned by Qatar 100%. Automobile manufacturers Volkswagen AG and Porsche Automobile Holding SE have also been targets of QIA investments. The wealth fund played a role in the Glencore International $29 billion USD takeover of Xstrata, putting it in the global commodities production and marketing sectors. QIA became one of the largest shareholders of France's Total SA oil company, as well as Royal Dutch Shell and British Airports Authority. (Lacqua and Tuttle 2014). These portfolio anchor investments have historical track records of financial success, plus as mentioned, Europe and North America have sturdy institutions that can protect the investments and ensure their value.

There is a clear logic behind these investments of Qatar in the Western developed countries. The financial crisis left corporations in need of capital, and Qatar has plenty of liquid assets. Additionally, Western investments are safe because of the institutional structures in those countries. Moreover, the brands that Qatar is purchasing are well known and trusted by the public; most are internationally known. Therefore, these purchases can be seen as an extension of Qatar's own branding campaign. This sort of investment focus brings Qatar closer to the current and previous global hegemons, the USA and Great Britain. On another front, Qatar is also investing in and building trade relations with China, a potential future hegemon. In addition to China, other Asian states such as Vietnam, Indonesia, and Japan are becoming Qatari partners in development. These too, are large investments, yet safe in terms of institutional protection, which maintains the value of the investments and secures their long-term productivity barring any crisis or strategic miscalculation. Infrastructure is in place in the West and in Asia that will facilitate Qatar's business growth.

Qatar's Asian interests are an example of the increasing thickness of South-South relations. Gulf States and Asia, China especially, have been partnering on energy trade (Ulrichsen 2010: 4–5). Qatar Petroleum and the China National Offshore Oil Company (CNOOC) agreed upon a number of arrangements in 2008–2009, a notable one is a twenty-five year Exploration and Production Sharing Agreement that will make Qatar the leading supplier of liquid natural gas (LNG) to China (ibid: 4–5). CNOOC president Fu Cheng Yu commented that, "the global economy is in fundamental reshaping and we have determined to build up strategic partnership in the energy field with Qatar" (Reuters 2014).

When analyzing Qatar's foreign policy, investment patterns and relations with other countries, particularly those in the West, it becomes clear that calculated decision-making by Qatari top officials is behind the manner in which Qatar is maneuvering through international politics and affairs. These calculated decisions to invest in soft/subtle power tools have allowed Qatar to create a sphere of influence in which it has become a legitimate and credible actor in international and regional affairs. Furthermore, these investments provide a form of economic, geographic, and resource security for Qatar, which in turn gives it the freedom and ability to secure its international and regional interests. The unique manner in which Qatar has managed to use and control these soft/subtle power tools, we argue, reflects Qatar's "nestedness," which will be further examined in the following section.

## From Soft to Nested Power

The prestige and influence that Qatar has been building over the years is a direct result of the Qatari government's ability to utilize several different instruments of power, in order to create an image and brand of the state and portray it to the rest of the world. As has been noted in the previous section, the Qatari government has come a long way in developing and implementing soft power tools in order to gain a high level of prestige and influence as an emerging global actor. We will argue that the approach the Qatari government has taken to international relations allows it to successfully implement various power tools at different levels, in order to secure its strategic interests and policy objectives. We refer to this as nested power.

We define nested power as the use of multiple tools and means, at all levels, and harnessing them to multi-dimensional purposes of branding, positioning, attracting, and hedging. In this context, nested power looks at different factors and levels of interaction in a non-hierarchical manner with carful calculations on how every factor or level of interaction affects the overall situation, making it a complex formula. In the nested power, the level of one factor or interaction makes sense within the level of another factor or interaction. Therefore, each case, decision, or interaction for any purpose of branding, positioning, hedging, or attracting is unique and has multiple sides and angles. According to nested power, a player navigates through multiple, nested levels using various kinds of forces—hard and soft—parallel to their best interests. Some of these levels and interactions are independent and some of them are interdependent. The concept of nested power represents the ability of a state to position, get attract, and become an international player by using its resources, relations, networking, and forces. With this approach of nested power, the player can establish relationships with multiple powers, even if these powers are at odds with one another. However, the player needs to be careful when managing these odds in order to mitigate negative consequences. The concept of nested power gives the player the flexibility to use different forces and tools at different levels to manage, balance, challenge, develop, and end the relationship.

The forces that make up nested power are hard and soft, such as the following: military intervention, security agreements, arms deals, military bases, investment, foreign policy, media, aviation, international events, labor agreements, education, research, art, sponsorship, scholarship, training, mediation, financial aid, international cooperation, partnership and alliances, sport, regional cooperation, entertainment, awards, branding, trade, lobbying, security agreements, and military bases.

To understand a case of political position or movement, it is crucial to identify the economic, social, political, historical, and geographical space in which the case is operated and exists. This space may be local, national, or global. It will more likely involve complex and evolving interactions at different levels: national, regional, and global. In this context of a multilevel and multidimensional model, we talk more about nested factors, which means that a political case or decision might fall under different folders or factors (Fig. 13.1).

The tools and mechanisms of nested power rest on all of these resources that a country may or may not possess. A state can use all or some of these forces and tools to position, get attraction, and become an international player. The resources and tools of nested power are utilized and leveraged through public diplomacy. No one particular tool or force of nested power can achieve meaningful influence or attraction alone. Therefore, the use of a combination of these tools is crucial to create the maximum attraction and impact. However, even with the use of a combination of tools and forces, results are not always guaranteed uniformly across all states at all times. It will always depend on the effectiveness and intelligence

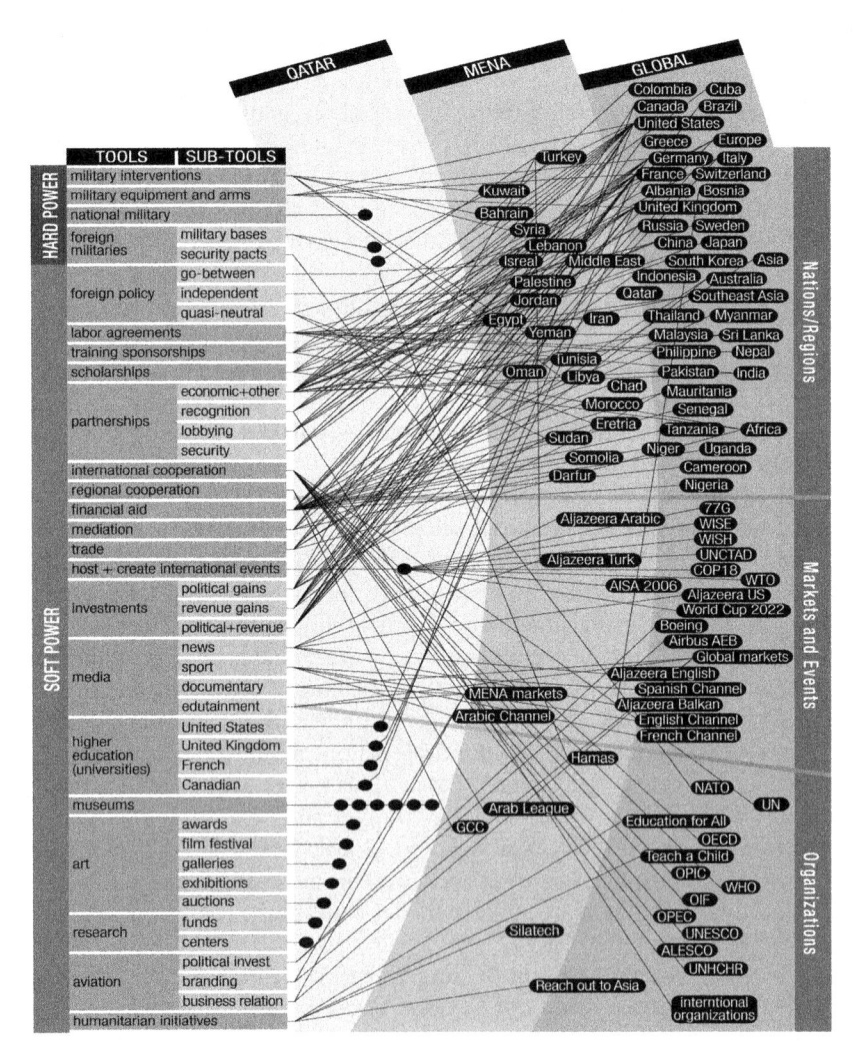

Fig. 13.1  Qatar's nested power

of public diplomacy. Using the concept of nested power at different levels with different tools can help a state achieve general goals and specific objectives. Moreover, a state can approach any objective, such as branding, from multiple directions at multiple levels. What becomes clear from this definition of nested power is that it serves as a more comprehensive way to characterize the steps the Qatari government has taken to build the "Qatar brand." By implementing and investing in education, media, world sporting events, aviation, mediation, and humanitarian aid, to name a few, Qatar has been able to capitalize on its resources and use them effectively to create a unique national brand and achieve its foreign policy objectives through becoming an influential regional and global actor.

In order to better understand the concept of nested power, we will investigate how the Qatari government is using various power tools at different levels of interaction in order to create a globally recognized and influential Qatari brand, which signifies the nested power the country maintains. In conjunction with this, it is important to note that a country's ability to successfully implement and utilize soft/hard power tools is often dependent on its reputation and relationship with members of the international community. Qatar's small size, geographic location, and historic association with oil wealth and conservative Islamic countries in the region are all reasons why Qatar is strongly invested in creating a strong, unique national brand that serves to diminish these existing stereotypes and narratives about the country and in turn secure its interests and foreign policy goals and objectives (Roberts 2012: 235–37). In reality, Qatar is a progressive, sovereign country, with diverse resources that have effectively managed to enhance its credibility regionally and globally (ibid: 235–37). By further analyzing the nested power tools of media, sports aviation, mediation, and humanitarian aid, it will become clear how these tools interact at the national, regional, and international levels to enhance Qatar's influence and credibility, allowing it to effectively pursue their foreign policy agenda.

The emergence of the media outlet al-Jazeera in 1996 is a clear example of a soft power tool that Qatar has strategically implemented and invested in, as a way of successfully creating a public diplomacy strategy that reflects the values and norms of the Qatari state (Samuel-Azran 2013: 1295–96). The establishment of Al-Jazeera has radically shifted Arab media and notions surrounding press freedom, allowing the media outlet to be a powerful advocate with particular political ambitions. The news channel offers new and different perspectives in delivering news, as the news channel is guided by the principles of free speech, democracy, and transparency. In recent years, with the political upheaval and tensions between Middle Eastern governments and citizens, Al-Jazeera has become a distinguished high-quality product for delivering Arab and Islamic issues in a broad and unbiased way (Antwi-Boateng 2013: 42).

The Qatari news channel has been cleverly created to operate as a dual power tool. On one hand, the news channel has the ability to stand as an independent and creditable actor, often protecting the rights of common Arab citizens. On the other hand, the media outlet has managed to effectively enhance the prestige and credibility of the Qatari state within the international community through its visibility and influence in Arab politics.

Censorship and lack of freedoms in Arab countries are key issues that the existence of Al-Jazeera has challenged. During the Egyptian uprising, while Egyptian media outlets censored the reality of protests and demonstrations, Al-Jazeera openly and transparently publicized the real situation on the ground and reinforced its commitment to freedom of press and speech. Due to the level of independence that Al-Jazeera operates with, Western governments are increasingly using it as credible news source with firsthand accounts of Middle Eastern news (Harb 2011).

Although Al-Jazeera appears to be a positive actor in Middle Eastern affairs, it has also come under heavy criticism for its involvement in Egypt, and it was accused of bias for supporting of the Muslim Brotherhood, which resulted in world-renowned journalists being imprisoned by the Egyptian government. The actions taken by Al-Jazeera serve to indicate how powerful and creditable the media outlet is. By Al-Jazeera having the ability to influence and shape public opinion in the Middle East, it presents Qatar as a progressive society dedicated to freedoms and democratic principles. Furthermore, the case of Al-Jazeera demonstrates the transformational state of the country as the country offers modern freedoms to its citizens and the surrounding region in the form of information and freedom of speech, but it is still concerned with being a culturally respectful Islamic state.

What becomes clear is that Al-Jazeera is a powerful, relevant, and influential public relations tool at the domestic, regional, and international levels. This in turn reflects the nested nature of Qatar's power because of the influence and credibility Al-Jazeera has at all levels of interaction, which gives the Qatari state the power and agency to maneuver through, influence, and shape regional politics according to its interests and despite being accused of harboring bias in recent situations.

A key component to Qatar's foreign policy objectives is to strengthen international peace and security. In order to achieve this goal Qatar has increasingly been assuming the role of a mediator and peacemaker in conflict areas. This, in part, gives Qatar the agency and ability to ensure its survival in the region and also enhances its legitimacy and credibility in global affairs (Barakat 2014: 11–13). By positioning itself as a mediator, the Qatari government aims to strategically minimize potential terror threats, conflict, and population displacement, and it seeks to promote country environments where conducive and peaceful business deals and investments can take place, as a form of meaningful development (ibid: 11–13).

Qatar's intervention and mediation in Lebanon is considered one of its most successful, as Qatari officials were able to bring various t Lebanese parties together to reach the Doha Agreement in May 2008 (Kamrava 2011: 547). The agreement appointed a presidential candidate and created the foundation for the formation of a national unity government (Kamrava 2011: 548). This form of mediation presented by Qatar serves to solidify Qatar's image as a credible actor in regional politics and further advance its foreign policy agenda.

In the case of Libya, critics argue that Qatar's intervention in the conflict has led to a shift in the balance of Qatar's identity as a peaceful mediator (Kamrava 2011: 553). Qatar's role in the intervention was based mainly on oil and securing national interests (Roberts 2011). In 2010, approximately 85 % of Libyan oil exports went to Italy, France, Britain, and Spain (EIA 2011). By using its credible and influential reputation, Qatar sought to secure the interests of important Western allies, an argument that can be applied to Qatar's actions in the Syrian conflict.

Qatar's brand of being a peacekeeper and contributing to international and domestic peace and security serves to signify the nestedness of Qatari foreign policy. At the international level, Qatar has been enhancing its reputation, solidifying its legitimacy, and strengthening its international alliances. At the domestic level, Qatari investment in mediation efforts allows the state to redefine its norms and values to encompass the interests of Qatari citizens.

The nested nature of Qatari power is in turn highlighted by the state's ability to be influential in its mediation efforts as a means of securing its regional interests and diminishing potential threats to the country. Furthermore, Qatari involvement in Libya allows us to see how Qatar can successfully transform its role by using its creditable image and influence in the region to further secure Western alliances.

In conjunction with its role as a peacemaker, Qatar has been instrumental in providing humanitarian assistance to countries in need. Through providing humanitarian aid, Qatar further demonstrates the country's shared values with others and its commitment to international cooperation, peace, and security initiatives, which ultimately serve to further its foreign policy objectives (Ministry of Foreign Affairs 2013). An example of Qatari humanitarian aid was the Qatar Friendship Fund, established in 2012 to provide aid and assistance to Japan after the 2012 earthquake and tsunami (Ministry of Foreign Affairs 2013). The fund supported the rehabilitation of damaged infrastructure and generated employment opportunities in the region. Initiatives such as this allow Qatar to further the legitimacy of its prestigious brand as it continues to carve out a space as an influential actor in international affairs. Here, the nested nature of Qatari power is made clear as its commitment to providing humanitarian assistance and support to countries in need signifies the multi-dimensional reach of the country. On one hand, Qatar has the ability to use military intervention in situations where necessary. On the other hand, Qatar can act as a peaceful mediator and give countries humanitarian assistance. However, the image of Qatar goes beyond that of an aggressor or a peacemaker and instead projects a uniquely prestigious Islamic country with various industries and political alliances and strongholds, which all contribute to the overall policy ambitions of the country.

Qatar's public diplomacy, mediation efforts, and aid initiatives are all working separately and together at the international, regional, and domestic levels in order to allow the country to pursue its foreign policy objectives.

Qatar has always been characterized by its oil and natural gas wealth and it is important to note that this has been strategically used in order to achieve certain economic objectives. However, it is also important to note that Qatar does not solely rely on its oil wealth and has taken significant steps to diversify its economy, industries, and trade (Beavis 2014: 416; see Chapter 3). The ways that Qatar is diversifying and opening up as a country have been by investing in sports, aviation, education and tourism, to name a few. By analyzing these soft power tools the nested power of Qatar will be illustrated, as these tools are effectively implemented to build the national Qatari brand and further the country's foreign policy objectives.

In 2010, among eleven other bidding counties, Qatar won the bid to host the FIFA 2022 World Cup, making it the first Middle East and Islamic country to host the games. Hosting a sporting event such as the

FIFA World Cup gives Qatar the ability to communicate its attractiveness through the shared cultural values of sport and in turn increase its international credibility, prestige, and potential for agency (Roberts 2012: 236–37). Historically, sports have been a powerful channel for countries to use and build relationships. Due to the centrality of universally admired values in international sporting events, hosting states have the ability to enhance and showcase their attractiveness, by demonstrating that they share in these values and aim to incorporate them within their own cultural, social, and political norms (Amara 2013). Qatar is set to spend over $200 billion on its preparations to host the games, which will be invested in building stadiums, training facilities, and transport infrastructure, which could potentially contribute to an increase of competitive athletes in the region (Amara 2013). What becomes clear is that hosting the World Cup provides Qatar with a unique opportunity to enhance its credibility both internally and externally, as the World Cup will put Qatar in the global spotlight with the potential of increased trade and investment, along with creating a sense of national pride among Qatari citizens.

Although it appears that Qatar stands to benefit greatly from hosting the World Cup, it is important to keep in mind the recent corruption allegations that have plagued FIFA and Qatar's alleged involvement. Along with this, Qatar has faced strong criticisms with regards to the treatment of migrant workers, which the Qatari government has responded to by promising labor reforms and norms, such as timely pay, decent living conditions, and decent working hours (Guardian 2012). Furthermore, the known hooliganism and high alcohol consumption associated with football calls into question the legitimacy of Qatar hosting the games (Dorsey 2012).

Qatar's sports diplomacy aims to increase the country's prestige by creating a unique brand that assures its legitimacy in international relations, which in turn signifies the nestedness of Qatar's foreign policy. In the case of the FIFA games, Qatar aims to create a positive impression and attract tourism and foreign investment; however, the negative implications arising indicate the fine line that states have to navigate in international relations in order to remain powerful and influential. Although hosting the FIFA games serves to build the Qatari brand, the side steps that have been taken in order to get there may be more detrimental to the state's reputation than beneficial. This in turn highlights the transformational state of Qatar, as opening up the country to the norms of football culture will, in a sense, force Qatar to tolerate Western norms, while working to preserve its own culture and tradition.

The nestedness of Qatari power is reflected here in the steps Qatar is willing to take in order to host the World Cup. Qatar seeks to establish itself as a modern sport oasis for years to come and is using the prestigious World Cup as a means of justifying its investment in facilities, infrastructure, and equipment. Although Qatar has come under heavy criticism (as is any country preparing for a major world sporting event), if it is able to successfully host the games, it could realize its ambition of becoming the Middle Eastern Sporting Hub and being an influential actor in the field.

Another way that Qatar is successfully diversifying its economy and furthering the national brand is through the establishment an efficient and prestigious national airline carrier. Qatar Airways is a state-owned and operated airline and operates services across all continents (Brannagan et al. 2014: 124). Qatar Airways has gained world renowned status and is known for its high quality of services and tasteful showcasing of Qatari culture and values (Brannagan et al. 2014: 125). Qatar Airways in turn serves to represent the Qatari state and has become another way in which the Qatari government can promote the country to potential business partners and other countries by sending a message of commitment to excellence, while also generating significant revenues (Brannagan et al. 2014: 125). Again, it becomes clear how the Qatari government is effectively using a soft power tool in order to create an image of the country that will in turn ensure the survival of the country and increase its legitimacy and agency as a regional and international actor.

By analyzing Qatari media, sports development, aviation development, mediation, and humanitarian assistance initiatives, what becomes clear is the strategic process that has gone into developing these power tools. This strategic process in turn reflects the nested nature of Qatari power and the transformative state of the country, as it aims to modernize while balancing issues of traditional society, religion, and social inclusion. By looking at the examples of Al-Jazeera, humanitarian assistance, Qatari mediation, and the recent military interventions made by the Qatari state, the driving force behind having the ability to maneuver through different levels of interaction and be influential at all levels signifies the nested nature of the state. Having built up a creditable news channel and being successful in pervious mediation efforts, Qatar has the ability to build on that by using their reputation and influence in order to pursue other foreign policy objectives, such as establishing closer ties with Western countries.

When looking at the examples of the FIFA World Cup and Qatar Airways, which are relatively new Qatar investments, again, the nested nature of Qatari power is highlighted. The controversy over Qatar winning the bid to host the games demonstrates the power they have to shift outcomes in their favor. However, in similar veins to that of Qatar Airways, the justifications behind them have long-term implications that are significant to Qatar's foreign policy agenda. If Qatar can overcome the negativity surrounding hosting the World Cup Games, it can position itself to be an instrumental sporting hub in the Middle East. Along with this, by establishing Qatar Airways a dominant international airline, Qatar can demonstrate its global power and influence in different industries. However, the criticism that Qatar has faced, especially with hosting the FIFA games, demonstrates that Qatar needs to be careful and avoid using its financial power to side-step processes.

## Conclusions

Qatar is a small, unique state that has been undergoing a period of transformation, in order to protect itself, remain competitively viable, and assert itself in international politics. The nested nature of Qatari power illustrates how the Qatari government has strategically invested in certain power tools and is using them independently and interdependently in order to create a modern, progressive, and unique society. No single power tool or its implications defines the Qatari state or its foreign policy agenda, they have the ability to be influential and creditable in various industries and secure legitimate alliances. However, it should be noted that formation of the nested power depended on visionary leadership that can orchestrate different actors and powers for the best interest of state. In the case of Qatar, one can easily raise questions on the sustainability of Qatar's nested power practice. Also, as Brannagan and Giulianotti (2014) argue, one needs to focus on the other side of soft power, that of soft disempowerment, which happens when soft power tools bring so much attention to the country and vulnerabilities are closely monitored by international actors; examples are the of migrant workers or debates pertaining to FIFA. Perhaps the key criteria would be the extent to which Qatari leadership, as the creators of Qatar's nested power, will critically improve, strategically manage, and cascade down the practice of nested power. The ability to deal with these challenges and concerns will determine the country's present and the future that awaits for generations to come.

## BIBLIOGRAPHY. QATAR: POLICY MAKING IN A TRANSFORMATIVE STATE

Amara, Mahfoud. 2013. The Pillars of Qatar's International Sports Strategy. E-International Relations. http://www.e-ir.info/2013/11/29/the-pillars-of-qatars-international-sport-strategy/

Antwi-Boateng, Osman. 2013. The rise of Qatar as a soft power and the challenges. *European Scientific Journal* 9(31): 350–368.

Barakat, Sultan. 2014. *Qatari Mediation: Between Ambition and Achievement.* Doha: Brookings Doha Centre.

Brannagan, Paul Michael, and Richard Giulianotti. 2014. Soft power and soft disempowerment: Qatar, global sport and football's 2022 World Cup Finals. *Leisure Studies.*

Brannagan, Paul, Jacqueline Mubanga, and Mads De Wolff. 2014. Qatar: Firsthand account of soft power. *E-International Relations.* Accessed May 15, 2015.

Beavis, J.; Fletcher, J. and Morakabati, Y. (2014). "Planning for a Qatar Without Oil: Tourism and Economic Diversification, a Battle of Perceptions," Tourism Planning and Development, 11(4).

Cooper, Andrew F., and Timothy M. Shaw. 2009. Diplomacy of small states at the start of the twenty-first century: How vulnerable? How resilient? In *The Diplomacies of Small States: Between Vulnerability and Resilience*, eds. Andrew F. Cooper, and Timothy M. Shaw, 1–18. Houndmills, Basingstoke: Palgrave Macmillan.

Cooper A. and Momani, B. (2011) "Qatar and Expanded Contours of Small State Diplomacy," The International Spectator 46, no. 3, 113–28, doi:10.1080/03932729.2011.576181.

Cooper, Andrew, and Timothy Shaw. 2013. "Diplomacy of Small States at the Start of the Twenty-First Century: How Vulnerable? How Resilient?" In The Diplomacies of Small States: Between Vulnerability and Resilience, 1–18. New York: Palgrave MacMillan

Dorsey, J. 2012. Alcohol ban raises specter of problems for Qatar's hosting of 2022 World Cup. *The World Post.* http://www.huffingtonpost.com/james-dorsey/alcohol-ban-raises-specte_b_1211377.html

Economist Intelligence Unit, GCC Trade and Investment Flows: The Emerging-Market Surge (Economist Intelligence Unit Limited, 2011).

Energy Information Administration, "Qatar," Qatar Analysis, 2014, http://www.eia.gov/countries/cab.cfm?fips=qa.
Harb, Z. 2011. Arab Revolutions and the Social Media Effect. *Media and Culture Journal* 14 (2).
Joseph Jr. Nye, Soft Power: The Means to Success in World Politics (New York: Public Affairs, 2004), x.
Kamrava, Mehran. 2009. Royal factionalism and political liberalization in Qatar. *Middle East Journal* 63(3): 401–420.
———. 2011. Mediation and Qatari foreign policy. *Middle East Journal* 65(4): 539–556.
———. 2013. *Qatar: Small State, Big Politics*. Ithaca, NY: Cornell University Press.
Lacqua, F., and R. Tuttle. 2014. Qatar Investment Fund to Boost Investments in UK. *Daily Star Lebanon*, February 13. http://www.dailystar.com.lb/Business/Middle-East/2014/Feb-13/247157-qatar-wealth-fund-to-boost-investments-in-uk.ashx
Mathisen, T. 1971. *The Functions of Small States in the Strategies of Great Powers*. Oslo: University of Olaget.
Roberts, D. 2011. Behind Qatar's Intervention in Libya. *Foreign Affairs*, September 28.
Roberts, D 2012. Understanding Qatar's foreign policy objectives. *Mediterranean Politics* 17(2): 233–239.
Reuters, "Gulf States Seek Food Security in Europe, US after African Problems," Gulf Business, January 4, 2014, http://gulfbusiness.com/2014/01/gulf-states-seek-food-security-in-europe-us-after-african-problems/
Samuel-Azran, T. 2013. Al-Jazeera, Qatar, and new tactics in state-sponsored media diplomacy. *American Behavioral Scientist* 57(9): 1293–1311.
State of Qatar, Ministry of Foreign Affairs (2013) Foreign Aid Report 2013 (Department of International Development: Doha).
SWF Institute, 2014. fund Rankings. Available at: http://www.swfinstitute.org/fund-rankings/[Accessed October 10, 2014]
Ulrichsen, Kristian Coates. 2010. *The GCC States and the Shifting Balance of Global Power*. Doha: Retrieved from https://repository.library.georgetown.edu/bitstream/handle/10822/558292/CIRSOccasionalPaper6KristianCoatesUlrichsen2010.pdf?sequence=5Center for International and Regional Studies, Georgetown University School of Foreign Service in Qatar.
Vital, D. 1971. *The Survival of Small States: Studies in Small Power/Great Power Conflict*. Oxford: Oxford University Press.

CHAPTER 14

# Conclusions

*Lolwah R.M. Alkhater, M. Evren Tok, and Leslie A. Pal*

This book has argued that the scale of Qatar's policy ambitions requires a fresh frame of reference as a "transformative state," which we defined as *a state that seeks to introduce and implement, over a comparatively short time, a radical re-configuration of social, economic, and political institutions in a country*. This definition has three key dimensions: (1) *time* (short, compressed, and intense), (2) *depth* (radical, deep), and (3) *scope* (almost simultaneously, across all sectors, public and private). By calling attention to its transformative character, we are not denying other important characteristics of the Qatari state, for example, its geo-political location in the Gulf and the Middle East, its dependence on hydrocarbons, and its Arab and Islamic nature, to name only the key ones. Our argument is simply that these characteristics, as crucial as they are, need to be weighed with and against the state's policy ambitions. Indeed, the ambition to transform Qatar into a modern state and society is one tempered by the exigencies of

---

L.R.M. Alkhater (✉)
Qatar Foundation and RAND-Qatar Policy Institute, Doha, Qatar

E.M. Tok
Public Policy in Islam Program, Qatar Faculty of Islamic Studies, Hamad bin Khalifa University, Doha, Qatar

L.A. Pal
School of Public Policy and Administration, Carleton University, Ottawa, ON, Canada

© The Author(s) 2016
M.E. Tok et al. (eds.), *Policy-Making in a Transformative State*,
DOI 10.1057/978-1-137-46639-6_14

geography, culture, history, and religion. Does its transformative character make Qatar unique? In some ways it does, and we will discuss these below. A "unique case" is somewhat troubling from a social science perspective, since it explains nothing but itself; it is *sui generis*. However, understanding Qatar does cast some light on challenges in the Gulf and the Middle East, as well as broader issues of governance and the management of public policy dynamics. For example, Qatar's challenges and opportunities are similar to those faced by some other Gulf states. In the field of foreign policy, as another example, it has been taken as an exemplar of "small state diplomacy" (Cooper and Momani 2011; Cooper and Shaw 2009).

A transformative state pursues its agenda in a short, compressed, and intense time frame. As Chapters 1 and 12 point out, while Qatar was a typical Gulf oil sheikhdom until the early 2000s, its oil wealth was relatively modest and the pace of development quite measured. The discovery of natural gas reserves in 1971 then took another twenty years to develop, and Qatar only emerged as an LNG superpower in the mid-2000s. As Chapter 3 showed, a choice was made at that time to launch a National Vision as well as a development strategy that would completely transform Qatar by 2030. Within thirty years, or one generation, Qatar set the goal of developing a completely modern health care system, a state-of-the art educational system, a new urban infrastructure both for Doha and surrounding smaller cities, a transportation infrastructure including a complete metro system in Doha, and a knowledge-based economy that would be the platform for a post-hydrocarbon future. These goals reflect the other two dimensions of transformation: its depth and its scope. It is deep in the sense that, in the aggregate, it is affecting the way in which ordinary Qataris live, learn, work, communicate, and understand each other and the place of their country in the world. It certainly poses challenges for balancing these changes with the retention of some sort of stable national identity as defined through history, the state itself, and Islam. The scope is obvious–where other states struggle to develop their economy or their educational system, or to modernize their health care, Qatar is doing them all at once.

Transformation has some elements of modernization—Qatar is openly adopting and importing what it considers the best international or "modern" standards—but it is distinct from an earlier modernization theory that predicted that a modern economy would compel modernization in culture and lifestyle, converging on Western capitalist and secularist models (Lerner 1958). Indeed, this earlier framework (as applied to the

Middle East) captured the element of time: modernization was characterized by "societies in a hurry," but it failed to capture the dynamics of a modernization that seems to be coupled with preservation of monarchy and Islamic, religious identity. Kamrava (2013) has tried to define Qatar's transformative character by relying on Scott's notion of "high modernism" (Scott 1998) and linking it to extensive "social engineering" through the creation of a completely new society. Scott (1998: 4) defines high modernism as "a strong, one might even say muscle-bound, version of the self-confidence about scientific and technical progress, the expansion of production, the growing satisfaction of human needs, the mastery of nature (including human nature), and, above all, the rational design of social order commensurate with the scientific understanding of natural laws." The brutality and arrogance of high modernism was best exemplified by the Stalinist project of collectivization of agriculture. Qatar's transformative ambitions may resemble high modernism in timing, scope, and depth, but not in its blunt force or even in its rationalism, given that societal change is to be calibrated by Islamic principles. And while the transformation has been deep, it has not been wrenching or savage. Why?

The answer takes us to some of the characteristics of Qatar that, in combination, make it unique or at least distinctive. Most obviously, it has resources or rents that do not require redistribution or the imposition of material losses on any segment of the native population. As a rentier state (discussed more below), it can "buy off" its citizens with material benefits, and indeed the transformations it envisages (e.g., health, education, economy) actually involve *raising the standards and levels of services and benefits* to its population. As chapters in this book have shown, these do entail some costs in terms of changing social structures and perhaps even dissatisfaction with exactly how the services are configured and delivered, but show none of the brutality of "high modernism." Qatar also has a tiny native population, for example, in comparison with Saudi Arabia (almost 30 million) or even Yemen (almost 25 million); therefore, the per capita benefits from resource wealth are uncommonly high. Not only is the native population small, but it is almost exclusively Arab Sunni, thereby avoiding the religious split between Shi'a and Sunni that afflicts most other Gulf states (Gengler 2015). Finally, Qatar has had unusually adept leadership in the person of Sheikh Hamad, the Father Emir. His hand was clearly evident in the adoption of the Constitution, in the National Vision and development strategy, and in Qatar's distinctive foreign policy. As we noted in Chapter 1, this combination of resource wealth, small population, and astute leadership has persuaded analysts that the ruling bargain in Qatar is more stable and legitimate than that in other Gulf states.

That is not to say that Qatar does not face challenges in its transformative agenda. The most obvious one is its reliance on oil and gas revenues, particularly as world prices have dropped since 2014. However, even in this, it is an outlier. While predicting the imminent collapse of all the other Gulf monarchies, Davidson admits that Qatar's future is a little rosier: "the state can actually sustain high spending and wealth distribution to its national population" (Davidson 2012: 237). Alkhater, in Chapter 12 in this volume, essentially agrees. He points out that Qatar has actually been reasonably astute in preparing for a decline in oil prices, as far back as 2013, and that among the GCC states, it alone has used a more independent monetary policy during the global financial crisis. Another challenge is the extraordinary imbalance in population: some 300,000 native Qataris and two million expatriate workers. Not only is the imbalance unique, but it is entangled with the *kafala* system and mistreatment of migrant workers that has attracted international criticism and undermined Qatar's branding efforts discussed in Chapter 13. At the time of writing, the FIFA scandal was generating demands that World Cup hosting rights be withdrawn from Russia and Qatar (in 2018 and 2022 respectively) on the grounds that those rights were won through bribes. This was yet another blow to the "Qatar brand," as well as a possible economic disaster given the investments already made in infrastructure to host the event.

However, most of the direct and immediate challenges Qatar faces are at the policy sector level, a level explored in detail in the preceding chapters. The next section will review the main findings and themes of those chapters, followed by reflections on theory and Qatar's future.

## Qatar's Transformative Agenda: Key Themes

The chapters in the book can leave no doubt about the reality of Qatar's transformative ambitions—they are not merely rhetorical, nor are they small-scale efforts to quell dissent through bribing Qataris. The Qatar National Vision (QNV), discussed in detail in Chapter 3, and which informs the Qatar National Development Strategy (QNDS), aims to transform Qatar into a "modern country" by 2030, essentially into a knowledge-based economy built on the investments made possible from its massive inflow of hydrocarbon revenues. These revenues were not automatic; while the North Field was discovered in 1971, there were a series

CONCLUSIONS 371

of key strategic decisions made over the next twenty years that enabled Qatar to break into global LNG markets, beat out existing competitors, and become the world's leading exporter. The result was that from 2004–2011 it had the highest rate of GDP growth in the world at 15.9 % per year, even outstripping China (Ibrahim and Harrigan 2012).

The preceding chapters have explored in detail the policy dimensions of this transformative agenda in education (K-12 and post-secondary), health, urban development, environment, and foreign and strategic policy. We will not revisit those details here, but we will instead draw insights from the chapters along two key dimensions: what they tell us about the policy-making and governance system in Qatar, and what they reveal about the stresses and tensions in implementing this transformative agenda.

*Policy-Making and Governance System*

Most of the normal tools or frameworks instinctively used to analyze policy systems do not easily apply to Qatar. Those frameworks usually assume embedded state institutions and their accompanying processes, a clear configuration of often disparate and large social groupings or classes, and a complex interplay over time between those groupings and those institutions (for example, see Fukuyama 2011; Fukuyama 2014; Mahoney and Thelen 2010; Migdal 1988, 2001; Steinmo et al. 1992; Teichman 2012). Qatar confounds this instinct in several ways. It is small in size and has a native Qatari population of only about 300,000. As discussed in Chapter 10, the overall population has exploded in recent years: in 1970 the total was barely over 100,000, with only 40,000 Qataris. This means that the scope or ambit of decision-making is extraordinarily narrow. Qatar never developed a strong merchant class (Crystal 1995), and so it has no strongly embedded social groupings or classes to oppose the ruling family, not even religious ones since the Qataris are overwhelmingly Sunni. The Al-Thani ruling family has been in place since 1868, and despite some turbulence over succession with soft coups by Sheikh Khalifa over Sheikh Ahmad in 1972, and Sheikh Hamad over Khalifa in 1995, it enjoyed stability with Sheikh Hamad from 1995 to 2013; and there was an orderly succession to his son, the current Emir Tamim. The Constitution came into effect only in 2005, and while it provides the scaffolding of a rule of law and institutional procedure, is still clearly a work-in-progress and overshadowed by the emir's executive powers and decisions, as Chapter 2 points out in detail.

This is not to deny the importance of history in understanding Qatar, but history in its case is not as clearly congealed in institutions, practices, or social structures as it is in other countries. The policy process in Qatar, as well as its institutions, is more fluid. It has a variable and fluctuating architecture that responds to and reflects immediate pressures and rolling policy priorities. Its institutional lava is still cooling. In this we agree with Kamrava: "Even by the highly personalized standards of political systems in the Arabian Peninsula, despite a proliferation of institutions in recent decades, the Qatari system stands out for its comparative lack of institutional depth and continued centrality of individual personalities as the founts of power" (Kamrava 2013: 122). Understanding this, as well as the newness of the system-independence came only in 1971—is an important backdrop to the insights that emerge from the preceding chapters.

Perhaps the key insight is that there is less one, single policy-making system in Qatar than a series of overlapping and loosely connected systems and sub-systems. This is of course true of any state (Migdal 1997), but particularly so in Qatar's case. Figure 14.1 presents a stylized map of the different players, institutions, and processes that comprise the policy-making system in Qatar. The system consists of three, interconnected but relatively distinct and sometimes autonomous levels. The first is the sphere of the ruling family, the Al-Thanis, and it is characterized primarily by the exercise of personal power through family and other immediate connections (see Kamrava 2013: 122). Of course, a good part of this power—particularly for the emir—is framed through the Constitution, so it is not purely personal or clientelistic. But as we saw in Chapters 1 and 2, the Constitution provides the emir with an extremely wide range of discretionary powers. At the center of the family sphere is the emir himself, the father emir, their wives and children, and immediate relatives. A second group consists of powerful technocrats in senior positions in key public agencies, along with key ministers and the prime minister. A third segment of the family dominates the oil and gas sector, state-owned enterprises, and the sovereign wealth funds. We include the Qatar Foundation here because of the scope of its formal activities in both education and foreign policy, but of course it is headed by Sheikha Moza, the second wife of the Father Emir. A fourth segment is active in real estate and other private sector developments. The figure depicts them as separate sub-spheres, but they overlap and are all embraced within the immediate Al-Thani family and other close leading families (Fromherz 2012:Chapter 8; Herb 1999: 109–126; Kamrava 2009).

CONCLUSIONS 373

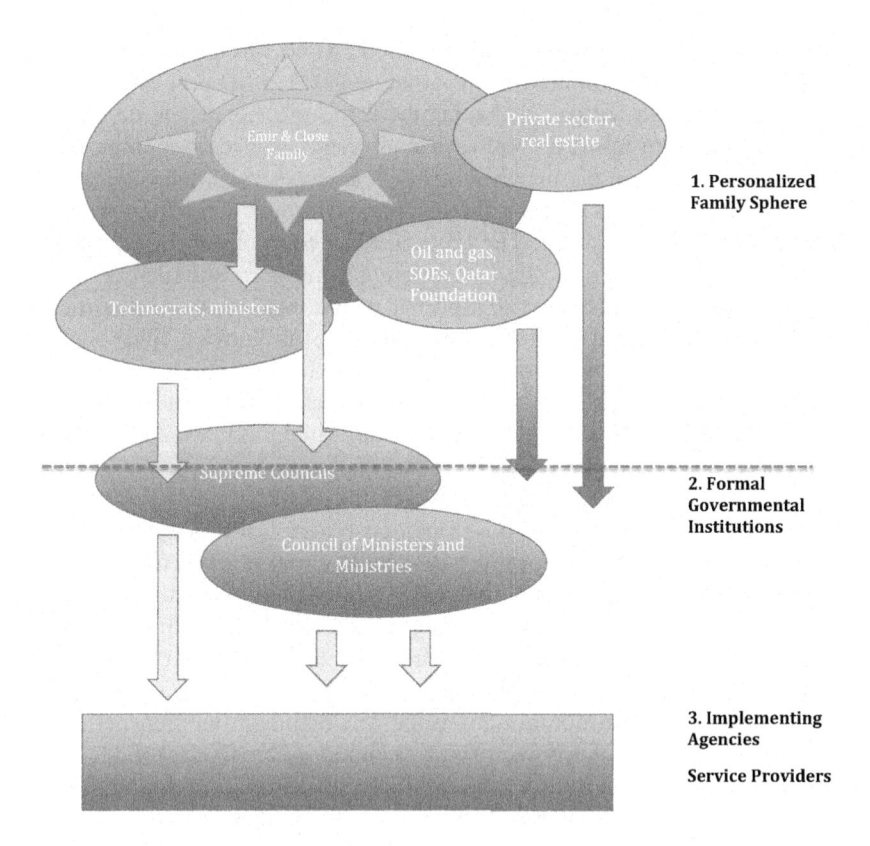

**Fig. 14.1** Qatar Policy-Making System

[Diagram labels: Emir & Close Family; Private sector, real estate; Oil and gas, SOEs, Qatar Foundation; Technocrats, ministers; Supreme Councils; Council of Ministers and Ministries. Right-side legend: 1. Personalized Family Sphere; 2. Formal Governmental Institutions; 3. Implementing Agencies / Service Providers]

The exercise of power within this family sphere is personalized and largely private. The Emir and immediate family are at the center, and Sheikh Hamad was astute in cementing both his informal and formal powers as Emir, not least in giving key roles in the management of the state to his son Tamim as Crown Prince, his wife Sheikha Moza, and his daughter Sheikha Al-Mayassa bint Hamad bin Khalifa Al-Thani (chairperson of Qatar Museums, the Doha Film Institute, and Reach Out to Asia). Key positions in various sectors, public and quasi-private, are appointed at the discretion of the Emir, but the Arab tradition of ruling families and tribes is less hierarchical and more dispersed than the Western tradition, so in this sense the ruling family and the Emir, while certainly pre-eminent, do not completely dominate. As Fromherz (2012: 131) points out, "The Emir continues to answer to his family. Although technically he has the ability to appoint ministers and review government decisions, some ministries function as miniature fiefdoms." This helps explain an observation from various chapters that the Qatari policy system is simultaneously centralized and de-centralized. The centralization comes from the power and centrality of the Emir and his immediate entourage, while the decentralization arises from the separate power base and legitimacy of other members of the Al-Thani tribe and other distinct, leading tribes. What is most important to note from a policy perspective is that key decisions are made within this level or sphere, and they consequently drive the system as a whole. The decision to launch the QNV and the QNDS were the Emir's; key decisions about the Qatar Foundation, Education City, and cultural institutions were made by Sheikha Moza and Sheikha Al-Mayassa. Close, senior family members have positions that bridge institutions and consequently allow them to be decision-makers in a variety of sectors. Perhaps one of the best illustrations of this is HH Abdullah bin Hamad Al-Attiyah. From 1992 to 2011 he was the Minister of Energy and Industry (which in 1999 assumed responsibility for electricity and water), but for a period from 2007 to 2011, he was simultaneously a director of Qatar Petroleum and Gulf Airways Corporation, as well as the deputy prime minister.

Various arrows point down from this family sphere to a second level of formal governmental institutions, including the key ones prescribed in the Constitution. The actual flows—the rivulets and eddies—of power are difficult to capture in a single graphic, but a key point is that the power flows down, it does not flow up from the formal institutions, let alone from popular or civic power through those institutions. In addition to the formal constitutional authorities in the council and ministries, several chapters have noted the use of Supreme Councils, most notably in health and education. Figure 14.1 has a dashed line through the Supreme Councils because they sit astride the personalized family sphere and the formal governmental institutional sphere. They can be seen as "super-ministries" in that they assemble ministers and other key decision-makers under the leadership of a member of the ruling family, combining both formal and informal powers, supercharging them to drive the policy sector.

The third sector or sphere consists of implementing agencies, service providers, private sector partners, and some civil society organizations. They are too numerous to list in the figure, but as every chapter has shown, they are essential to understanding the dynamics of policy-making in Qatar. Chapters 4 and 5 highlighted the role of private schools, international universities, Qatar University, community colleges, and even the role of the media in reflecting public discontent with some of the reforms. Chapter 6 showed the role of private developers (though these are connected with leading families) in implementing (or not) the detailed provisions of the Qatar National Master Plan. An even more arresting example is in the health care field, with the Supreme Council on Health (SCH) launching and managing a National Health Strategy in cooperation with a host of health professional associations, private hospitals, the Hamad Medical Corporation, and employers. It is precisely these types of bodies and implementation mechanisms that are leading the transformation agenda (though as of early 2016 the Supreme Councils were disbanded in favour of Ministry control). Concentrating exclusively on the personalized family sphere, and the ruling family in particular, leads to the almost total omission of the modern machinery of state that has to be created and mobilized in order for the transformative agenda to become real. And these are not merely transmission belts—they have to harness resources and capacities in order to deal with technically complex issues like urban transportation, medical care, environmental regulation, or water and food supplies. Doing all these things requires decision-making at the highest levels of the state, and in Qatar's case, the ruling family—and these clearly cannot and should not be ignored. However, it also demands serious calibration of institutional and administrative capacities.

While stylized, Fig. 14.1 helps us diagnose some of the governance and policy-making challenges that are discussed in various chapters in this book. At a macro-level, there is the problem of balancing the three sectors and the tensions within them. For example, excessive dominance by the Emir, his immediate family members, or indeed of the ruling family itself would risk overwhelming and alienating the necessary expertise to run and deliver complex social services. There is also the challenge of maintaining harmony among the various leading families or tribes. The Al-Thanis, and in particular Sheikh Hamad when he was Emir, have been relatively successful to date in both. There has been strong personalistic leadership as noted above in cases like the Qatar Foundation and the Qatar Museums, but the overall development process and associated institutions have been managed competently, and indeed professionals in every key sphere have been given their due weight. More troubling has been the habit of using ad hoc Supreme Council-type mechanisms to drive the policy process. These have worked—particularly in the case of the Supreme Health Council, as seen in Chapter 7—but they reinforce the impotence of the Council of Ministers and the constitutional role of formal institutions. Also, the habit of relying on familial authority, even if it is harnessed to a formal governmental ministerial position, means that legitimacy continues to be centered on family connections and not on constitutional responsibilities. Of course, those constitutional responsibilities would be buttressed if they flowed from some sort of popular mandate. In the absence of that, the real source of power and legitimacy in the Qatar system will continue to be the ruling family and the Emir himself. An example of where this can lead is the FIFA World Cup bid. It seems from evidence presented in Chapter 3 that the idea for the bid came from the Emir, as has the broader enthusiasm for positioning Qatar as a center for international sports competitions. But winning the bid for the FIFA World Cup in 2022 effectively overshadows and to some degree sidelines the QNDS. FIFA demands major construction projects: arenas, hotels, and transportation infrastructure, not to mention unknown cultural and logistical challenges in accommodating international, beer-thirsty soccer fans in a devout Muslim nation.

We will return to this theme in discussing rentier state theory at the end of this chapter, but clearly this institutional challenge is reminiscent of Huntington's classic discussion of the "King's Dilemma," citing the cases of the traditional monarchies (as they were then) of Morocco, Iran, Ethiopia, Libya, Afghanistan, Saudi Arabia, Cambodia, Nepal, Kuwait, and Thailand (Huntington 1968: 177–191): "On the one hand, centralization of power in the monarchy was necessary to promote social, cultural, and economic reform. On the other hand, this centralization made difficult or impossible the expansion of the power of the traditional polity and the assimilation into it of the new groups produced by modernization. The participation of these groups in politics seemingly could come only at the price of the monarchy" (Huntington 1968: 177). For Huntington, the essential problem was the "relation between traditional and modern authority," and this is certainly inscribed in the tension between the effective machinery of state (Council of Ministers, ministries, and agencies) and monarchial and ruling family/tribal authority. It makes itself evident in the paradox of centralization/decentralization discussed in various chapters—power is very much centralized in the Emir Diwan and the ruling family, but because power is personalized in family and tribe, it is also fragmented and decentralized through key ministries and agencies, depending on which leading figure happens to be in charge. Centrifugal forces have been kept in check through three mechanisms: (1) despite the existence of other tribes, relative harmony among them and obeisance to the Al-Thanis, (2) the personal dominance and leadership of the Father Emir when he was in power, and (3) sufficient wealth or "rents" to avoid internal competition over resources. So far, the internal coherence and small size of the native Qatari population has simply not generated the oppositional forces that Huntington assumed would accompany significant modernization. We return to these issues below; for the time being, what other features of the policy-making system are observed in our chapters? We can highlight three: capacity, implementation, and public engagement.

Most of our chapters revealed that the ambitions of a transformative agenda have strained the capacity of the state to both plan sectoral agendas and to carry them through. The major exception has been the oil and gas sector (see Chapter 3), and even then it is an exception only because it has been assiduously developed through extensive cooperation with international oil and gas companies since the early 1970s. In its early days, the sector depended on international advice and on consultants, a pattern that our chapters repeatedly confirmed, from economic development planning to health care. The RAND-Qatar Policy Institute was particularly important in the health and education sectors, as well as in recommending the architecture of a national economic planning secretariat. Its ten-year agreement with the Qatar government (2003–2013) was not renewed, in part because of muted complaints that it had unduly influenced policy decisions, sometimes—as with the K-12 reforms discussed in Chapter 4—with unpopular results. Capacity was an issue in establishing the General Secretariat for Development Planning (GSDP), as Chapter 3 showed, and it continues to be in the next phase of the QNDS. Indeed, the QNDS itself addressed the public sector administrative capacity as a focus for development of a modern Qatari state. The scope and intensity of the transformational agenda in almost every sector, from health to food security, requires capacity. International consultants helped in the early, development phase through the 2000s, but ultimately, the training and educational initiatives discussed in Chapter 5 are intended to develop the necessary expertise among Qataris themselves.

Implementation is linked to capacity and the mobilization of necessary expertise, but it is distinct in that it is about the actual fulfillment of plans, the organizational mobilization of capacity through oversight and compliance. The chapters show repeated weaknesses here as well. They start at the top with the lack of oversight and coordination through the General

Secretariat for the Council of Ministers, basically a cabinet-office type of institution. For the QNDS, the GSDP was the oversight and coordinating agency for the first phase of the plan, but it was weakened in the 2013 government re-organization under the new Emir. Chapter 6 showed the fragmentation in the urban development sector, partly as the model moved to embrace PPPs and away from a central planning approach to a more case-by-case approach. For example, initial plans for an eight-floor limit on buildings in the West Bay area of Doha were abandoned, and large parts of the city are given over to the developers themselves (the Qatar Foundation and its "Education City" is a prime example) to implement zoning and other construction requirements. On the other hand, the hugely complex implementation challenges in developing a modern health care system almost overnight are being addressed successfully. Chapter 7 points out that from 1970 to 2005 the Ministry of Health was responsible both for policy and for some service delivery through its control over the Hamad Medical Corporation. The creation of the national Health Corporation in 2005 and the SCH in 2009 were designed to sharpen the distinction between regulator and service provider. As a signal of the importance of the health care sector, the chapter notes that the chairman of the board of the SCH was the crown prince, and when he became Emir the role was assumed by the Prime Minister, Sheikh Abdullah bin Nasser bin Khalifa Al-Thani (who is also the Minister of the Interior). Until 2014, the vice-chair of the SCH board was Sheikha Moza. Not surprisingly, the chapter notes how effective the SCH has been in pursuing the agenda of health care system transformation. The chapter notes that the SCH has a program management office that provides daily monitoring of the implementation of the National Health Strategy (NHS), which itself is closely coordinated with the full spectrum of stakeholders. The NHS was divided into 35 projects and over 200 measureable outputs, all under dedicated managers overseen by a monthly steering group. Other sectors with reasonable records of implementation are the oil and gas sector, and the variety of state-owned enterprises such as the Qatar Investment Authority, Qatar Holding LLC, Qatari Diar (real estate and development), and Qatar Sports Investment (see Chapter 13). None of these are as rigorously managed or as transparent as the SCH, but their effectiveness can be judged by results.

Other examples would include the post-secondary sector and the development of Education City—the cluster of international institutions described in Chapter 5 is producing graduates, and increasingly Qatari graduates. The chapter describes some setbacks and reversals, but overall the program has moved ahead successfully. In terms of transportation, while traffic in Doha is often a snarl, and famously dangerous with erratic driving, the road system is functional and continues to expand, and it will soon be supplemented by an extensive metro system (underground in the central core around the Souk Waqif, ground-level light rail in the rest). The city has been transformed over the past five years, and by 2022 will be even further transformed and close to "finished." When the initiatives across all these sectors are totaled, whatever their immediate limitations, they constitute significant implementation successes in terms of achieving intentions and delivering services. As Chapter 1 noted in citing the Worldwide Governance Indicators on "government effectiveness," Qatar compares favorably with the OECD average. Everyday life for Qataris and for most expatriate professionals "works," and often works quite well by any reasonable standard.

The bigger issue about implementation is cost-effectiveness. Office towers get built, but remain half-empty. Government services get delivered, but often with what seems like twice or three times the staff that is actually needed, usually because of the drive to "Qatarization" (see Chapter 10). The Western universities in Education City received generous terms (all physical and operational costs covered), and they occupy massive, state-of-the art facilities that would be the envy of any North American dean. But their student bodies are miniscule, ranging from 250 to 450, and graduating classes are often as small as 50 or less. The metro and rail system promises to be a marvel, but given the scattered nature of the urban design discussed in Chapter 6, as well as the Qatari cultural preference for large vehicles and hired drivers as a status symbol, it is unclear what the actual demand will be. These and other examples point to the problem of over-capacity. Some of this is simply due to unavoidable issues of scale—a medical school needs certain basic facilities, whether it has 50 students or 500. But there does seem to be a frenetic appetite in Qatar to build the best, irrespective of initial scale and uptake, possibly reflecting an attitude shaped by almost limitless resources. If one can build the best—even if it is underutilized at first—why not?

A third theme on policy-making and governance that emerges from the chapters is the issue of public engagement. Article 1 of the Constitution states that Qatar's "political system is democratic." Under any conventional definition of democracy, this is a fiction, even with the limited elections to the Central Municipal Council (CMC). However, the engagement of the public can be seen differently in the Arab tribal and Islamic traditions of *majlis* and consultations with leaders, and so the absence of Western style political parties and national parliamentary voting should not be seen as a complete short-circuiting of public feedback. As Lewis (2008: 21) points out: "The notion of consultation as an obligation of the ruler goes back to the advent of Islam; the attempt to organize some sort of apparatus of consultation goes back at least a thousand years in the history of the Turkish people. The practice of consultation and deliberation was already familiar in pre-Islamic Arabia, as is attested by Arabic references to the meetings of bodies, variously called *majlis* and *mala*, as well as in some old South Arabian inscriptions. Two verses in the Qur'ān, Chapter III, 153/159 and XLII, 36/38 are frequently cited as imposing a duty of consultation on rulers" (see also, Al-Mulk 1978; Asad 1961; Moten 1996).

Aside from principle, there is the reality of public reactions to state initiatives. Again, we will take up rentier state theory below, but the classic version of that theory assumes a passive populace, bought off by the rulers. Several chapters in this book cast doubt on this, and they show both strong public reactions in some cases, such as the K-12 reforms (Chapter 4), the post-secondary reforms (Chapter 5), as well as reactions and even policy reversals by the authorities. Chapter 9 on identity issues reveals the internal debate among young Qataris on social as well as conventional media about tradition and culture. In health care, the SCH has been assiduous in engaging stakeholders in both policy design and in implementation, and gauging levels of satisfaction and making necessary corrections in service levels, for example. Indeed, ordinary life in Doha is similar in the routine public-private interfaces that take place on a daily basis in any advanced country: posters in shopping centers remind customers of their rights and obligations when they make purchases; street signs encourage water and energy conservation as well as safe driving; newspapers have their community activity sections announcing charitable and other public events. This is not democratic engagement in the conventional sense of routinized stakeholder consultation, but it shows a wide range and variety of interactions among individuals, families, and civil society organizations and the state. Again, the smallness of Qatar and the effective concentration of almost the entire population in the city of Doha makes that level of interaction and engagement more feasible. But what it suggests is that a seriously *service-oriented* rentier state can operate and behave in ways that engage the citizenry as *consumers* of services, and if it is willing to accommodate customer dissatisfaction and respond to it, it can have a level of interaction with the population that is not democratic in a political sense, but responsive in a service sense. This may be more than enough to ensure stability, coupled with sufficient employment opportunities and reasonable (in Qatar's case, high) personal and family incomes.

*Stresses and Tensions*

Before discussing the pressures that Qatar's transformative agenda has created, we should acknowledge its successes. Despite the problems of capacity and implementation in the policy-making system, and the concentrations and dispersion of power due to the attempt to graft a tribal, personalized monarchial system to a modern state bureaucracy, Qatar has enjoyed remarkably astute leadership and intelligent policy design. It won nature's lottery in discovering the North Field, but it had to make difficult, strategic decisions over twenty years to profitably exploit the resource and leverage its benefits into growth, not only directly in LNG exports but in petrochemical feedstock. It was lucky once again when its production came on stream during a prolonged period of high oil prices, yielding almost unimaginable levels of revenue. But again, it astutely invested those revenues through its sovereign wealth fund and in domestic investments guided by the QNV and the QNDS. As we pointed out at the beginning of this chapter, Qatar is perhaps uniquely positioned with respect to its transformative agenda in that in pursuing that agenda it did not require the imposition of dramatic losses or social dislocation on its population. Indeed, given its small population and the starting point for its economy and society, the transformative agenda has involved almost exclusively an *increase in benefits and in services* to the native Qatari population. To this point, for Qataris, "transformation" in the material sense (incomes, jobs, housing), and in the sense of government services and other benefits, has been almost entirely about improvements, not surprisingly since Qataris enjoy the highest per capita GDP on the planet. Chapters in this book have highlighted these achievements: a health care system that currently—before continued improvements and development—compares favorably with the best in the world; effectively a zero-unemployment rate; access to some of the world's best universities; a positive (barring the fall-out from FIFA scandals) international "brand;" and stability and security in a very troubled and turbulent neighborhood both in the Gulf and the Middle East.

Nonetheless, these accomplishments have produced stresses and tensions, and not every policy initiative has been entirely successful. Some of the causes for this lie with the policy system itself—we noted the problems of coordination, fragmentation, implementation, and capacity. Fortunately, there do not appear to be internecine struggles within the Al-Thanis or with other leading families, and the leadership of both Hamad and now Tamim as Emir has been steady. But we noted some of the liabilities of personalized and familial power, as well as the somewhat surprising FIFA bid, and some of the extravagances of the educational and cultural sector reflect that. Nonetheless, in standing back and reviewing the chapters, there are some policy initiatives that have not worked well, and others which, while we have characterized them as successes, still have problematic aspects:

- K-12 education: The "Education for a New Era" initiative (Chapter 4) was clearly flawed and as a result the reform policies were reversed. A voucher system gives parents the flexibility to choose the best (and often expensive) forms of private education for their children, though there is no evidence that all private schools in Qatar provide high quality education. Normally those schools that are known for their excellent record, such as Qatar Academy, the Sherborne, or the American school, get filled quickly and have long waiting lists.
- Post-secondary education: This is in many respects a major success, but Chapter 5 showed some of the problems with the Education City model and the implementation of high admission standards. These were addressed by revisions to the mandate and operations of Qatar University and the introduction of a community college system, but questions remain about the effective channeling of students from the K-12 system into post-secondary institutions.
- Urban development: Doha's futuristic cluster of gleaming office towers in West Bay has become, along with the Corniche and the Museum of Islamic Art, the city's signature. To these will be added other cultural institutions such as the National Museum, the Orientalist Museum, and the Olympic and Sports Museum. But as Chapter 6 pointed out, the city is developing along radial lines of dispersed clusters of shopping centers and attractions with little connection to each other. Builders have been given discretion to manage their own projects, leaving regulatory gaps. Also, some projects such as the Pearl or Katara Village are underutilized by the locals, and it

CONCLUSIONS 383

is unclear to how they will attract an external audience of visitors or tenants.
- Identity and heritage: One of the key pressures and stresses that has been produced by Qatar's rapid transformation is in the sense of national identity and culture in the face of rapid modernization, and the policy response described in Chapter 9 has been mixed. Some of it entails inventing an ersatz "history" through restoration projects of mosques, forts, souks, and other "heritage" sites. These do not always align well with modernist aspirations and characterizations, as in West Bay or the Pearl. The National Museum will, when it opens, try to square the circle by giving voice to history while celebrating the future. In all these efforts, there is a subtle and sometimes not-so-subtle celebration of the ruling family. Layered on top of these efforts is the mania for international sporting events, to be crowned by the FIFA World Cup in 2022. Casual observation shows that Qataris are not particularly sports-minded or especially interested in athletics, so this "branding" exercise seems to float without any strong social moorings. Chapter 9 suggests that there may be better prospects for the revival of "traditional" sports through developing national competitions, giving the examples of the Fourth Traditional Dhow Festival (November 2014); the Sixth Qatar International Falcon Hunting Festival (January 2015); the Annual Arabian Camel Festival (January–February 2015); the H.H. The Emir 24th International Equestrian Sword Festival (February 2015); and the Senyar (Marine) Championship (April 2015).
- Labor market policies: The two key policies in this field are Qatarization and the *kafala* system of managing the expatriate work force. Chapter 10 revealed the success of the first in providing employment for Qataris in the public sector, but its failure to stimulate employment in the private sector. That failure is partly due to the absence of opportunities, since the private sector (outside of the petroleum and related industries) is small. But Qataris are not interested in service occupations, and to date employment in the public sector has been more attractive. This has led to odd outcomes: overemployment in public services and especially in clerical and support positions in the public service; formal positions occupied by Qataris while expatriates are actually doing the work; and high instances of absenteeism or underperformance since Qataris are rarely fired. This is changing in the face of new economies due to lower oil prices and

revenues, and greater pressure on performance, but it remains a problem. The *kafala* system is not unique to Qatar, and it is used by other GCC states. Nonetheless, it has attracted international criticism from human rights organizations and Western media (e.g., Britain's *The Guardian* ran a series in 2014–2015 on Qatar's "modern slavery"). While migrant workers voluntarily sign contracts and earn incomes that are important sources of remittances for their home countries, there are instances of abuse by employers, and worker mobility and other rights are tightly constrained.

- Food and water security: The water consumption of Qataris exceeds the available renewable resources that exist in their country, and so is their consumption of food since Qatar imports 80–90 % of its needs from abroad. Although Qatar started a unique attempt to develop an integrative management framework of water and food resources, as indicated in Chapter 11, there is no evidence that such a framework is being implemented. In fact, there is ambiguity surrounding the Qatar National Food Security Program (QNFSP) which was mandated in 2008 by the Emir to develop a food security plan and oversee its implementation. Contradictory media reports in 2014 talked about trimming QNFSP due to budget constraints while they highlighted the changing and inconsistent targets and objectives that the entity had been announcing (Scott 13, February 2014). Around the same time, the QNFSP's Chairman Fahad Al-Attiya stepped down, leaving speculations about the reasons as well as the future of the Food Security Strategy. QNFSP is keeping a very low profile, if it even exists anymore, and there is almost no official mention of the strategy. After the cabinet reshuffle in 2013, the Ministry of Environment apparently inherited agricultural affairs under a department with the same name, while Hassad continues its investments in agricultural lands outside Qatar to secure more sustainable food resources. As for water security, there are increasingly more visible public awareness campaigns about restraining consumption, but no significant policy changes can be observed in this regard.
- Foreign policy and branding: Analysts and international observers usually hail Qatar's foreign policy and branding as successes. Chapter 13 takes a more sophisticated look at the "nested" tools at Qatar's disposal and how it has used them deftly on a variety of fronts simultaneously to achieve its strategic objectives. Nonetheless, there have been stumbles. The possible blowback from the FIFA

bribery scandal may be the most visible and damaging—something that was to be the jewel in its international sports-franchise crown may taint the ruling family and the country as corrupt and vainglorious. The adverse publicity around the *kafala* system is entangled with FIFA, since a large number of migrant laborers are in Qatar to build the stadiums, the metro system, and the five-star hotels that will support the Cup. Beyond sports, Qatar took some foreign policy decisions that angered its GCC partners, particularly Saudi Arabia, most notably its support for the Muslim Brotherhood after the Arab Spring and during the Egyptian uprisings and the Morisi government. Hosting Afghani Taliban for several years and allowing them to open an office in Doha, while apparently being supported by the United States as a step toward opening negotiations, struck an odd note in international public opinion.

This is a list of policy failures or at least policy problems—they are shortcomings in deliberate state initiatives in different sectors when trying to implement its transformative agenda. But these failures or shortcomings are both the result of and contributions to the stresses and pressures of transformation itself. We argue that these have been relatively mild when compared to the "high modernist" transformative agendas of the past, but they are not negligible, and indeed if they are not navigated and managed adroitly, they could undermine the modernization project as a whole. Again, our chapters have provided repeated examples of the key stresses and pressures, all in one way or another hinging on the clichéd but real challenge of balancing rapid (almost supersonic) modernization with a society that remains small, and retains its character as tribal, traditional, and Islamic.

- Pathologies of high income (I): As stresses go, this would seem to be a minor one, and probably devoutly wished by anyone not suffering from it. From a policy perspective, however, it poses a major problem of induced lethargy, declining ambition, laziness, and a lack of discipline. In the context of Dubai, for example, Davidson (2008) calls this the "paradox of rentierism," but notes that it was remarked upon by Sheikh Muhammad bin Rashid al-Maktum himself, who complained of the "voluntary unemployment" of young Dubai nationals, where 54 % of nationals receiving social security benefits were of working age. A similar problem was noted by two of the architects of Qatar's QNDS in addressing the question, why rush into diversification of the economy when resource rents were so comfortably high? "[A] strategy focused exclusively on building a financial endowment could foreshadow a future in which income levels are high but in which Qataris' capabilities, creativity, resilience and even 'happiness' are undermined" (Ibrahim and Harrigan 2012: 20).

- Pathologies of high income (II): There are a host of health problems (e.g., diabetes, diet) that typically accompany rapid modernization, and they have been evident in Qatar as well. Add geography and the heat, and these health issues are compounded by lifestyle factors that discourage outdoor activities and exercise.
- Population growth: In 1908, the population of Qatar was estimated to be 27,000, with non-Qataris accounting for about 22 % of the total. Even in 1999, the total population was only slightly over half a million. It now stands at 2.3 million, with only about 300,000 Qataris. There are three aspects to this that have been highlighted in previous chapters: the rapidity of the growth, the imbalance of natives and expatriates, and the gender imbalance with 75 % of the population being male (mostly migrant laborers). This population growth has been at the root of other pressures around housing, services, transportation, and the security of food, water, and energy.
- Qatari women and the Qatari family: The tribe, the family, and the roles of men and women had a coherence and homology with traditional economic and political structures before the resource boom and transformation. Chapter 8 highlighted the policy contortions through the boom as the government has tried to retain key elements of those traditional templates while accommodating and even driving modernity. The extended family has become nuclear; women have become more independent economically; divorce rates have increased; fertility is declining; children are being cared for by foreign domestic workers. Reconciling and balancing these forces is not impossible, but it is challenging, especially when compounded by demographic pressures.
- Resistances: As various chapters noted, despite the relative homogeneity of the Qatari population in terms of Arabic identity and religion, not everyone has been happy with the leadership's transformative agenda. Chapter 9 pointed to the recalcitrance of traditionalists who fear the loss of identity and authenticity in the reflected

glare of shopping malls and consumerism. The Emir and his immediate family are cosmopolitans, and they need to be careful not to go too fast, too far in the modernization project; there have been examples of backpedalling (e.g., the shrouding of a series of artistic statues outside the Sidra Hospital—a maternity hospital—depicting the stages of fetal gestation). On the other hand, again as Chapter 9 suggested, there may be newly created segments in society that are more modern than traditional, and indeed more modern than the ruling family itself. This is a species of the "King's Dilemma" that we will take up in a moment.

- Regional tensions: This is not specific to Qatar or indeed to its transformative agenda, but we should not ignore the geopolitical facts on the ground. Qatar is a GCC state that has to cooperate as well as compete with its partners. Bahrain and Kuwait pose awkward examples of monarchies with more active parliaments and elections; the UAE (particularly Dubai) is both a model and a competitor; Saudi Arabia considers itself the dominant actor in the region, and it is currently engaged in armed conflict in Yemen, just south of Qatar. As an Arab state, Qatar is entangled in the turmoil of the Middle East in Syria and Iraq, and it supported the Muslim Brotherhood when the Brotherhood was considered a pariah by Egypt and Saudi Arabia. As an Islamic nation, it engages with the larger Islamic world, from Pakistan and Afghanistan to Indonesia and Malaysia. It has to calibrate its transformative agenda of modernization against these overlapping and sometimes contradictory backdrops.

Are these policy failures and these stresses and tensions fatal to the transformative project? To date, the record has been quite good by any reasonable standard. There have been no street demonstrations or intra-family struggles (at least in public). The level and quality of basic services (at least for nationals and for the professional class of expatriate workers) are at or above the best in the developed world. The society is wealthy, prosperous, and stable. Though a monarchy, it is a monarchy that has exercised self-restraint and some self-binding through a Constitution and the rule of law, and by regional standards the social atmosphere is comparatively benign. But these might all be superficial impressions. A deeper analysis requires us to ask about the nature of the regime and its underlying logic.

## Qatar: What Kind of "Rentier State" and What Kind of Future?

Given its location, its hydrocarbon wealth, and its monarchy, Qatar typically has been analyzed through the lens of "rentier state theory." As we noted in our discussion in Chapter 1, that theory itself has evolved, and in terms of Qatar has had to come to grips with the nuance of a country that confounds some of the theory's basic assumptions. For that reason, the label of "rentier" is usually qualified in some fashion: "late rentier," or "extreme rentier." Additionally, the political system has been qualified as either "pluralized autocracy" or "soft authoritarian" (Brumberg 2002; Gray 2011, 2013). Indeed, some analysts have suggested that in the case of Qatar (along with Kuwait and the UAE), "gradual adoption of democratic trends, civil society and political culture, coupled with economic prosperity, may allow for democratic consolidations over time" (Gregg 2013: 112). But for others, the continued link between resource rents and authoritarianism seems clear: "The availability of resource rents accruing from abroad strengthens the incumbent's chances to retain power, through either coercion, use of government expenditure to buy off opposition, or simply better opportunities to deliver services and engage in populist policies" (Luciani 2012: 4). Some analysts have predicted the collapse of all the Gulf monarchies by 2017 (Davidson 2012), while others have suggested, at least for cases like Qatar (high rents) and Dubai (apparently successful transition to a post-hydrocarbon economy), continued stability (Herb 2014). During the turmoil of the Arab Spring, which Kamrava persuasively argues marked the collapse of the "ruling bargains" among most of the Middle East states (Kamrava 2014), Qatar emerged more or less unscathed: "In terms of domestic politics, Qatar seems to have been almost completely unaffected by the Arab Spring. Public protests against the regime, or even specific government policies, have been conspicuously absent. The expression of dissent online has also been muted when compared to the rest of the Arab world" (Lucas 2014: 315). In assessing political risk in the MENA region (based on GDP per capita and proportion of youth in the population and youth unemployment), Qatar serves as a "shining example" of low-risk, "due to its all-but-nonexistent unemployment, record GDP per capita, and phenomenal reserves" (Farha 2015: 55).

Each rentier state needs to be assessed separately and empirically (Al-Azoby and Baskan 2014), and the Gulf monarchies differ in sometimes dramatic ways—Bahrain is only 40 kilometers from Qatar, but a world away in terms of political and economic instability (Gengler 2015). We have noted some of the key distinguishing features of the Qatari state system and economy above, and we need on just highlight them again here. *First*, the state and its native population are small. *Second*, it sits atop a massive resource endowment of natural gas (and more modest amounts of oil) that it has astutely developed. *Third*, while there are several tribes and leading families, the Al-Thanis have firm prominence and control, especially since the consolidation of power under Hamad when he was emir (1995–2013). Family and tribal relations have to be managed, but they do not appear to pose regime challenges. *Fourth*, there are no competing centers of power in the military or the security apparatus, as was characteristic of many of the MENA regimes that were shocked by the Arab Spring. *Fifth*, and to some extent based on these features, Qatar seems able to escape Huntington's "King's Dilemma." The essence of the dilemma was that modernization was implacable and unavoidable, and a monarch who supports and champions it will inevitably create new interests ("modern" ones that Huntington implied would be materialistic and egalitarian) that will ultimately challenge the sovereign. The chances of transitioning to constitutional monarchies were slim, but Huntington argued that continuing to actively rule while modernizing was unlikely as well, again assuming the creation of new groups and interests aligned with a modernizing agenda ("upwardly mobile individuals" as he put it). One strategy is to assimilate these groups into the centralized, modernizing bureaucracy, but Huntington thought that the "ability of the traditional monarchy to reduce discontent through this process of individual absorption declines, however, as modernization progresses" (Huntington 1968: 186). Importantly, he did qualify this conclusion by noting that the Middle East monarchies had a higher absorptive capacity because they were more "fluidly endowed." And so we come back again to the rentier bargain, and in the case of Qatar, the ability to make good on that bargain simply because of resource endowments that eclipse those of any of the other GCC states (even Saudi Arabia, on a per capita basis). And this in turn brings us back to rentier state theory, but we know from the chapters in this book that Qatar's situation is not simply one of a "ruling bargain" based on mountains of money. So, to the preceding five characteristics we would add, in continuing numerical order, five more.

The *sixth* feature of Qatar is that its social, religious, and cultural configuration seems capable of balancing modernization and tradition, and, with tradition, the active role of the Emir and the ruling family. Huntington assumed that modernization would corrode traditionalism and thereby undermine the legitimacy of a traditional and active monarch. As various chapters in this book on the family and on Qatari identity demonstrated, while transformative and modernizing forces have been turbulent and challenging, they have not dissolved tradition or religion. Moreover, the ruling family has been astute in building up "tradition" and its own place in that tradition. The *seventh* feature is the ruling family itself, and in particular the leadership of the Hamad when he was Emir. "Modern" Qatar merged under his leadership, and the strategic decisions around developing the country's gas reserves and launching the QNV and the QNDS were his. Social science rightly avoids hagiography, but there are rare cases when leadership is decisive in public affairs. This is one of them. Emir Tamim seems to have inherited his father's strategic abilities, and the Father Emir Hamad remains very much on the scene.

An *eighth* feature, not completely unique to Qatar (Dubai demonstrates it as well), is an extraordinary openness to adopting best practices and leading models in public services, and to subject Qatari policy and institutions to rigorous international standards. Our chapters have shown those instances where Qatar has fallen short, either because of design or implementation, but the ambitions are there—in health and education, in transportation and urban design, and even in foreign policy. The injunction that "Qatar Deserves the Best," of course, is grounded in the resources that can purchase the best, but the results are clear in a host of policy sectors. To date, the design and implementation of these best practices and models have relied on external consultants and highly trained expatriates, but they gradually may be taken over by educated Qataris themselves.

The *ninth* feature is the depth, detail, and scope of the modernization agenda itself – what we have called the transformative agenda. Huntington assumed that "modernization" had to be disruptive of tradition, so it would simultaneously create traditionalist resistance and new, demanding social groups. Qataris have expressed dissatisfaction with some aspects of the agenda, particularly education reform, but on the whole, modernization in the Qatari context has meant employment, higher incomes, material wealth, and some of the best public services in the world. And this transformative agenda is fully committed to an economic transformation to a post-hydrocarbon, knowledge-based economy. As Chapter 12 argued, this poses enormous challenges, particularly with limited macroeconomic policy instruments, but it is not impossible. In this respect, Qatar has some advantages over its rival Dubai, which more or less accomplished that transition earlier. A final, *tenth* feature of Qatar is the regime's adaptability. We saw how, when confronted with resistance by Qataris over educational reforms, the regime adapted those reforms, introducing new provisions regarding Arabic instruction and new institutions like community colleges. It has taken modest steps in the direction of elections for the CMC, with the participation of women not only in those elections but in leadership positions in key institutions. The leadership is not blind—they are familiar with rentier state theory, can see the turmoil in other Gulf states, and are well aware that the oil and gas will eventually run out, or that at the very least, anything past the next thirty years is unpredictable.

These ten characteristics comprise a distinct country profile and help us understand Qatar's governance system and the transformative policy agenda that it has pursued for the past 15 years. That agenda continues—the destination is a "modern country" by 2030. It faces both internal challenges of public sector capacity that we have mentioned earlier, regional tensions and turbulence, water-food-energy challenges, and of course low oil and gas prices. For the first time in 15 years, Qatar is expecting a deficit in 2016 (Arabian Business 2015). This may be the first distant thunder of possible financial resource constraints that have been completely absent for the past two decades. To this point, anything and everything has been possible. The question now is whether what has been accomplished, built, and provided in the form of services and lifestyle is sustainable and will continue paving its way toward a post-hydrocarbon, knowledge-based economy.

### Bibliography. Qatar: Policy Making in a Transformative State

Al-Azoby, Mazhar, and Birol Baskan. 2014. State-society relations in the Arab Gulf region: Dilemmas and prospects. In *State-Society Relations in the Arab Gulf States*, eds. Mazhar Al-Azoby and Birol Baskan, 1–12. Berlin: Gerlach Press.

Al-Mulk, Nizam. 1978. *The Book of Government or Rules for Kings: The Siyar al-Muluk or Siyasat-nama of Nizam Al-Mulk*. Translated by Hubert Darke. 2nd ed. London: Routledge and Kegan Paul.

Arabian Business. 2015. Qatar expects budget deficit in 2016. *Arabian Business. com*. Retrieved from http://www.arabianbusiness.com/qatar-expects-budget-deficit-in-2016-595518.html, June 9.

Asad, Muhammad. 1961. *The Principles of State and Government in Islam*. Berkeley, CA: University of California Press.

Brumberg, Daniel. 2002. "Democratization in the Arab World? The trap of liberalized autocracy." *Journal of Democracy* 13 (4):56-68.
Cooper, Andrew F., and Bessma Momani. 2011. Qatar and the expanded contours of small state diplomacy. *International Spectator* 46(2): 127–142.
Cooper, Andrew F., and Timothy M. Shaw. 2009. Diplomacy of small states at the start of the twenty-first century: How vulnerable? How resilient? In *The Diplomacies of Small States: Between Vulnerability and Resilience*, eds. Andrew F. Cooper and Timothy M. Shaw, 1–18. Houndmills, Basingstoke: Palgrave Macmillan.
Crystal, Jill. 1995. *Oil and Politics in the Gulf: Rulers and Merchants in Kuwait and Qatar*, Rev. edn. Cambridge: Cambridge University Press.
Davidson, Christopher M. 2008. *Dubai: The Vulnerability of Success*. New York: Columbia University Press.
Davidson, Christopher M. 2012. *After the Sheikhs: The Coming Collapse of the Gulf Monarchies*. London: Hurst and Company.
Farha, Mark. 2015. The Arab revolts: Local, regional, and global catalysts and consequences. In *The Arab Uprisings: Catalysts, Dynamics, and Trajectories*, eds. Fahed Al-Sumait, Nele Lenze, and Michael C. Hudson, 47–68. London: Rowman and Littlefield.
Fromherz, Allen J. 2012. *Qatar: A Modern History*. London: I.B. Tauris.
Fukuyama, Francis. 2011. *The Origins of Political Order: From Prehuman Times to the French Revolution*, vol 1. New York: Farrar, Straus and Giroux.
———. 2014. *Political Order and Political Decay: From the Industrial Revolution to the Globalization of Democracy*, vol 2. New York: Farrar, Straus and Giroux.
Gengler, Justin. 2015. *Group Conflict and Political Mobilization in Bahrain and the Arab Gulf: Rethinking the Rentier State*. Bloomington, IN: Indiana University Press.
Gray, Matthew. 2011. *A Theory of "Late Rentierism" in the Arab States of the Gulf*. Doha, Qatar: Occasional Paper No. 7. Center for International and Regional Studies. Georgetown University School of Foreign Service in Qatar.
———. 2013. *Qatar: Politics and the Challenges of Development*. Boulder, CO: Lynne Rienner Publishers.
Gregg, Heather S. 2013. The prospects for democratization in the Middle East. In *Governance in the Middle East and North Africa: A Handbook*, ed. Abbas Kadhim, 112–132. London: Routledge.
Herb, Michael. 1999. *All in the Family: Absolutism, Revolution, and Democracy in the Middle East Monarchies*. Albany, NY: State University of New York.
———. 2014. *The Wages of Oil: Parliaments and Economic Development in Kuwait and the UAE*. Ithaca, NY: Cornell University Press.
Huntington, Samuel P. 1968. *Political Order in Changing Societies*. New Haven: Yale University Press.
Ibrahim, Ibrahim, and Frank Harrigan. 2012. Qatar's economy: Past, present and future. *QScience Connect* 9: 1–24.

Kamrava, Mehran. 2009. Royal factionalism and political liberalization in Qatar. *Middle East Journal* 63(3): 401–420.
———. 2013. *Qatar: Small State, Big Politics*. Ithaca, NY: Cornell University Press.
———. 2014. The rise and fall of ruling bargains in the Middle East. In *Beyond the Arab Spring: The Evolving Ruling Bargain in the Middle East*, ed. Mehran Kamrava, 17–45. London: Hurst and Company and Centre for International and Regional Studies, School of Foreign Service in Qatar, Georgetown University.
Lerner, Daniel. 1958. *The Passing of Traditional Society: Modernizing the Middle East*. New York: The Free Press.
Lewis, Bernard. 2008. *Political Words and Ideas in Islam*. Princeton, NJ: Markus Wiener Publishers.
Lucas, Russell E. 2014. The Persian Gulf monarchies and the Arab Spring. In *Beyond the Arab Spring: The Evolving Ruling Bargain in the Middle East*, ed. Mehran Kamrava, 313–340. London: Hurst and Company and Centre for International and Regional Studies, School of Foreign Service in Qatar, Georgetown University.
Luciani, Giacomo. 2012. Introduction: The resource curse and the Gulf development challenges. In *Resources Blessed: Diversification and the Gulf Development Model*, ed. Giacomo Luciani, 1–28. Berlin: Gerlach Press.
Mahoney, James, and Kathleen Thelen, eds. 2010. *Explaining Institutional Change: Ambiguity, Agency, and Power*. Cambridge: Cambridge University Press.
Migdal, Joel S. 1988. *Strong Societies and Weak States: State-Society Relations and State Capabilities in the Third World*. Princeton, NJ: Princeton University Press.
Migdal, Joel S. 1997. Studying the state. In *Comparative Politics: Rationality, Culture, and Structure*, eds. Mark Irving Lichbach, and Alan S. Zuckerman, 208–235. Cambridge: Cambridge University Press.
——— 2001. *State in Society: Studying How States and Societies Transform and Constitute Each Other*. Cambridge: Cambridge University Press.
Moten, Abdul Rashid. 1996. *Political Science: An Islamic Perspective*. London: Macmillan Press.
Scott, James C 1998. *Seeing Like a State: How Certain Schemes to Improve the Human Condition Have Failed*. New Haven: Yale University Press.
Steinmo, Sven, Kathleen Thelen, and Frank Longstreith, eds. 1992. *Structuring Politics: Historical Institutionalism in Comparative Analysis*. Cambridge: Cambridge University Press.
Teichman, Judith A. 2012. *Social Forces and States: Poverty and Distributional Outcomes in South Korea, Chile, and Mexico*. Stanford, CA: Stanford University Press.

# INDEX

**A**
Abdullah bin Jassim Al-Thani, 6
absolute monarchy, 38
Adjudication of Constitutional
 Disputes, 55, 57
Administrative Dispute Adjudication,
 55, 57
administrative justice system, 57–9
Al-Band Al-Markazi, 105
Al-Hajri, Hamad, 226–7
Ali bin Abdullah Al-Thani, 5
Al Jazeera, 161, 163, 243, 244, 357, 358
Al-Rayyan TV, 257–61
*Al-Taqweem Al-Mustamir Lil-Talib*,
 119
Al-Thanis
 Abdullah bin Jassim Al-Thani, 6
 Ali bin Abdullah Al-Thani, 5
 Hamad bin Khalifa Al-Thani, 78,
  136, 158, 162, 220, 350
 Jassim bin Mohammed bin
  Al-Thani, 252
 Khalifa bin Hamad Al-Thani, 6, 44,
  98, 243, 263
 Tamim bin Hamad Al-Thani, 3, 84,
  249, 251, 297, 306

Amended Provisional Basic Law, 42
Arab Human Development Report
 2005 (AHDR), 228
Arab nationalism, 241, 242
Arab Spring, 2, 19, 65, 86, 333, 385,
 389
 Qatar's rile in, 68, 388
*arda*, 215
Aspire Park, 171

**B**
Basic Law (1970). *See* constitutional
 and legal system, Basic Law
Boston Consulting Group, 299
British protectorate agreement, 4, 5

**C**
Cassation Court, 55
Central Municipal Council (CMC), 7,
 380, 391
Central Planning Organisation (CPO),
 174
charter educational system, 112–13
childcare, 233–4

© The Author(s) 2016
M.E. Tok et al. (eds.), *Policy-Making in a Transformative State*,
DOI 10.1057/978-1-137-46639-6

395

China National Offshore Oil Company (CNOOC), 371, 372
citizenship *vs.* national identity, 245–8
climate change, 298, 299, 304
CMC. *See* Central Municipal Council (CMC)
CNOOC. *See* China National Offshore Oil Company (CNOOC)
competitive sectors, 291
constitutional and legal system
  Basic Law (1970), Provisional and Amended; Article 37, 45; Article 40, 49; Article 51, 49; Article 67, 54; Article 138, 57; Emir's ratification, 49; family protection by, 216; vs. Permanent Constitution, 54; public participation, 42
  Deputy Ruler, 44–5
  legislative process; administrative justice system, 57–9; constitutional court, 53–7; draft laws, 45–8; official gazette, 50–2; proposal, 44–5; ratification and refusal, 48–50; time needed to promulgate law, 52–3
  monarchy; absolute and limited, 38; Al-Thani family, 37–8; Emir and state public authorities, 39–40; Emir's prerogatives, 40; people participation, 42–4; pro-forma political bodies, 38; Shura Council's prerogatives, 41–2
  Permanent Constitution, 43
  Shura Council (the legislature); Art. 10, 46; Cabinet proposals, 45; committees, 47; discussion of drafts laws, 46; president, 48; ratification, 49
constitutional court, 53–7

context and constitution
  elections, 7
  2004 Law on Private Associations and Foundations, 14
  population imbalance, 7
  powers and articles, 8–9
  public rights and duties, 9
  sponsorship system, 14
  WGI Qatar and MENA, 14, 15
Council of Information and Communication Technology (ictQATAR), 84
culture and sports development, 162
culture of Qatar, 261–6

D
democratic governance, 16–17
demographic imbalance, 224
demographic policy
  challenges, 277–9
  trends, 272–7
Department of Human Rights, 307
Deputy Ruler, 44–5
Diplomatic District in West Bay, 171
divorce rates, 225–6
Doha, global hub in
  culture and sports, 162
  education and science, 162–3
  governance by new form; fragmented organisational structure, 166; legal rights of master developers, 167–8; out-dated plans and policies, 166–7; staff capacity deficits, 165–6
  infrastructure and services, 161
  investments, 156–7
  investment strategies; emerging contrasting typologies, 171–2; fragmented development, 168–9; low building standards,

172–3; privatised urban landscapes, 170–1; urban peripheries predominance, 170
large-scale investments, 173–4
methodological approach, 158
news and media, 163–4
real estate investments, 160–1
domestic help and childcare, 233–4
domestic workers, 226–7
draft laws, 45–8

# E
economic development, 74–5
economic diversification, 71–2
economic policy, 291–2
Economist Intelligence Unit (EIU), 352
economy, 309
  annual inflation in, 314
  economic cycle channel, 334
  exchange rate channel, 335–8
  financial sector, 312
  flexible labor supply, 317–8
  global economy and policy divergence, 322–8
  government revenue and expenditure, 313
  income channel, 333–334
  macroeconomic policy model, 318–9
  macroeconomic stabilization policies, 339–40
  monetary policy crisis approach, 329–32
  narrow and undiversified production base, 317
  post-independence oil economy, 310–1
  pre-independence oil economy, 310
  pro-cyclical population growth, 319–22
  rapid economic expansion period, 311–6
  real sector, 312
  slow growth period, 311
  small open economy, 316–7
educational policy, 291
education, K-12 system, 382
  charter system in context, 112–13
  design and implementation; abstract analysis, 106; Central Provision, 105; educational statistics, 109; MOE organization chart, 107; rational analysis, 106; reformed structure, 107; SEC announcement, 105; social controversy, 109; societal dissatisfaction, 110; teachers and staff, 104
  education in Qatar today, 121–2
  history of reform, 98–101
  national assessments, 120
  procedures vs. content, 117–21
  Qatar education Strategy 2000–2010 proposal, 99
  RAND study; accountability, 102–3; autonomy, 102; choice, 103; independent school system, 102; options for reform, 100; variety, 103
  rational-choice theory; assumed rational behavior, 114; de-facto model of governance, 115; student demand and school supply, 116
  reform, 255–7
  types of schools, 101
education and science development, 162–3
Education City, 163
education gap, 232–3
education reforms, 69–70

education system, K–12 education system
EIU. *See* Economist Intelligence Unit (EIU)
Emir
  and state public authorities, 39–40
  backing and initiative, 82
  prerogatives, 40
energy challenge, 298–299
entrepreneurship, 291
environmental challenges
  energy sector, 298–299
  food production, 299–300
  water resources, 297–8
environmental development, 75
environmental governance, 304–6
ethnic nationalism, 244–9
executive authority, 39
Executive Groups, 80–1
Exploration and Production Sharing Agreement, 353–4

F
facilities and devices license, 185
family intersectional policies
  authoritarian model *vs.* laissez-faire model, 230–2
  continuity and change, 229
  current attitudes, 218–19
  historical development, of family; Basic Law in 1970, 216; nuclear family, 215; tribal allegiances, 214; women, predicament of, 215–16
  institutional instability, 229–30
  institutions and legislation, 221–3
  policy recommendations; domestic help and childcare, 233–4; education gap and marriage barriers, 232–3
  Qatari women in labor force, 223
  state interventions and perceived threats; demographic imbalance, 224; divorce rates, 225–6; domestic workers, 226–7; tensions in state policy, 227–8
*faz'a*, 216
*fereej*, 217
FIFA World Cup 2022, 1, 26, 31, 73, 90, 162, 195, 263, 272, 279, 330, 339, 360–1, 363, 376, 383
financial autonomy, 66–7
financial crisis, 328, 353
  global financial crisis, 30, 70, 80, 327, 329, 331, 334, 336, 337, 370
  monetary policy crisis, 329–32
financing system, in health care
  burden of health spending, 190
  collection, 192–3
  financial risk protection, 189
  healthcare coverage, 191
  pooling, 193
  purchasing, 193–4
  Seha, 191
  total health expenditure, 188, 189
food challenge, 299–300
foreign policy, 278, 348–52, 354, 357–61, 363, 368, 369, 372, 384–5, 390

G
GCC economic model, 320–2
General Secretariat for Development Planning (GSDP), 377–8
global financial crisis, 30, 70, 80, 327, 329, 331, 334, 336, 337, 370
globalization, 241
governance system, 371–81
GSDP. *See* General Secretariat for Development Planning (GSDP)

INDEX 399

Gulf Central Committee for Drug Registration (GCC-DR), 204
Gulf Cooperation Council (GCC), 242, 243, 350
post-secondary education, 132–6
private higher education, 135–6
private universities, 133–4
scholarship programs, 133
universities, 132–3

## H
Hamad bin Jassim bin Jaber bin Muhammad Al-Thani (HBJ), 60n7, 83n2
Hamad bin Khalifa Al-Thani, 78, 136, 158, 162, 220, 349
Hamad Bin Khalifa University (HBKU), 140
Hamad Medical Corporation (HMC), 181
health policy-making
financing system; burden of health spending, 190; collection, 192–3; financial risk protection, 189; healthcare coverage, 191; pooling, 193; purchasing, 193–4; Seha, 191; total health expenditure, 188, 189
governance; accountability mechanisms, 181; healthcare service providers, 184; health risks, 185–6; licensing, of facilities and devices, 185; Ministry of Public Health, 181; National Health Authority, 182; National Health Strategy, 184; nonclinical services, 187; regulatory and monitoring mechanisms, 185; strategic policy, 187; Supreme Council of Health, 182; transparent governance, 183

information systems, 202–3
medical products, 204–5
service delivery; monitoring, 201–2; organization, 198–200; planning, 197; provision, 200–1
technologies, 204–5
vaccines, 204–5
workforce, 194–6
heritage projects, Qatar, 261–6
higher education, 255–7
high modernism, 254, 369
human development, 73–4

## I
immigration policies, 290
information systems, in health care, 202–3
infrastructure and services development, 161
integrated policy, need for, 300–1
international legislation, 288
International Society for Quality in Health Care (iSQua), 201
Islam, Islamic, 3, 7, 8, 17, 74, 98, 122, 242, 243, 250–3, 263, 264, 357, 358, 360, 367, 368, 369, 380, 385, 387
Islamic values, 75, 250

## J
Jassim bin Mohammed bin Al Thani, 252
judiciary, 39–40

## K
*Kafala,* 14
Katara Cultural Village, 170, 264
Katatib, 98

Khalifa bin Hamad, 6, 44, 98, 243, 263
knowledge-based economy, 136, 256, 272, 283, 318, 368, 390
Kuttab girls' school, 98

## L
labor market policies, 383–4
labor supply flexibility, Qatari economy, 317–8
labour market
  females' participation, 281
  policy, 290
  trends, 279–6
Law on Associations and Private Foundations, 58
legislative process
  administrative justice system, 57–9
  constitutional court, 53–7
  draft laws, 45–8
  official gazette, 50–2
  proposal, 44–5
  ratification and refusal, 48–50
  time needed to promulgate law, 52–3
legislature, 39
limited monarchy, 38
liquefied natural gas (LNG), 311, 368

## M
macroeconomic management framework (MMF), 310, 314, 315
macroeconomic policy model, Qatari economy, 318–19
macroeconomic stabilization policy, Qatari economy, 339–40
marriage barriers, 232–3
medical products, 204–5
medium power, 351

MIA. *See* Museum of Islamic Art (MIA)
migrant, 28, 186, 246
migrant labor, 86, 385, 271, 288, 385, 386
migrant workers, 156, 189, 224, 282, 361, 363, 370, 384
migrant Arabs, 277
Ministry of Administrative Development, 83, 84
Ministry of Culture, Arts, and Heritage, 264
Ministry of Education (MOE), 3, 24, 25, 98–102, 104, 106–8, 137, 142, 143
Ministry of Energy and Industries, 305
Ministry of the Environment, 303
Ministry of Foreign Affairs, 289, 303, 360
Ministry of Information and Communication, 84
Ministry of Interior, 43, 283, 289
Ministry of Justice, 51, 56
Ministry of Labour, 284, 286, 289, 291
Ministry of Municipal Affairs and Agriculture (MMAA), 164
Ministry of Municipalities and Urban Planning (MMUP), 158
Ministry of Public Health (MPH), 181
Ministry of Social Affairs, 14, 225
MMF. *See* macroeconomic management framework (MMF)
monarchy, 16, 18–19
  absolute and limited, 38
  Al-Thani family, 37–8
  Emir and state public authorities, 39–40
  Emir's prerogatives, 40
  people participation, 42–4

INDEX  401

pro-forma political bodies, 38
Shura Council's prerogatives, 41–2
monetary policy crisis, 329–32
Moza Bint Nasser
  HH Sheikha Moza, 182, 221
  Sheikha Moza, 25, 73, 372–4, 378
  Shiekha Moza bint Nasser, 25, 101, 162, 220
multiculturalism, 241
Municipal Spatial Development Plans (MSDP), 174
Museum of Islamic Art (MIA), 263
Muslim Brotherhood (MB), 243

N
National Day, 252
National Health Authority (NHA), 182
National Health Insurance Company (NHIC), 193
National Health Strategy (NHS), 184, 378
national identity, 241
  citizenship vs., 245–8
  ethnicity, 244–49
  higher education, 255–7
  K-12 education reform, 255–7
  state discourse, 249–54
  tradition vs. modernity, 254–5
  women as second-class citizens, 248–9
national legislation, 288–9
national visions and development, 71
natural gas production, 298, 299
natural resources policy, 301–2
nested power
  nature of, 348
  soft to, 354–63
nested power in, 354–63
news and media development, 163–4

O
Official Gazette, 50–2
oil revenue stability, in Qatar, 335
operationalized resilience, 349
optimum currency area (OCA), 325

P
Permanent Constitution, 42–3, 45, 46, 49, 51, 54, 55, 57, 60n7, 62n25, 62n26, 62n34, 73, 78
Petroleum Development Qatar Limited (pDQL), 5
Planning Council, 79
policy divergence, in Qatar, 322–30
policy-making, 371–81
  economic diversification, 71–2
  education reforms, 69–70
  empirical limitations, 67–8
  financial autonomy, 66–7
  financial crisis, 70
  national visions and development, 71
  neo-Weberian polities, 67
  rentier state theory, 67, 388–90
population growth in Qatar, 274, 275
Population Planning Committee (PPC), 224
post-secondary education (PSE), 382
  achievements, 144
  branch campuses, 134
  challenges; K-12 education reform impacts, 147–8; pace of reform, 148; societal response, 148–9
  economic challenges, 136–7
  GCC region, 132–3
  government scholarship system, 142–4
  knowledge-based economy, 136
  Qatar University reformation, 140–2
  scholarship programs, 133

post-secondary education (PSE) (*cont.*)
   societal responses, 144–7
   university branch campuses and colleges establishment, 137–40
power, 8–9
   medium power, 351
   nested power, 348, 354–63
   soft power, 349–63
   subtle power, 17, 348, 349, 351, 352, 354
price stability, in Qatar, 335
Private Associations and Foundations, 2004 Law, 14
private sector challenge, 282–3
privatised urban landscapes, 170–1
Protection of Society Law, 58
Provisional Basic Law, 1970, 42, 54
public management, drivers and levers of, 84–5
public policy, 305–7
   international legislation, 306
   national legislation, 306–7

# Q
Qatar
   context and constitution; elections, 7; 2004 Law on Private Associations and Foundations, 14; population imbalance, 7; powers and articles, 8–9; public rights and duties, 9; sponsorship system, 14; WGI Qatar and MENA, 14, 15
   contradictions, 16–17
   democratic governance, 16–17
   economic development, 1–2
   historical background; British protectorate agreement, 4, 5; foreign worker influx, 5; oil and gas development, 4–5; 1949 succession agreement, 5
   modern lifestyle, 17
   monarchy, 16, 18–19
   political development, 3
   Qatar National Development Strategy, 21
   Qatar National vision 2030, 3, 20
   Qatar time line, 10–13
   rentier state, 19, 389–9
   social development, 3
Qatar Airways, 161, 362, 363
Qatar Comprehensive Educational Assessment, 118
Qatar education Strategy 2000–2010 proposal, 99
Qatar Foundation, 25, 82, 160–3, 221–2
Qatari Diar Real Estate Investment Company, 160–1
Qatari food security plan, 302–3
Qatari nationality, 57
Qatar Investment Authority (QIA), 160, 352
Qatarization challenge, 283–5
Qatar Monetary agency, 311
Qatar National Development Framework (QNDF), 174
Qatar National Development Strategy (QNDS) 2011–2016, 21, 251, 370
   advisor, 79
   challenges for, 76–7
   development planning secretariat, 80
   drivers and levers of public management, 84–5
   economic development, 74–5
   Emir's backing and initiative, 82
   environmental development, 75
   Executive Groups, 80–1
   human development, 73–4
   inter-related factors, 82–3
   Planning Council, 79
   political reforms, 78
   QP role, 81–2

INDEX  403

situational analyses, 76
social development, 74
stakeholder consultations, 76, 81
state management institutions, 76
substantive and operational
  challenges, 78
Supreme Oversight Committee, 80
Qatar National Food Security Program
  (QNFSP), 302–3, 384
Qatar National Vision 2030 (QNV),
  3, 20, 174, 249–250
economic development, 74–5
environmental development, 75
human development, 73–4
social development, 74
Supreme Oversight Committee, 80
Qatar University, 140–2
QCB deposit policy rate (QCBDR),
  329–2
QCB lending policy rate (QCBLR),
  329–2
QNDS. *See* Qatar National
  Development Strategy (QNDS)
QNSFP. *See* Qatar National Food
  Security Program (QNSFP)
QNV2030. *See* Qatar National Vision
  2030 (QNV2030)


R
RAND-Qatar Policy Institute, 377
RAND study
  accountability, 102–3
  autonomy, 102
  choice, 103
  independent school system, 102
  options for reform, 100
  variety, 103
ratification and refusal, legislative
  system, 48–50
real estate investments, 160–1
rentier state theory, 67, 388–90

S
SCH. *See* Supreme Council on Health
  (SCH)
second-class citizens, women as,
  248–49
Seha, 191, 193
service delivery, in health care
  monitoring, 201–2
  organization, 198–200
  planning, 197
  provision, 200–1
Shura Council (the legislature)
  Art. 10, 46
  Cabinet proposals, 45
  committees, 47
  discussion of drafts laws, 46
  president, 48
  ratification, 49
small open economy, in Qatar, 316–7
small state, 16, 17, 213, 368
  policies, 350, 351
  powers, 349–54
social development, 74
social engineering, 369
social media, 257–63, 265
soft power
  concept of, 349–63
  to nested power, 349–63
soft power in, 349–63
Souq Waqif, 171
sovereign wealth fund (SWF), 352
state discourse, 249–55
state-owned enterprises (SOEs), 352
structural liquidity surplus (SlS), 325
subtle power, 17, 348, 349, 351, 352,
  354
Supreme Constitutional Court, 53, 55
Supreme Council of Health (SCH),
  182–8, 375, 376, 378
Supreme Education Council (SEC),
  100, 105
Supreme Oversight Committee, 80

## T

Tamim bin Hamad Al-Thani, 3, 84, 249, 251, 297, 306
Teach for Qatar, 121
transformative state. *See also* health policy-making; constitutional and legal system
  architectural identity, 262
  context and constitution; elections, 7; 2004 Law on Private Associations and Foundations, 14; population imbalance, 7; powers and articles, 8–9; public rights and duties, 9; sponsorship system, 14; WGI Qatar and MENA, 14, 15
  contradictions, 16–17
  democratic governance, 16–17
  economic development, 1–2
  historical background; British protectorate agreement, 4, 5; foreign worker influx, 5; oil and gas development, 4–5; 1949 succession agreement, 5
  modern lifestyle, 17
  monarchy, 16, 18–19
  political development, 3
  Qatar National Development Strategy, 21
  Qatar National vision 2030, 3, 20
  Qatar time line, 10–13
  rentier state, 19, 389–9
  social development, 3
tribal identity, 253, 260, 267
tribes
  allegiances, 28, 214
  identity, 253, 260
  society, 5, 19
  tribalism, 29, 260

## U

unemployment challenge, 285–6
urban development, 382–3
urbanism
  current megaprojects map, 169
  economic visions, 157
  effective hub vision, 173–5
  governance by new form; fragmented organisational structure, 166; legal rights of master developers, 167–8; out-dated plans and policies, 166–7; staff capacity deficits, 165–6
  investments, 156–7
  investment strategies; emerging contrasting typologies, 171–2; fragmented development, 168–9; low building standards, 172–3; privatised urban landscapes, 170–1; urban peripheries predominance, 170
  large-scale investments, 173–4
  methodological approach, 158

## V

vaccines, 204–5
vertical diversification, Qatari economy, 316–7

## W

water challenge, 297–8
water-energy food (WEF) nexus, 300–1
water scarcity, 296
WeF Nexus tool 2.0, 301–2, 306
West Bay, Diplomatic District in, 171
WHO health systems, 180

World's economic Center of Gravity (WECG), 322
Worldwide Governance Indicators (WGI), 14, 15

Z
zero lower bound (ZLB), 325, 327

Printed by Printforce, the Netherlands